Garfield out to lunch

BY: JIM DAVIS

BALLANTINE BOOKS · NEW YORK

Published in the United States by Ballantine Books, a division of Random House, Inc., New York, and simultaneously in Canada by Random House of Canada Limited, Toronto.

Library of Congress Catalog Card Number: 85-90865
ISBN: 0-345-33118-4

Manufactured in the United States of America

First Edition: March 1986

10 9 8 7 6 5 4 3 2 1

EARLIEST KNOWN GARFIELD!

Presented here for the first time anywhere is the earliest known Garfield strip.

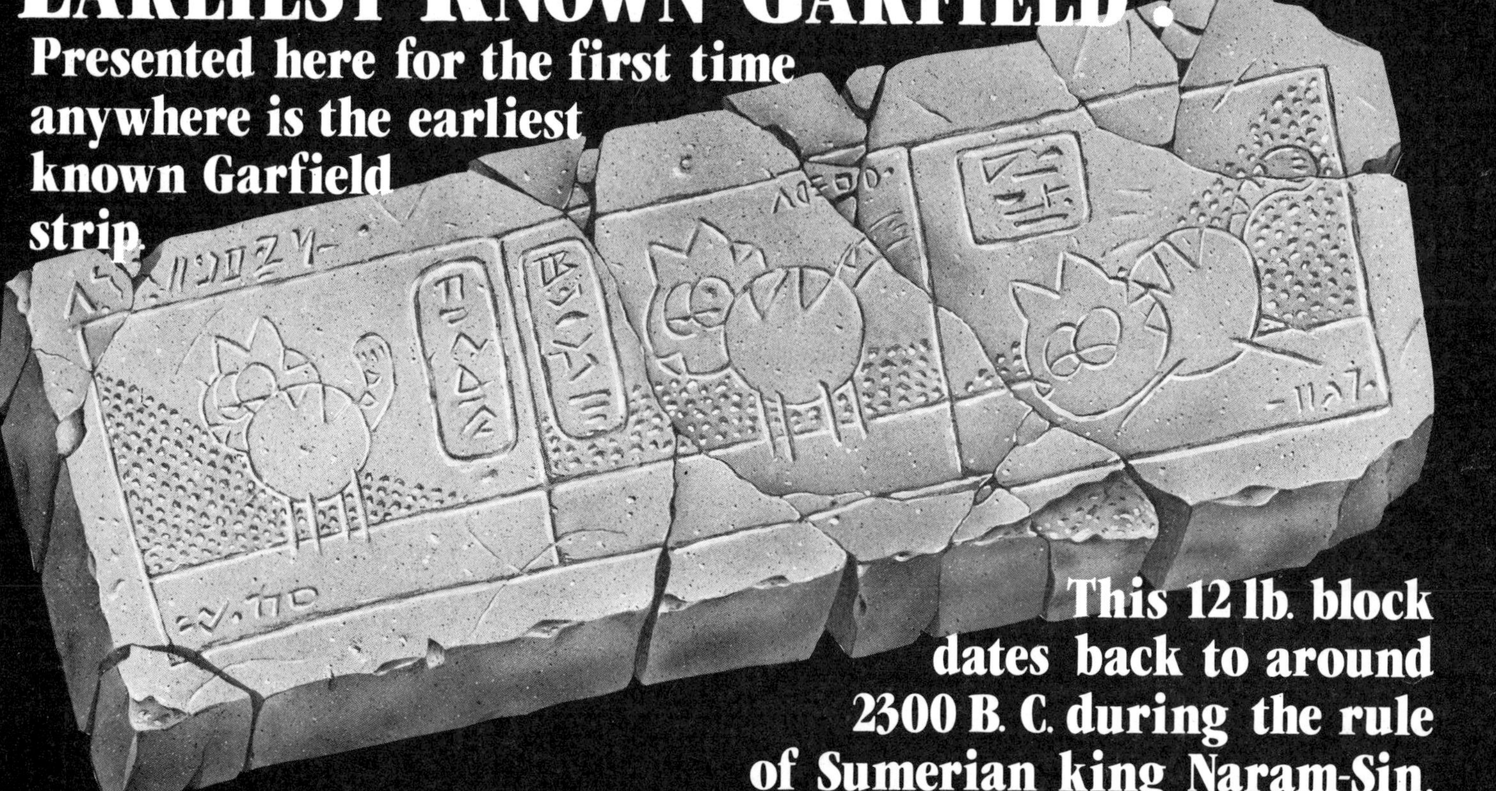

This 12 lb. block dates back to around 2300 B. C. during the rule of Sumerian king Naram-Sin. Jim Davis' name appears in lower right.

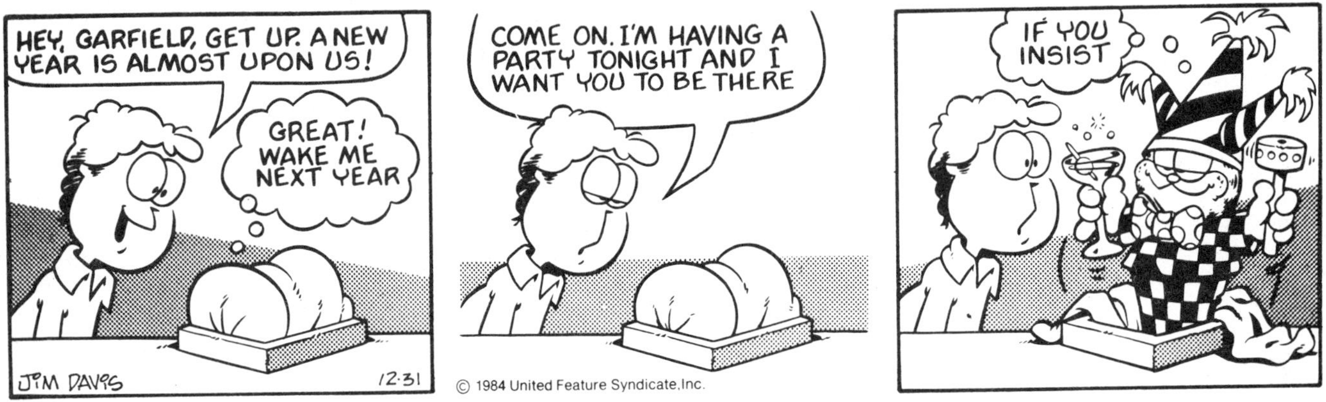
HEY, GARFIELD, GET UP. A NEW YEAR IS ALMOST UPON US!
GREAT! WAKE ME NEXT YEAR
COME ON. I'M HAVING A PARTY TONIGHT AND I WANT YOU TO BE THERE
IF YOU INSIST
JIM DAVIS
12·31

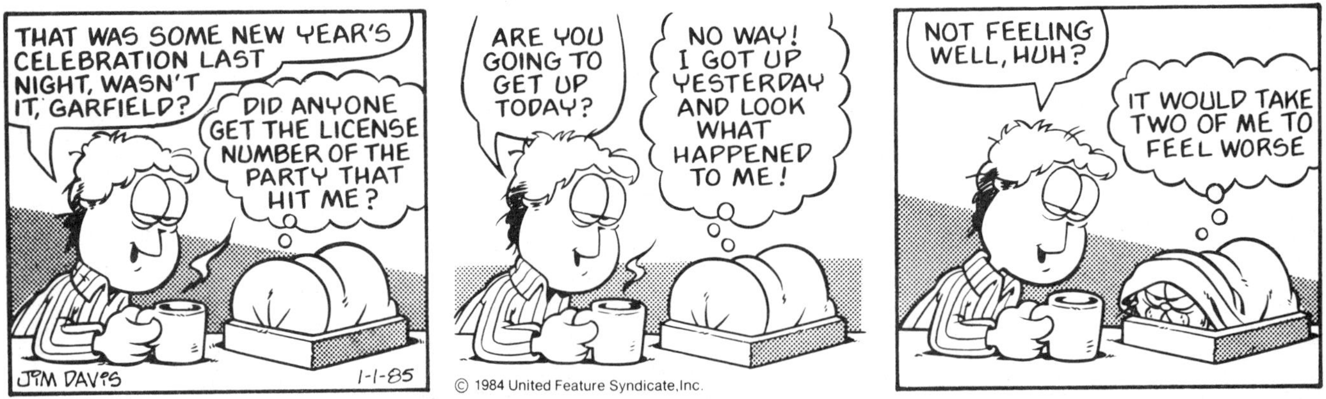
THAT WAS SOME NEW YEAR'S CELEBRATION LAST NIGHT, WASN'T IT, GARFIELD?
DID ANYONE GET THE LICENSE NUMBER OF THE PARTY THAT HIT ME?
ARE YOU GOING TO GET UP TODAY?
NO WAY! I GOT UP YESTERDAY AND LOOK WHAT HAPPENED TO ME!
NOT FEELING WELL, HUH?
IT WOULD TAKE TWO OF ME TO FEEL WORSE
JIM DAVIS
1-1-85

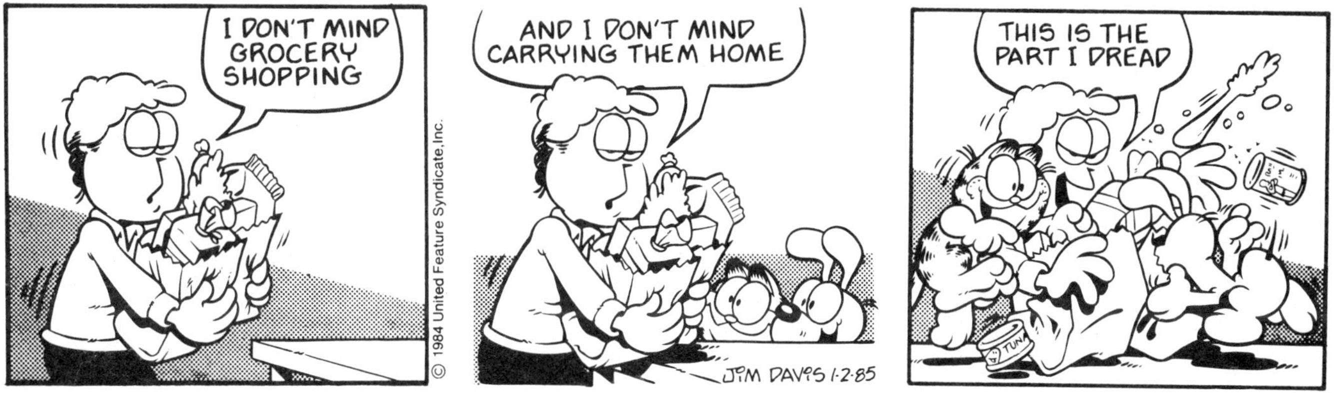
I DON'T MIND GROCERY SHOPPING
AND I DON'T MIND CARRYING THEM HOME
JIM DAVIS 1-2-85
THIS IS THE PART I DREAD
TUNA

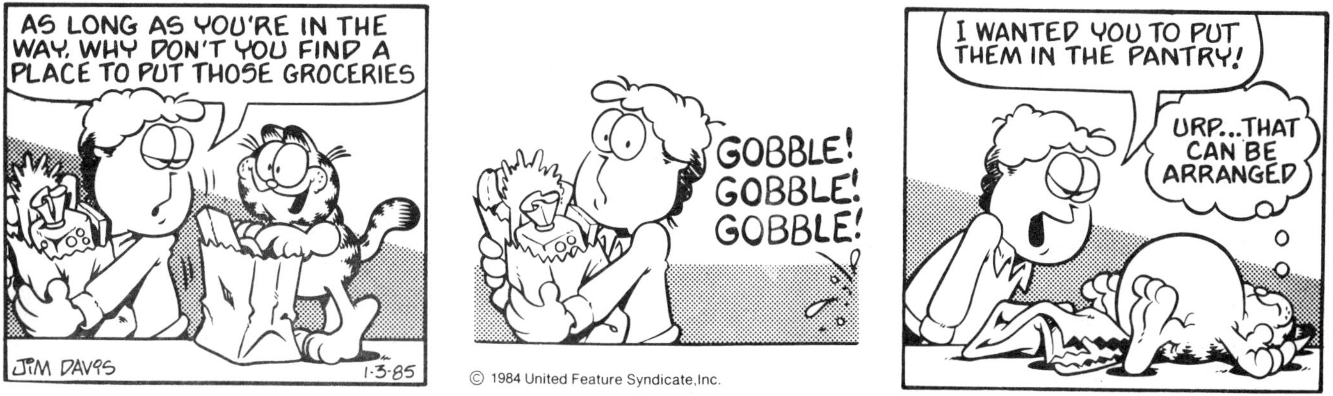
AS LONG AS YOU'RE IN THE WAY, WHY DON'T YOU FIND A PLACE TO PUT THOSE GROCERIES
JIM DAVIS
1-3-85
GOBBLE! GOBBLE! GOBBLE!
I WANTED YOU TO PUT THEM IN THE PANTRY!
URP...THAT CAN BE ARRANGED

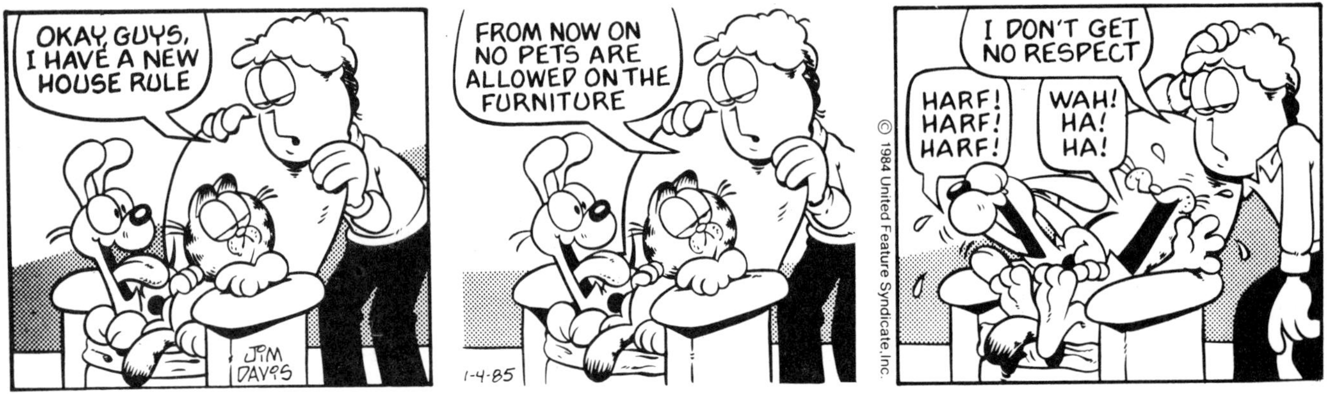
OKAY, GUYS, I HAVE A NEW HOUSE RULE
JIM DAVIS
FROM NOW ON NO PETS ARE ALLOWED ON THE FURNITURE
1-4-85
© 1984 United Feature Syndicate, Inc.
I DON'T GET NO RESPECT
HARF! HARF! HARF!
WAH! HA! HA!

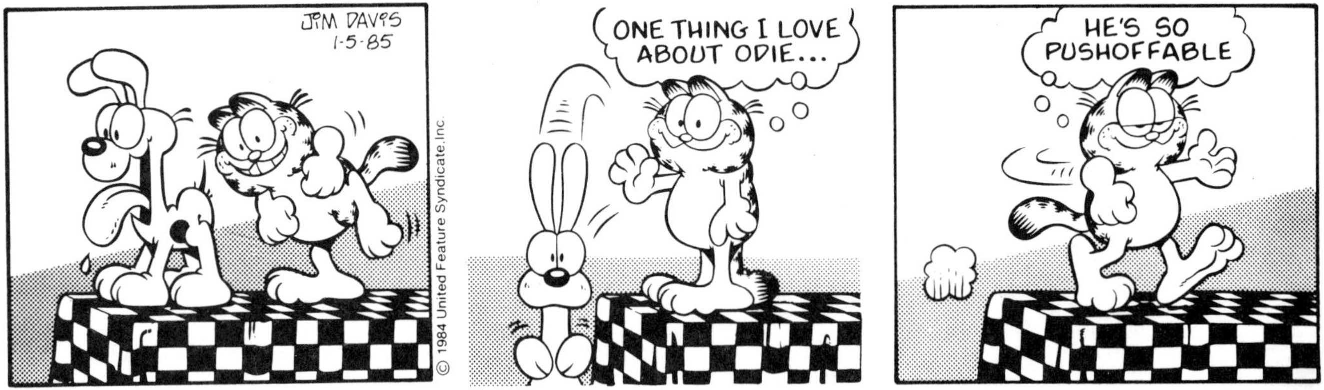
JIM DAVIS
1-5-85
© 1984 United Feature Syndicate, Inc.
ONE THING I LOVE ABOUT ODIE...
HE'S SO PUSHOFFABLE

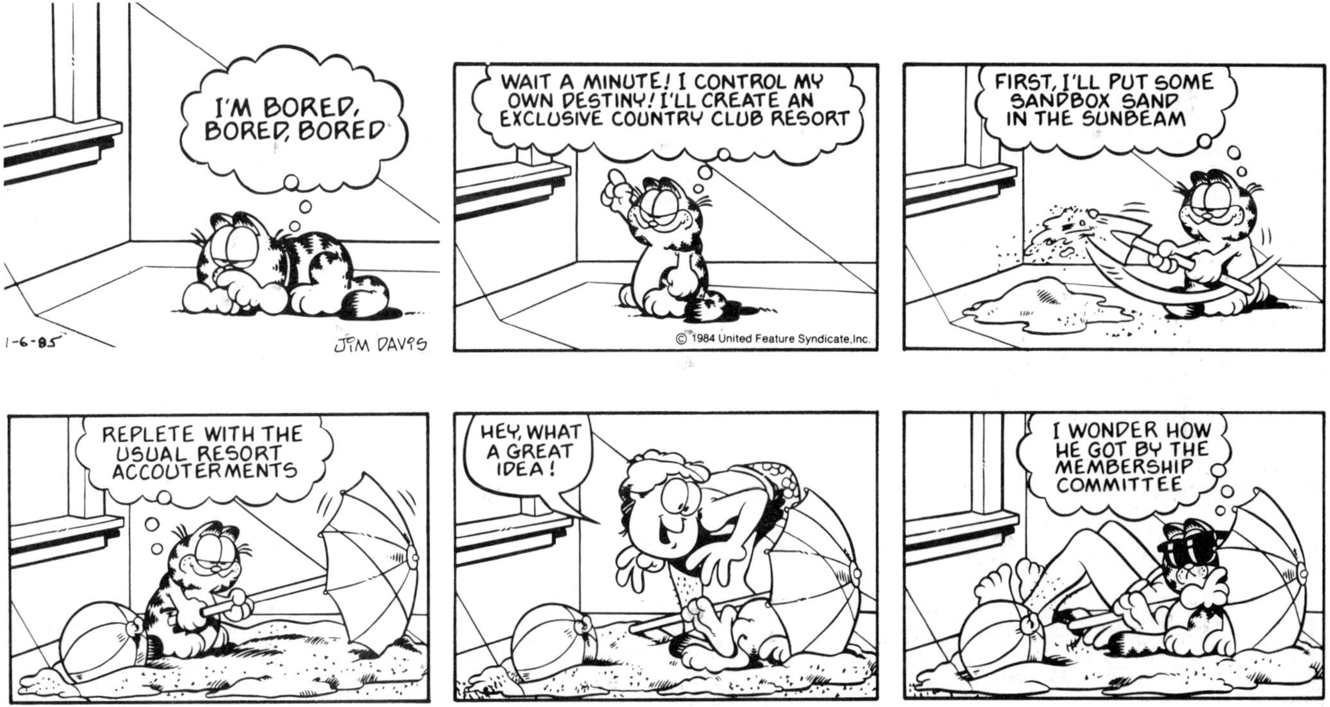
I'M BORED, BORED, BORED
1-6-85
JIM DAVIS
WAIT A MINUTE! I CONTROL MY OWN DESTINY! I'LL CREATE AN EXCLUSIVE COUNTRY CLUB RESORT
© 1984 United Feature Syndicate, Inc.
FIRST, I'LL PUT SOME SANDBOX SAND IN THE SUNBEAM
REPLETE WITH THE USUAL RESORT ACCOUTERMENTS
HEY, WHAT A GREAT IDEA!
I WONDER HOW HE GOT BY THE MEMBERSHIP COMMITTEE

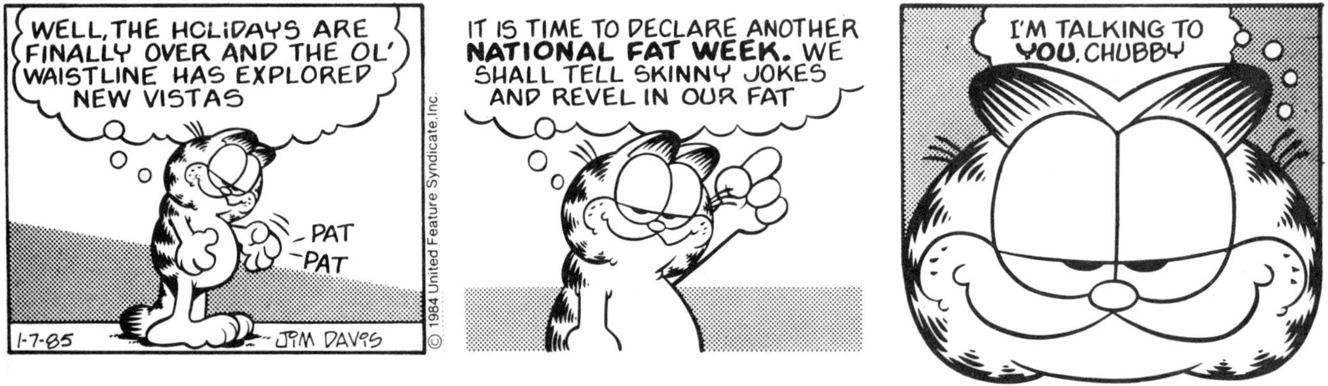
WELL, THE HOLIDAYS ARE FINALLY OVER AND THE OL' WAISTLINE HAS EXPLORED NEW VISTAS
PAT PAT
1-7-85
JIM DAVIS
© 1984 United Feature Syndicate, Inc.
IT IS TIME TO DECLARE ANOTHER **NATIONAL FAT WEEK.** WE SHALL TELL SKINNY JOKES AND REVEL IN OUR FAT
I'M TALKING TO **YOU**, CHUBBY

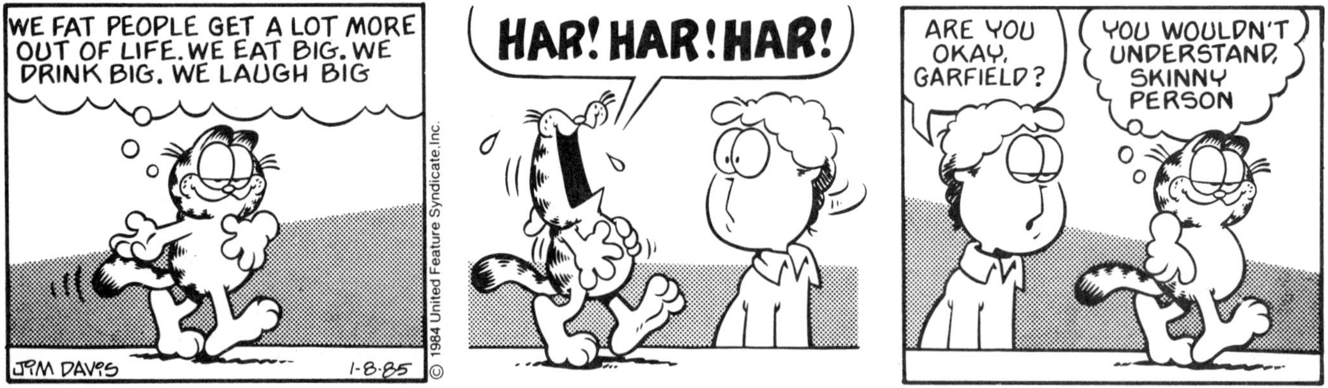
WE FAT PEOPLE GET A LOT MORE OUT OF LIFE. WE EAT BIG. WE DRINK BIG. WE LAUGH BIG
JIM DAVIS
1-8-85
© 1984 United Feature Syndicate, Inc.
HAR! HAR! HAR!
ARE YOU OKAY, GARFIELD?
YOU WOULDN'T UNDERSTAND, SKINNY PERSON

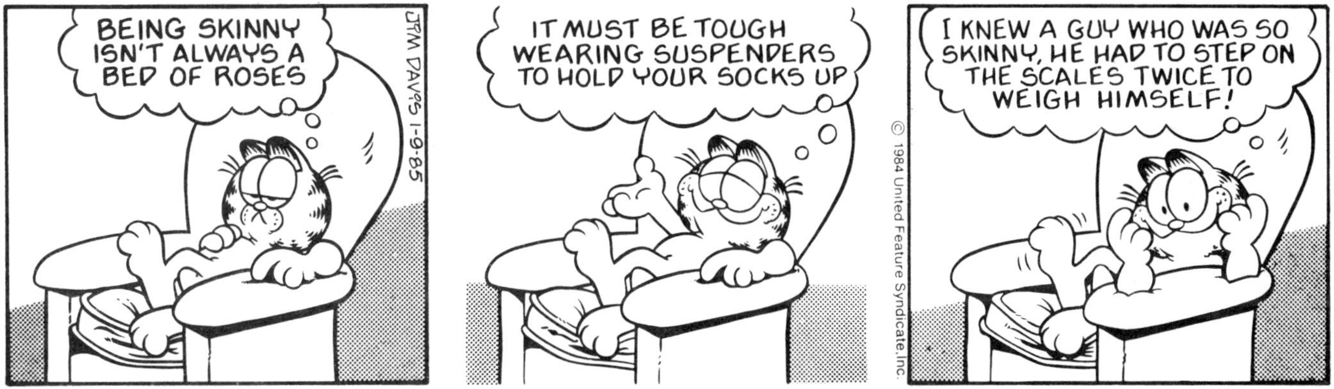
BEING SKINNY ISN'T ALWAYS A BED OF ROSES
JIM DAVIS 1-9-85
IT MUST BE TOUGH WEARING SUSPENDERS TO HOLD YOUR SOCKS UP
© 1984 United Feature Syndicate, Inc.
I KNEW A GUY WHO WAS SO SKINNY, HE HAD TO STEP ON THE SCALES TWICE TO WEIGH HIMSELF!

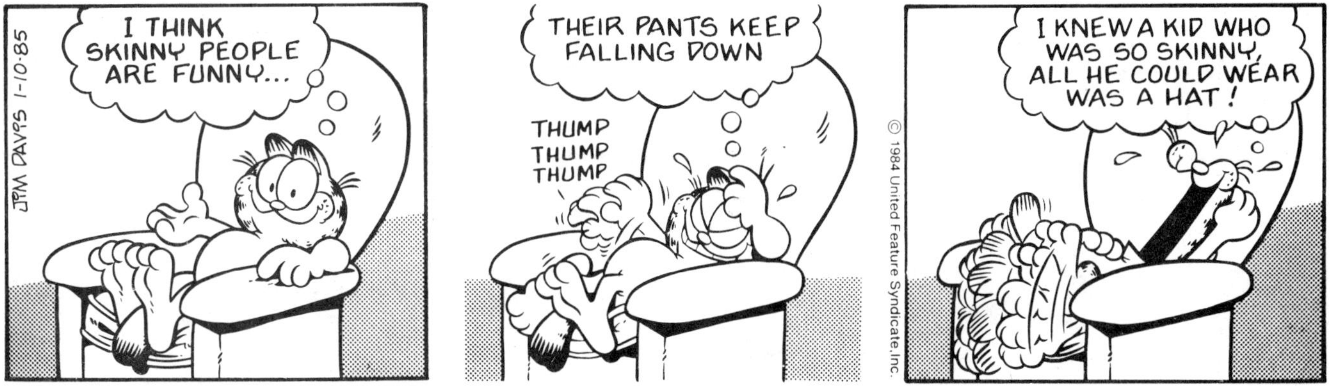
JIM DAVIS 1-10-85
I THINK SKINNY PEOPLE ARE FUNNY...
THEIR PANTS KEEP FALLING DOWN
THUMP THUMP THUMP
© 1984 United Feature Syndicate, Inc.
I KNEW A KID WHO WAS SO SKINNY, ALL HE COULD WEAR WAS A HAT!

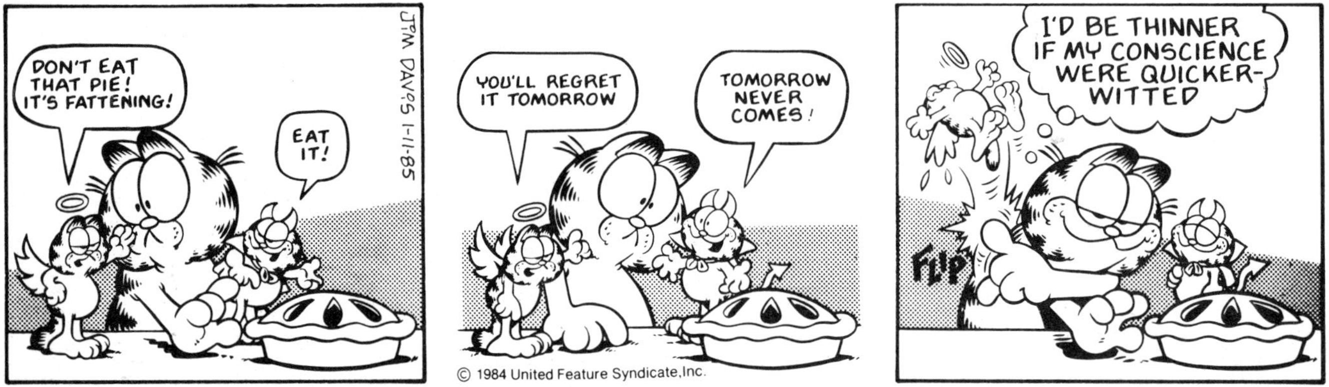
JIM DAVIS 1-11-85
DON'T EAT THAT PIE! IT'S FATTENING!
EAT IT!
YOU'LL REGRET IT TOMORROW
TOMORROW NEVER COMES!
FLIP
I'D BE THINNER IF MY CONSCIENCE WERE QUICKER-WITTED

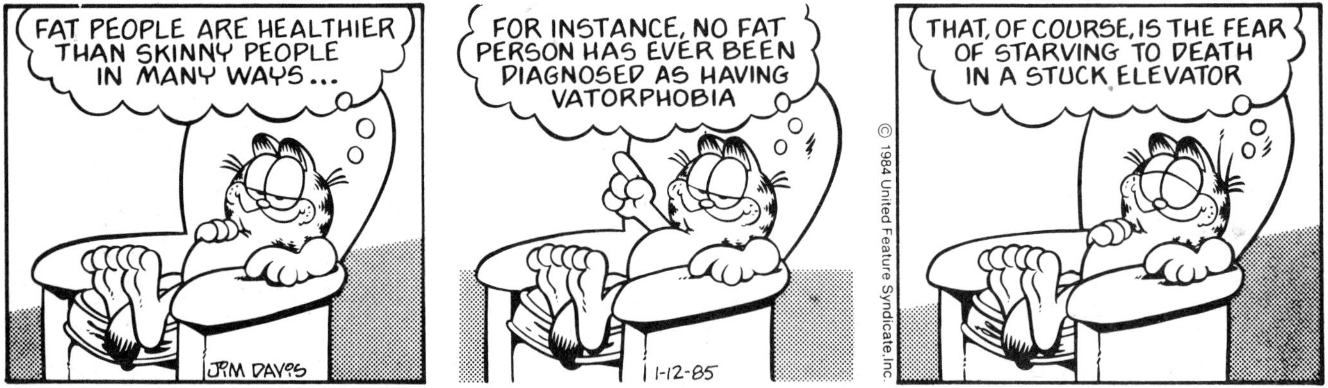
FAT PEOPLE ARE HEALTHIER THAN SKINNY PEOPLE IN MANY WAYS...
JIM DAVIS
FOR INSTANCE, NO FAT PERSON HAS EVER BEEN DIAGNOSED AS HAVING VATORPHOBIA
1-12-85
THAT, OF COURSE, IS THE FEAR OF STARVING TO DEATH IN A STUCK ELEVATOR

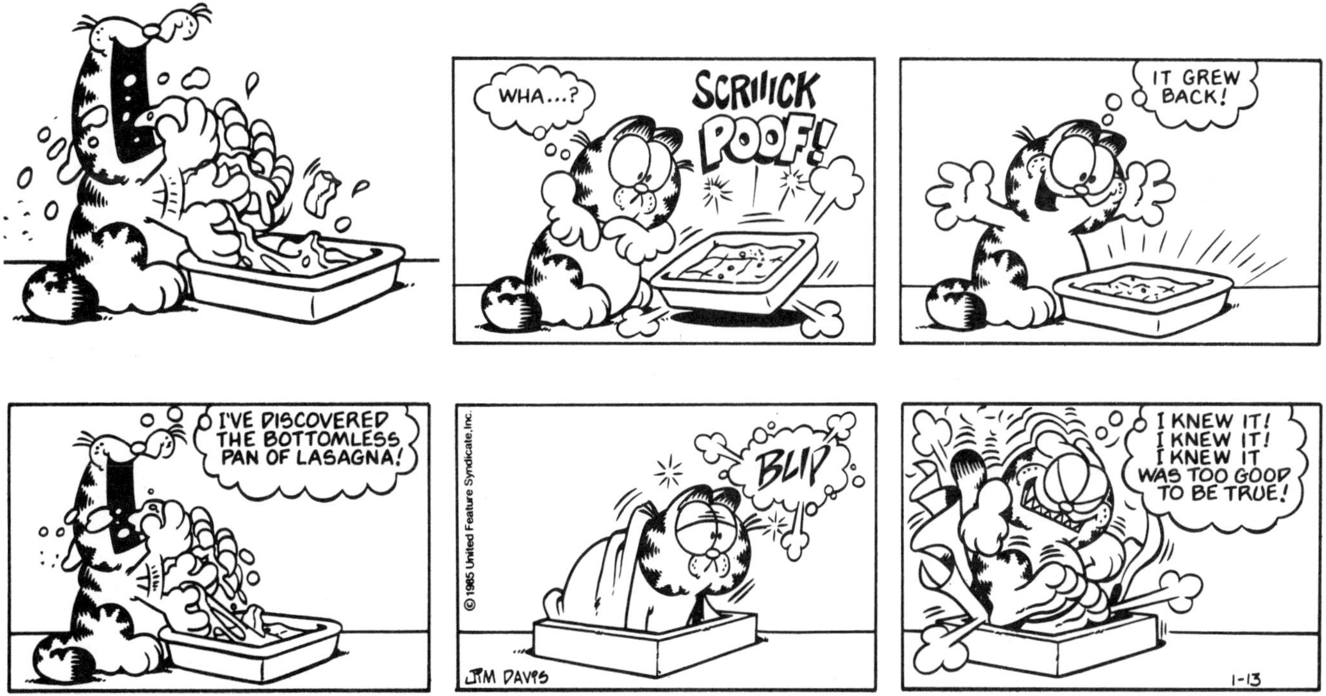

WHA...?
SCRIIICK
POOF!
IT GREW BACK!
I'VE DISCOVERED THE BOTTOMLESS PAN OF LASAGNA!
© 1985 United Feature Syndicate, Inc.
BLIP
JIM DAVIS
I KNEW IT! I KNEW IT! I KNEW IT WAS TOO GOOD TO BE TRUE!
1-13

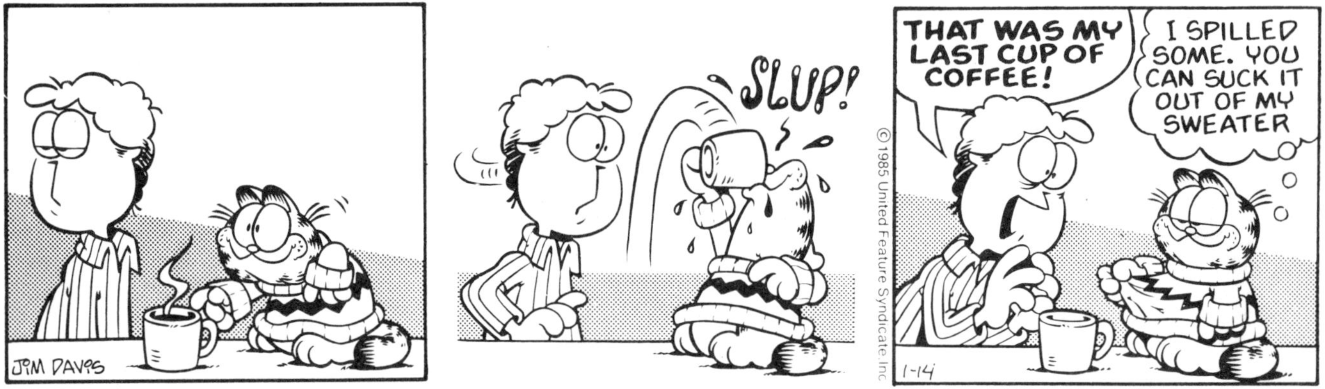
JIM DAVIS
SLUP!
© 1985 United Feature Syndicate, Inc.
THAT WAS MY LAST CUP OF COFFEE!
I SPILLED SOME. YOU CAN SUCK IT OUT OF MY SWEATER
1-14

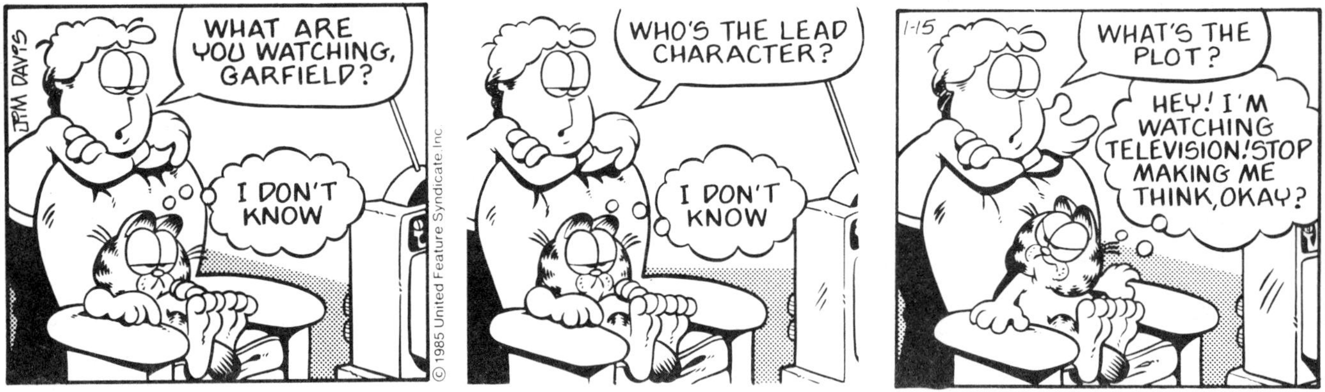
JIM DAVIS
WHAT ARE YOU WATCHING, GARFIELD?
I DON'T KNOW
© 1985 United Feature Syndicate, Inc.
WHO'S THE LEAD CHARACTER?
I DON'T KNOW
1-15
WHAT'S THE PLOT?
HEY! I'M WATCHING TELEVISION! STOP MAKING ME THINK, OKAY?

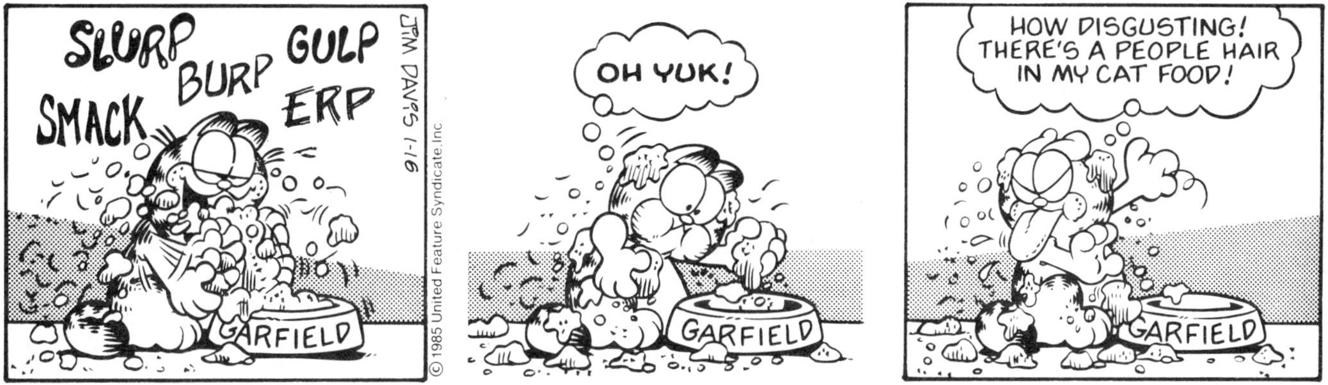
SLURP
SMACK
BURP
GULP
ERP
JIM DAVIS 1-16
© 1985 United Feature Syndicate, Inc.
GARFIELD
OH YUK!
GARFIELD
HOW DISGUSTING! THERE'S A PEOPLE HAIR IN MY CAT FOOD!
GARFIELD

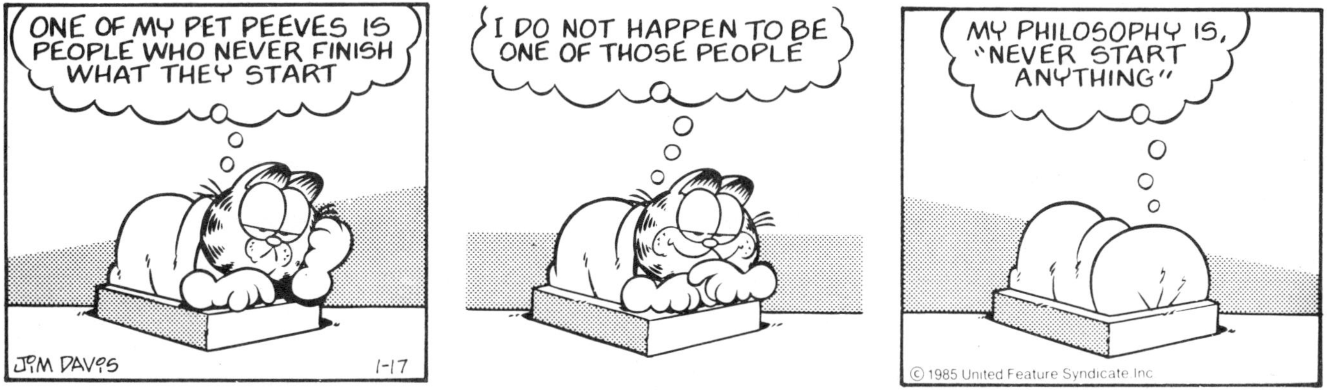
ONE OF MY PET PEEVES IS PEOPLE WHO NEVER FINISH WHAT THEY START
JIM DAVIS
1-17
I DO NOT HAPPEN TO BE ONE OF THOSE PEOPLE
MY PHILOSOPHY IS, "NEVER START ANYTHING"
© 1985 United Feature Syndicate Inc.

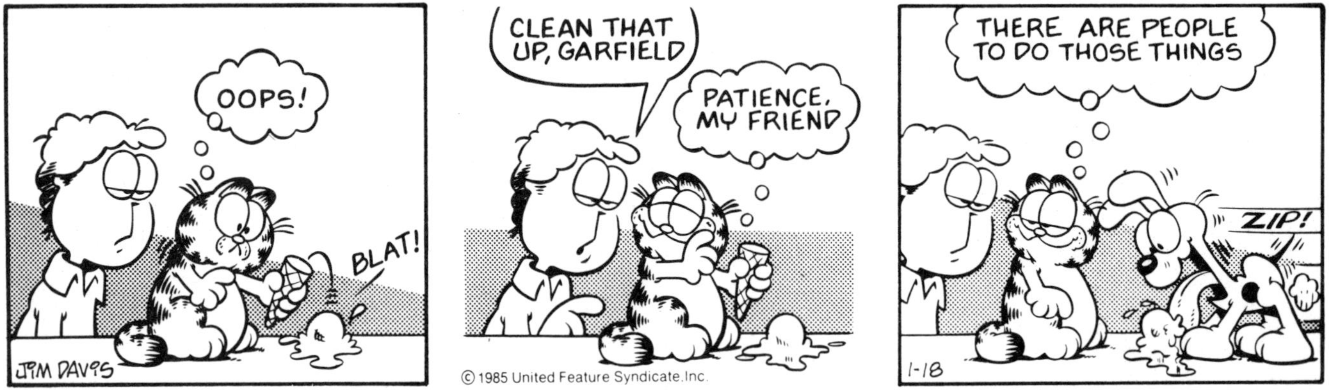
OOPS!
BLAT!
JIM DAVIS
CLEAN THAT UP, GARFIELD
PATIENCE, MY FRIEND
© 1985 United Feature Syndicate, Inc.
THERE ARE PEOPLE TO DO THOSE THINGS
ZIP!
1-18

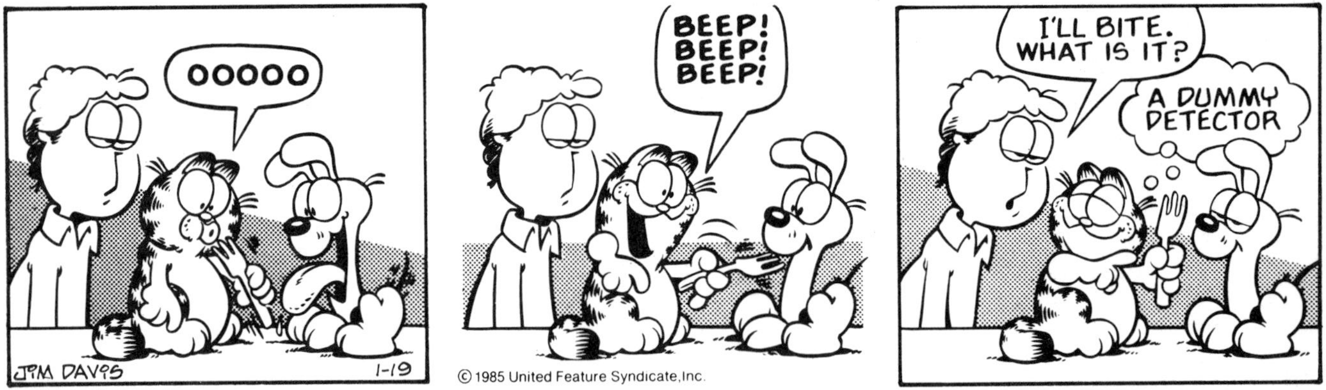
OOOOO
JIM DAVIS
1-19
BEEP! BEEP! BEEP!
© 1985 United Feature Syndicate, Inc.
I'LL BITE. WHAT IS IT?
A DUMMY DETECTOR

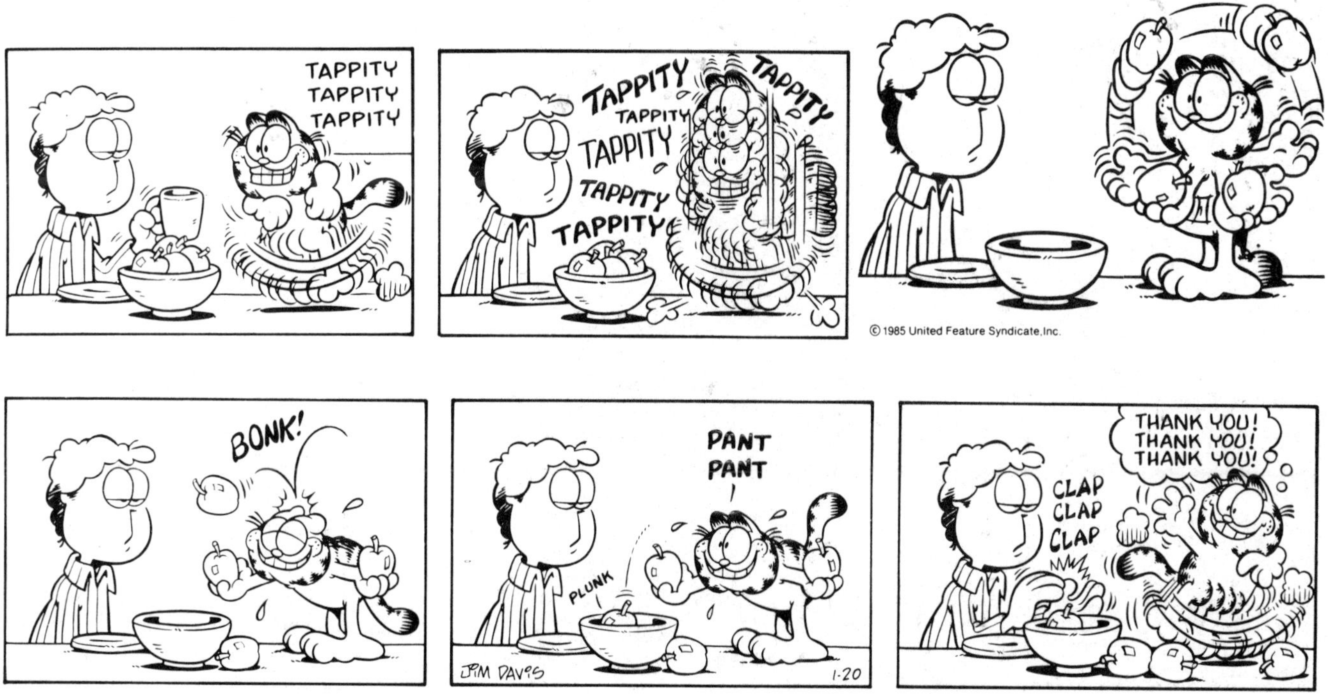
TAPPITY
TAPPITY
TAPPITY
TAPPITY
TAPPITY
TAPPITY
TAPPITY
TAPPITY
TAPPITY
BONK!
PANT
PANT
PLUNK
JIM DAVIS
1-20
CLAP
CLAP
CLAP
THANK YOU!
THANK YOU!
THANK YOU!

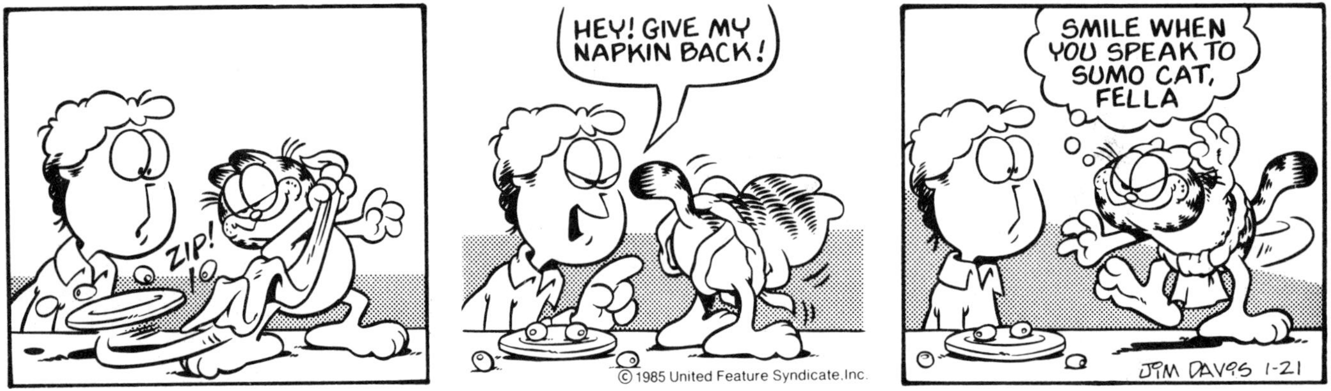
ZIP!
HEY! GIVE MY NAPKIN BACK!
SMILE WHEN YOU SPEAK TO SUMO CAT, FELLA
JIM DAVIS 1-21

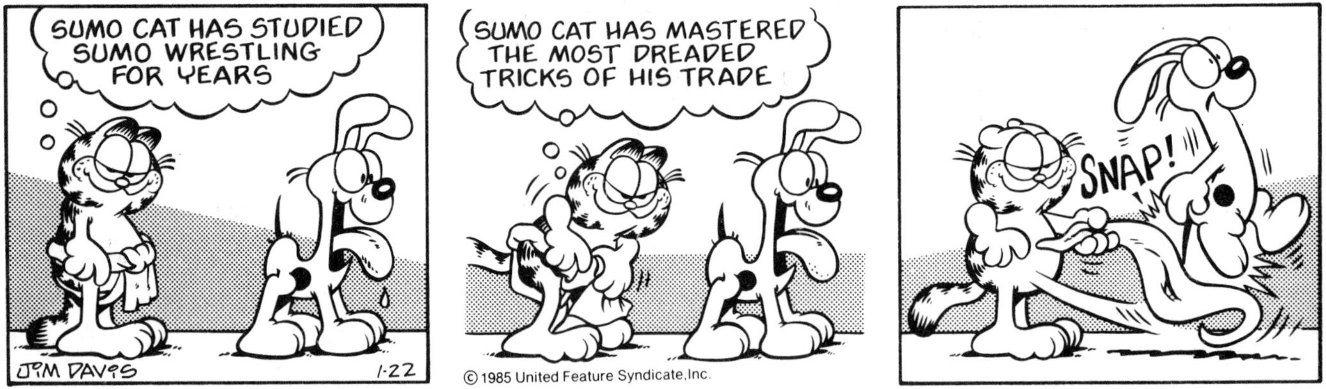
SUMO CAT HAS STUDIED SUMO WRESTLING FOR YEARS
JIM DAVIS 1-22
SUMO CAT HAS MASTERED THE MOST DREADED TRICKS OF HIS TRADE
SNAP!

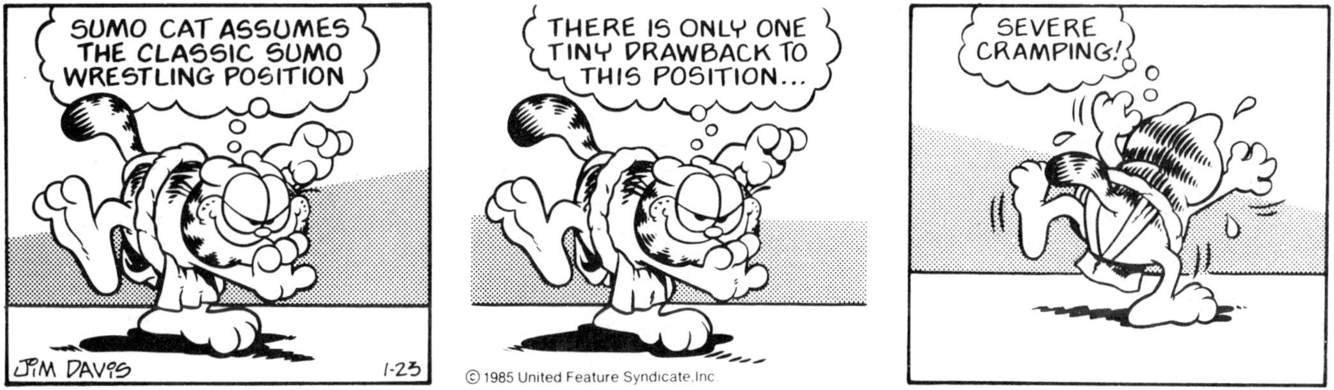
SUMO CAT ASSUMES THE CLASSIC SUMO WRESTLING POSITION
JIM DAVIS
1-23
THERE IS ONLY ONE TINY DRAWBACK TO THIS POSITION...
© 1985 United Feature Syndicate, Inc.
SEVERE CRAMPING!

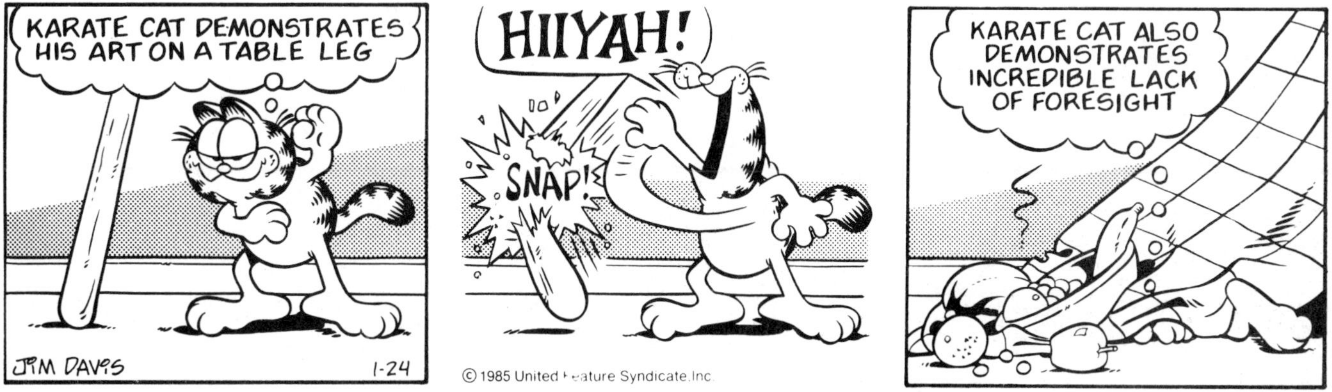
KARATE CAT DEMONSTRATES HIS ART ON A TABLE LEG
JIM DAVIS
1-24
HIIYAH!
SNAP!
© 1985 United Feature Syndicate, Inc.
KARATE CAT ALSO DEMONSTRATES INCREDIBLE LACK OF FORESIGHT

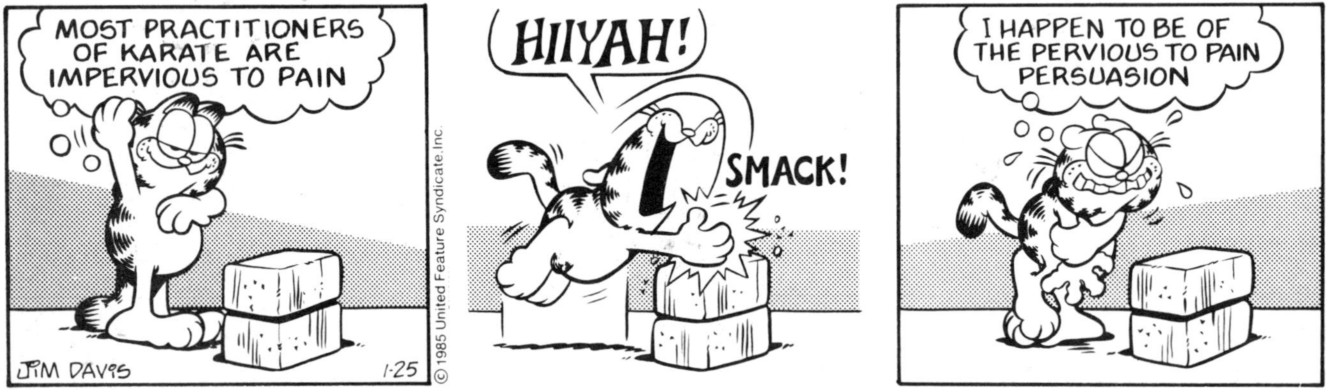
MOST PRACTITIONERS OF KARATE ARE IMPERVIOUS TO PAIN
JIM DAVIS
1-25
© 1985 United Feature Syndicate, Inc.
HIIYAH!
SMACK!
I HAPPEN TO BE OF THE PERVIOUS TO PAIN PERSUASION

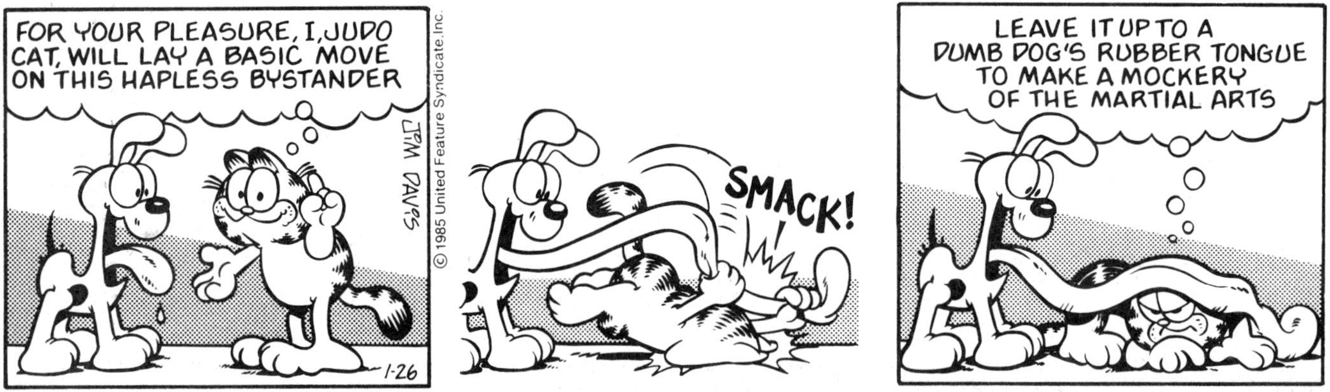
FOR YOUR PLEASURE, I, JUDO CAT, WILL LAY A BASIC MOVE ON THIS HAPLESS BYSTANDER
JIM DAVIS
1-26
© 1985 United Feature Syndicate, Inc.
SMACK!
LEAVE IT UP TO A DUMB DOG'S RUBBER TONGUE TO MAKE A MOCKERY OF THE MARTIAL ARTS

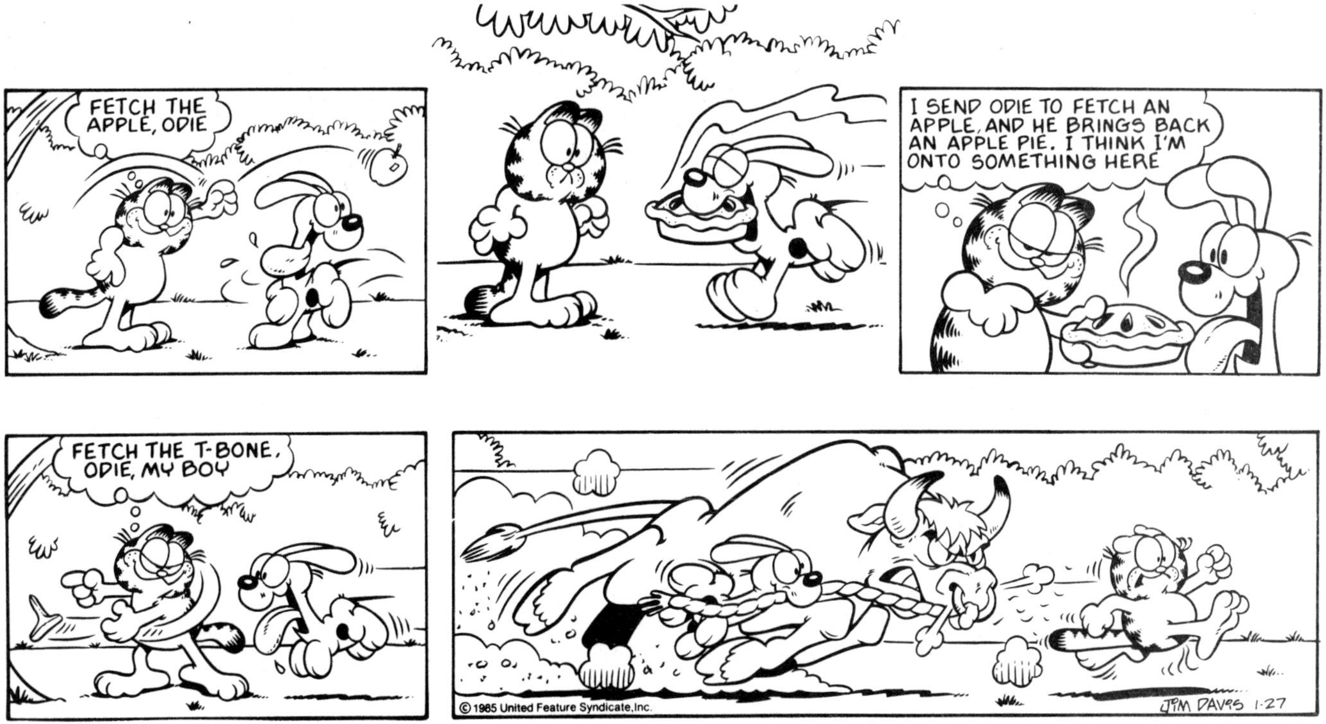
FETCH THE APPLE, ODIE
I SEND ODIE TO FETCH AN APPLE, AND HE BRINGS BACK AN APPLE PIE. I THINK I'M ONTO SOMETHING HERE
FETCH THE T-BONE, ODIE, MY BOY
© 1985 United Feature Syndicate, Inc.
JIM DAVIS 1-27

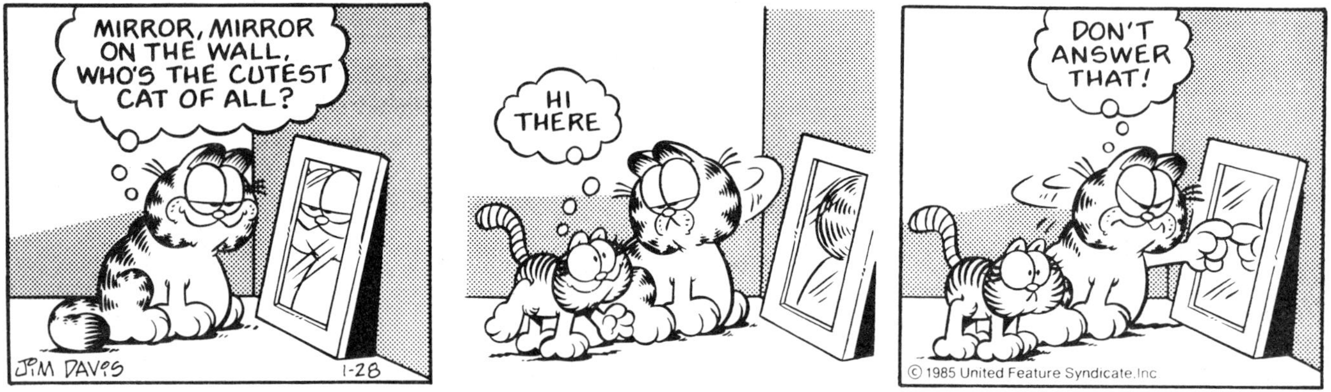
MIRROR, MIRROR ON THE WALL, WHO'S THE CUTEST CAT OF ALL?
JIM DAVIS
1-28
HI THERE
DON'T ANSWER THAT!
© 1985 United Feature Syndicate, Inc.

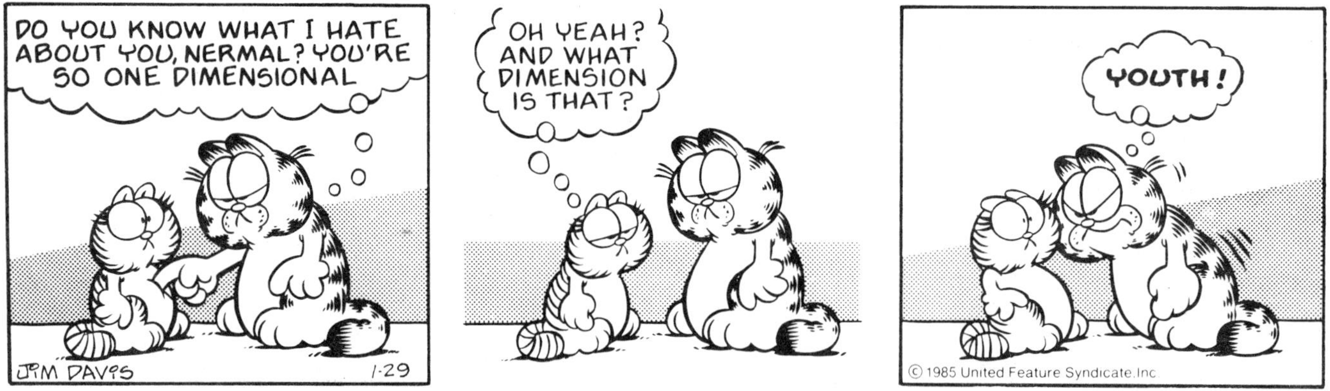
DO YOU KNOW WHAT I HATE ABOUT YOU, NERMAL? YOU'RE SO ONE DIMENSIONAL
JIM DAVIS
1-29
OH YEAH? AND WHAT DIMENSION IS THAT?
YOUTH!
© 1985 United Feature Syndicate, Inc.

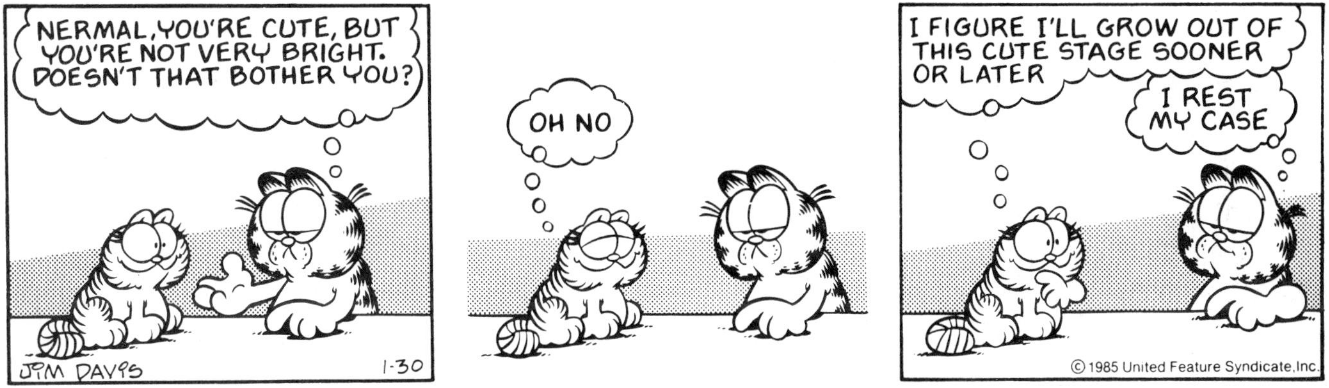
NERMAL, YOU'RE CUTE, BUT YOU'RE NOT VERY BRIGHT. DOESN'T THAT BOTHER YOU?
JIM DAVIS
1-30
OH NO
I FIGURE I'LL GROW OUT OF THIS CUTE STAGE SOONER OR LATER
I REST MY CASE
© 1985 United Feature Syndicate, Inc.

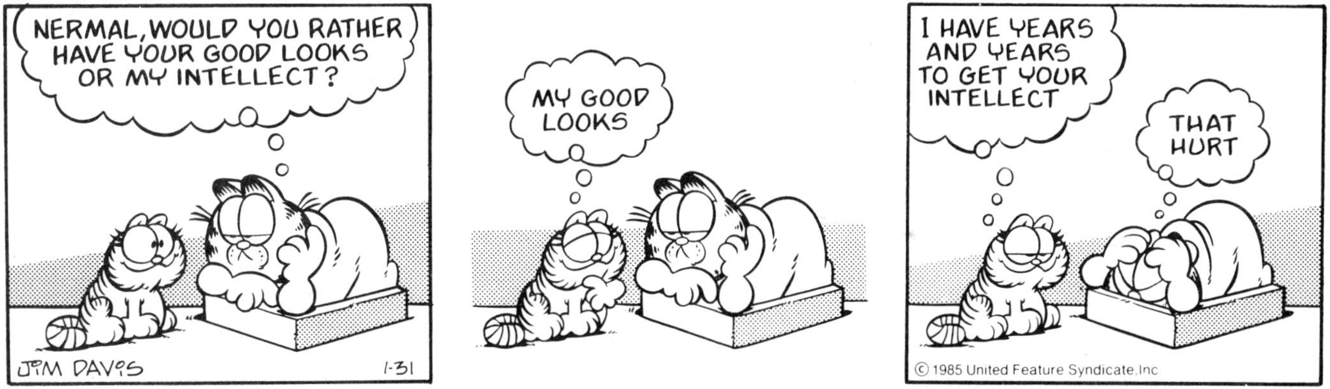
NERMAL, WOULD YOU RATHER HAVE YOUR GOOD LOOKS OR MY INTELLECT?
JIM DAVIS
1-31
MY GOOD LOOKS
I HAVE YEARS AND YEARS TO GET YOUR INTELLECT
THAT HURT
© 1985 United Feature Syndicate, Inc.

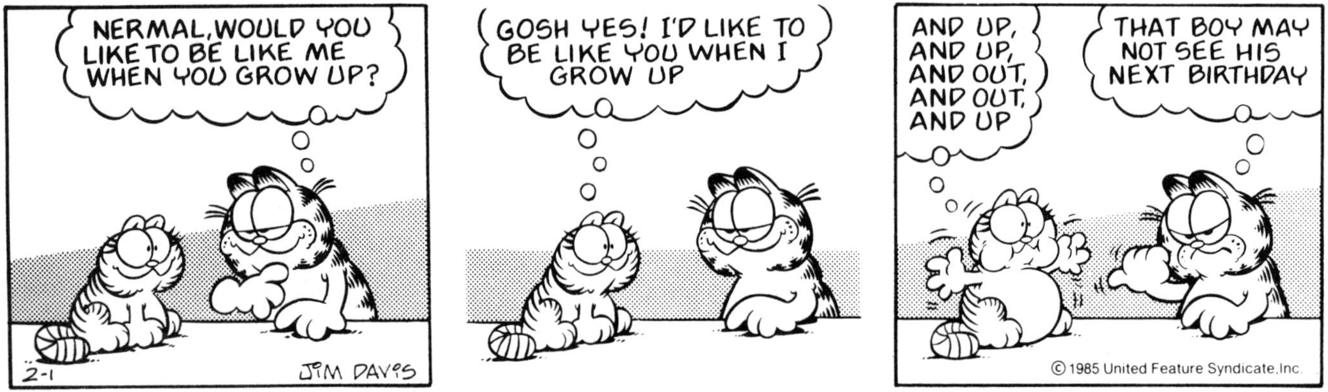
NERMAL, WOULD YOU LIKE TO BE LIKE ME WHEN YOU GROW UP?
2-1
JIM DAVIS
GOSH YES! I'D LIKE TO BE LIKE YOU WHEN I GROW UP
AND UP, AND UP, AND OUT, AND OUT, AND UP
THAT BOY MAY NOT SEE HIS NEXT BIRTHDAY
© 1985 United Feature Syndicate, Inc.

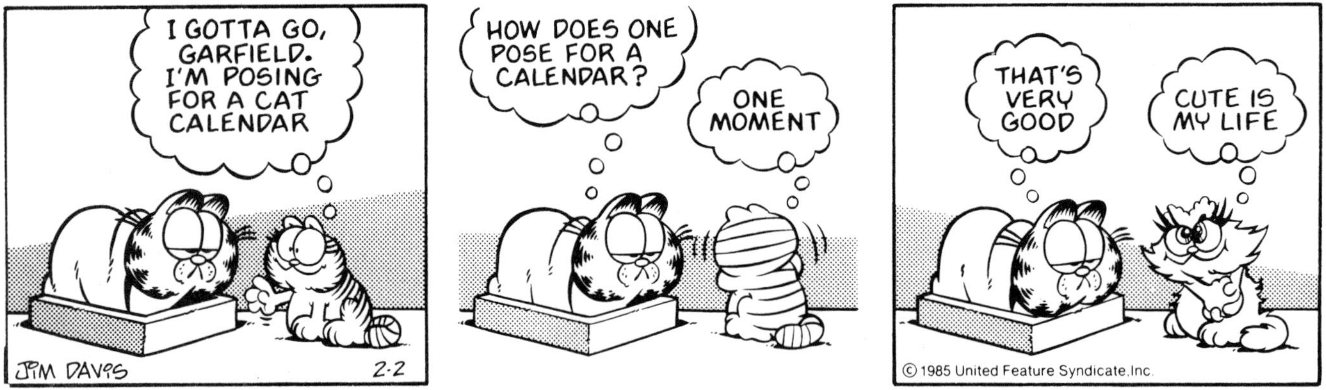
I GOTTA GO, GARFIELD. I'M POSING FOR A CAT CALENDAR
JIM DAVIS
2-2
HOW DOES ONE POSE FOR A CALENDAR?
ONE MOMENT
THAT'S VERY GOOD
CUTE IS MY LIFE
© 1985 United Feature Syndicate, Inc.

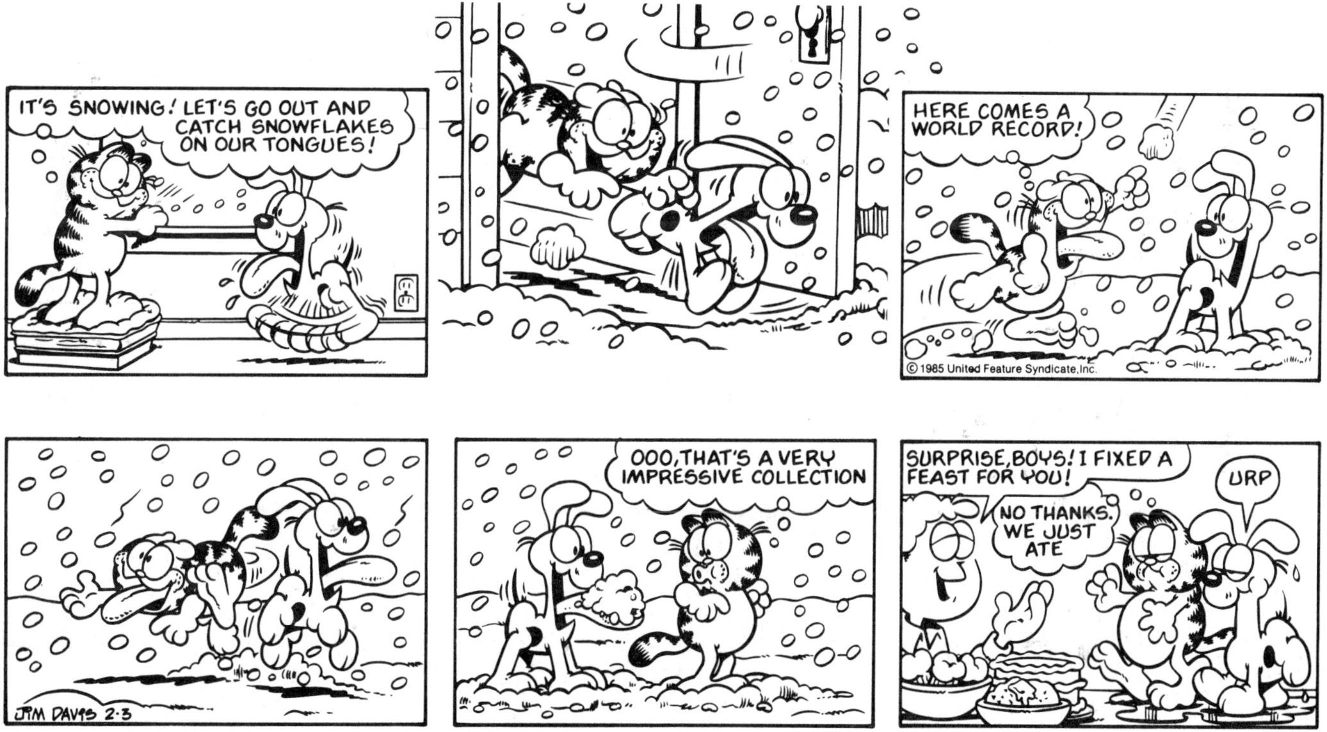

IT'S SNOWING! LET'S GO OUT AND CATCH SNOWFLAKES ON OUR TONGUES!
HERE COMES A WORLD RECORD!
© 1985 United Feature Syndicate, Inc.
JIM DAVIS 2·3
OOO, THAT'S A VERY IMPRESSIVE COLLECTION
SURPRISE, BOYS! I FIXED A FEAST FOR YOU!
NO THANKS. WE JUST ATE
URP

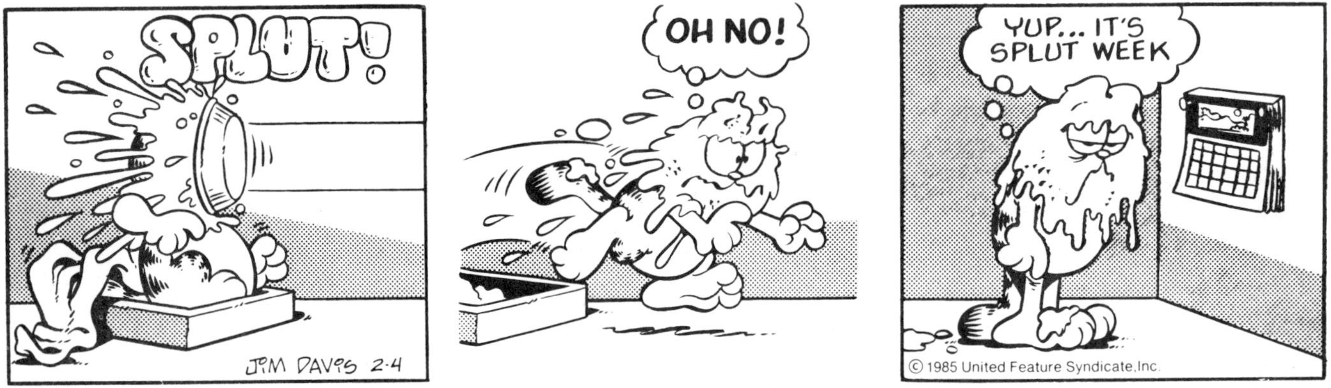
SPLUT!
JIM DAVIS 2·4
OH NO!
YUP... IT'S SPLUT WEEK
© 1985 United Feature Syndicate, Inc.

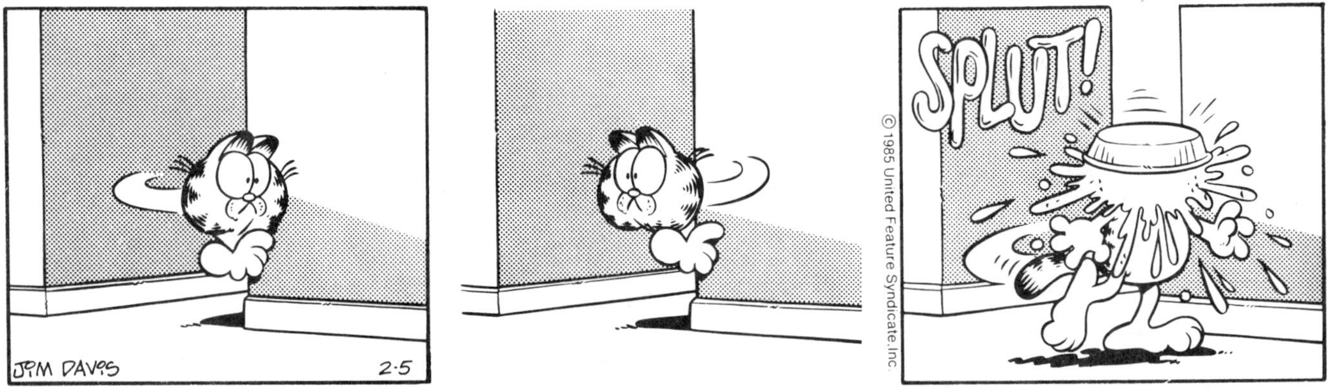
JIM DAVIS 2·5
© 1985 United Feature Syndicate, Inc.
SPLUT!

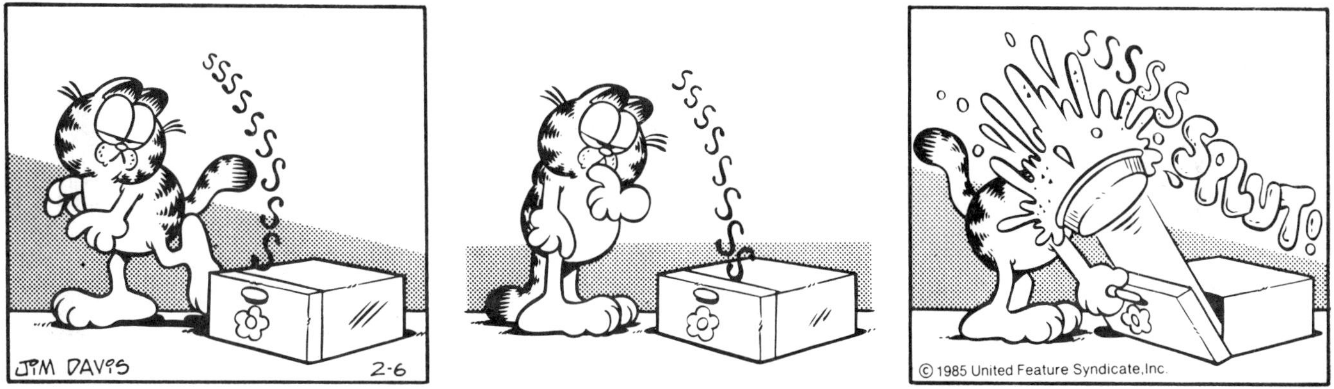
SSSSSSSS
JIM DAVIS
2-6
SSSSSSSS
SSSSS
SPLUT!

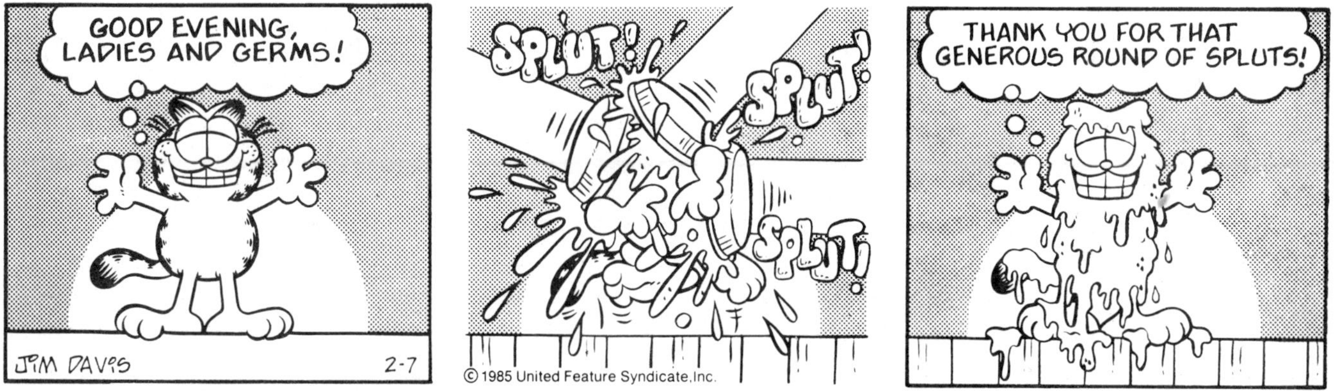
GOOD EVENING, LADIES AND GERMS!
JIM DAVIS
2-7
SPLUT!
SPLUT!
SPLUT!
THANK YOU FOR THAT GENEROUS ROUND OF SPLUTS!

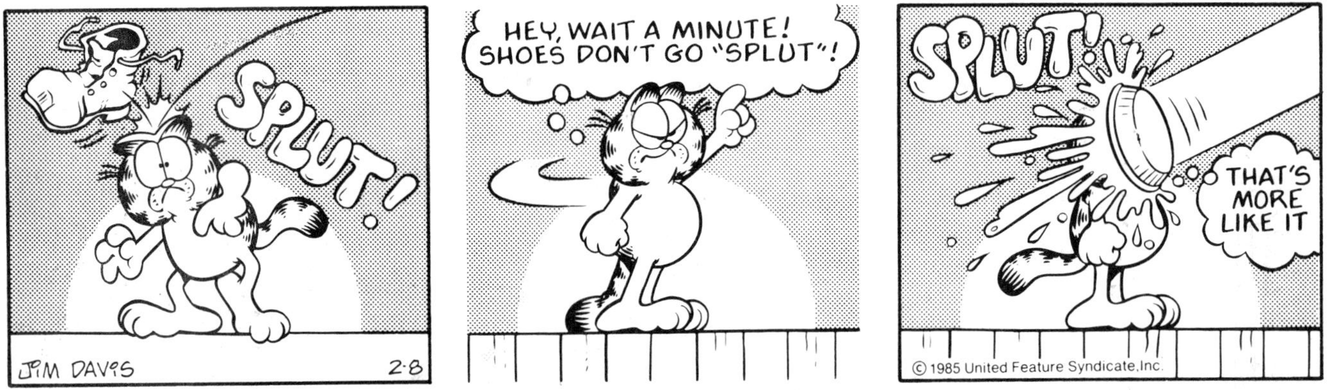
SPLUT!
JIM DAVIS
2-8
HEY, WAIT A MINUTE! SHOES DON'T GO "SPLUT"!
SPLUT!
THAT'S MORE LIKE IT
© 1985 United Feature Syndicate, Inc.

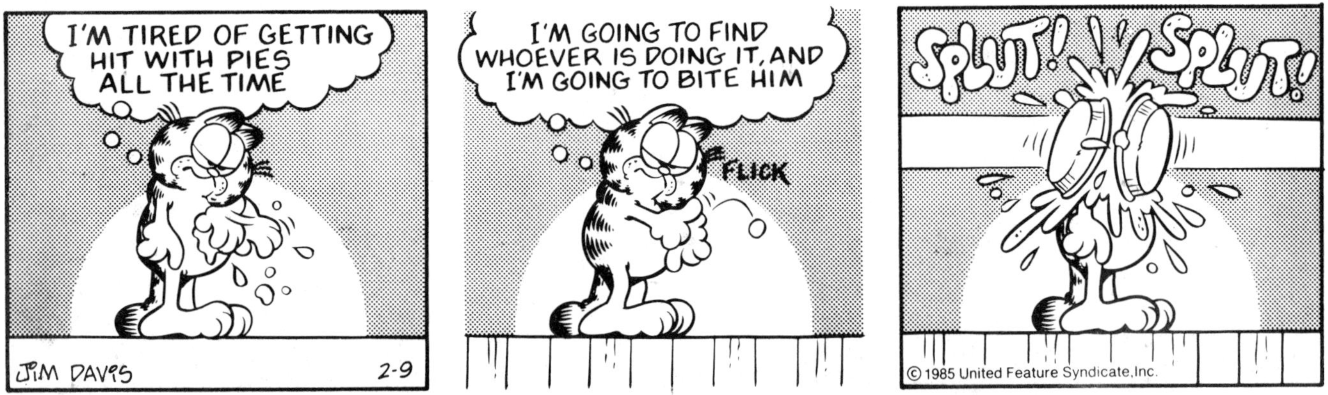
I'M TIRED OF GETTING HIT WITH PIES ALL THE TIME
JIM DAVIS
2-9
I'M GOING TO FIND WHOEVER IS DOING IT, AND I'M GOING TO BITE HIM
FLICK
SPLUT!
SPLUT!
© 1985 United Feature Syndicate, Inc.

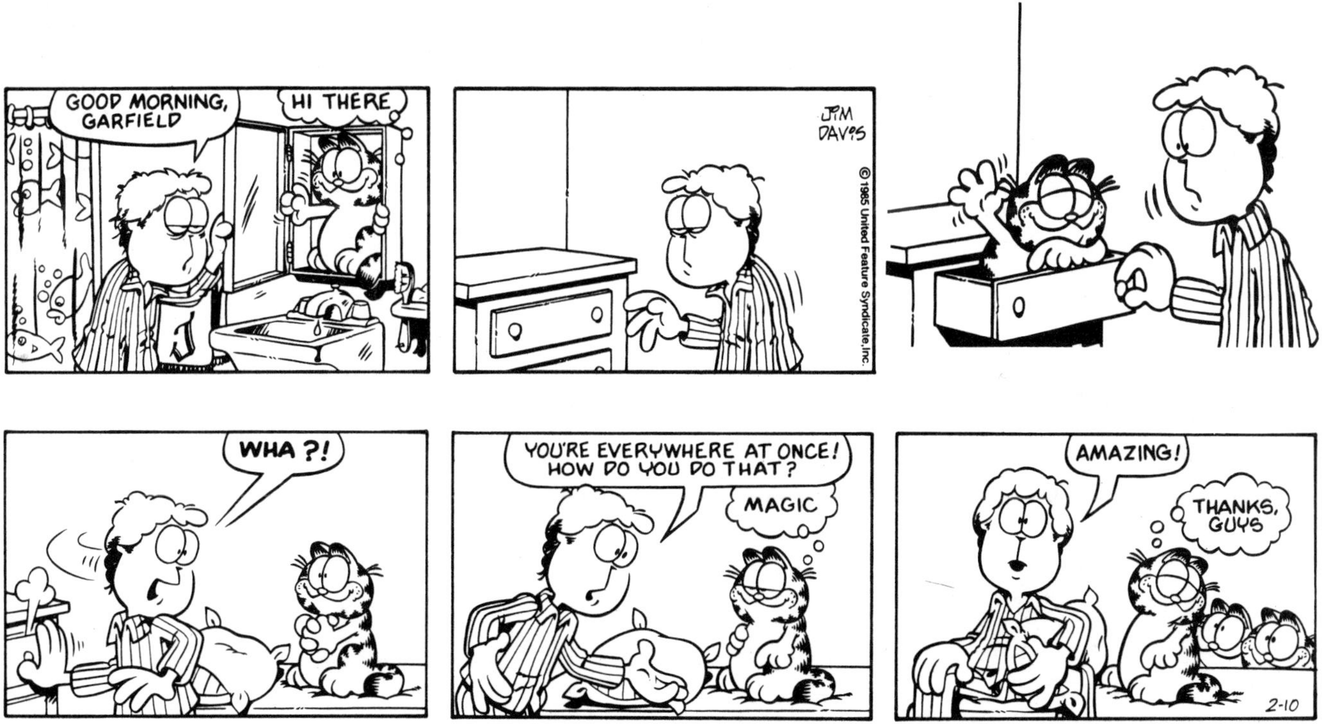
GOOD MORNING, GARFIELD
HI THERE
JIM DAVIS
© 1985 United Feature Syndicate, Inc.
WHA ?!
YOU'RE EVERYWHERE AT ONCE! HOW DO YOU DO THAT?
MAGIC
AMAZING!
THANKS, GUYS
2-10

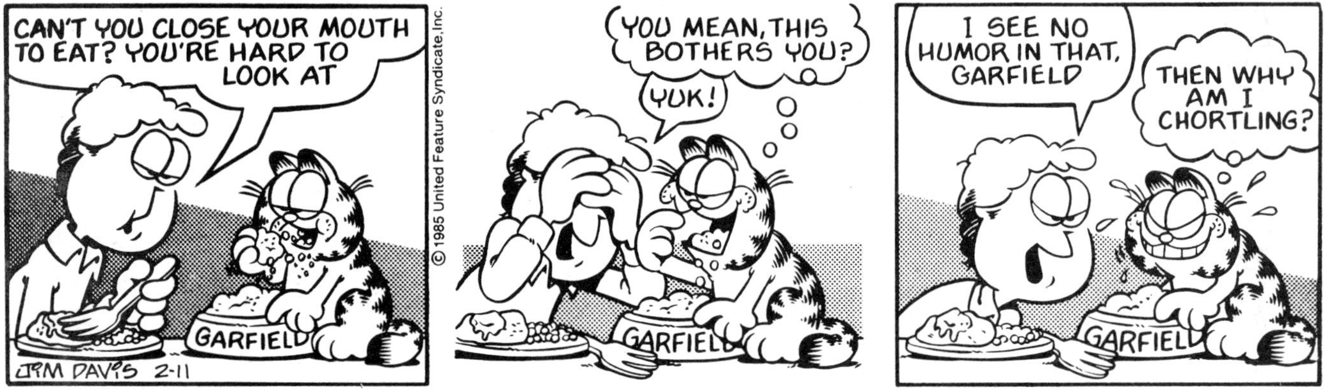
CAN'T YOU CLOSE YOUR MOUTH TO EAT? YOU'RE HARD TO LOOK AT
GARFIELD
JIM DAVIS 2-11
© 1985 United Feature Syndicate, Inc.
YOU MEAN, THIS BOTHERS YOU?
YUK!
GARFIELD
I SEE NO HUMOR IN THAT, GARFIELD
THEN WHY AM I CHORTLING?
GARFIELD

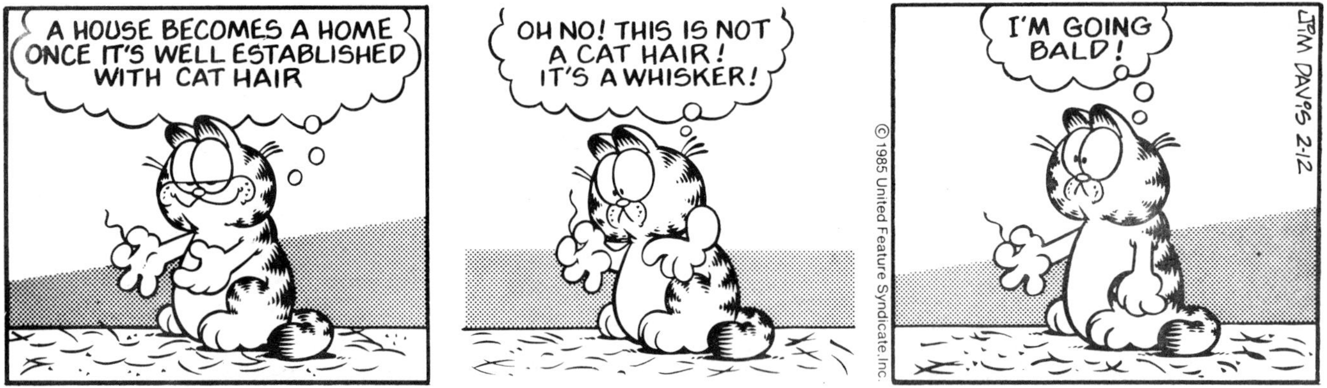
A HOUSE BECOMES A HOME ONCE IT'S WELL ESTABLISHED WITH CAT HAIR
OH NO! THIS IS NOT A CAT HAIR! IT'S A WHISKER!
© 1985 United Feature Syndicate, Inc.
I'M GOING BALD!
JIM DAVIS 2-12

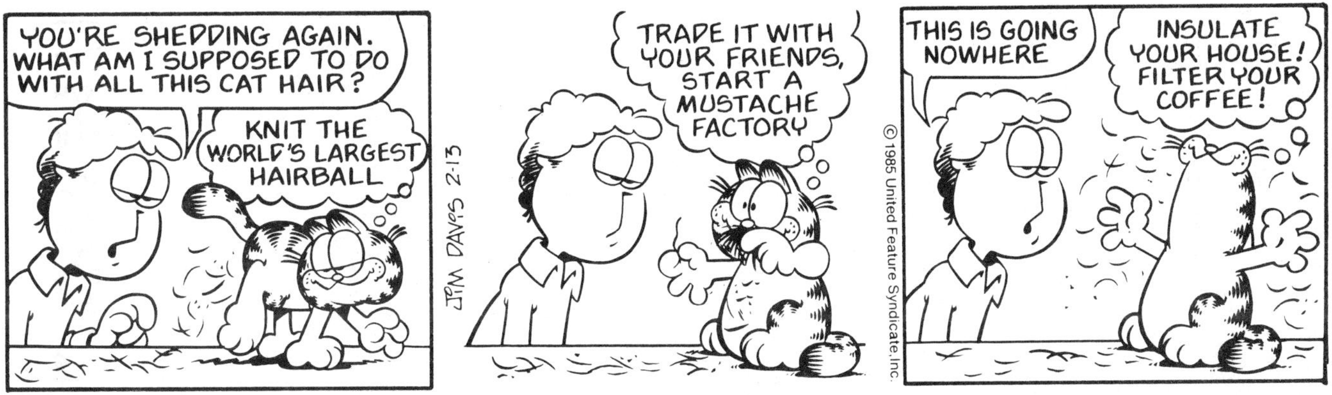
YOU'RE SHEDDING AGAIN. WHAT AM I SUPPOSED TO DO WITH ALL THIS CAT HAIR?
KNIT THE WORLD'S LARGEST HAIRBALL
JIM DAVIS 2-13
TRADE IT WITH YOUR FRIENDS, START A MUSTACHE FACTORY
THIS IS GOING NOWHERE
INSULATE YOUR HOUSE! FILTER YOUR COFFEE!
© 1985 United Feature Syndicate, Inc.

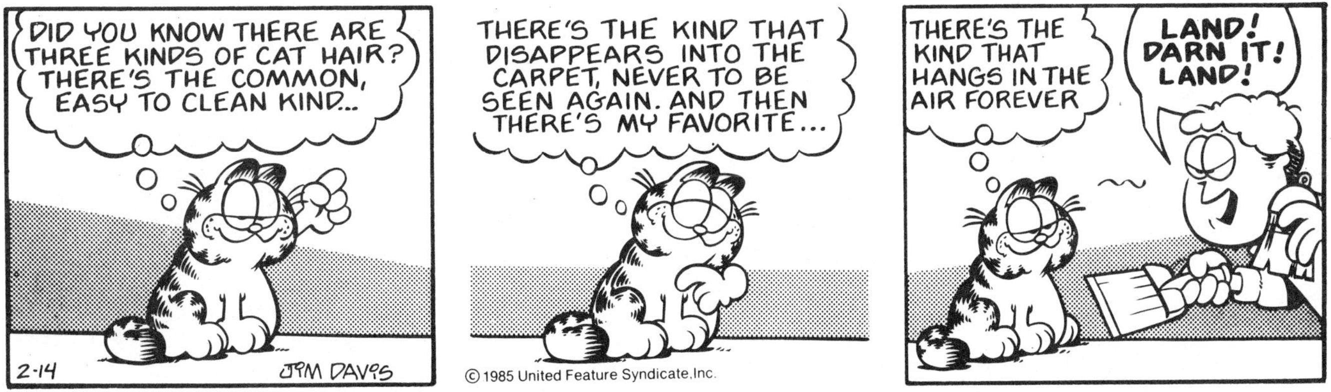
DID YOU KNOW THERE ARE THREE KINDS OF CAT HAIR? THERE'S THE COMMON, EASY TO CLEAN KIND...
2-14
JIM DAVIS
THERE'S THE KIND THAT DISAPPEARS INTO THE CARPET, NEVER TO BE SEEN AGAIN. AND THEN THERE'S MY FAVORITE...
© 1985 United Feature Syndicate, Inc.
THERE'S THE KIND THAT HANGS IN THE AIR FOREVER
LAND! DARN IT! LAND!

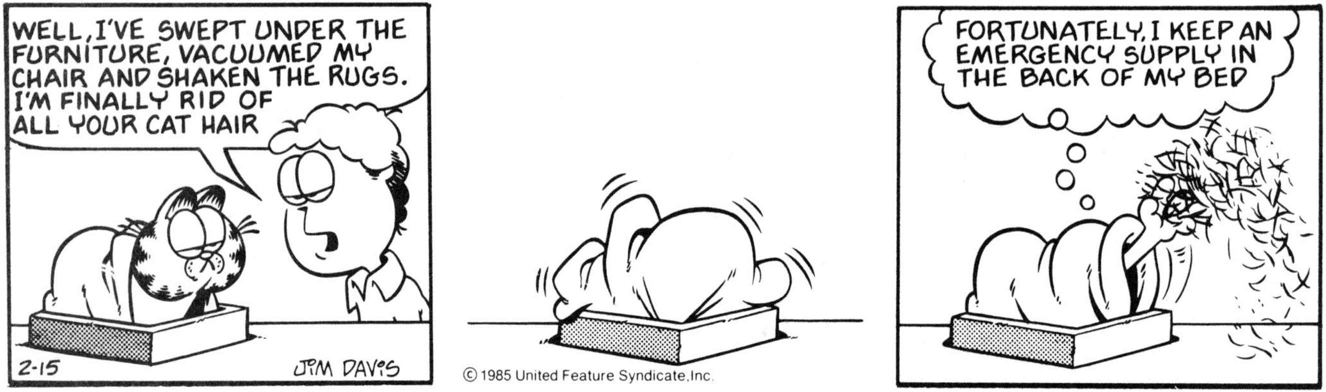
WELL, I'VE SWEPT UNDER THE FURNITURE, VACUUMED MY CHAIR AND SHAKEN THE RUGS. I'M FINALLY RID OF ALL YOUR CAT HAIR
2-15
JIM DAVIS
© 1985 United Feature Syndicate, Inc.
FORTUNATELY, I KEEP AN EMERGENCY SUPPLY IN THE BACK OF MY BED

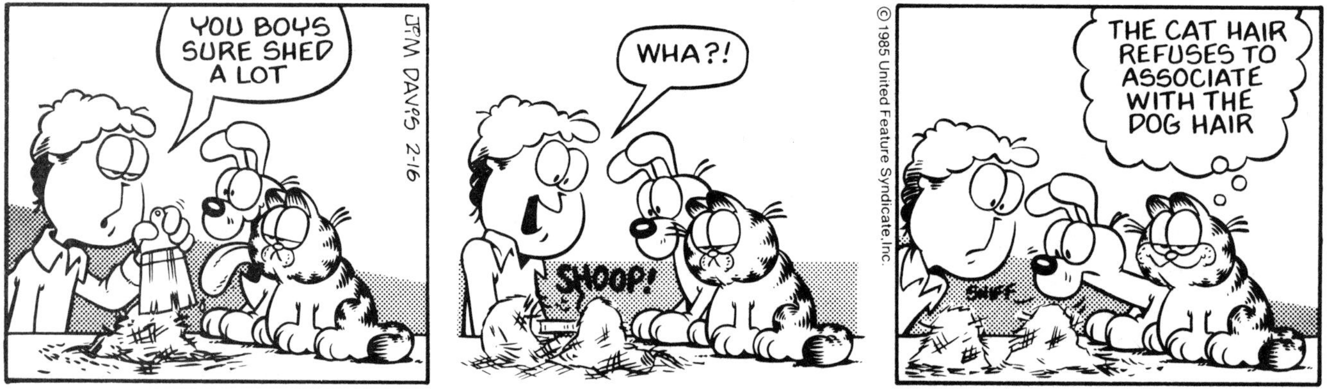
YOU BOYS SURE SHED A LOT
JIM DAVIS 2-16
WHA?!
SHOOP!
© 1985 United Feature Syndicate, Inc.
SNIFF
THE CAT HAIR REFUSES TO ASSOCIATE WITH THE DOG HAIR

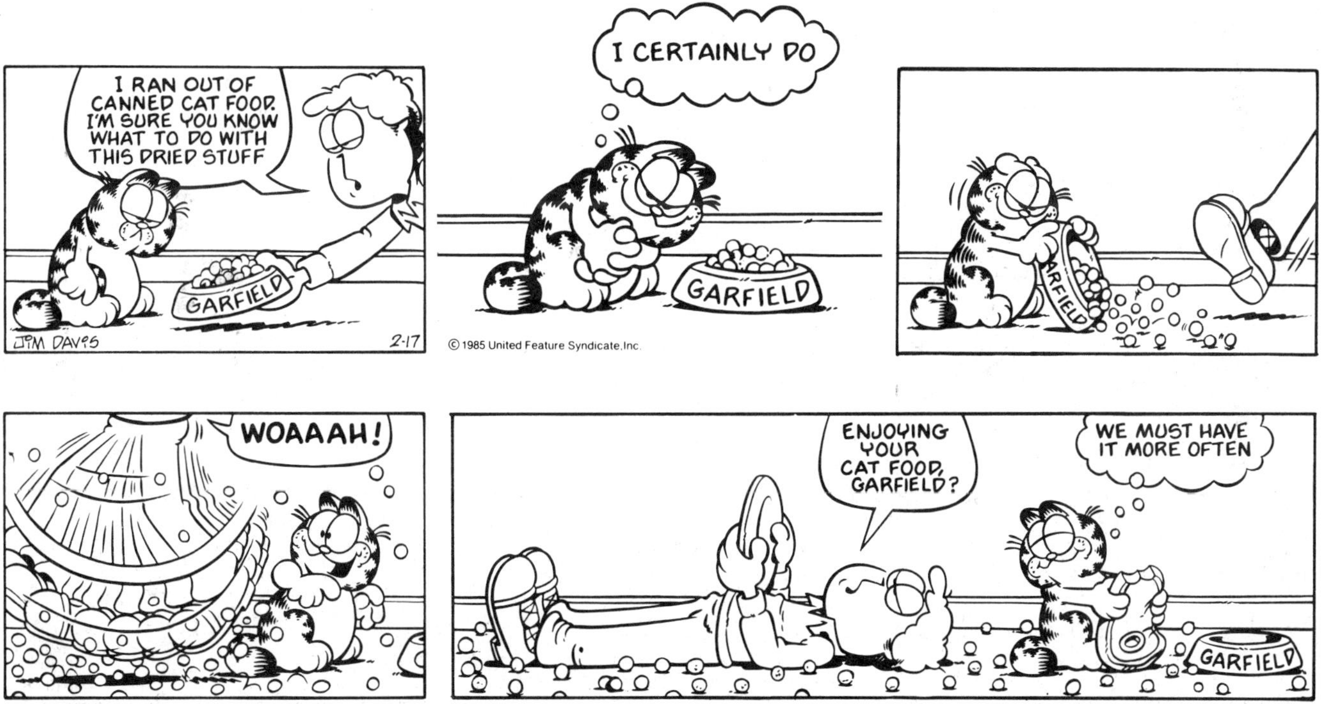
I RAN OUT OF CANNED CAT FOOD. I'M SURE YOU KNOW WHAT TO DO WITH THIS DRIED STUFF
GARFIELD
JIM DAVIS
2-17
I CERTAINLY DO
GARFIELD
GARFIELD
WOAAAH!
ENJOYING YOUR CAT FOOD, GARFIELD?
WE MUST HAVE IT MORE OFTEN
GARFIELD

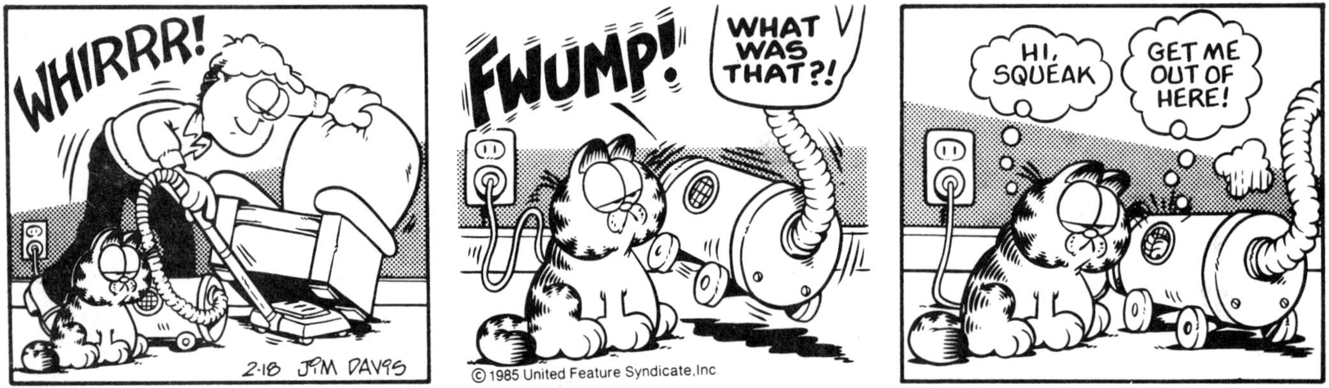
WHIRRR!
2-18 JIM DAVIS
FWUMP!
WHAT WAS THAT?!
© 1985 United Feature Syndicate, Inc
HI, SQUEAK
GET ME OUT OF HERE!

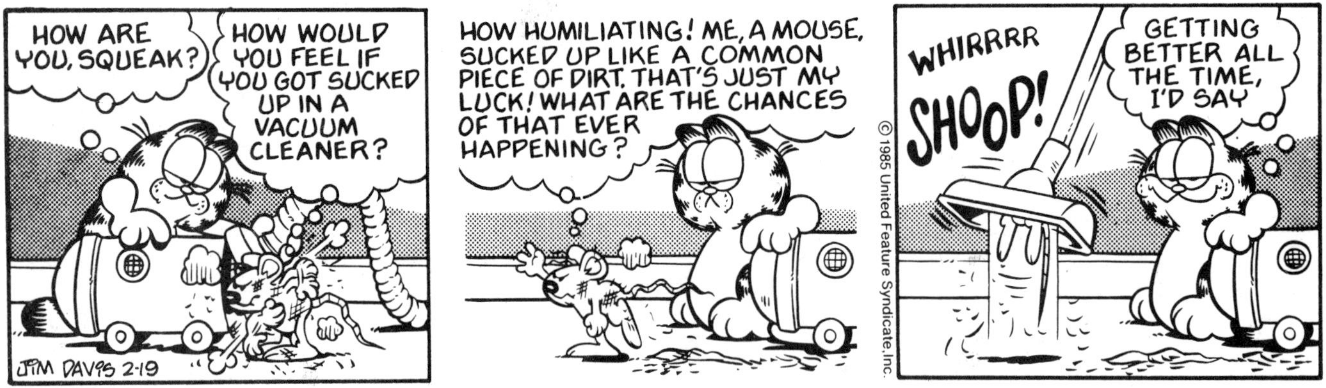
HOW ARE YOU, SQUEAK?
HOW WOULD YOU FEEL IF YOU GOT SUCKED UP IN A VACUUM CLEANER?
JIM DAVIS 2-19
HOW HUMILIATING! ME, A MOUSE, SUCKED UP LIKE A COMMON PIECE OF DIRT. THAT'S JUST MY LUCK! WHAT ARE THE CHANCES OF THAT EVER HAPPENING?
© 1985 United Feature Syndicate, Inc.
WHIRRRR
SHOOP!
GETTING BETTER ALL THE TIME, I'D SAY

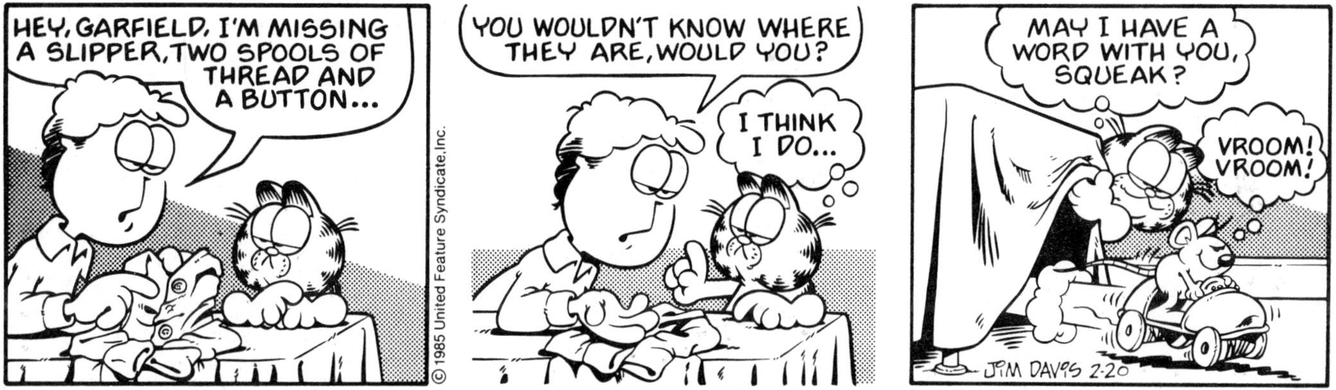
HEY, GARFIELD, I'M MISSING A SLIPPER, TWO SPOOLS OF THREAD AND A BUTTON...
© 1985 United Feature Syndicate, Inc.
YOU WOULDN'T KNOW WHERE THEY ARE, WOULD YOU?
I THINK I DO...
MAY I HAVE A WORD WITH YOU, SQUEAK?
VROOM! VROOM!
JIM DAVIS 2-20

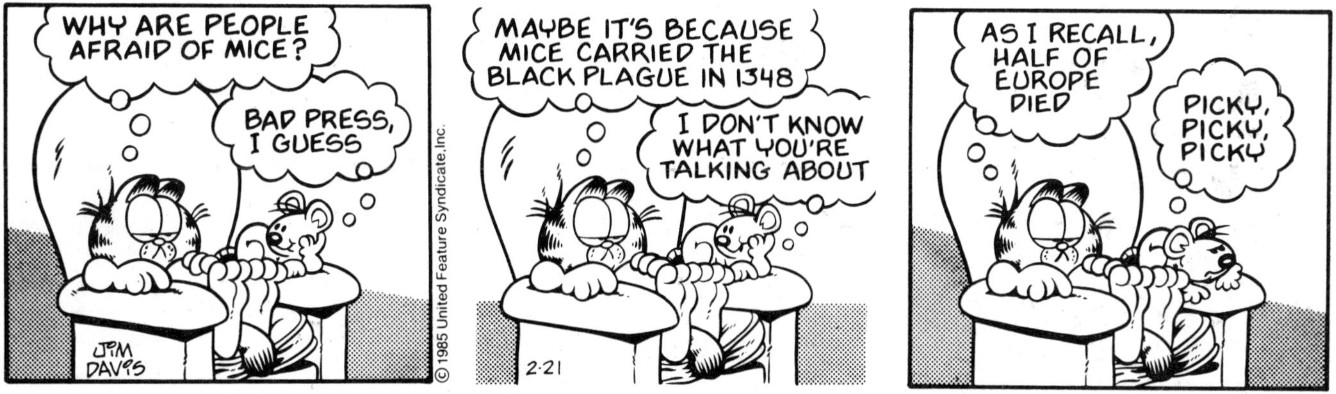
WHY ARE PEOPLE AFRAID OF MICE?
BAD PRESS, I GUESS
JIM DAVIS
© 1985 United Feature Syndicate, Inc.
MAYBE IT'S BECAUSE MICE CARRIED THE BLACK PLAGUE IN 1348
I DON'T KNOW WHAT YOU'RE TALKING ABOUT
2-21
AS I RECALL, HALF OF EUROPE DIED
PICKY, PICKY, PICKY

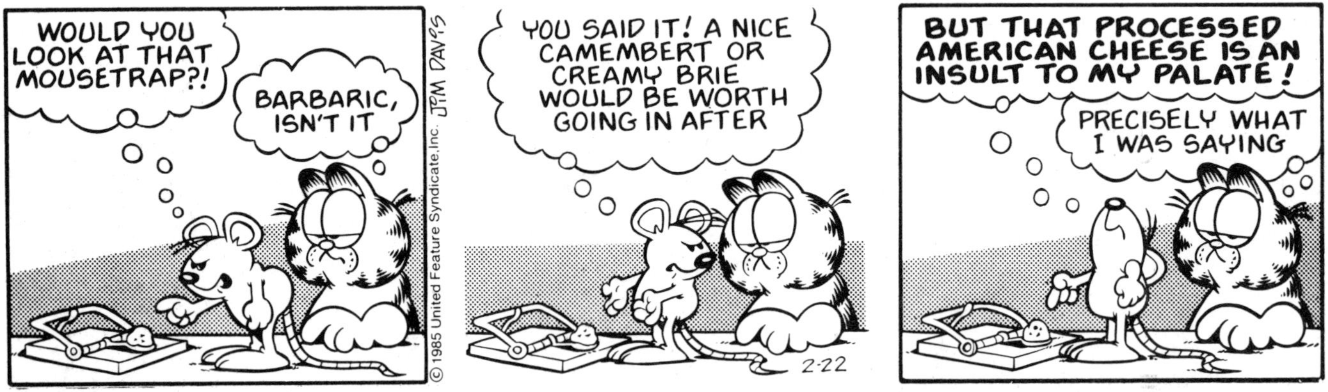
WOULD YOU LOOK AT THAT MOUSETRAP?!
BARBARIC, ISN'T IT
JIM DAVIS
© 1985 United Feature Syndicate, Inc.
YOU SAID IT! A NICE CAMEMBERT OR CREAMY BRIE WOULD BE WORTH GOING IN AFTER
2-22
BUT THAT PROCESSED AMERICAN CHEESE IS AN INSULT TO MY PALATE!
PRECISELY WHAT I WAS SAYING

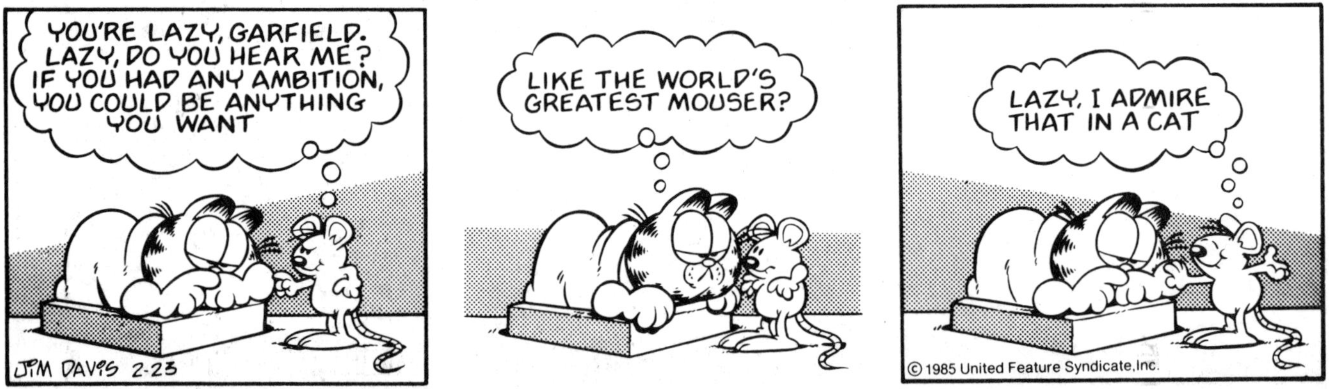
YOU'RE LAZY, GARFIELD. LAZY, DO YOU HEAR ME? IF YOU HAD ANY AMBITION, YOU COULD BE ANYTHING YOU WANT
JIM DAVIS 2-23
LIKE THE WORLD'S GREATEST MOUSER?
LAZY, I ADMIRE THAT IN A CAT
© 1985 United Feature Syndicate, Inc.

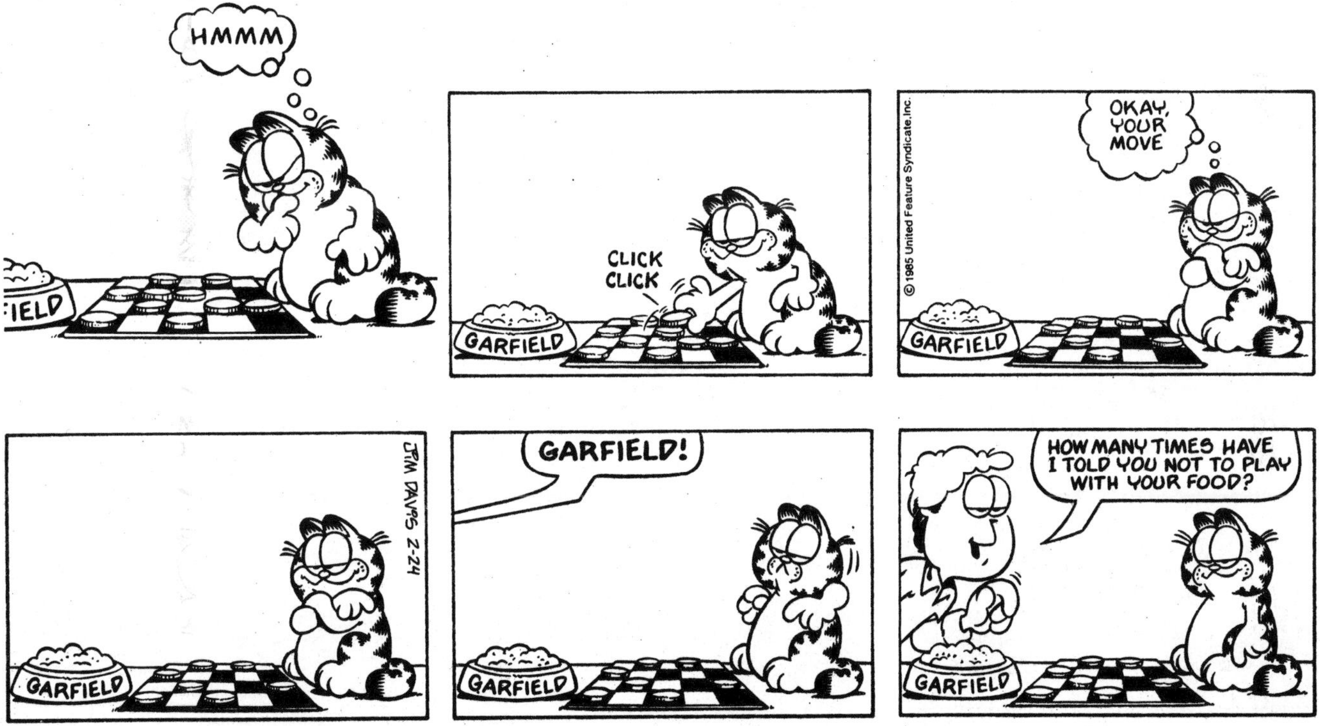
HMMM
FIELD
CLICK CLICK
GARFIELD
© 1985 United Feature Syndicate, Inc.
OKAY, YOUR MOVE
GARFIELD
JIM DAVIS 2-24
GARFIELD
GARFIELD!
GARFIELD
HOW MANY TIMES HAVE I TOLD YOU NOT TO PLAY WITH YOUR FOOD?
GARFIELD

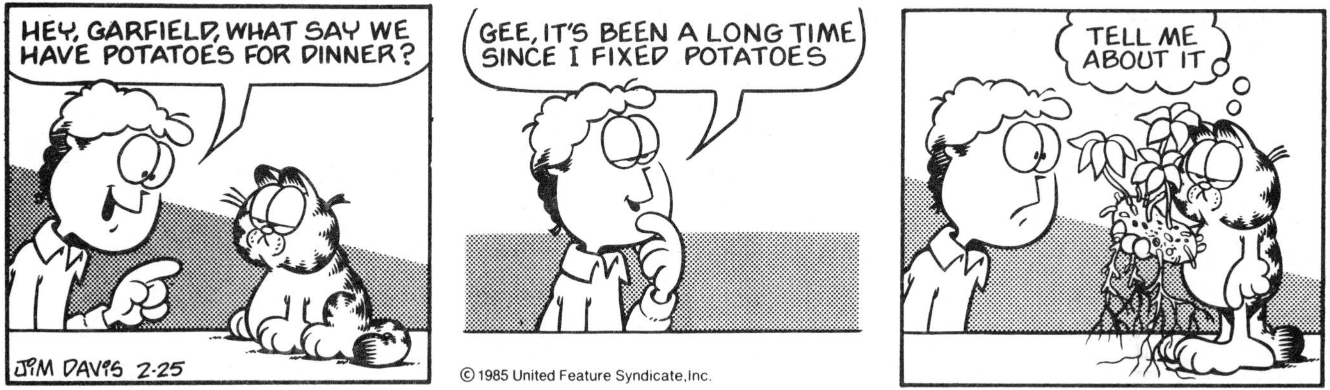
HEY, GARFIELD, WHAT SAY WE HAVE POTATOES FOR DINNER?
JIM DAVIS 2-25
GEE, IT'S BEEN A LONG TIME SINCE I FIXED POTATOES
© 1985 United Feature Syndicate, Inc.
TELL ME ABOUT IT

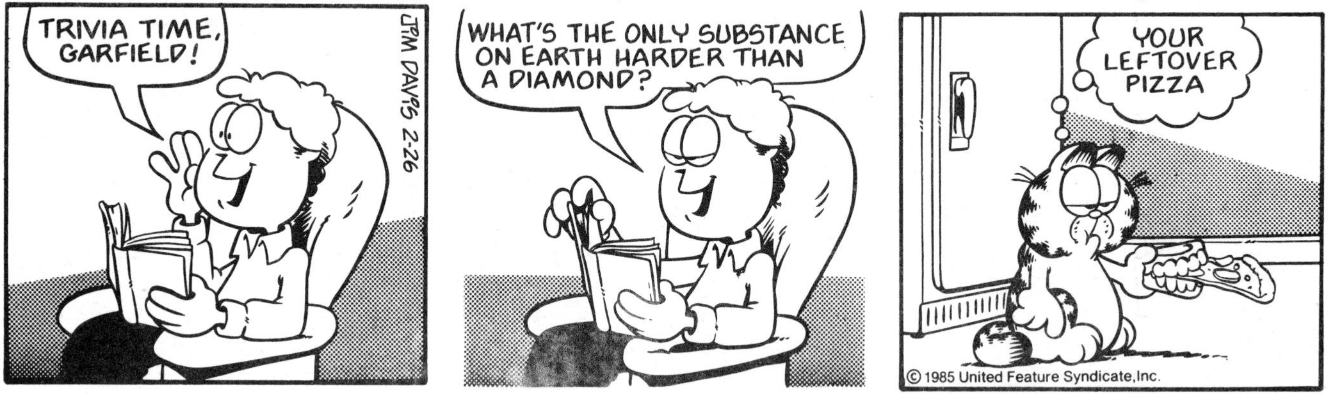
TRIVIA TIME, GARFIELD!
JIM DAVIS 2-26
WHAT'S THE ONLY SUBSTANCE ON EARTH HARDER THAN A DIAMOND?
YOUR LEFTOVER PIZZA
© 1985 United Feature Syndicate, Inc.

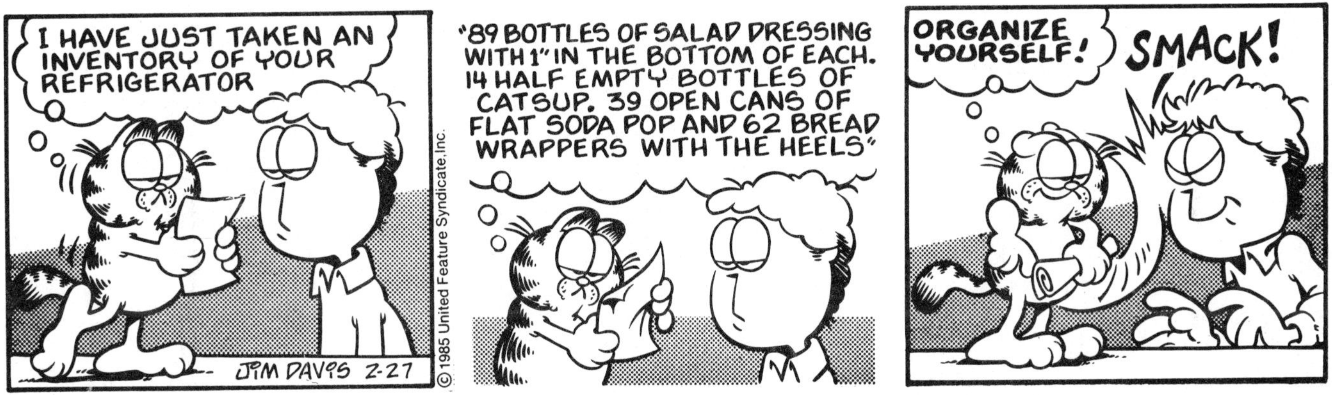
I HAVE JUST TAKEN AN INVENTORY OF YOUR REFRIGERATOR
JIM DAVIS 2-27
© 1985 United Feature Syndicate, Inc.
"89 BOTTLES OF SALAD DRESSING WITH 1" IN THE BOTTOM OF EACH. 14 HALF EMPTY BOTTLES OF CATSUP. 39 OPEN CANS OF FLAT SODA POP AND 62 BREAD WRAPPERS WITH THE HEELS"
ORGANIZE YOURSELF!
SMACK!

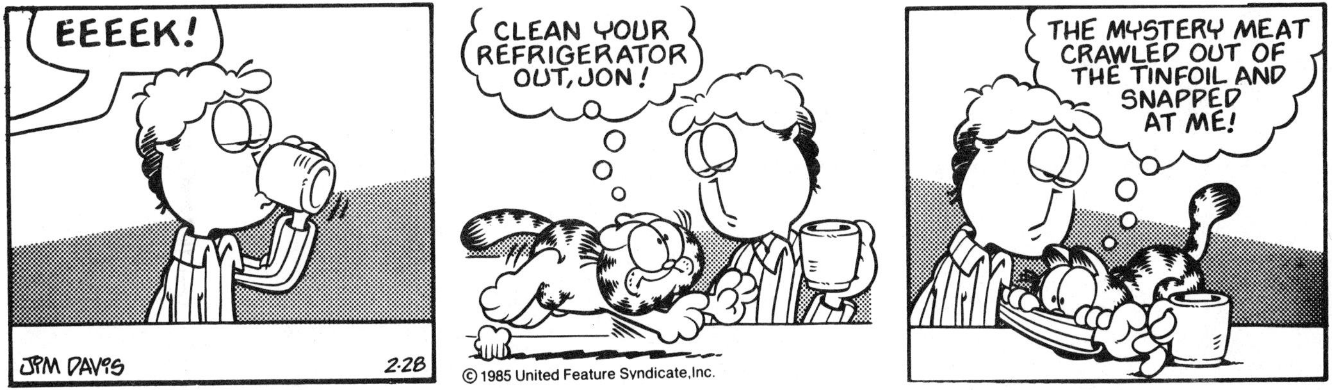
EEEEK!
JIM DAVIS
2-28
CLEAN YOUR REFRIGERATOR OUT, JON!
© 1985 United Feature Syndicate, Inc.
THE MYSTERY MEAT CRAWLED OUT OF THE TINFOIL AND SNAPPED AT ME!

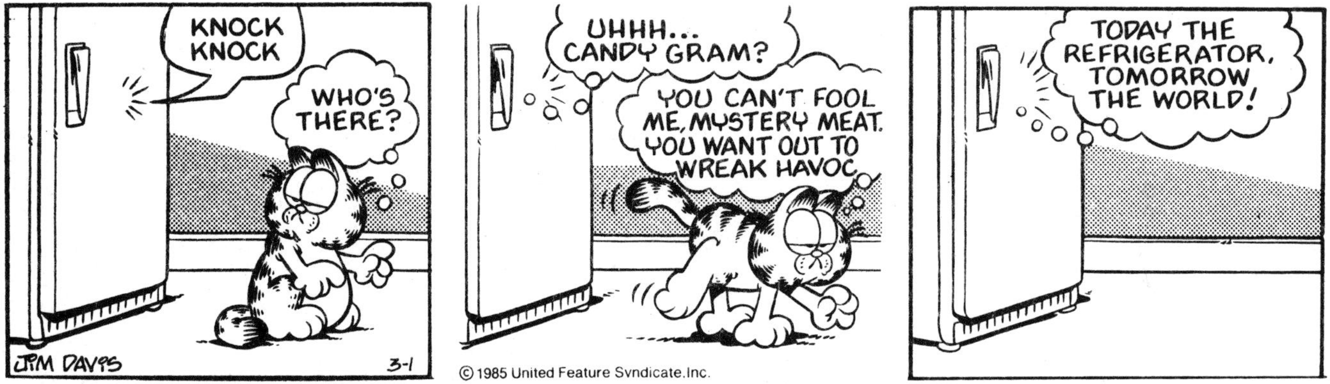
KNOCK KNOCK
WHO'S THERE?
UHHH... CANDY GRAM?
YOU CAN'T FOOL ME, MYSTERY MEAT. YOU WANT OUT TO WREAK HAVOC
TODAY THE REFRIGERATOR, TOMORROW THE WORLD!
JIM DAVIS 3-1
© 1985 United Feature Syndicate, Inc.

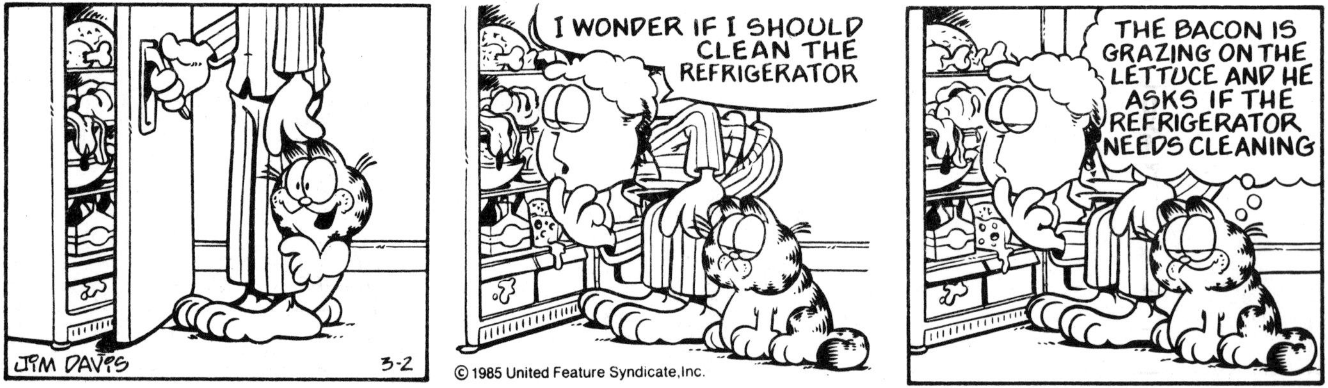
I WONDER IF I SHOULD CLEAN THE REFRIGERATOR
THE BACON IS GRAZING ON THE LETTUCE AND HE ASKS IF THE REFRIGERATOR NEEDS CLEANING
JIM DAVIS 3-2
© 1985 United Feature Syndicate, Inc.

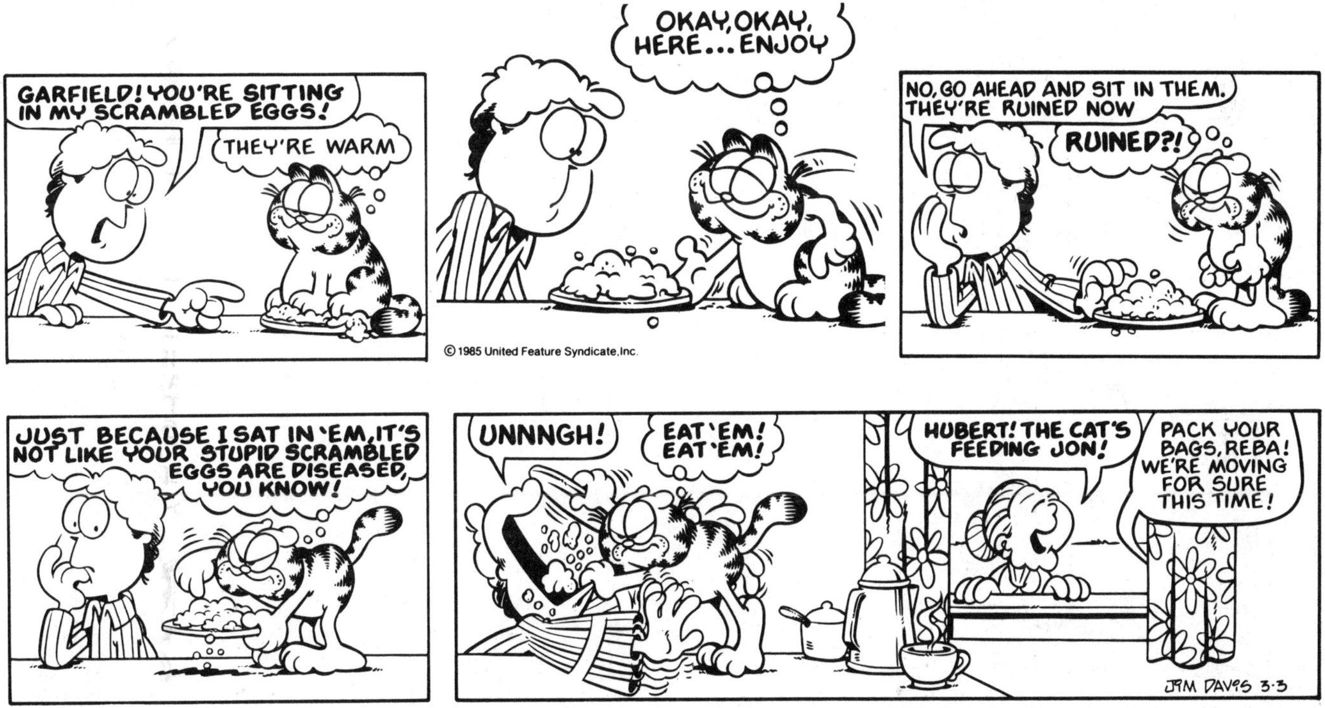
GARFIELD! YOU'RE SITTING IN MY SCRAMBLED EGGS!
THEY'RE WARM
OKAY, OKAY, HERE... ENJOY
NO, GO AHEAD AND SIT IN THEM. THEY'RE RUINED NOW
RUINED?!
JUST BECAUSE I SAT IN 'EM, IT'S NOT LIKE YOUR STUPID SCRAMBLED EGGS ARE DISEASED, YOU KNOW!
UNNNGH!
EAT 'EM! EAT 'EM!
HUBERT! THE CAT'S FEEDING JON!
PACK YOUR BAGS, REBA! WE'RE MOVING FOR SURE THIS TIME!
JIM DAVIS 3-3

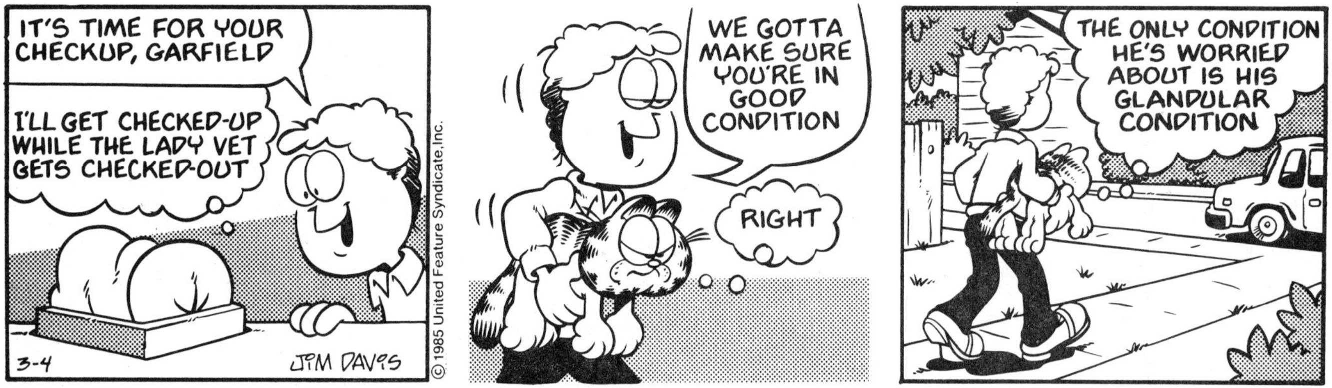
IT'S TIME FOR YOUR CHECKUP, GARFIELD
I'LL GET CHECKED-UP WHILE THE LADY VET GETS CHECKED-OUT
3-4
JIM DAVIS
WE GOTTA MAKE SURE YOU'RE IN GOOD CONDITION
RIGHT
THE ONLY CONDITION HE'S WORRIED ABOUT IS HIS GLANDULAR CONDITION

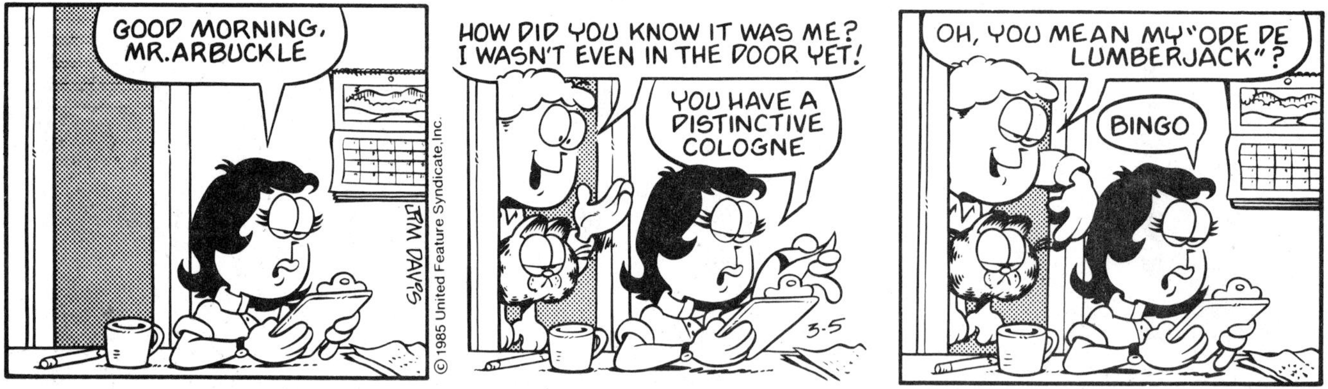
GOOD MORNING, MR. ARBUCKLE
JIM DAVIS
HOW DID YOU KNOW IT WAS ME? I WASN'T EVEN IN THE DOOR YET!
YOU HAVE A DISTINCTIVE COLOGNE
3-5
OH, YOU MEAN MY "ODE DE LUMBERJACK"?
BINGO

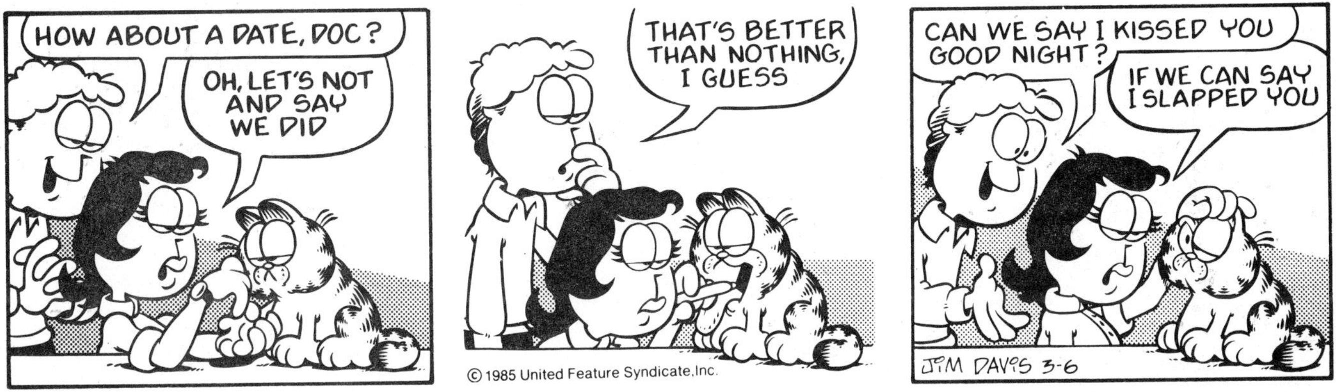
HOW ABOUT A DATE, DOC?
OH, LET'S NOT AND SAY WE DID
THAT'S BETTER THAN NOTHING, I GUESS
CAN WE SAY I KISSED YOU GOOD NIGHT?
IF WE CAN SAY I SLAPPED YOU
JIM DAVIS 3-6

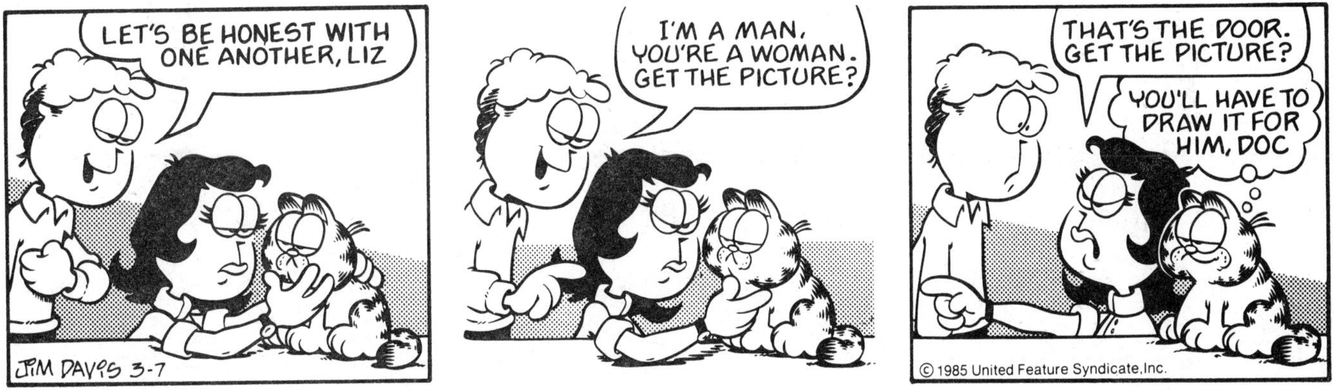
LET'S BE HONEST WITH ONE ANOTHER, LIZ
JIM DAVIS 3-7
I'M A MAN, YOU'RE A WOMAN. GET THE PICTURE?
THAT'S THE DOOR. GET THE PICTURE?
YOU'LL HAVE TO DRAW IT FOR HIM, DOC

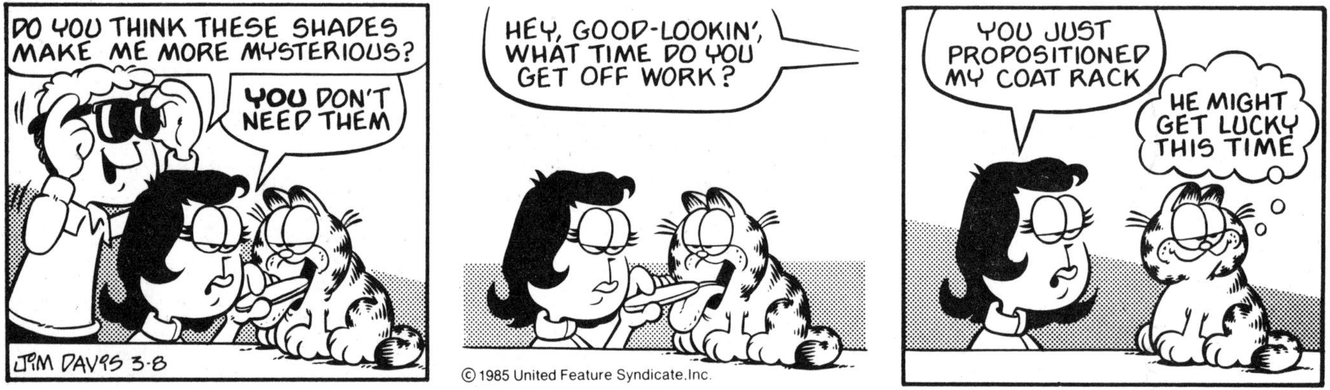
DO YOU THINK THESE SHADES MAKE ME MORE MYSTERIOUS?
YOU DON'T NEED THEM
JIM DAVIS 3-8
HEY, GOOD-LOOKIN', WHAT TIME DO YOU GET OFF WORK?
YOU JUST PROPOSITIONED MY COAT RACK
HE MIGHT GET LUCKY THIS TIME

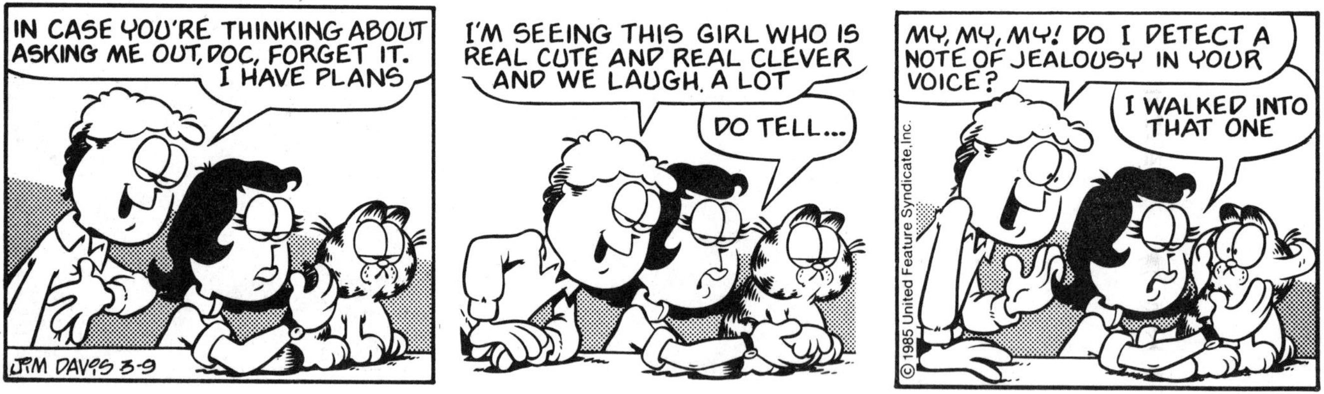
IN CASE YOU'RE THINKING ABOUT ASKING ME OUT, DOC, FORGET IT. I HAVE PLANS
JIM DAVIS 3-9
I'M SEEING THIS GIRL WHO IS REAL CUTE AND REAL CLEVER AND WE LAUGH A LOT
DO TELL...
MY, MY, MY! DO I DETECT A NOTE OF JEALOUSY IN YOUR VOICE?
I WALKED INTO THAT ONE

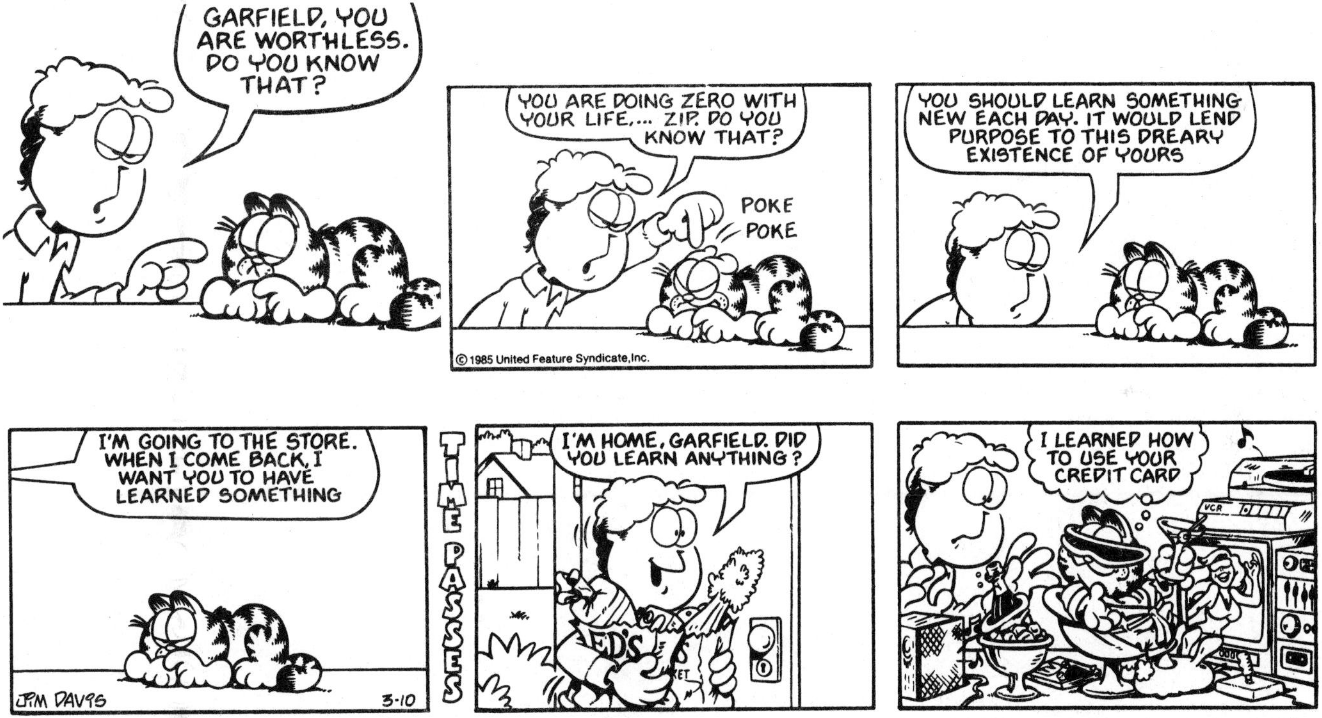

GARFIELD, YOU ARE WORTHLESS. DO YOU KNOW THAT?
YOU ARE DOING ZERO WITH YOUR LIFE,... ZIP. DO YOU KNOW THAT?
POKE POKE
© 1985 United Feature Syndicate, Inc.
YOU SHOULD LEARN SOMETHING NEW EACH DAY. IT WOULD LEND PURPOSE TO THIS DREARY EXISTENCE OF YOURS
I'M GOING TO THE STORE. WHEN I COME BACK, I WANT YOU TO HAVE LEARNED SOMETHING
JIM DAVIS
3-10
TIME PASSES
I'M HOME, GARFIELD. DID YOU LEARN ANYTHING?
ED'S
I LEARNED HOW TO USE YOUR CREDIT CARD
VCR

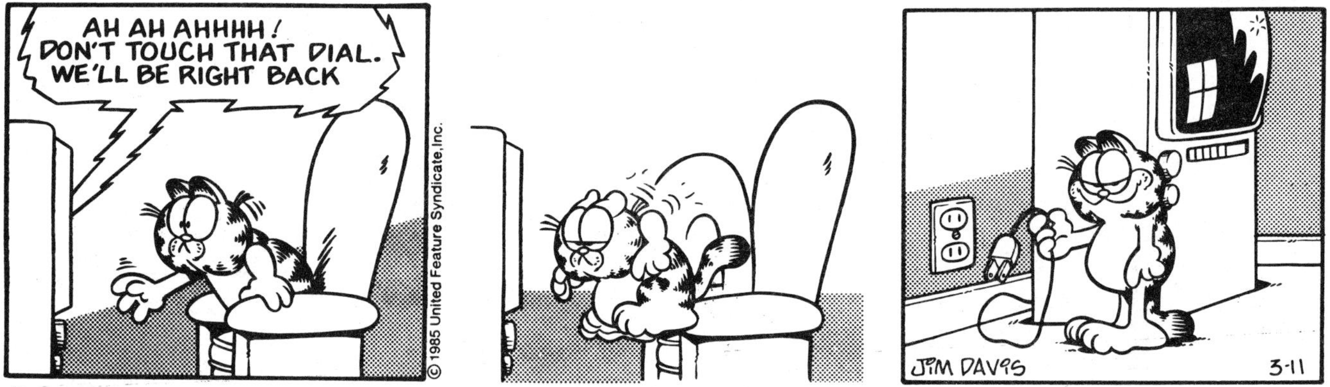
AH AH AHHHH! DON'T TOUCH THAT DIAL. WE'LL BE RIGHT BACK
© 1985 United Feature Syndicate, Inc.
JIM DAVIS
3-11

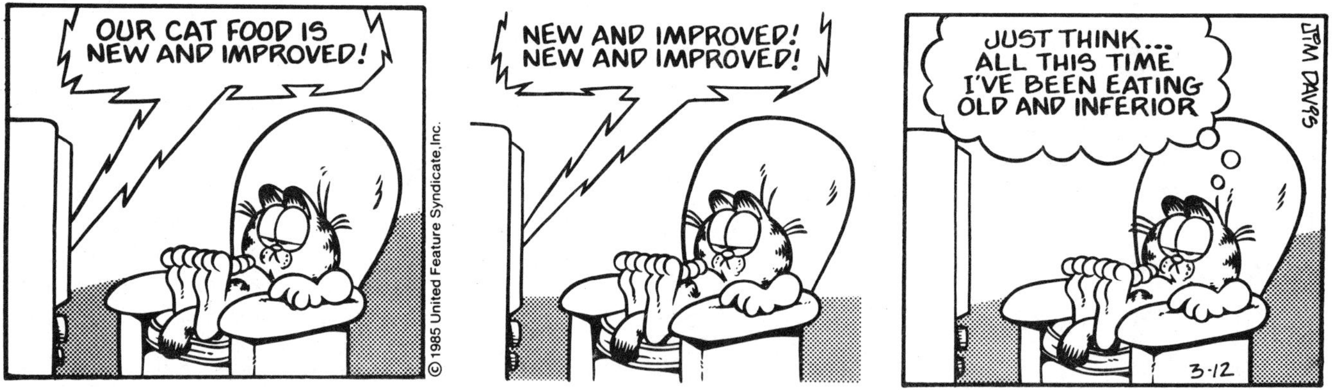
OUR CAT FOOD IS NEW AND IMPROVED!
© 1985 United Feature Syndicate, Inc.
NEW AND IMPROVED! NEW AND IMPROVED!
JUST THINK... ALL THIS TIME I'VE BEEN EATING OLD AND INFERIOR
JIM DAVIS
3-12

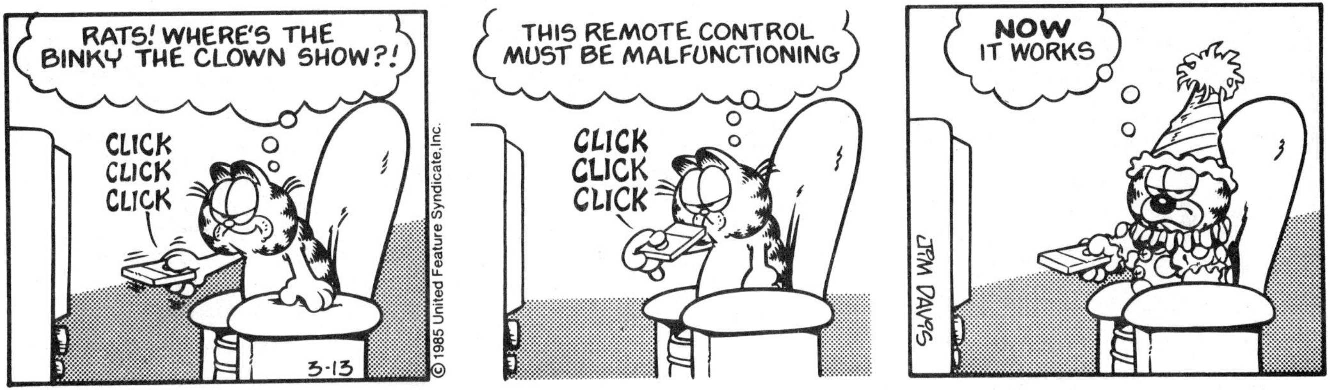
RATS! WHERE'S THE BINKY THE CLOWN SHOW?!
CLICK CLICK CLICK
3-13
© 1985 United Feature Syndicate, Inc.
THIS REMOTE CONTROL MUST BE MALFUNCTIONING
CLICK CLICK CLICK
NOW IT WORKS
JIM DAVIS

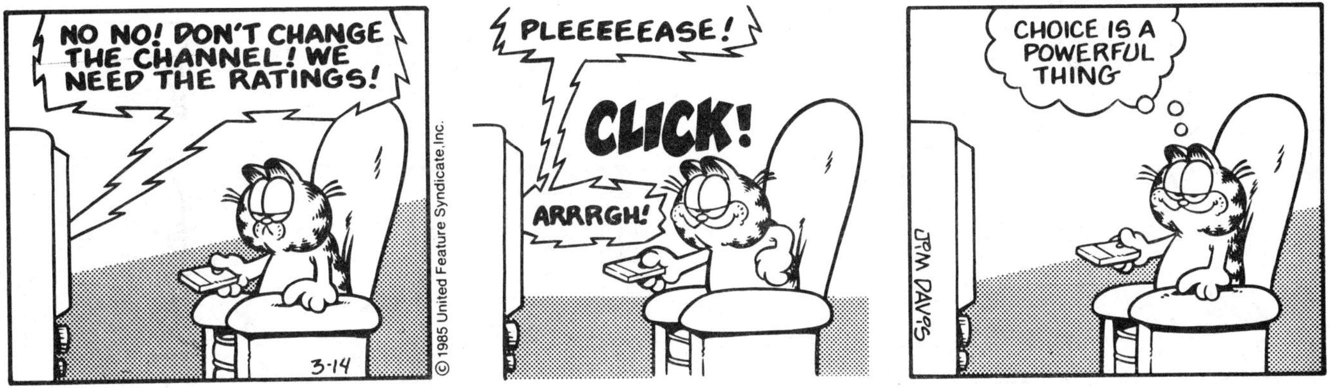
NO NO! DON'T CHANGE THE CHANNEL! WE NEED THE RATINGS!
3-14
© 1985 United Feature Syndicate, Inc.
PLEEEEEEASE!
CLICK!
ARRRGH!
CHOICE IS A POWERFUL THING
JIM DAVIS

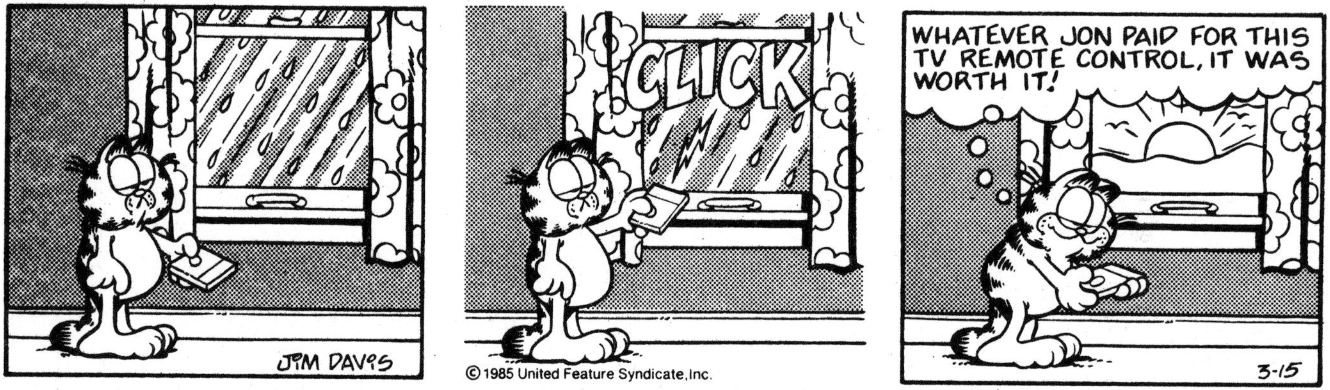
CLICK
WHATEVER JON PAID FOR THIS TV REMOTE CONTROL, IT WAS WORTH IT!
JIM DAVIS
3-15

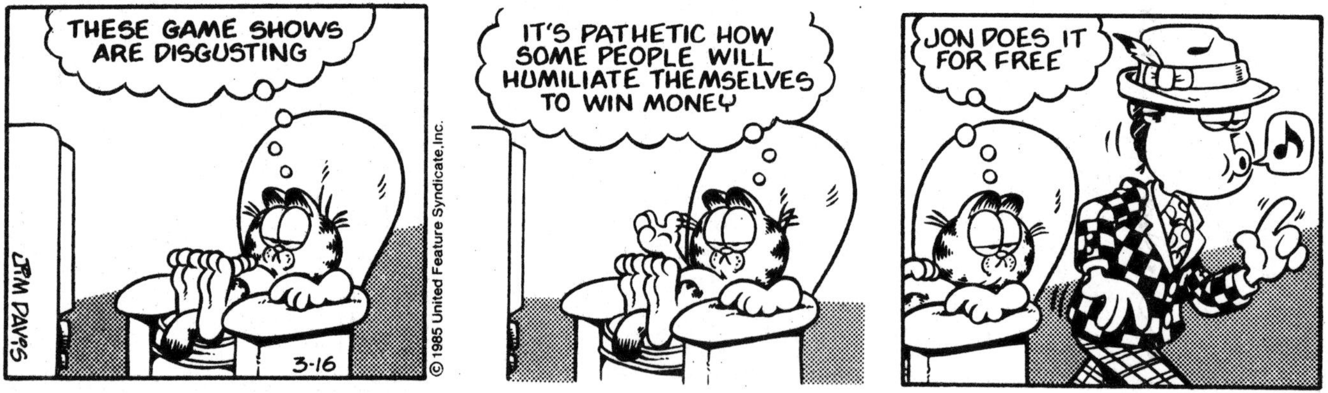
THESE GAME SHOWS ARE DISGUSTING
IT'S PATHETIC HOW SOME PEOPLE WILL HUMILIATE THEMSELVES TO WIN MONEY
JON DOES IT FOR FREE
JIM DAVIS
3-16

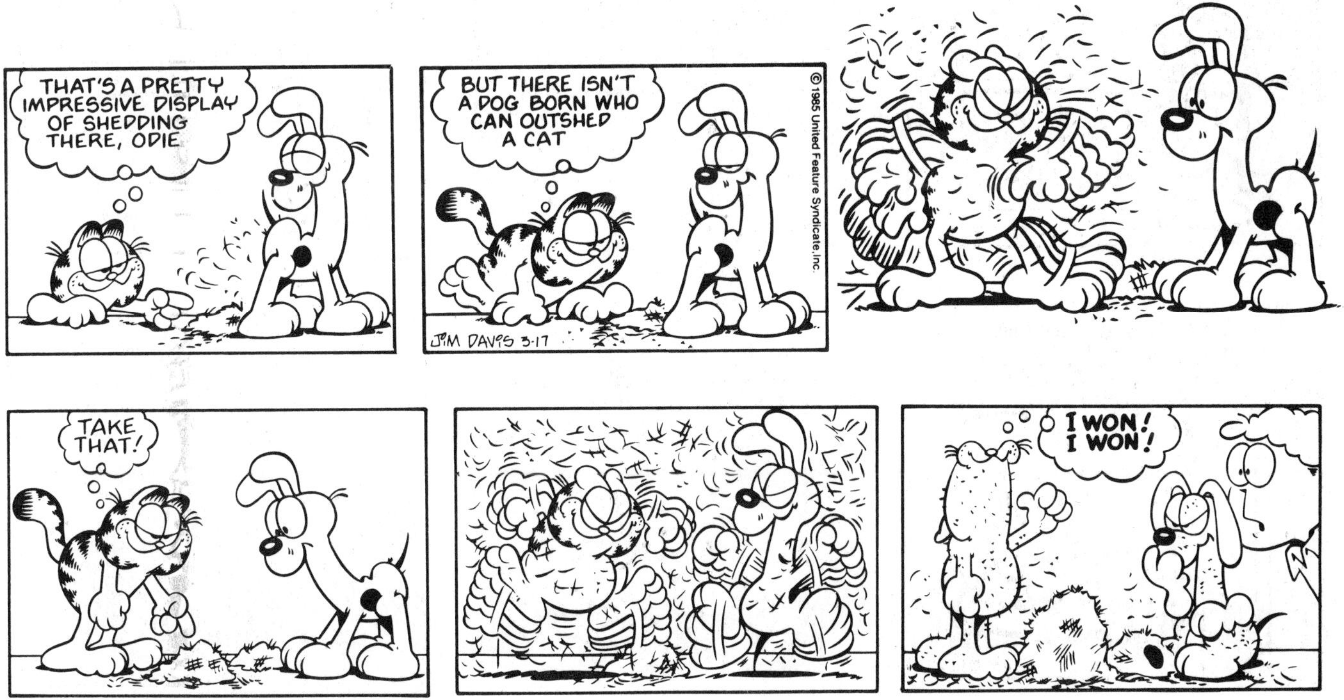
THAT'S A PRETTY IMPRESSIVE DISPLAY OF SHEDDING THERE, ODIE
BUT THERE ISN'T A DOG BORN WHO CAN OUTSHED A CAT
© 1985 United Feature Syndicate, Inc.
JIM DAVIS 3-17
TAKE THAT!
I WON! I WON!

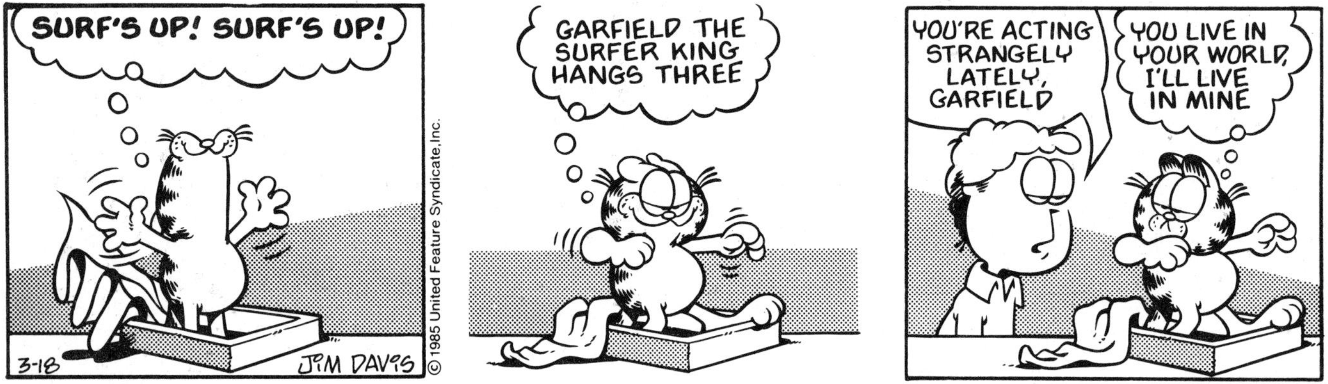
SURF'S UP! SURF'S UP!
3-18
JIM DAVIS
© 1985 United Feature Syndicate, Inc.
GARFIELD THE SURFER KING HANGS THREE
YOU'RE ACTING STRANGELY LATELY, GARFIELD
YOU LIVE IN YOUR WORLD, I'LL LIVE IN MINE

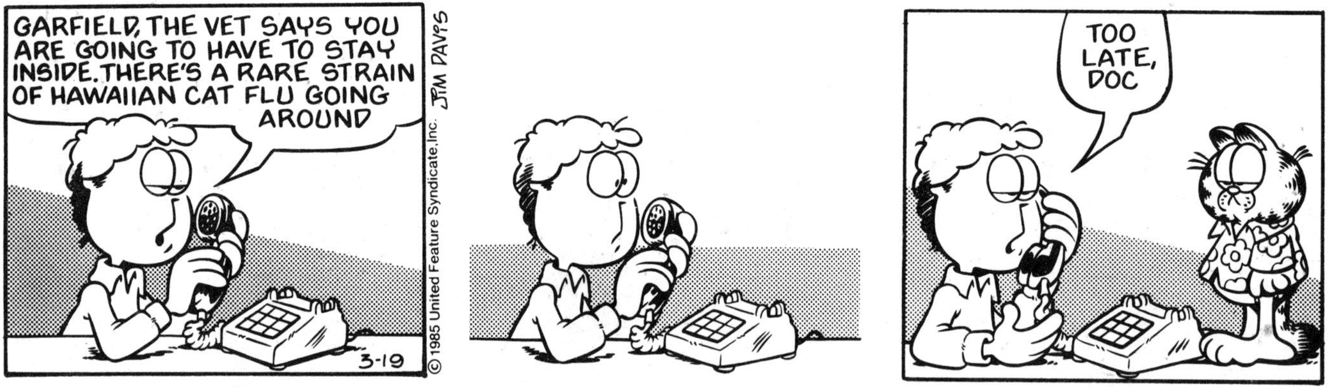
GARFIELD, THE VET SAYS YOU ARE GOING TO HAVE TO STAY INSIDE. THERE'S A RARE STRAIN OF HAWAIIAN CAT FLU GOING AROUND
JIM DAVIS
© 1985 United Feature Syndicate, Inc.
3-19
TOO LATE, DOC

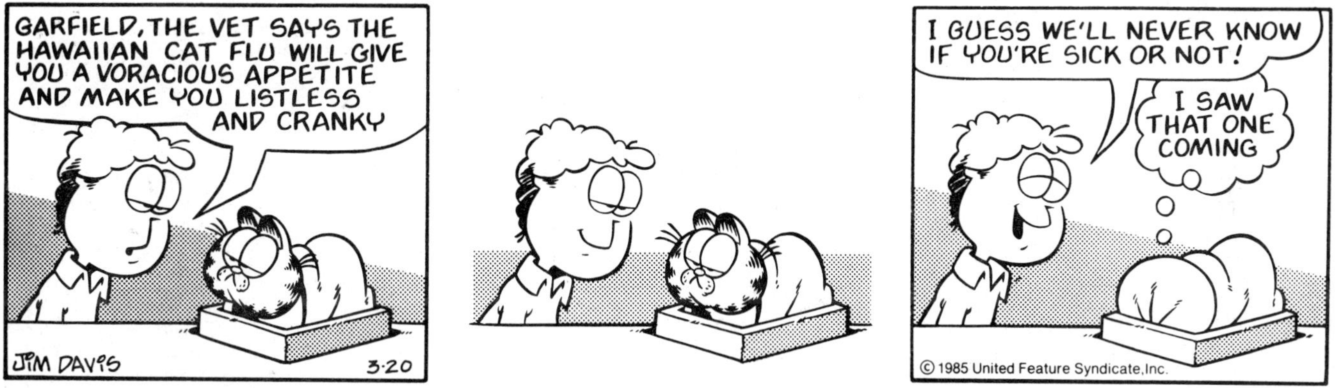
GARFIELD, THE VET SAYS THE HAWAIIAN CAT FLU WILL GIVE YOU A VORACIOUS APPETITE AND MAKE YOU LISTLESS AND CRANKY
JIM DAVIS
3-20
I GUESS WE'LL NEVER KNOW IF YOU'RE SICK OR NOT!
I SAW THAT ONE COMING
© 1985 United Feature Syndicate, Inc.

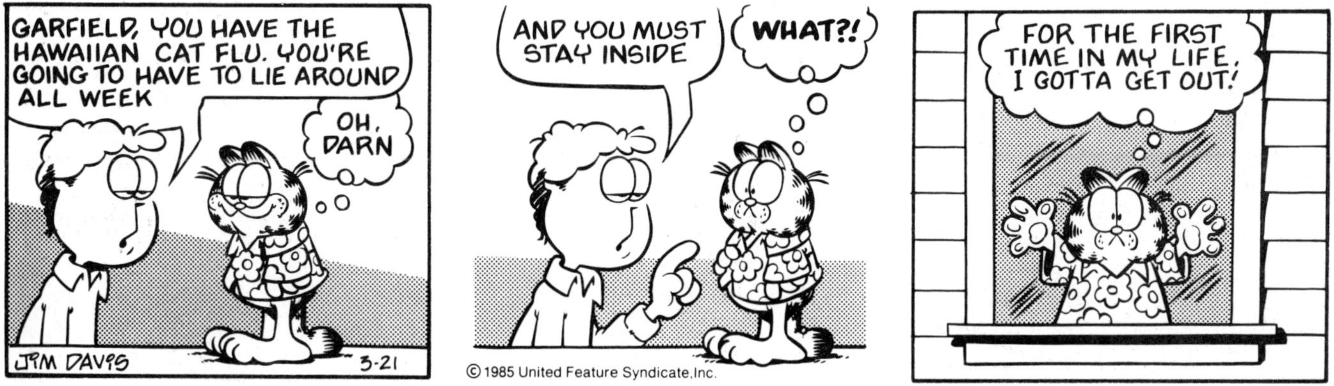
GARFIELD, YOU HAVE THE HAWAIIAN CAT FLU. YOU'RE GOING TO HAVE TO LIE AROUND ALL WEEK
OH, DARN
JIM DAVIS
3-21
AND YOU MUST STAY INSIDE
WHAT?!
© 1985 United Feature Syndicate, Inc.
FOR THE FIRST TIME IN MY LIFE, I GOTTA GET OUT!

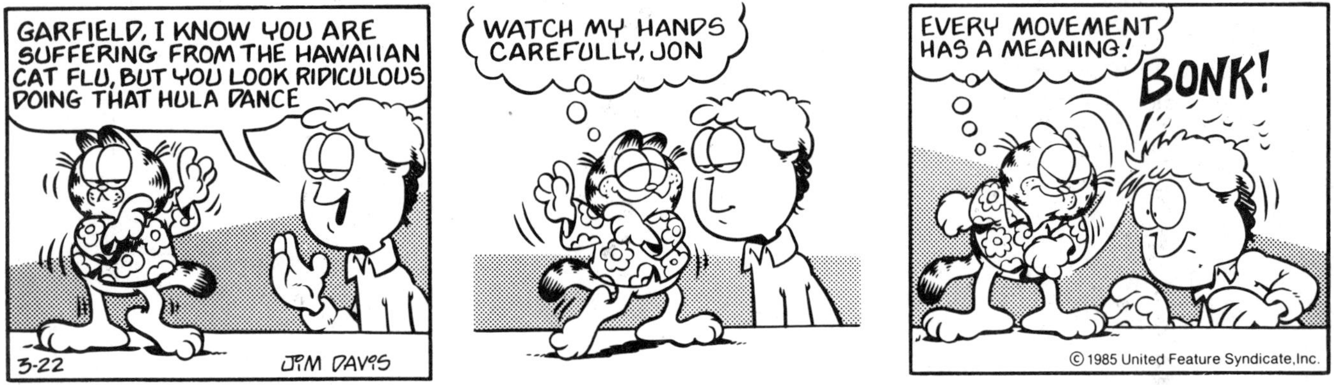
GARFIELD, I KNOW YOU ARE SUFFERING FROM THE HAWAIIAN CAT FLU, BUT YOU LOOK RIDICULOUS DOING THAT HULA DANCE
3-22
JIM DAVIS
WATCH MY HANDS CAREFULLY, JON
EVERY MOVEMENT HAS A MEANING!
BONK!
© 1985 United Feature Syndicate, Inc.

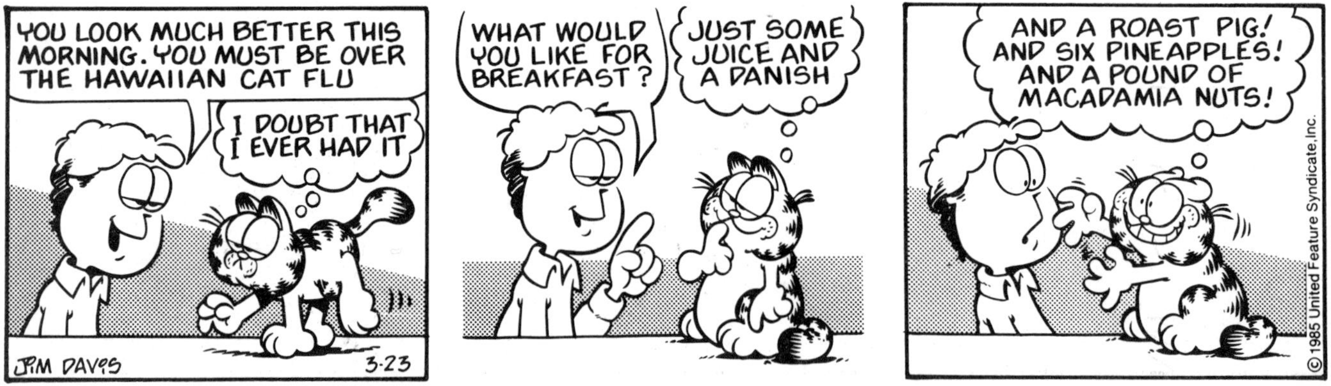
YOU LOOK MUCH BETTER THIS MORNING. YOU MUST BE OVER THE HAWAIIAN CAT FLU
I DOUBT THAT I EVER HAD IT
JIM DAVIS
3-23
WHAT WOULD YOU LIKE FOR BREAKFAST?
JUST SOME JUICE AND A DANISH
AND A ROAST PIG! AND SIX PINEAPPLES! AND A POUND OF MACADAMIA NUTS!
© 1985 United Feature Syndicate, Inc.

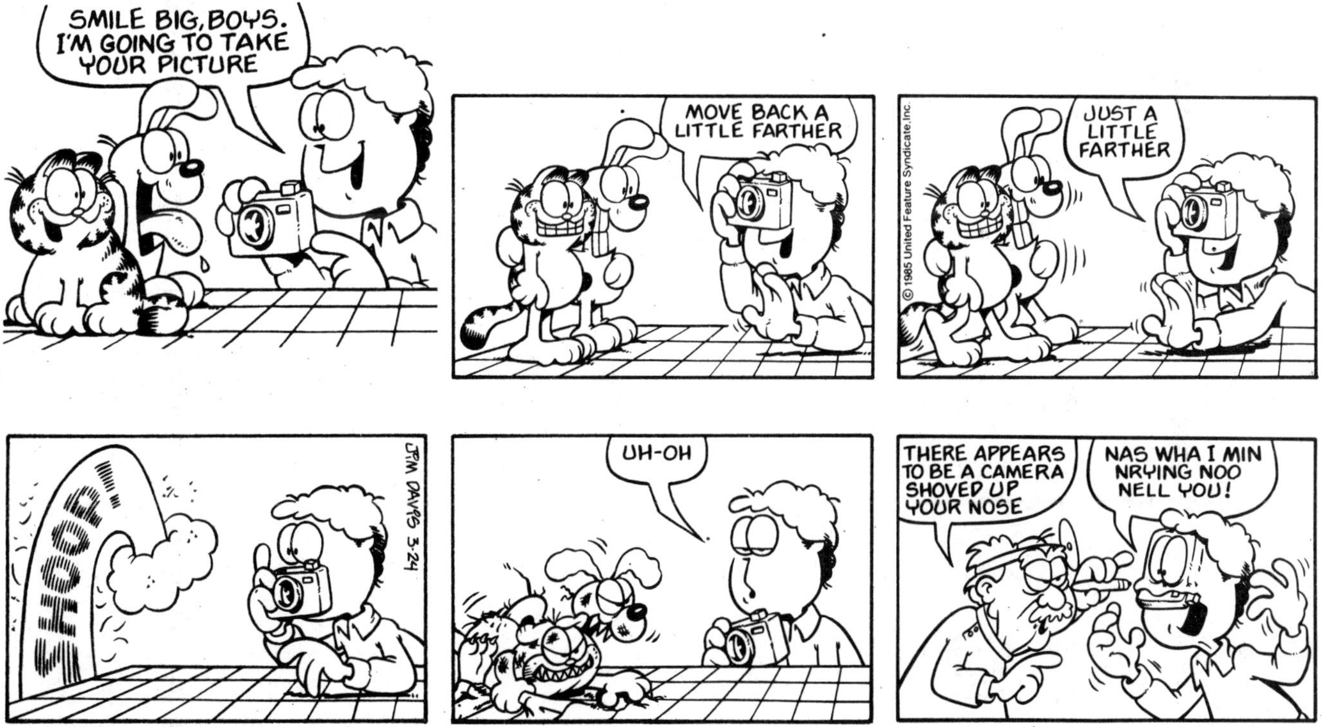
SMILE BIG, BOYS. I'M GOING TO TAKE YOUR PICTURE
MOVE BACK A LITTLE FARTHER
© 1985 United Feature Syndicate, Inc.
JUST A LITTLE FARTHER
SHOOP!!
JIM DAVIS 3-24
UH-OH
THERE APPEARS TO BE A CAMERA SHOVED UP YOUR NOSE
NAS WHA I MIN NRYING NOO NELL YOU!

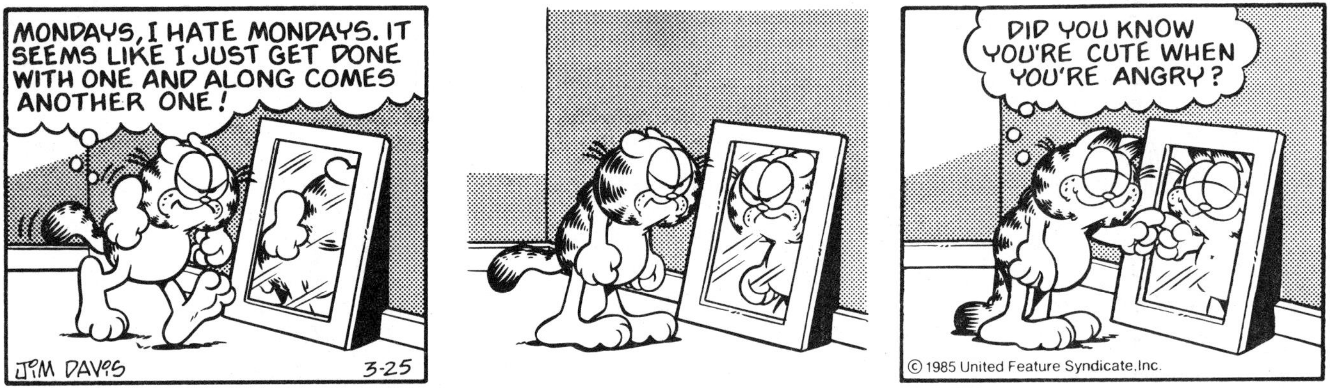
MONDAYS, I HATE MONDAYS. IT SEEMS LIKE I JUST GET DONE WITH ONE AND ALONG COMES ANOTHER ONE!
JIM DAVIS
3-25
DID YOU KNOW YOU'RE CUTE WHEN YOU'RE ANGRY?
© 1985 United Feature Syndicate, Inc.

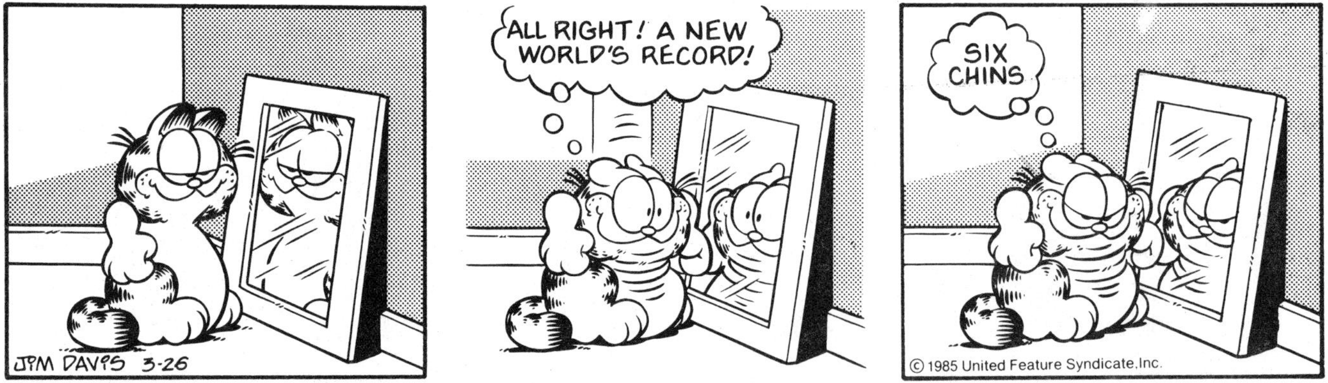
JIM DAVIS 3-26
ALL RIGHT! A NEW WORLD'S RECORD!
SIX CHINS
© 1985 United Feature Syndicate, Inc.

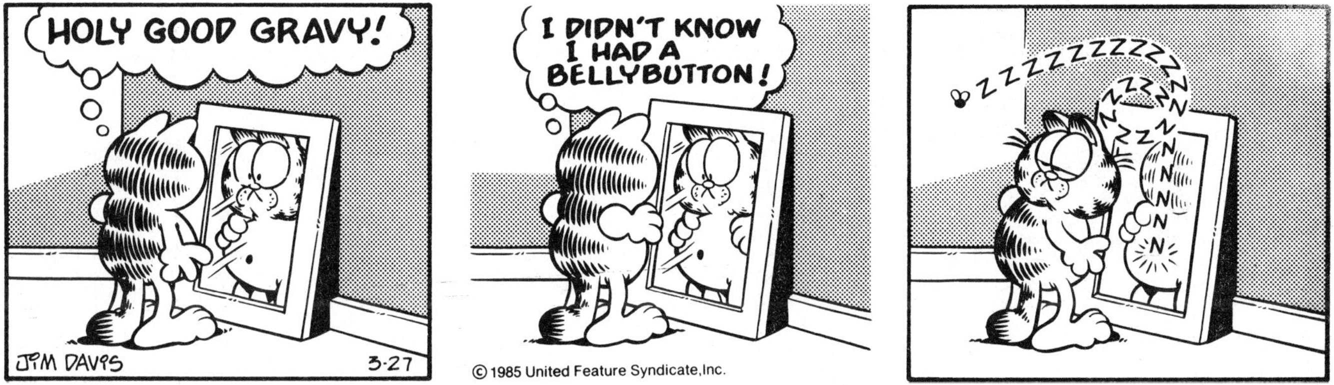
HOLY GOOD GRAVY!
JIM DAVIS
3-27
I DIDN'T KNOW I HAD A BELLYBUTTON!
© 1985 United Feature Syndicate, Inc.
ZZZZZZZZZZZZZZZZZZZNNNNNN

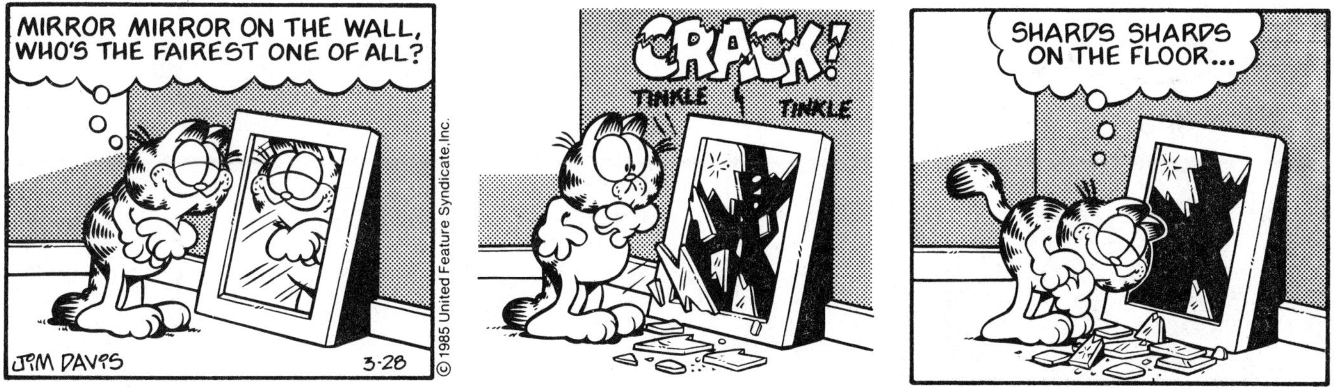
MIRROR MIRROR ON THE WALL, WHO'S THE FAIREST ONE OF ALL?
JIM DAVIS
3-28
© 1985 United Feature Syndicate, Inc.
CRACK!
TINKLE
TINKLE
SHARDS SHARDS ON THE FLOOR...

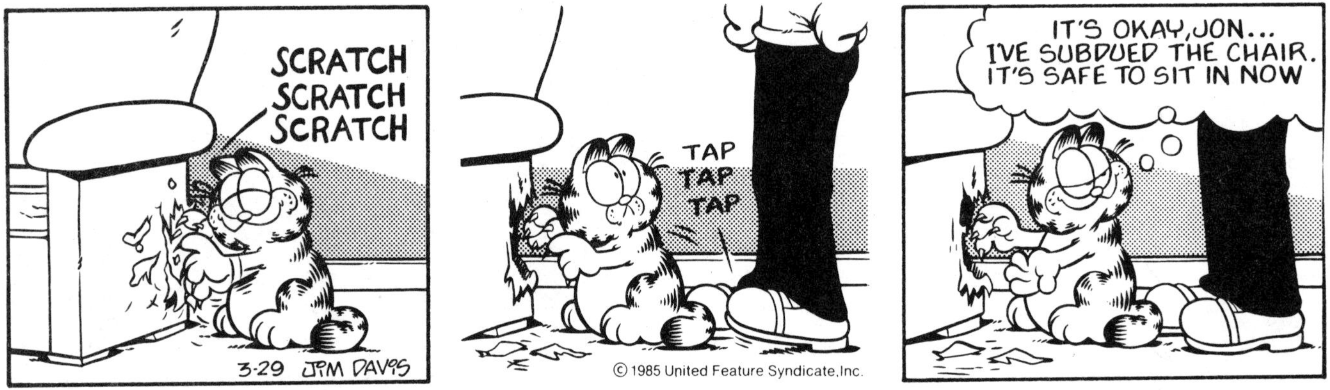
SCRATCH
SCRATCH
SCRATCH
3-29 JIM DAVIS
TAP
TAP
TAP
© 1985 United Feature Syndicate, Inc.
IT'S OKAY, JON... I'VE SUBDUED THE CHAIR. IT'S SAFE TO SIT IN NOW

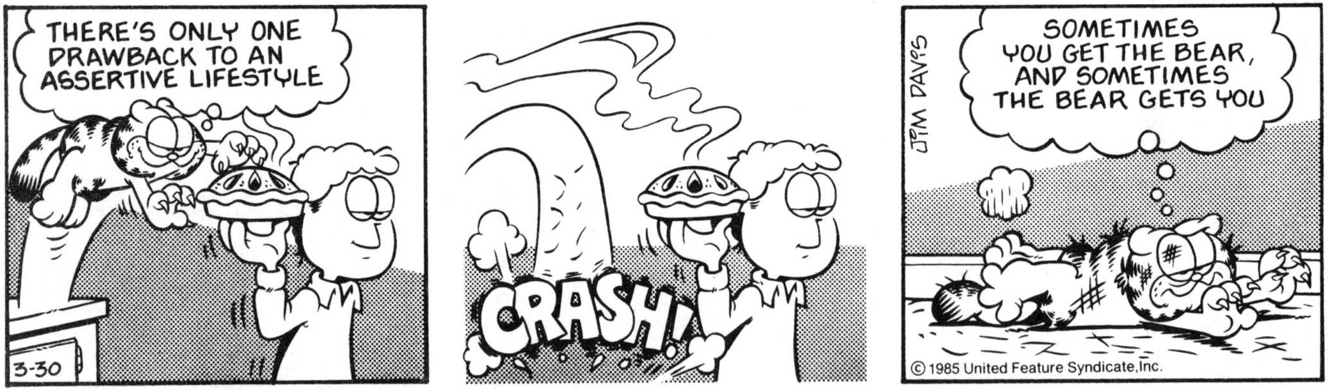
THERE'S ONLY ONE DRAWBACK TO AN ASSERTIVE LIFESTYLE
3-30
CRASH!
JIM DAVIS
SOMETIMES YOU GET THE BEAR, AND SOMETIMES THE BEAR GETS YOU
© 1985 United Feature Syndicate, Inc.

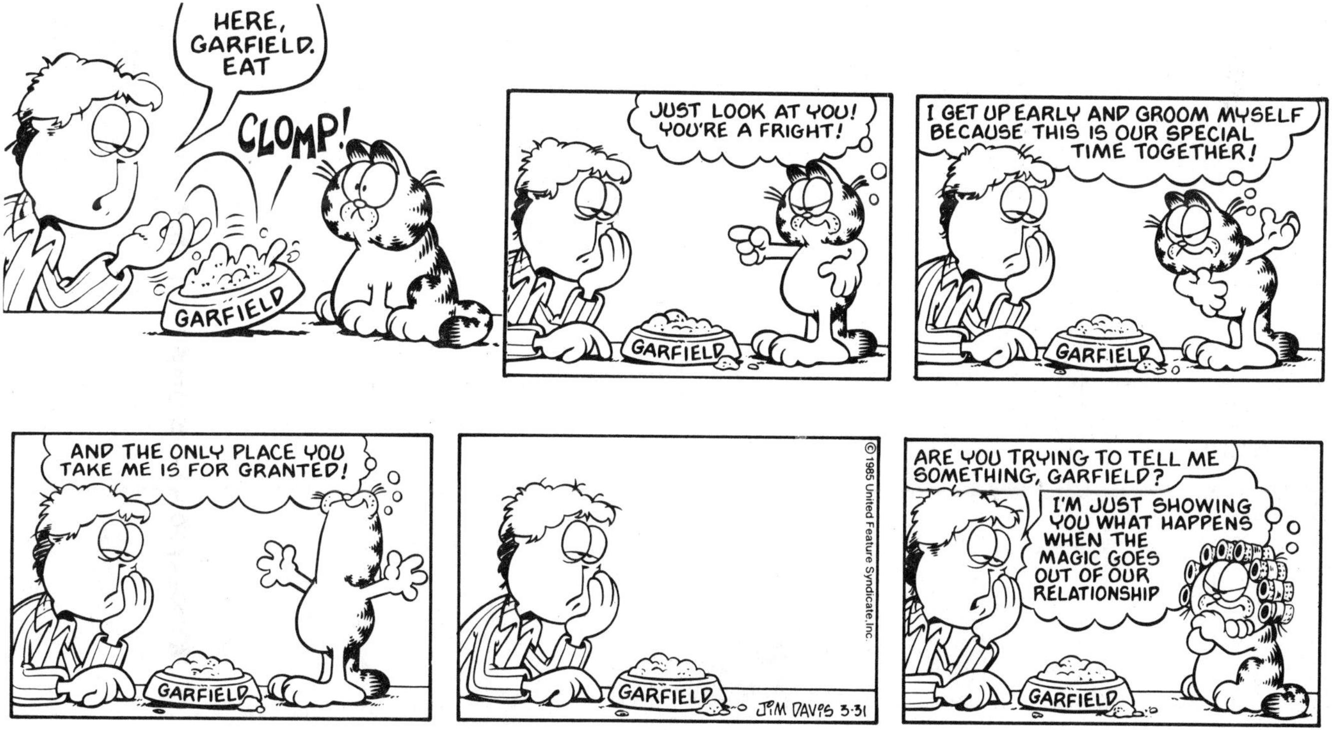

HERE, GARFIELD. EAT
CLOMP!
GARFIELD
JUST LOOK AT YOU! YOU'RE A FRIGHT!
GARFIELD
I GET UP EARLY AND GROOM MYSELF BECAUSE THIS IS OUR SPECIAL TIME TOGETHER!
GARFIELD
AND THE ONLY PLACE YOU TAKE ME IS FOR GRANTED!
GARFIELD
GARFIELD
JIM DAVIS 3-31
© 1985 United Feature Syndicate, Inc.
ARE YOU TRYING TO TELL ME SOMETHING, GARFIELD?
I'M JUST SHOWING YOU WHAT HAPPENS WHEN THE MAGIC GOES OUT OF OUR RELATIONSHIP
GARFIELD

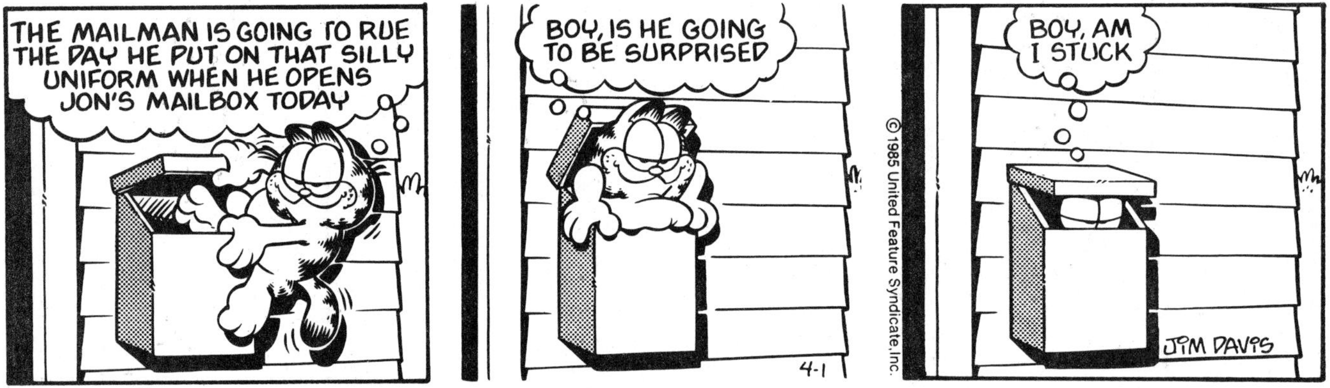
THE MAILMAN IS GOING TO RUE THE DAY HE PUT ON THAT SILLY UNIFORM WHEN HE OPENS JON'S MAILBOX TODAY
BOY, IS HE GOING TO BE SURPRISED
4-1
© 1985 United Feature Syndicate, Inc.
BOY, AM I STUCK
JIM DAVIS

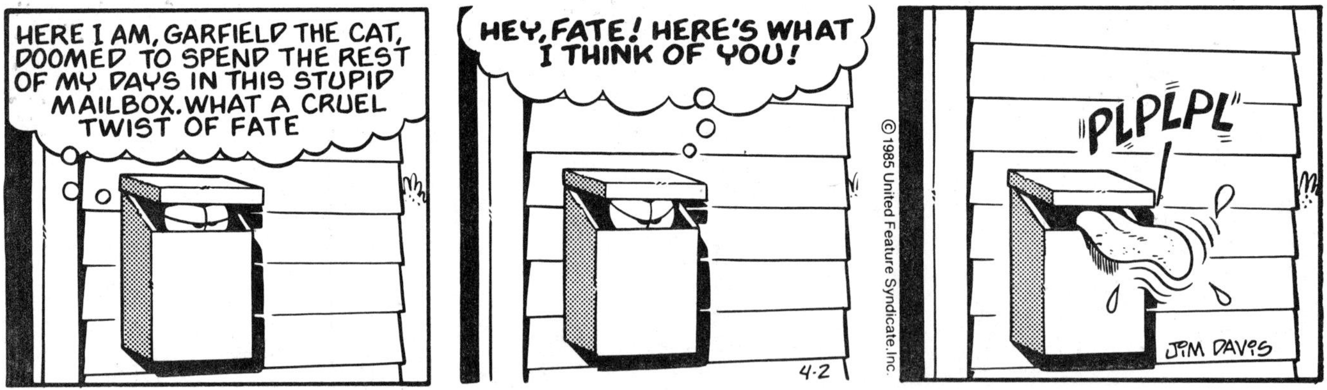
HERE I AM, GARFIELD THE CAT, DOOMED TO SPEND THE REST OF MY DAYS IN THIS STUPID MAILBOX. WHAT A CRUEL TWIST OF FATE
HEY, FATE! HERE'S WHAT I THINK OF YOU!
4-2
© 1985 United Feature Syndicate, Inc.
"PLPLPL"
JIM DAVIS

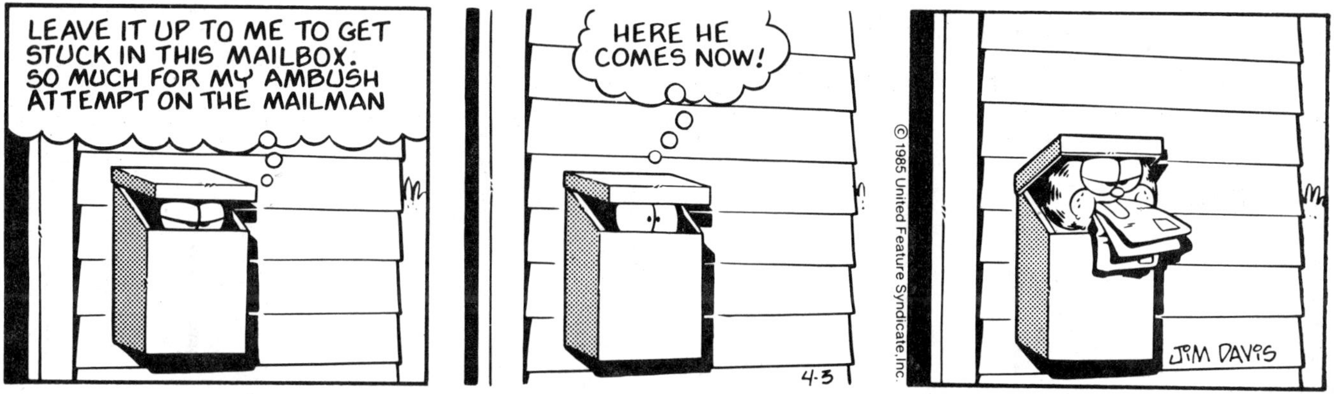
LEAVE IT UP TO ME TO GET STUCK IN THIS MAILBOX. SO MUCH FOR MY AMBUSH ATTEMPT ON THE MAILMAN
HERE HE COMES NOW!
4-3
© 1985 United Feature Syndicate, Inc.
JIM DAVIS

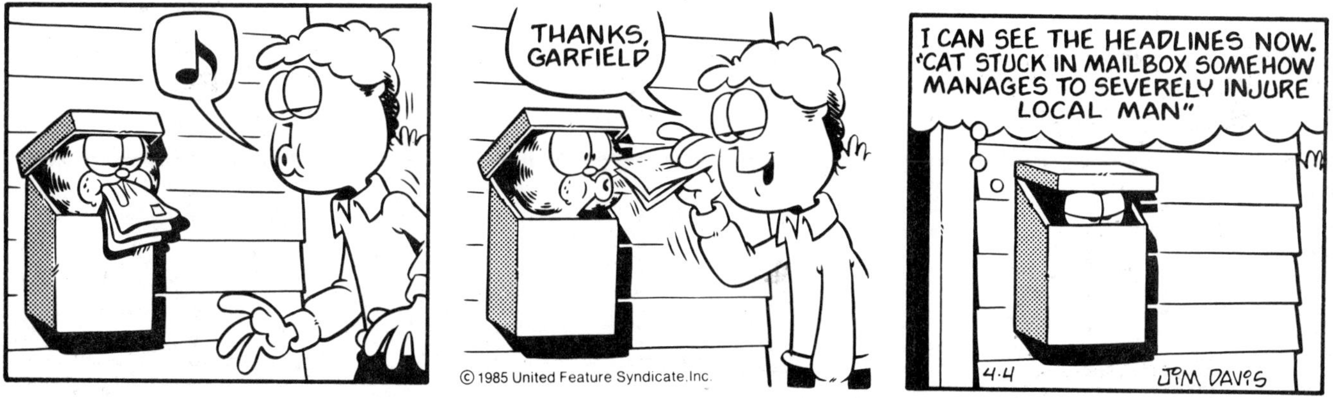
THANKS, GARFIELD
© 1985 United Feature Syndicate, Inc.
I CAN SEE THE HEADLINES NOW. "CAT STUCK IN MAILBOX SOMEHOW MANAGES TO SEVERELY INJURE LOCAL MAN"
4-4
JIM DAVIS

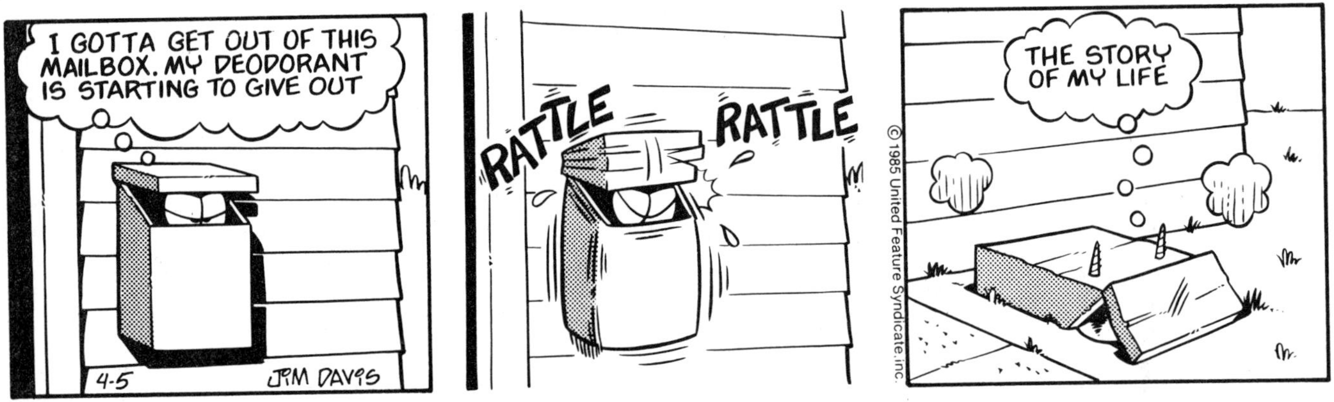
I GOTTA GET OUT OF THIS MAILBOX. MY DEODORANT IS STARTING TO GIVE OUT
4-5
JIM DAVIS
RATTLE
RATTLE
© 1985 United Feature Syndicate, inc.
THE STORY OF MY LIFE

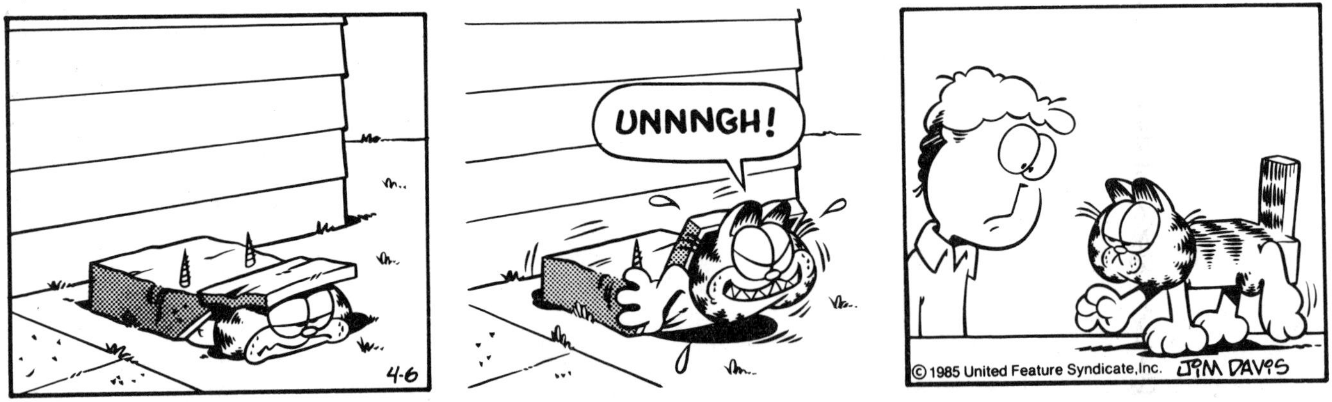
4-6
UNNNGH!
© 1985 United Feature Syndicate, Inc.
JIM DAVIS

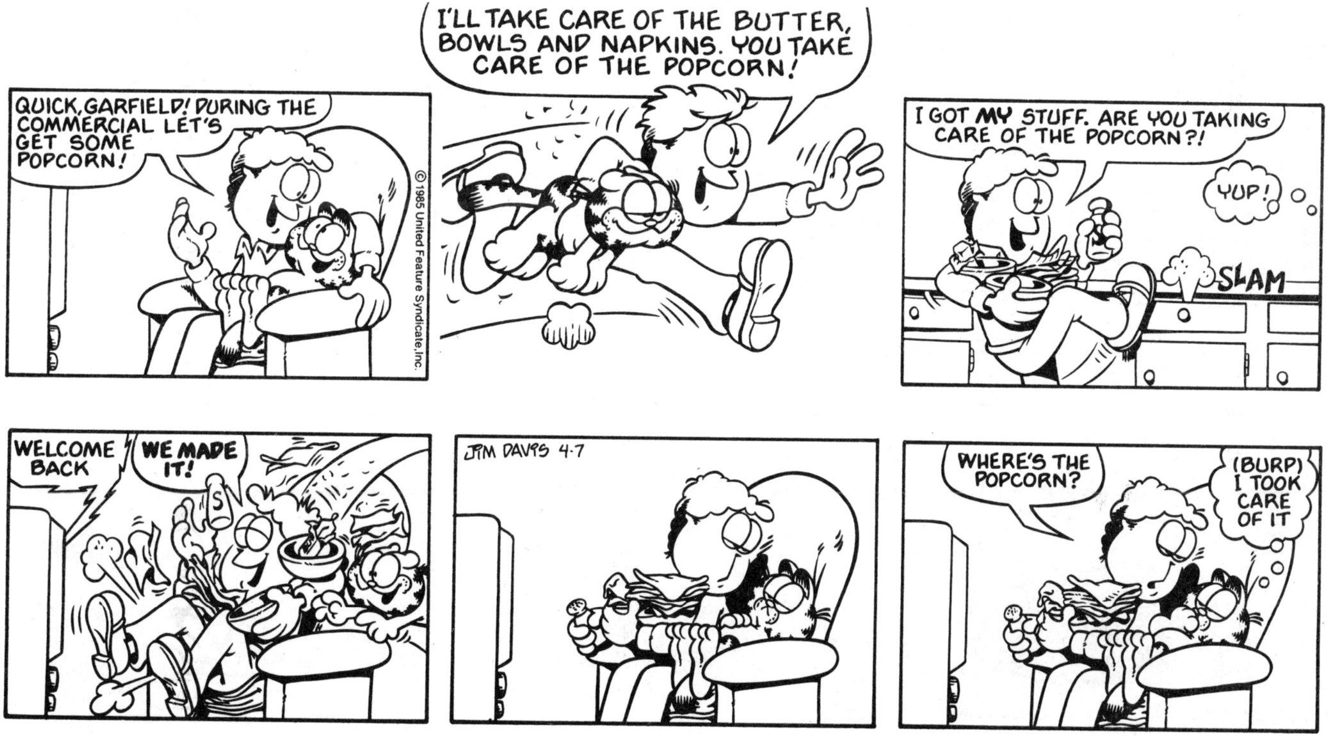

QUICK, GARFIELD! DURING THE COMMERCIAL LET'S GET SOME POPCORN!
© 1985 United Feature Syndicate, Inc.
I'LL TAKE CARE OF THE BUTTER, BOWLS AND NAPKINS. YOU TAKE CARE OF THE POPCORN!
I GOT MY STUFF. ARE YOU TAKING CARE OF THE POPCORN?!
YUP!
SLAM
WELCOME BACK
WE MADE IT!
S
JIM DAVIS 4-7
WHERE'S THE POPCORN?
(BURP) I TOOK CARE OF IT

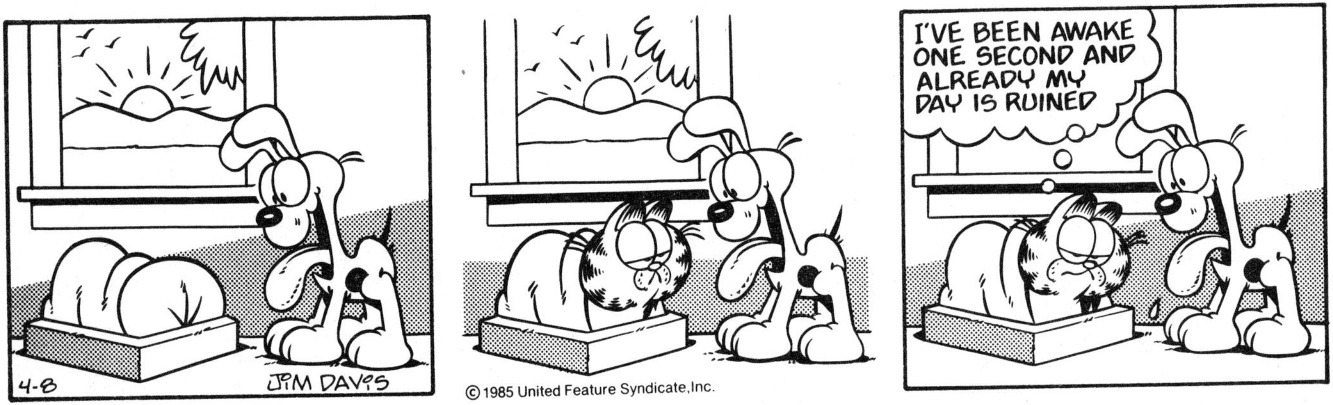
4-8
JIM DAVIS
I'VE BEEN AWAKE ONE SECOND AND ALREADY MY DAY IS RUINED

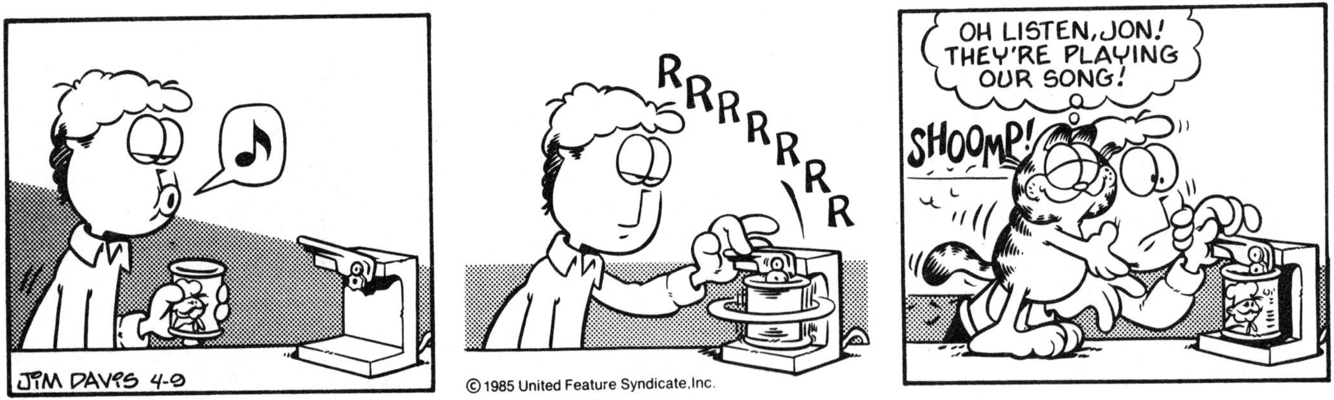
JIM DAVIS 4-9
♪
RRRRRRRRR
OH LISTEN, JON! THEY'RE PLAYING OUR SONG!
SHOOMP!

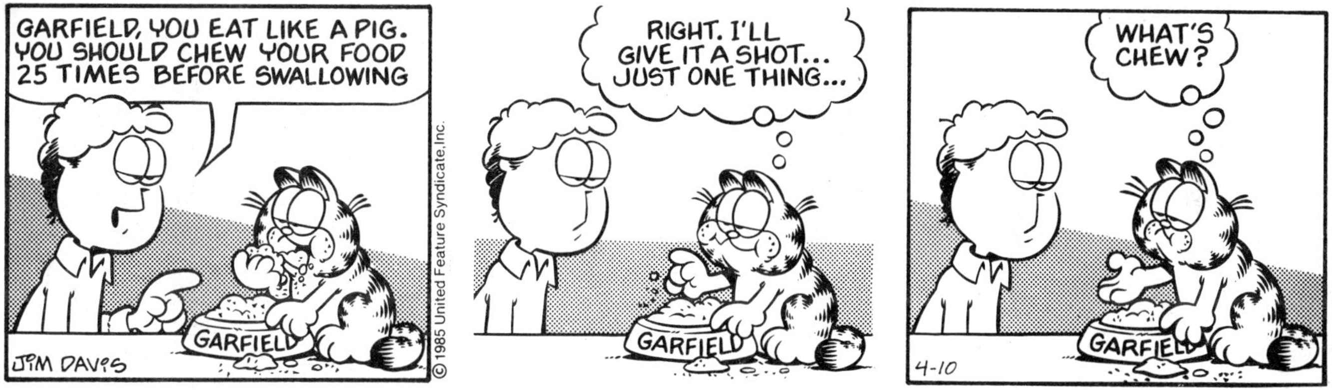
GARFIELD, YOU EAT LIKE A PIG. YOU SHOULD CHEW YOUR FOOD 25 TIMES BEFORE SWALLOWING
GARFIELD
JIM DAVIS
© 1985 United Feature Syndicate, Inc.
RIGHT. I'LL GIVE IT A SHOT... JUST ONE THING...
GARFIELD
WHAT'S CHEW?
GARFIELD
4-10

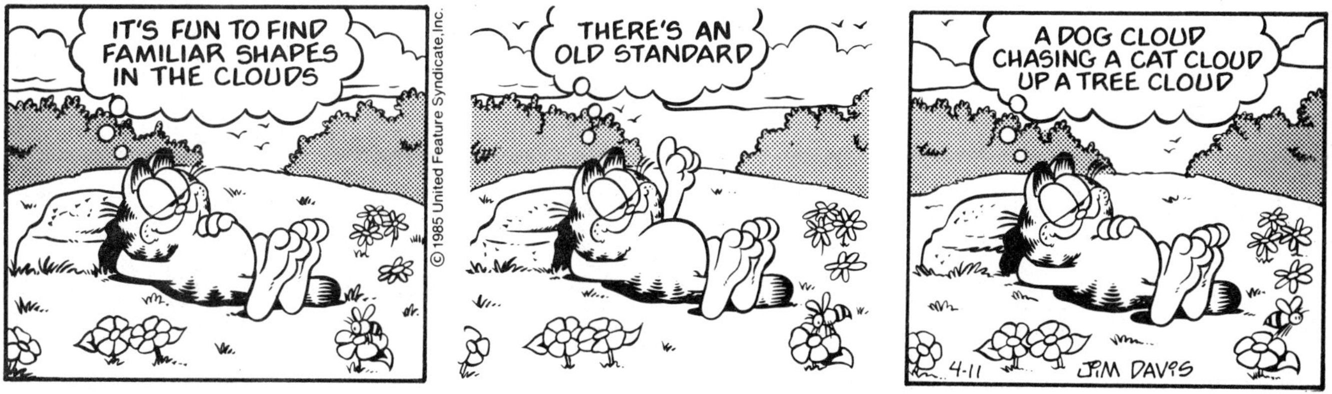
IT'S FUN TO FIND FAMILIAR SHAPES IN THE CLOUDS
© 1985 United Feature Syndicate, Inc.
THERE'S AN OLD STANDARD
A DOG CLOUD CHASING A CAT CLOUD UP A TREE CLOUD
4-11
JIM DAVIS

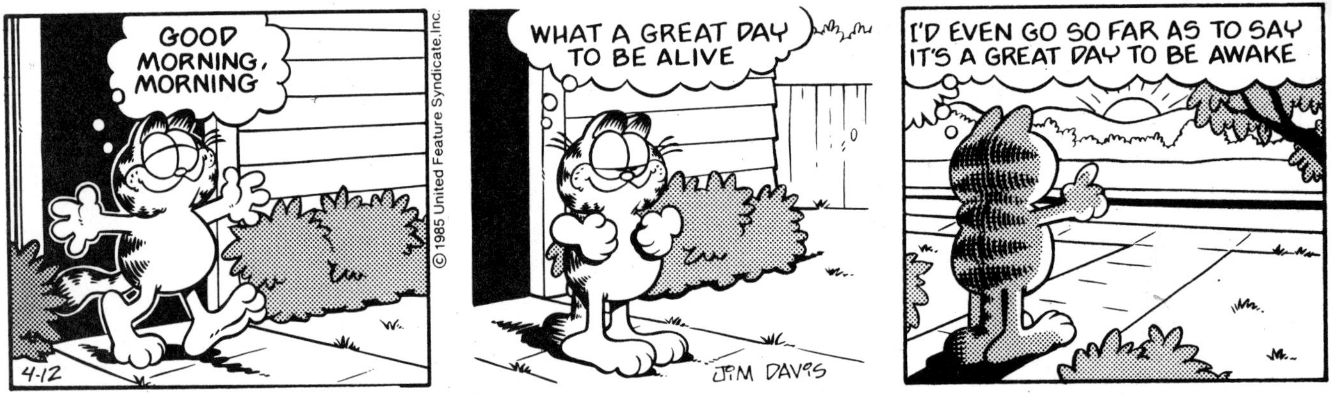
GOOD MORNING, MORNING
4-12
WHAT A GREAT DAY TO BE ALIVE
JIM DAVIS
I'D EVEN GO SO FAR AS TO SAY IT'S A GREAT DAY TO BE AWAKE

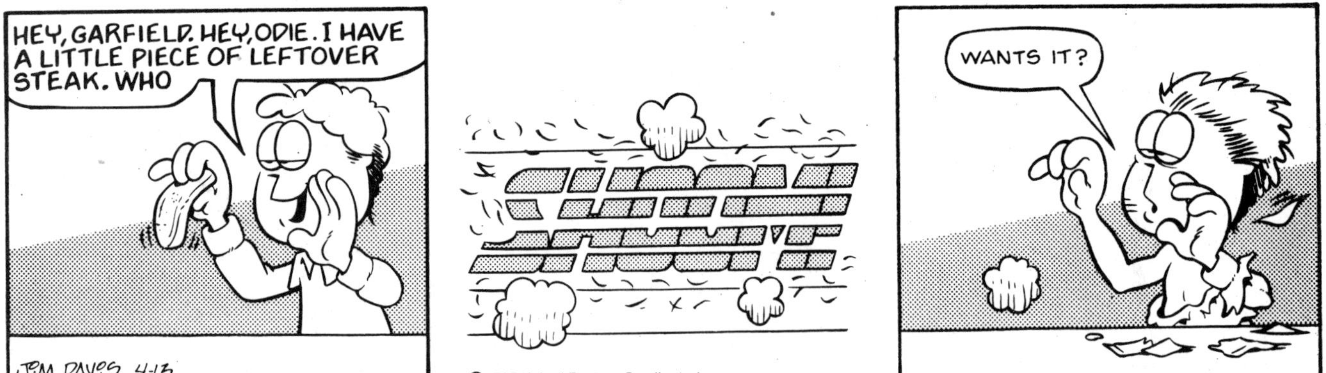
HEY, GARFIELD. HEY, ODIE. I HAVE A LITTLE PIECE OF LEFTOVER STEAK. WHO
JIM DAVIS 4-13
WANTS IT?

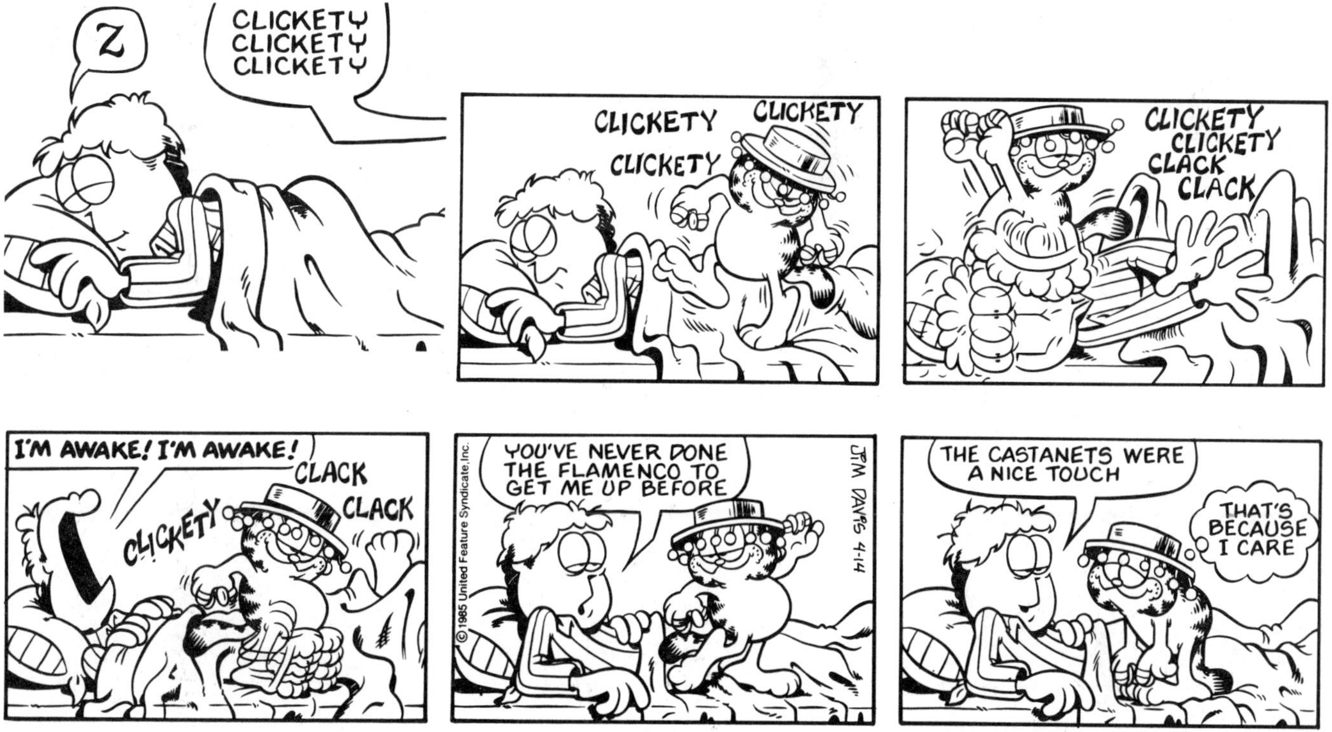
Z
CLICKETY CLICKETY CLICKETY
CLICKETY
CLICKETY
CLICKETY
CLICKETY CLICKETY CLACK CLACK
I'M AWAKE! I'M AWAKE!
CLICKETY
CLACK
CLACK
YOU'VE NEVER DONE THE FLAMENCO TO GET ME UP BEFORE
JIM DAVIS 4-14
© 1985 United Feature Syndicate, Inc.
THE CASTANETS WERE A NICE TOUCH
THAT'S BECAUSE I CARE

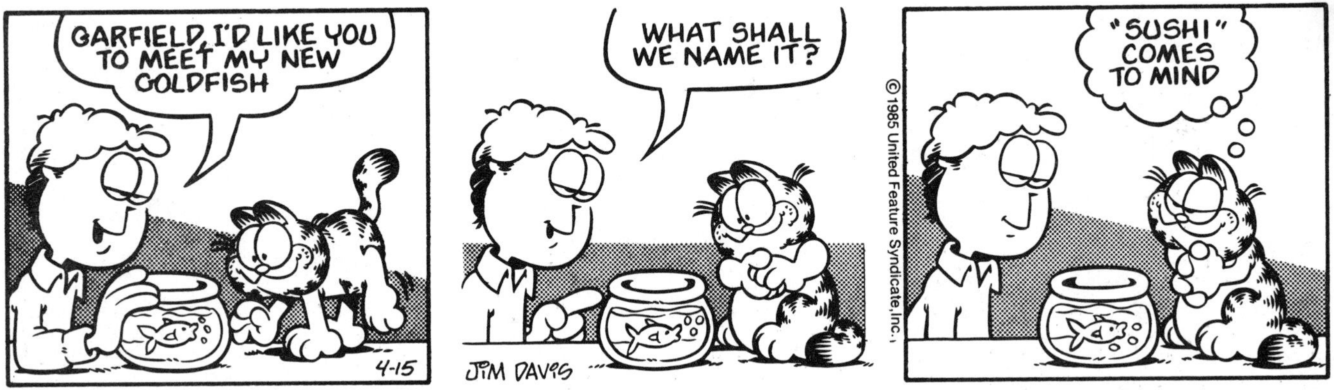
GARFIELD, I'D LIKE YOU TO MEET MY NEW GOLDFISH
4-15
WHAT SHALL WE NAME IT?
JIM DAVIS
© 1985 United Feature Syndicate, Inc.
"SUSHI" COMES TO MIND

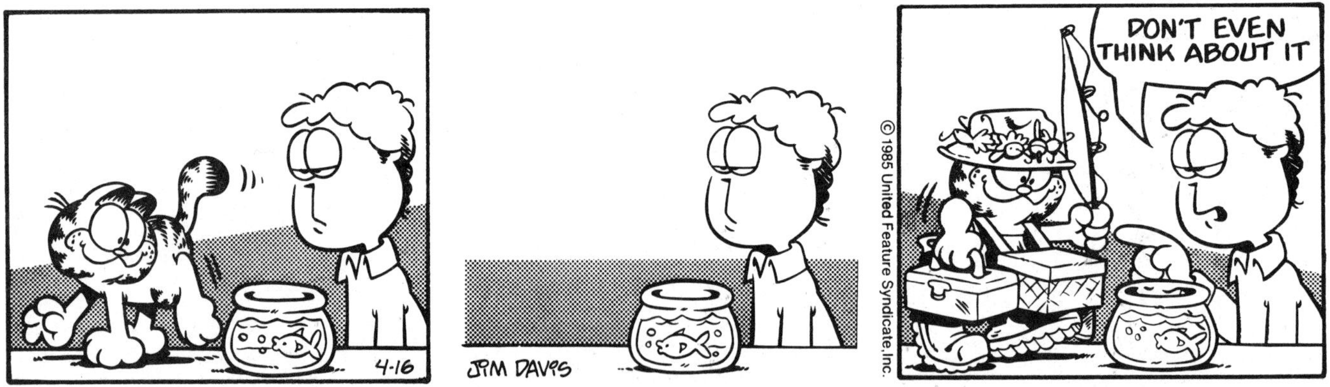
4-16
JIM DAVIS
© 1985 United Feature Syndicate, Inc.
DON'T EVEN THINK ABOUT IT

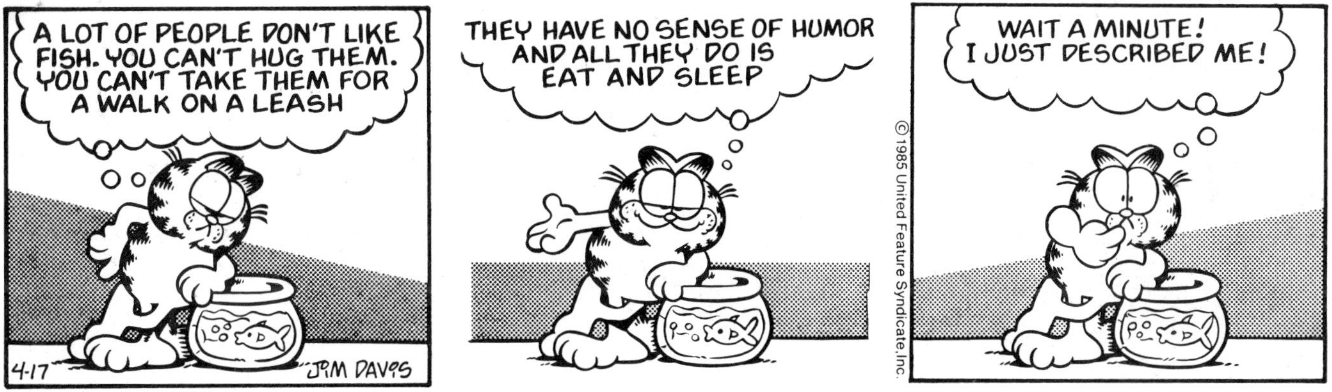
A LOT OF PEOPLE DON'T LIKE FISH. YOU CAN'T HUG THEM. YOU CAN'T TAKE THEM FOR A WALK ON A LEASH
4-17
JIM DAVIS
THEY HAVE NO SENSE OF HUMOR AND ALL THEY DO IS EAT AND SLEEP
© 1985 United Feature Syndicate, Inc.
WAIT A MINUTE! I JUST DESCRIBED ME!

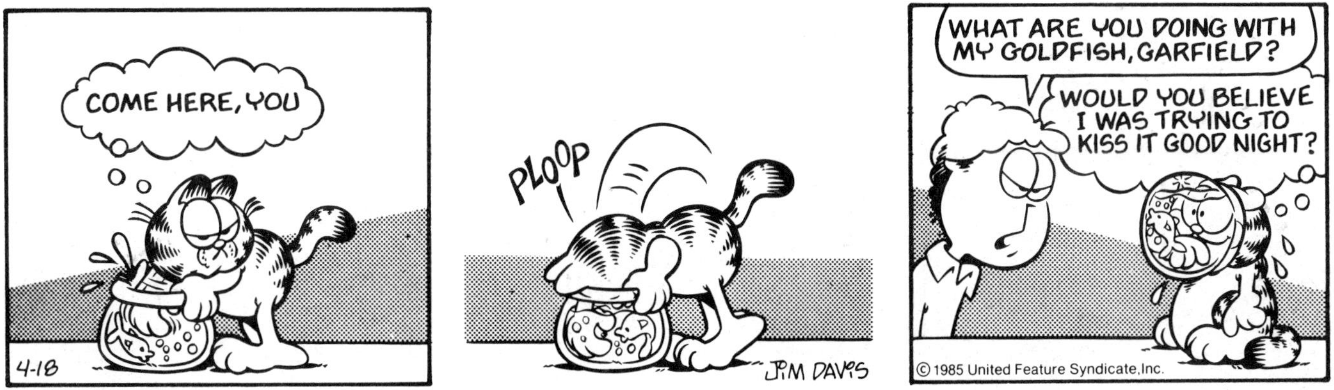
COME HERE, YOU
4-18
PLOOP
JIM DAVIS
WHAT ARE YOU DOING WITH MY GOLDFISH, GARFIELD?
WOULD YOU BELIEVE I WAS TRYING TO KISS IT GOOD NIGHT?
© 1985 United Feature Syndicate, Inc.

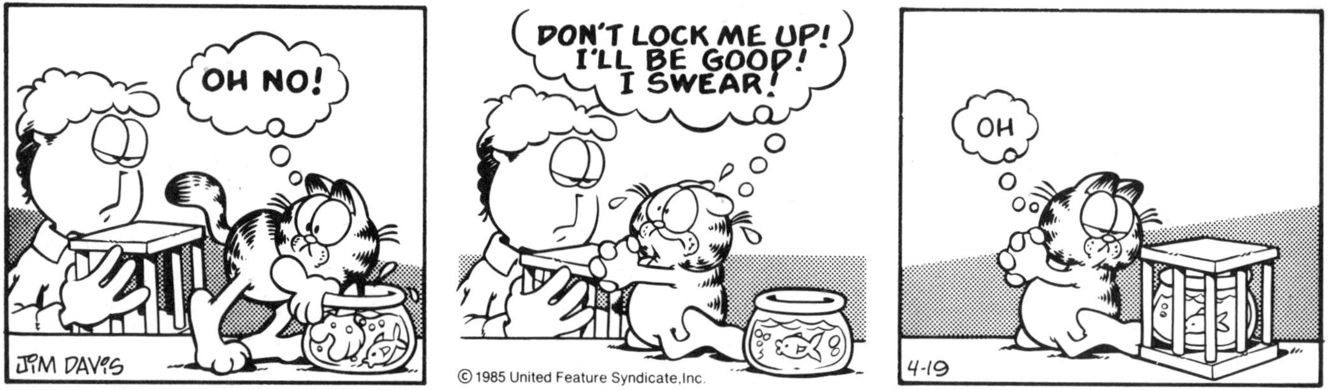
OH NO!
JIM DAVIS
DON'T LOCK ME UP! I'LL BE GOOD! I SWEAR!
© 1985 United Feature Syndicate, Inc.
OH
4-19

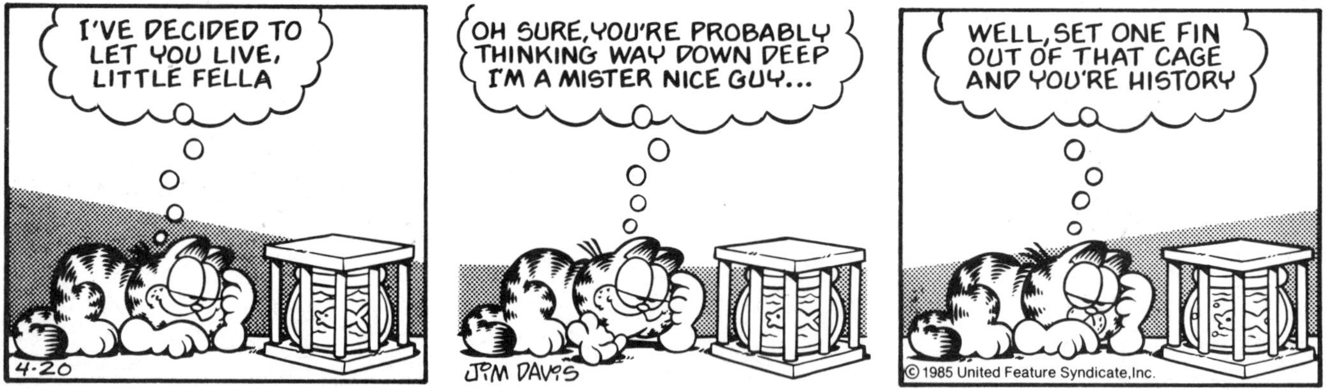
I'VE DECIDED TO LET YOU LIVE, LITTLE FELLA
4-20
OH SURE, YOU'RE PROBABLY THINKING WAY DOWN DEEP I'M A MISTER NICE GUY...
JIM DAVIS
WELL, SET ONE FIN OUT OF THAT CAGE AND YOU'RE HISTORY
© 1985 United Feature Syndicate, Inc.

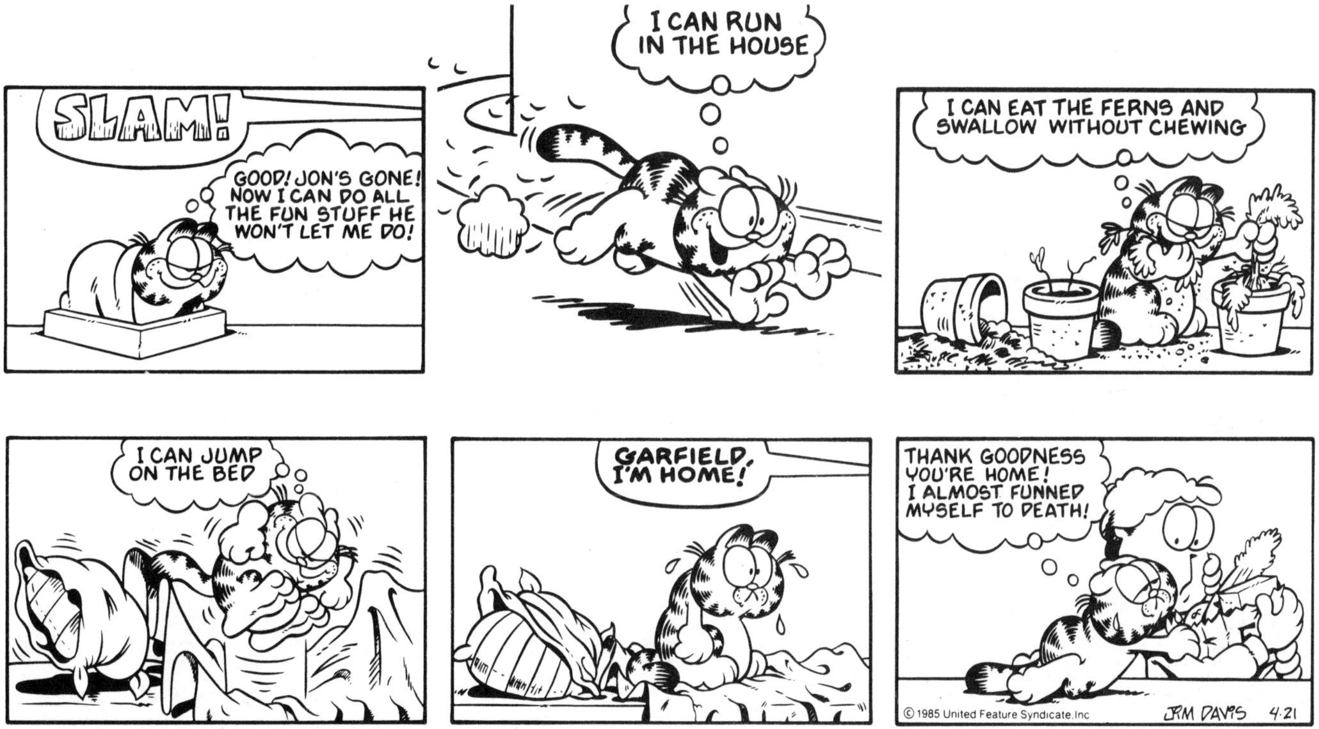
SLAM!
GOOD! JON'S GONE! NOW I CAN DO ALL THE FUN STUFF HE WON'T LET ME DO!
I CAN RUN IN THE HOUSE
I CAN EAT THE FERNS AND SWALLOW WITHOUT CHEWING
I CAN JUMP ON THE BED
GARFIELD, I'M HOME!
THANK GOODNESS YOU'RE HOME! I ALMOST FUNNED MYSELF TO DEATH!
© 1985 United Feature Syndicate, Inc
JIM DAVIS 4·21

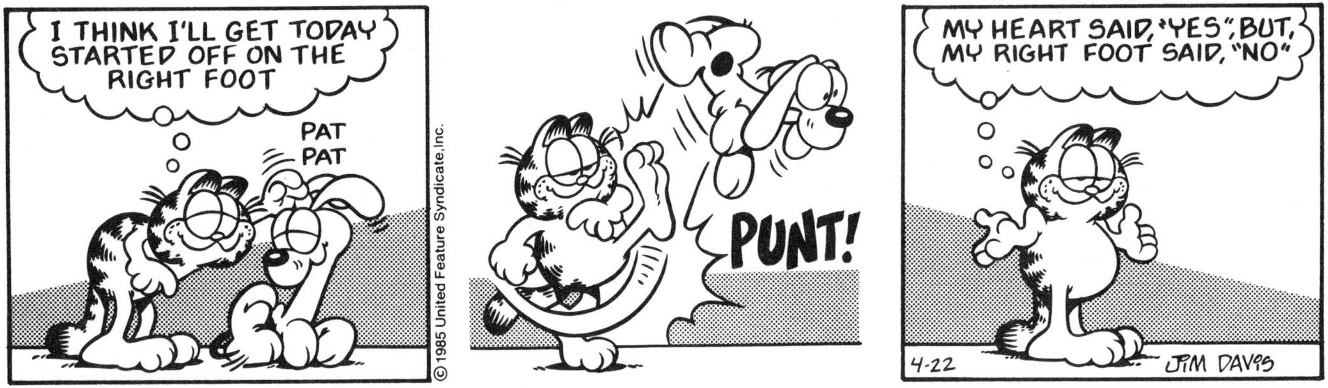
I THINK I'LL GET TODAY STARTED OFF ON THE RIGHT FOOT
PAT PAT
© 1985 United Feature Syndicate, Inc.
PUNT!
MY HEART SAID, "YES", BUT, MY RIGHT FOOT SAID, "NO"
4-22
JIM DAVIS

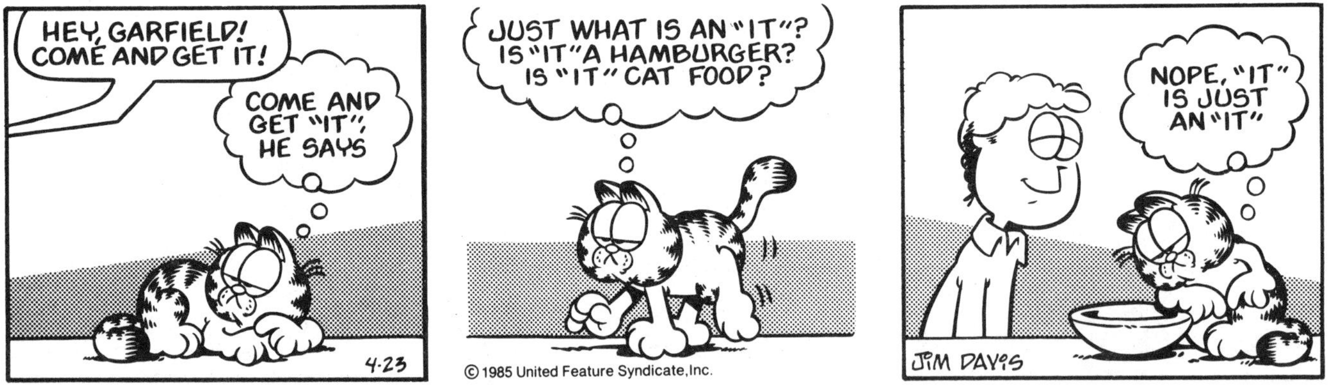
HEY, GARFIELD! COME AND GET IT!
COME AND GET "IT", HE SAYS
4-23
JUST WHAT IS AN "IT"? IS "IT" A HAMBURGER? IS "IT" CAT FOOD?
NOPE, "IT" IS JUST AN "IT"
JIM DAVIS

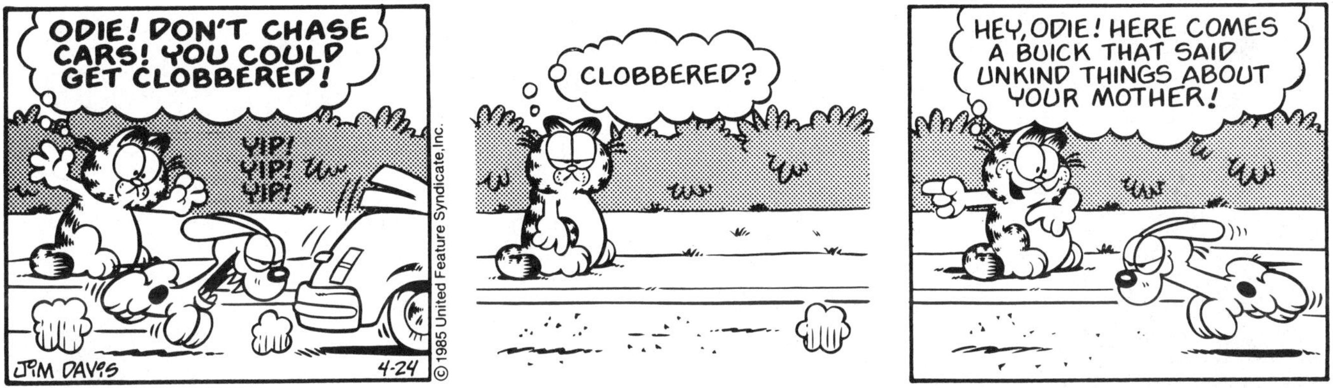
ODIE! DON'T CHASE CARS! YOU COULD GET CLOBBERED!
YIP! YIP! YIP!
JIM DAVIS 4-24
© 1985 United Feature Syndicate, Inc.
CLOBBERED?
HEY, ODIE! HERE COMES A BUICK THAT SAID UNKIND THINGS ABOUT YOUR MOTHER!

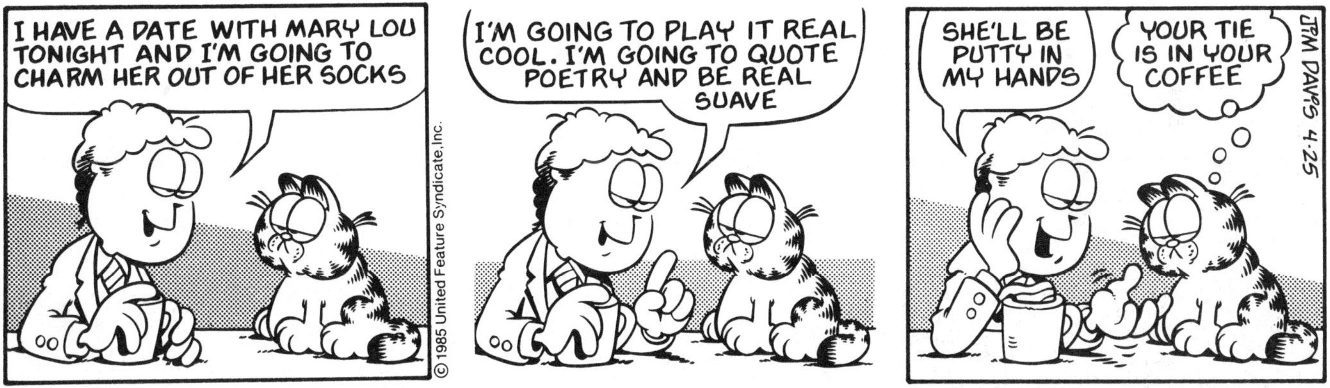
I HAVE A DATE WITH MARY LOU TONIGHT AND I'M GOING TO CHARM HER OUT OF HER SOCKS
© 1985 United Feature Syndicate, Inc.
I'M GOING TO PLAY IT REAL COOL. I'M GOING TO QUOTE POETRY AND BE REAL SUAVE
SHE'LL BE PUTTY IN MY HANDS
YOUR TIE IS IN YOUR COFFEE
JIM DAVIS 4-25

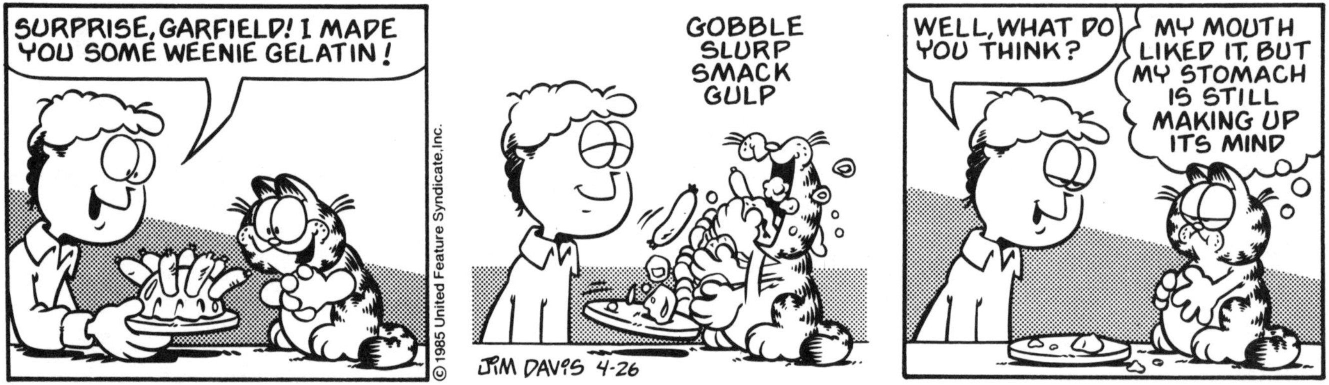
SURPRISE, GARFIELD! I MADE YOU SOME WEENIE GELATIN!
© 1985 United Feature Syndicate, Inc.
GOBBLE SLURP SMACK GULP
JIM DAVIS 4-26
WELL, WHAT DO YOU THINK?
MY MOUTH LIKED IT, BUT MY STOMACH IS STILL MAKING UP ITS MIND

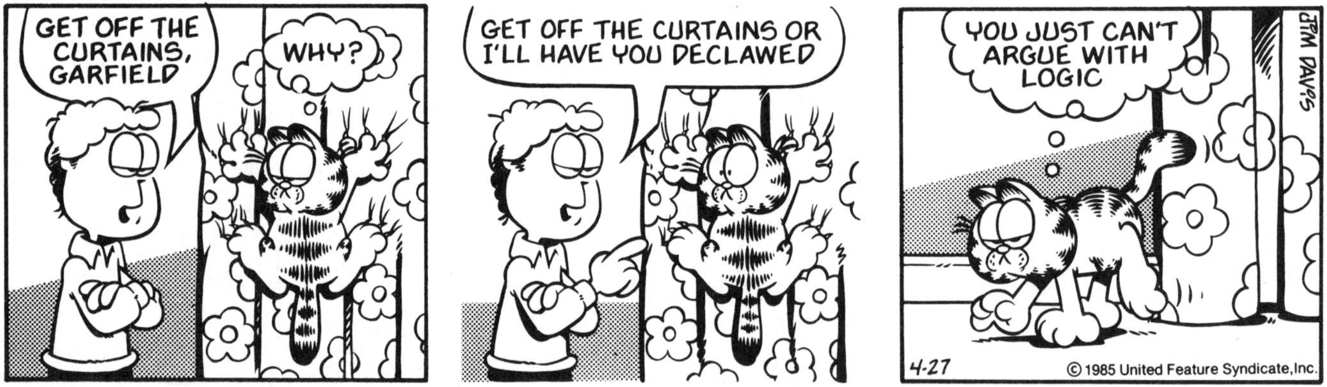
GET OFF THE CURTAINS, GARFIELD
WHY?
GET OFF THE CURTAINS OR I'LL HAVE YOU DECLAWED
YOU JUST CAN'T ARGUE WITH LOGIC
JIM DAVIS
4-27
© 1985 United Feature Syndicate, Inc.

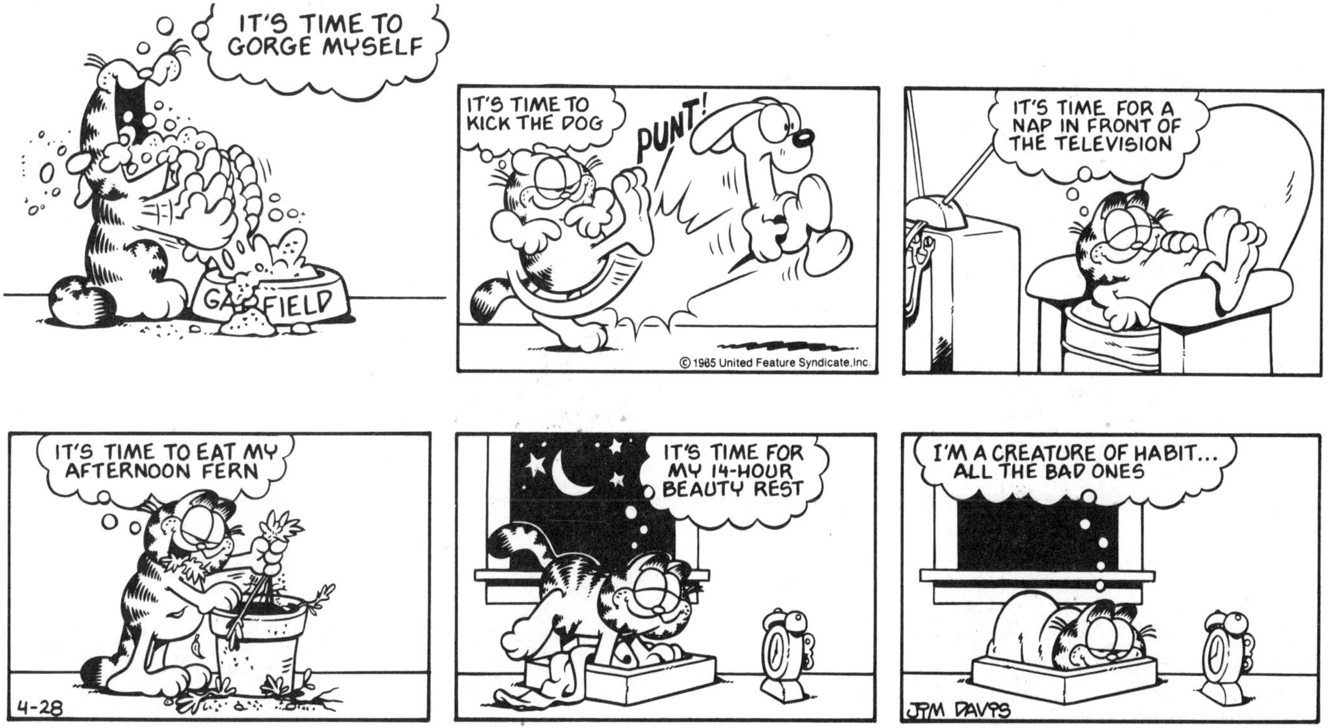
IT'S TIME TO GORGE MYSELF
GARFIELD
IT'S TIME TO KICK THE DOG
PUNT!
© 1985 United Feature Syndicate, Inc.
IT'S TIME FOR A NAP IN FRONT OF THE TELEVISION
IT'S TIME TO EAT MY AFTERNOON FERN
4-28
IT'S TIME FOR MY 14-HOUR BEAUTY REST
I'M A CREATURE OF HABIT... ALL THE BAD ONES
JIM DAVIS

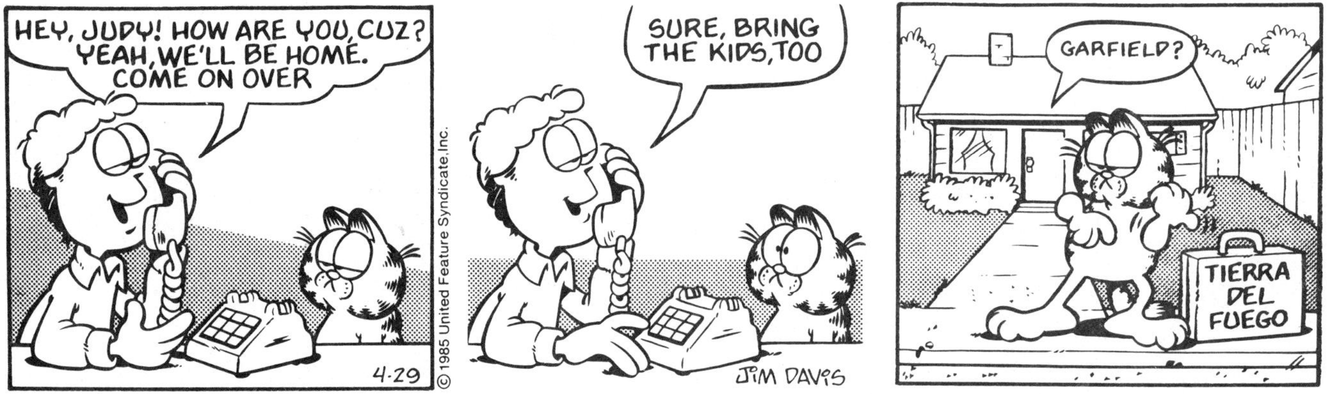

HEY, JUDY! HOW ARE YOU, CUZ? YEAH, WE'LL BE HOME. COME ON OVER
4-29
© 1985 United Feature Syndicate, Inc.
SURE, BRING THE KIDS, TOO
JIM DAVIS
GARFIELD?
TIERRA DEL FUEGO

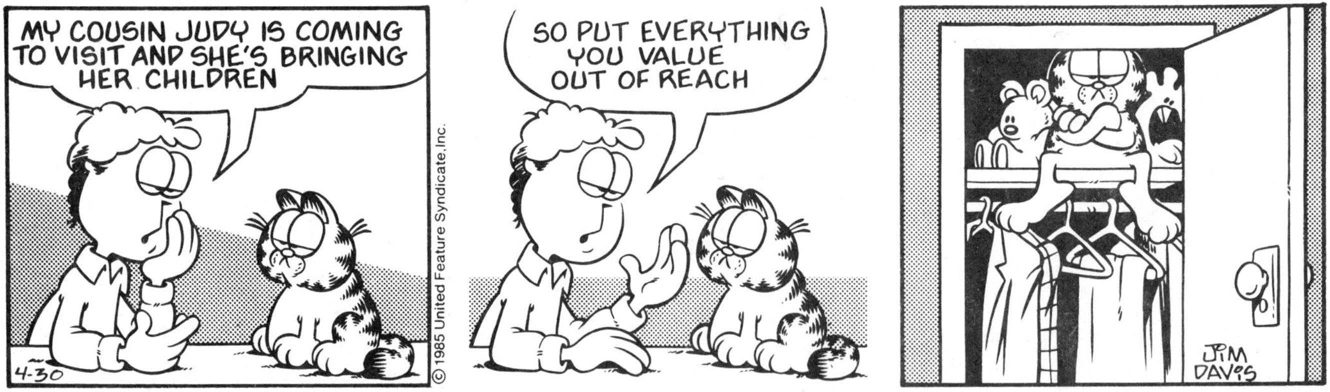

MY COUSIN JUDY IS COMING TO VISIT AND SHE'S BRINGING HER CHILDREN
4-30
© 1985 United Feature Syndicate, Inc.
SO PUT EVERYTHING YOU VALUE OUT OF REACH
JIM DAVIS

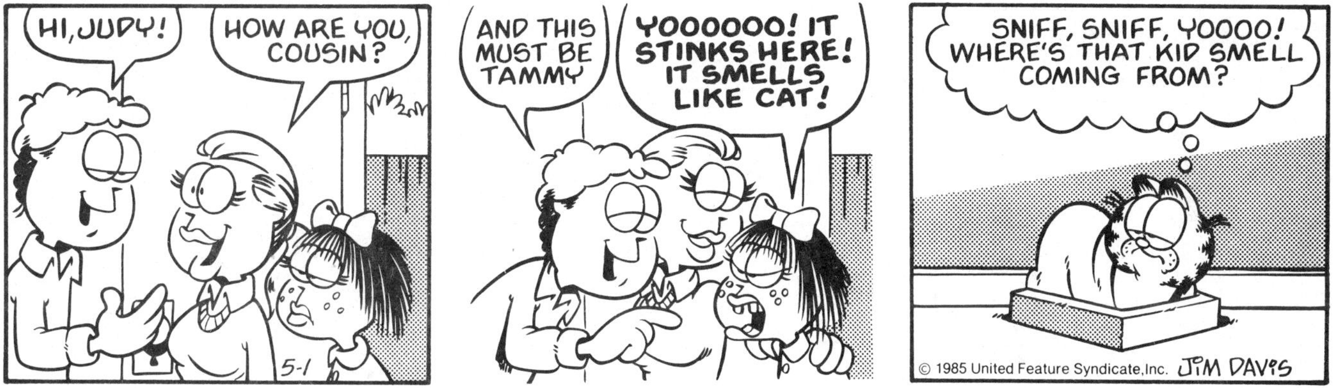
HI, JUDY!
HOW ARE YOU, COUSIN?
5-1
AND THIS MUST BE TAMMY
YOOOOOO! IT STINKS HERE! IT SMELLS LIKE CAT!
SNIFF, SNIFF, YOOOO! WHERE'S THAT KID SMELL COMING FROM?
© 1985 United Feature Syndicate, Inc. JIM DAVIS

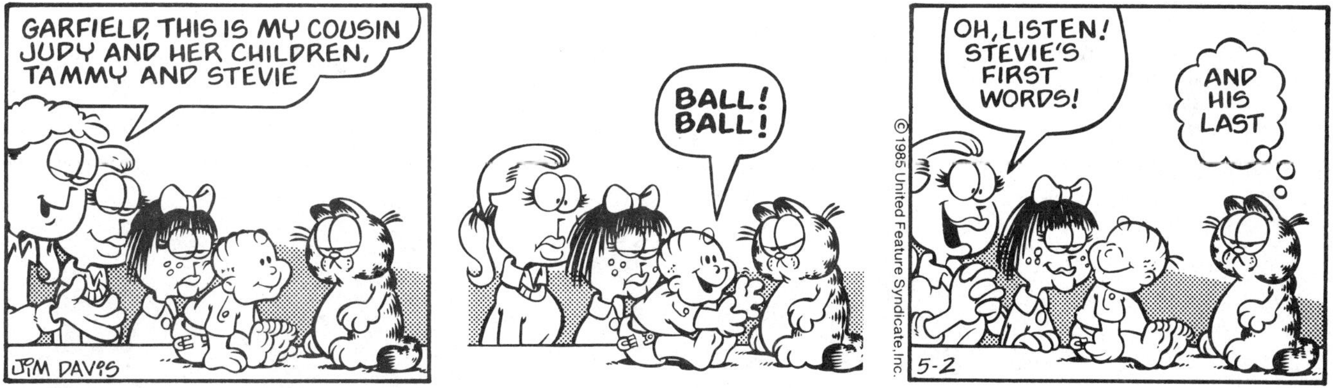
GARFIELD, THIS IS MY COUSIN JUDY AND HER CHILDREN, TAMMY AND STEVIE
JIM DAVIS
BALL! BALL!
© 1985 United Feature Syndicate, Inc.
OH, LISTEN! STEVIE'S FIRST WORDS!
AND HIS LAST
5-2

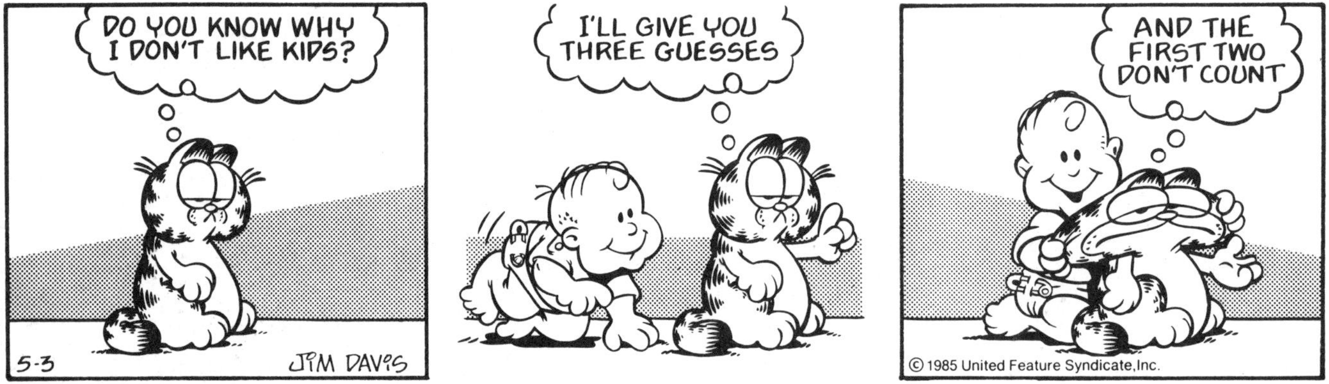
DO YOU KNOW WHY I DON'T LIKE KIDS?
5-3
JIM DAVIS
I'LL GIVE YOU THREE GUESSES
AND THE FIRST TWO DON'T COUNT
© 1985 United Feature Syndicate, Inc.

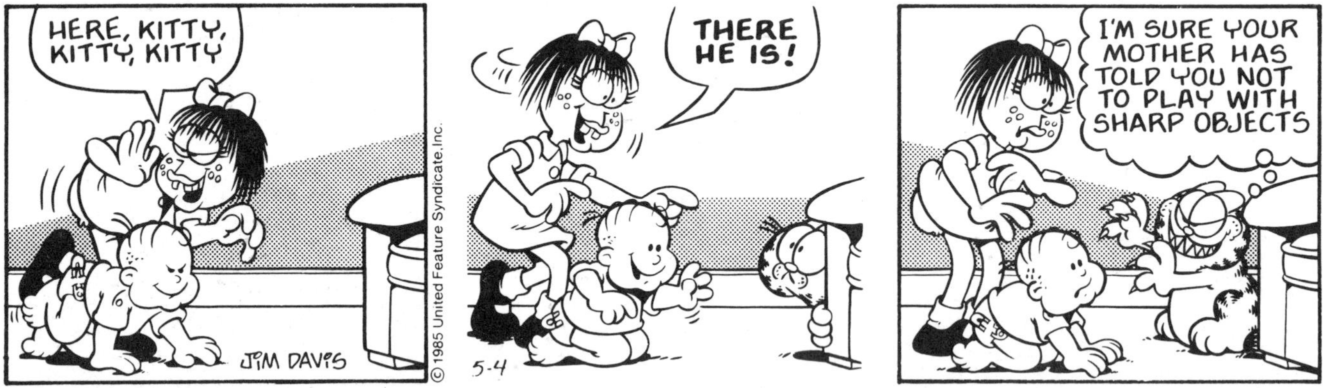
HERE, KITTY, KITTY, KITTY
JIM DAVIS
© 1985 United Feature Syndicate, Inc.
5-4
THERE HE IS!
I'M SURE YOUR MOTHER HAS TOLD YOU NOT TO PLAY WITH SHARP OBJECTS

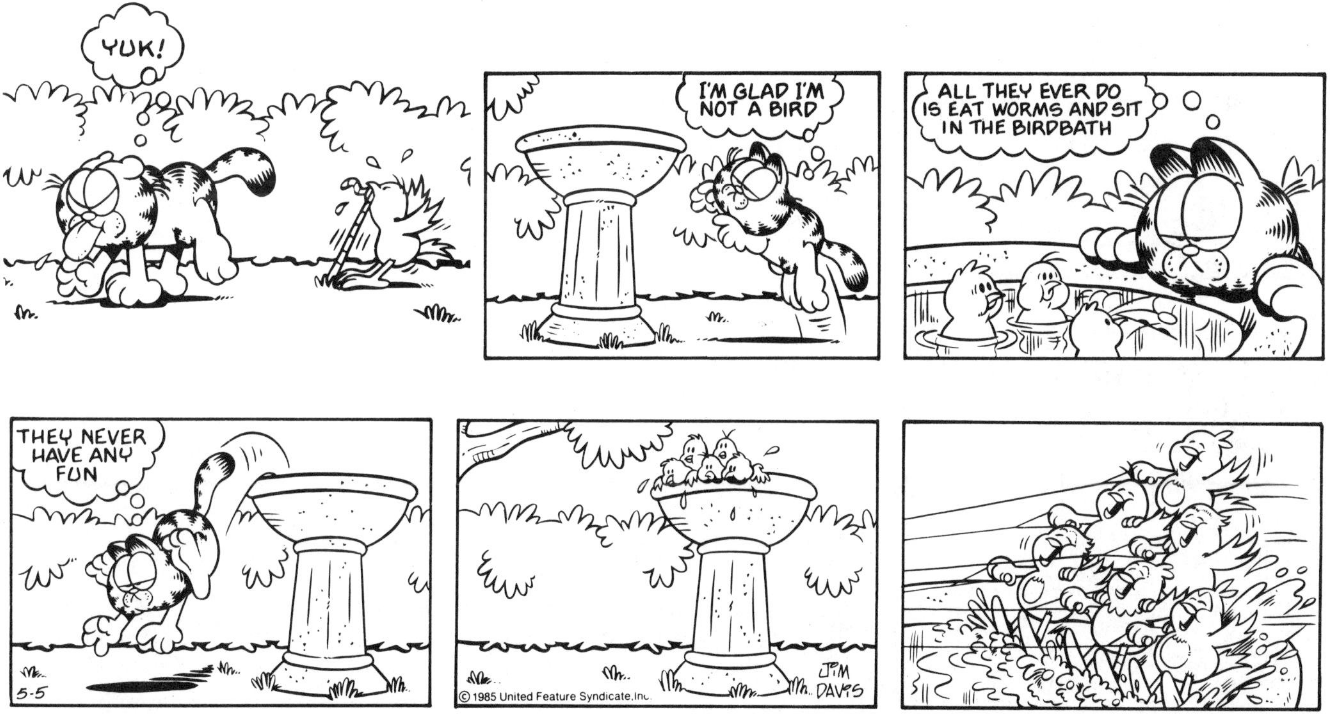
YUK!
I'M GLAD I'M NOT A BIRD
ALL THEY EVER DO IS EAT WORMS AND SIT IN THE BIRDBATH
THEY NEVER HAVE ANY FUN
5-5
© 1985 United Feature Syndicate, Inc.
JIM DAVIS

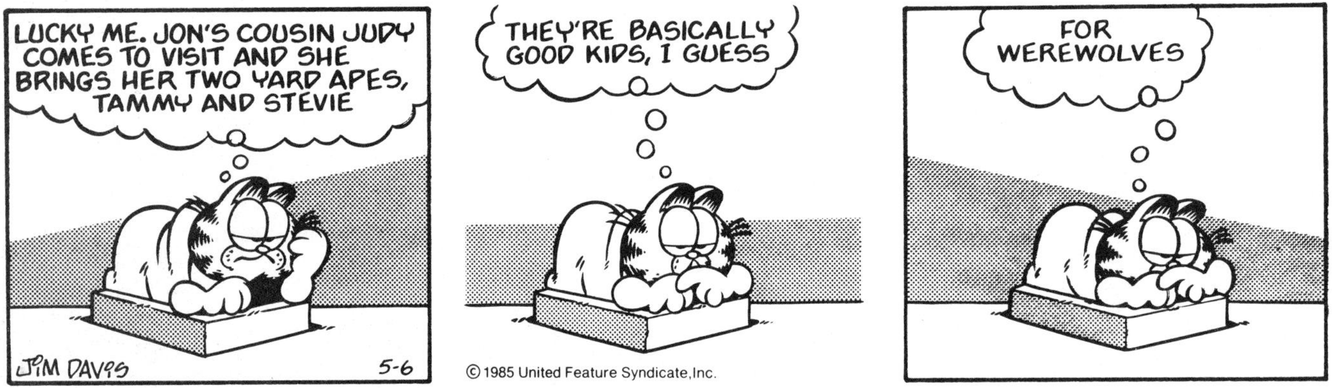
LUCKY ME. JON'S COUSIN JUDY COMES TO VISIT AND SHE BRINGS HER TWO YARD APES, TAMMY AND STEVIE
JIM DAVIS
5-6
THEY'RE BASICALLY GOOD KIDS, I GUESS
© 1985 United Feature Syndicate, Inc.
FOR WEREWOLVES

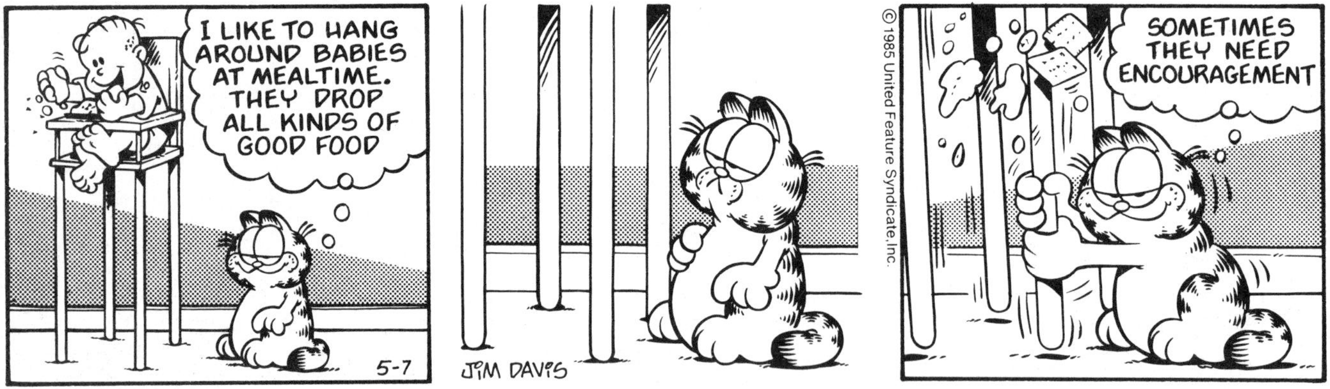
I LIKE TO HANG AROUND BABIES AT MEALTIME. THEY DROP ALL KINDS OF GOOD FOOD
5-7
JIM DAVIS
© 1985 United Feature Syndicate, Inc.
SOMETIMES THEY NEED ENCOURAGEMENT

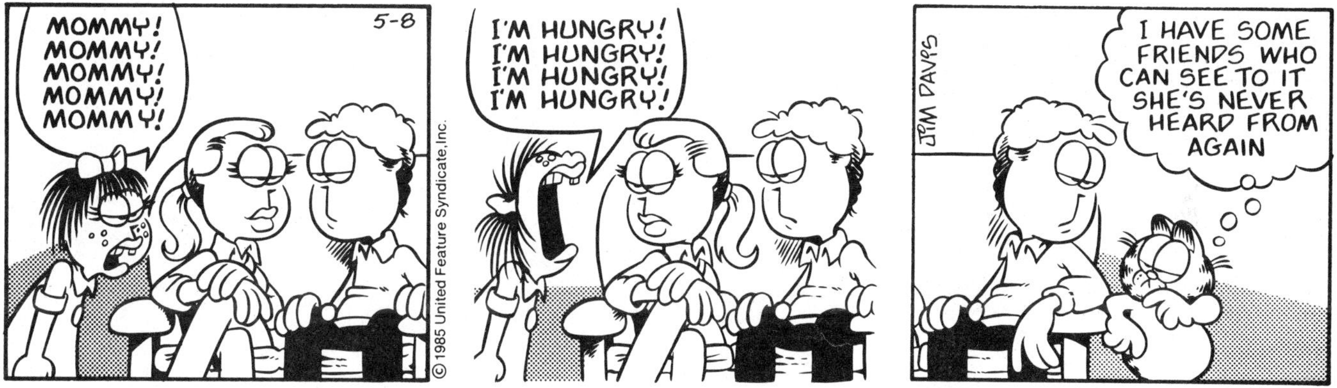
MOMMY! MOMMY! MOMMY! MOMMY! MOMMY!
5-8
© 1985 United Feature Syndicate, Inc.
I'M HUNGRY! I'M HUNGRY! I'M HUNGRY! I'M HUNGRY!
JIM DAVIS
I HAVE SOME FRIENDS WHO CAN SEE TO IT SHE'S NEVER HEARD FROM AGAIN

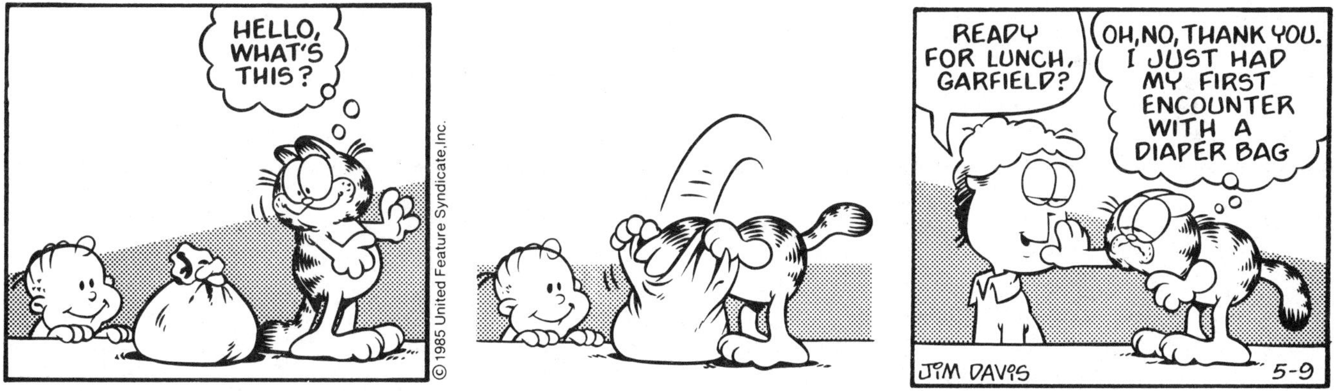
HELLO, WHAT'S THIS?
© 1985 United Feature Syndicate, Inc.
READY FOR LUNCH, GARFIELD?
OH, NO, THANK YOU. I JUST HAD MY FIRST ENCOUNTER WITH A DIAPER BAG
JIM DAVIS
5-9

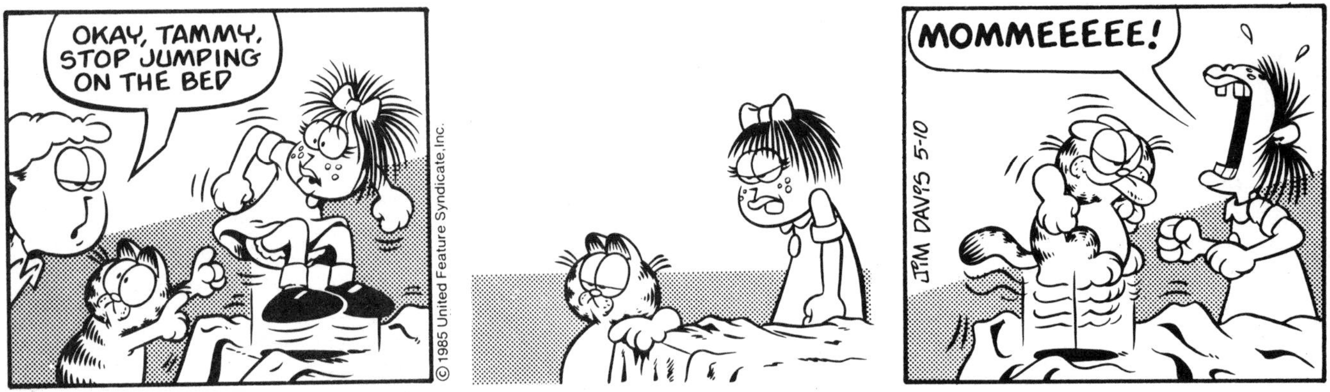
OKAY, TAMMY, STOP JUMPING ON THE BED
© 1985 United Feature Syndicate, Inc.
MOMMEEEEE!
JIM DAVIS 5-10

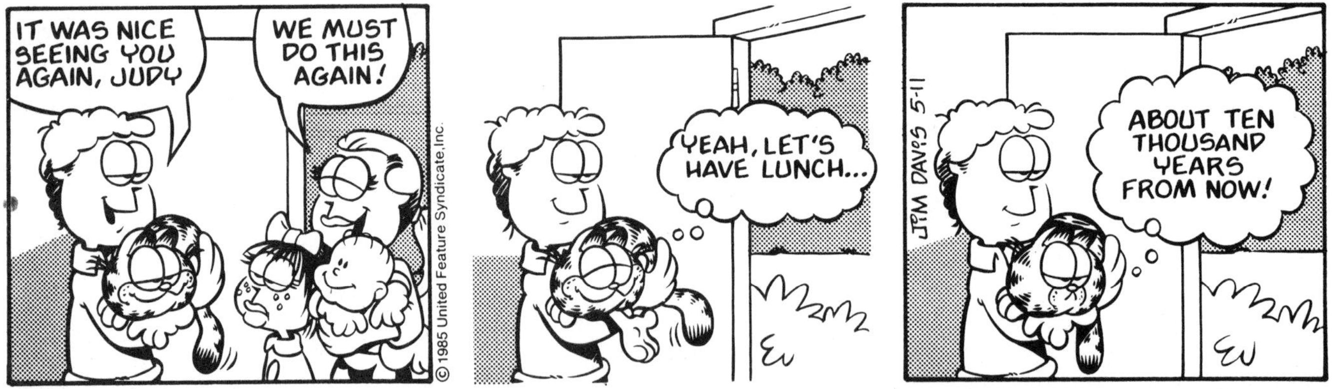
IT WAS NICE SEEING YOU AGAIN, JUDY
WE MUST DO THIS AGAIN!
© 1985 United Feature Syndicate, Inc.
YEAH, LET'S HAVE LUNCH...
ABOUT TEN THOUSAND YEARS FROM NOW!
JIM DAVIS 5-11

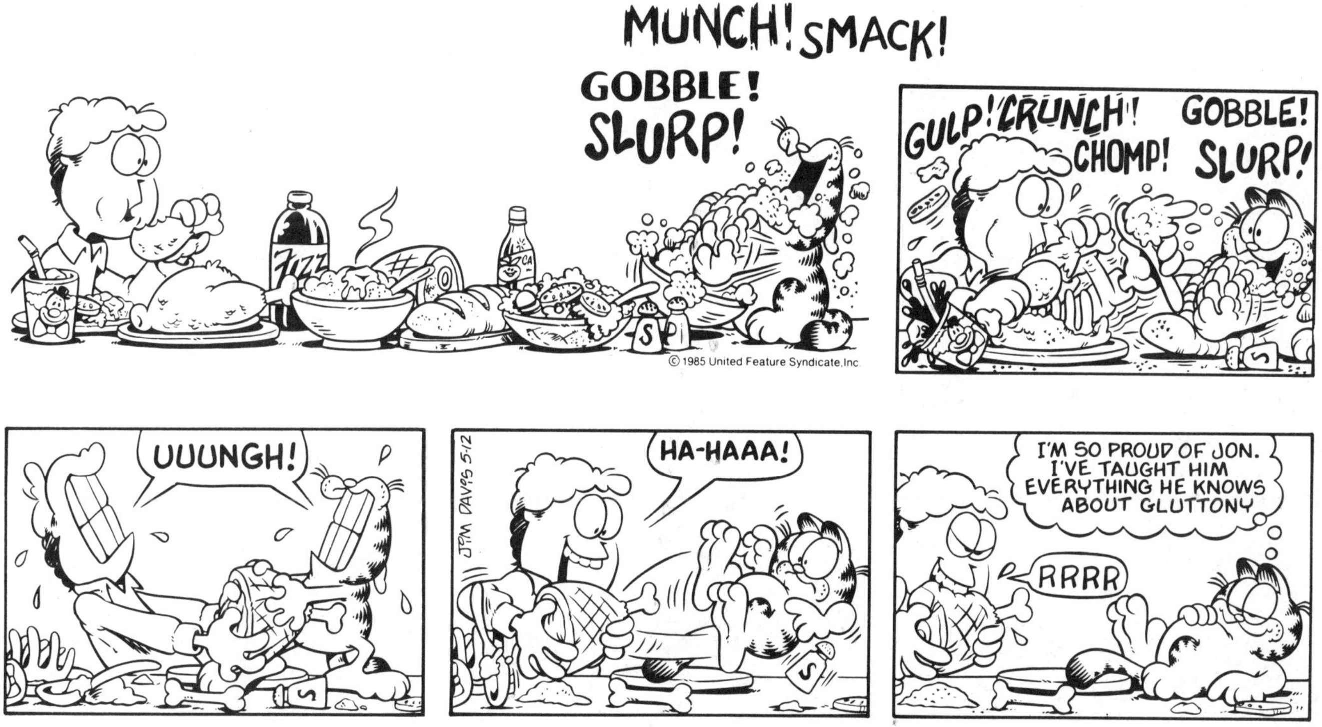

MUNCH! SMACK!
GOBBLE! SLURP!
© 1985 United Feature Syndicate, Inc.
GULP! CRUNCH! CHOMP!
GOBBLE! SLURP!
UUUNGH!
JIM DAVIS 5-12
HA-HAAA!
I'M SO PROUD OF JON. I'VE TAUGHT HIM EVERYTHING HE KNOWS ABOUT GLUTTONY
RRRR

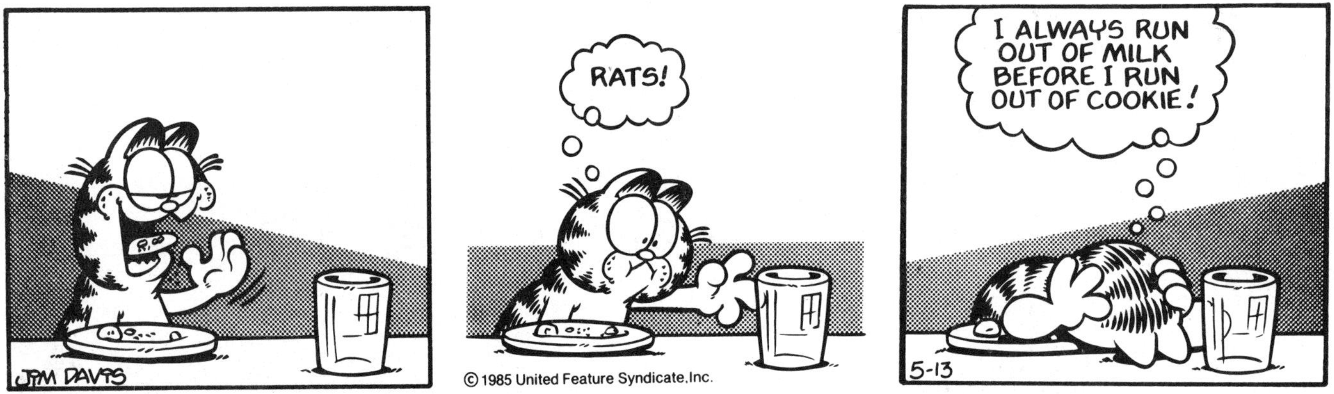
RATS!
I ALWAYS RUN OUT OF MILK BEFORE I RUN OUT OF COOKIE!
JIM DAVIS
5-13

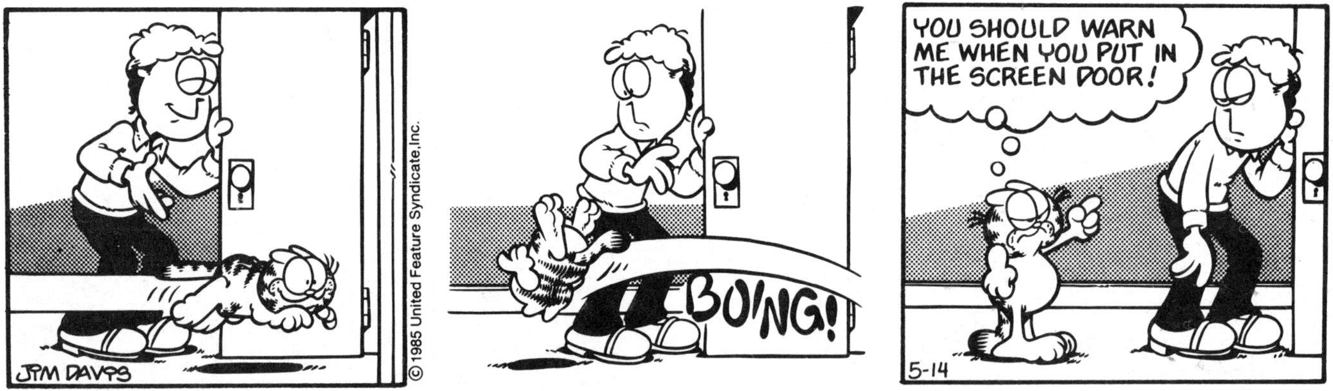
BOING!
YOU SHOULD WARN ME WHEN YOU PUT IN THE SCREEN DOOR!
JIM DAVIS
5-14

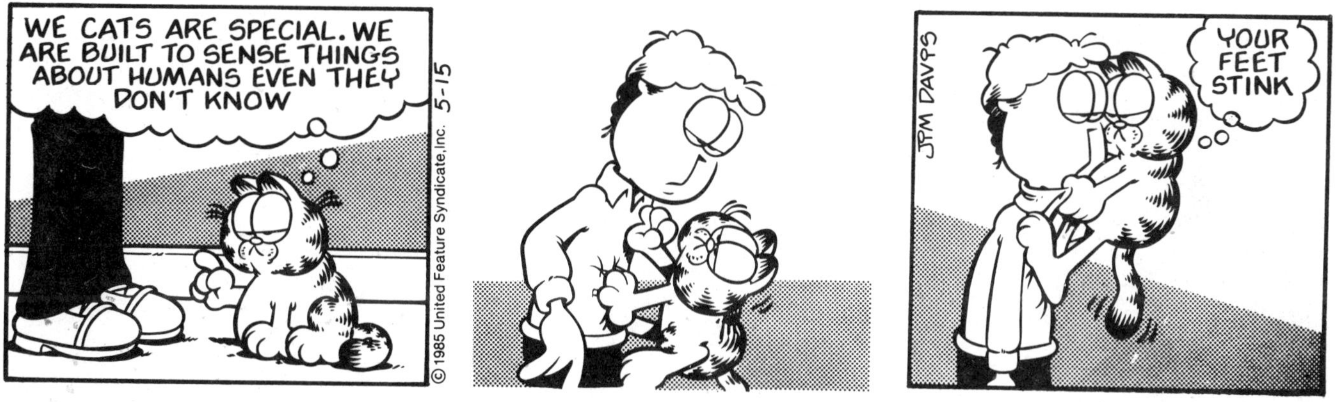
WE CATS ARE SPECIAL. WE ARE BUILT TO SENSE THINGS ABOUT HUMANS EVEN THEY DON'T KNOW
5-15
© 1985 United Feature Syndicate, Inc.
JIM DAVIS
YOUR FEET STINK

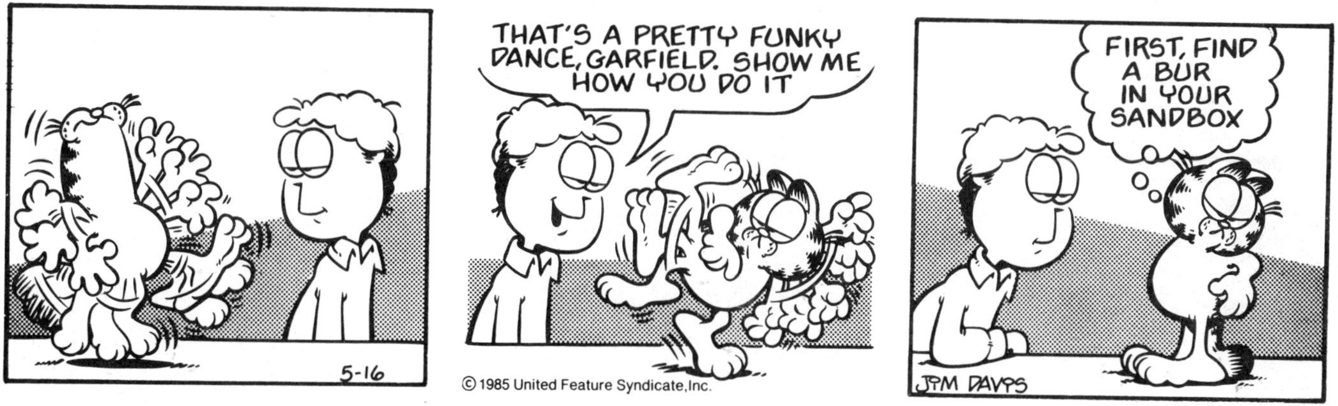
5-16
THAT'S A PRETTY FUNKY DANCE, GARFIELD. SHOW ME HOW YOU DO IT
© 1985 United Feature Syndicate, Inc.
FIRST, FIND A BUR IN YOUR SANDBOX
JIM DAVIS

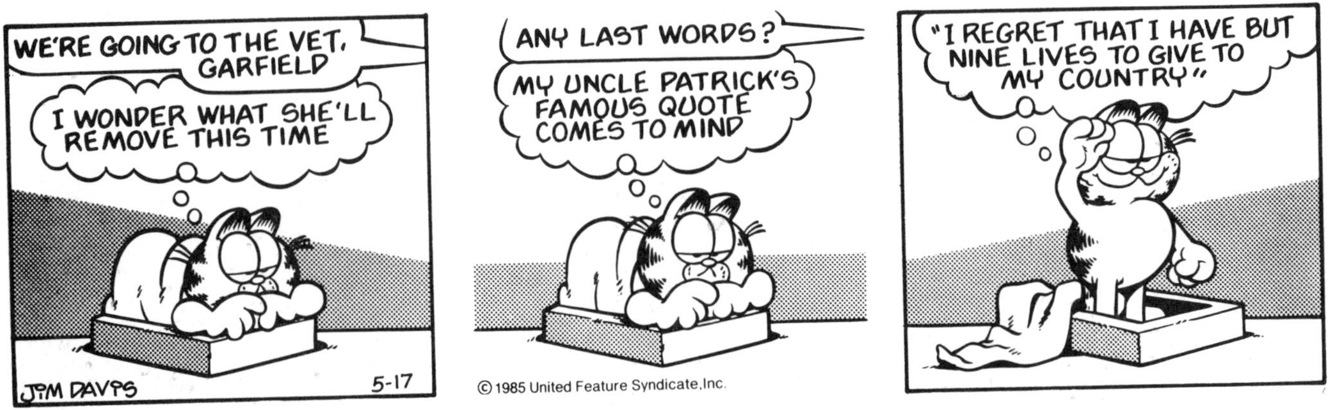
WE'RE GOING TO THE VET, GARFIELD
I WONDER WHAT SHE'LL REMOVE THIS TIME
JIM DAVIS
5-17
ANY LAST WORDS?
MY UNCLE PATRICK'S FAMOUS QUOTE COMES TO MIND
© 1985 United Feature Syndicate, Inc.
"I REGRET THAT I HAVE BUT NINE LIVES TO GIVE TO MY COUNTRY"

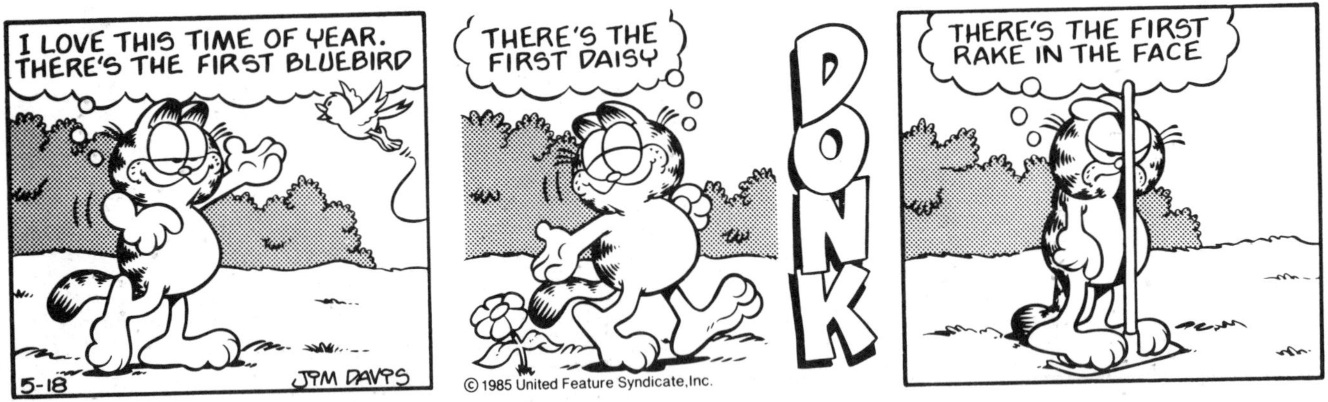
I LOVE THIS TIME OF YEAR. THERE'S THE FIRST BLUEBIRD
5-18
JIM DAVIS
THERE'S THE FIRST DAISY
© 1985 United Feature Syndicate, Inc.
DONK
THERE'S THE FIRST RAKE IN THE FACE

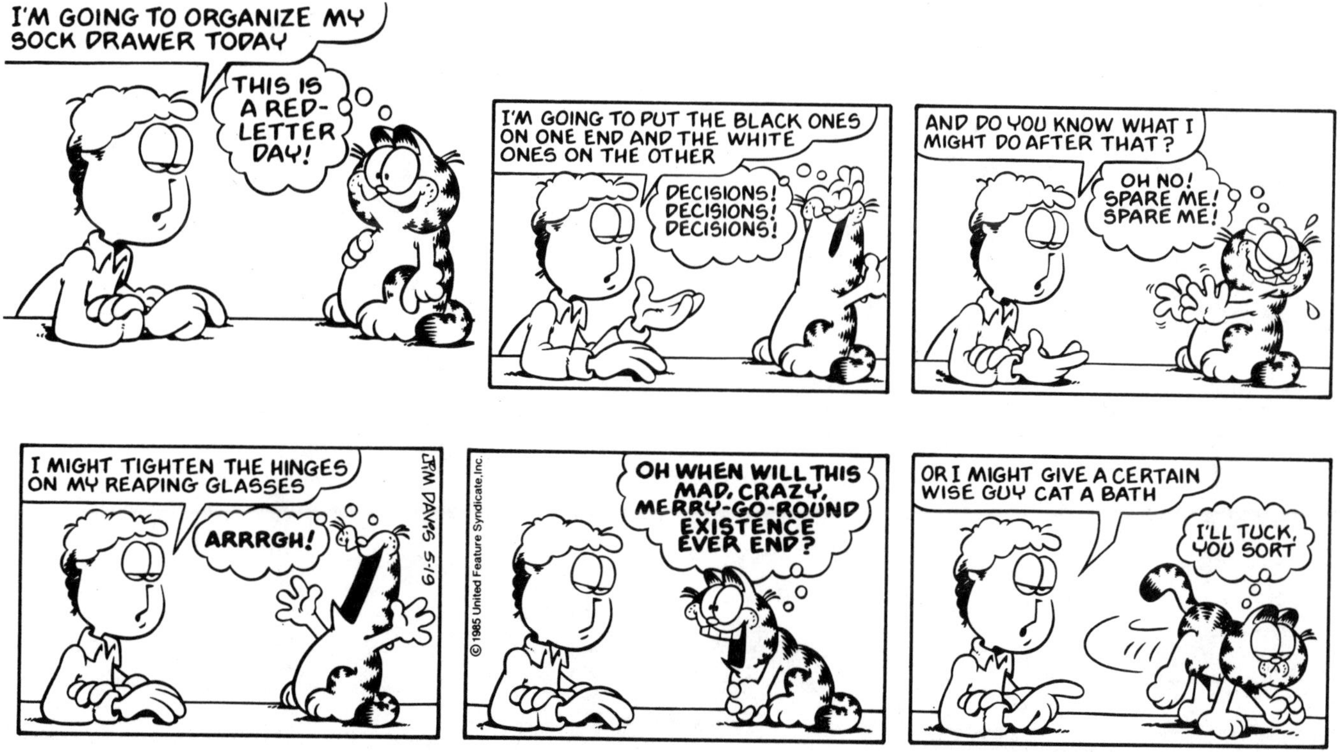
I'M GOING TO ORGANIZE MY SOCK DRAWER TODAY
THIS IS A RED-LETTER DAY!
I'M GOING TO PUT THE BLACK ONES ON ONE END AND THE WHITE ONES ON THE OTHER
DECISIONS! DECISIONS! DECISIONS!
AND DO YOU KNOW WHAT I MIGHT DO AFTER THAT?
OH NO! SPARE ME! SPARE ME!
I MIGHT TIGHTEN THE HINGES ON MY READING GLASSES
ARRRGH!
JIM DAVIS 5-19
© 1985 United Feature Syndicate, Inc.
OH WHEN WILL THIS MAD, CRAZY, MERRY-GO-ROUND EXISTENCE EVER END?
OR I MIGHT GIVE A CERTAIN WISE GUY CAT A BATH
I'LL TUCK, YOU SORT

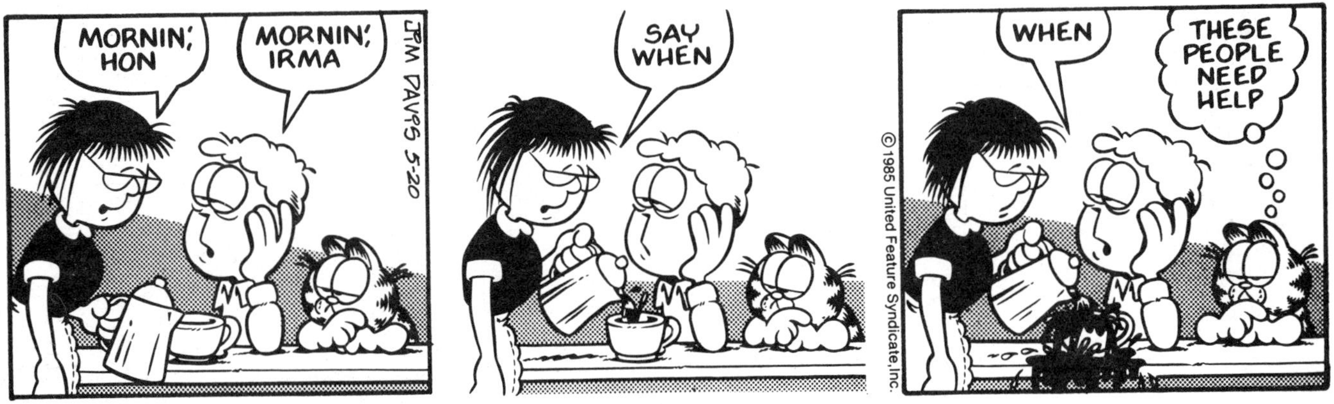
MORNIN', HON
MORNIN', IRMA
JIM DAVIS 5-20
SAY WHEN
© 1985 United Feature Syndicate, Inc.
WHEN
THESE PEOPLE NEED HELP

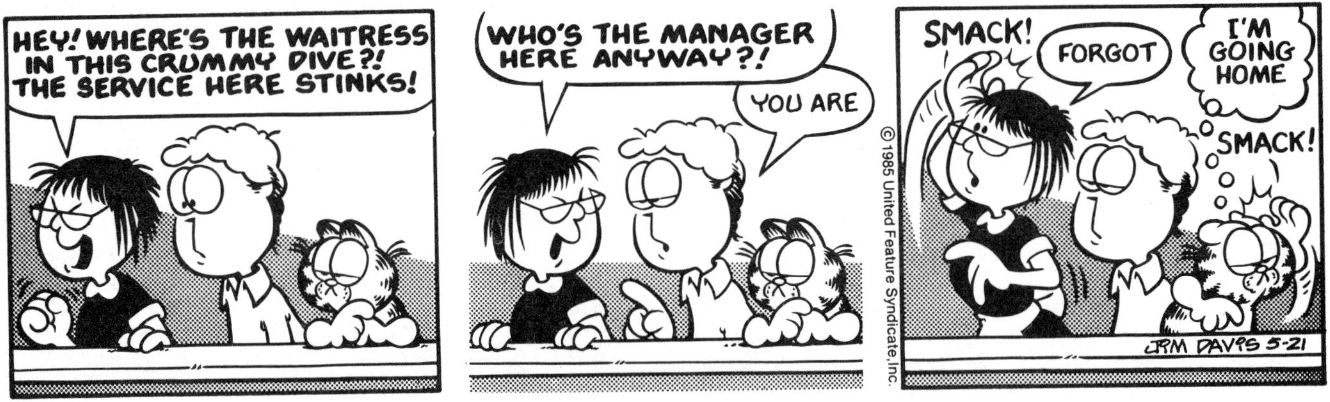
HEY! WHERE'S THE WAITRESS IN THIS CRUMMY DIVE?! THE SERVICE HERE STINKS!
WHO'S THE MANAGER HERE ANYWAY?!
YOU ARE
© 1985 United Feature Syndicate, Inc.
SMACK!
FORGOT
I'M GOING HOME
SMACK!
JIM DAVIS 5-21

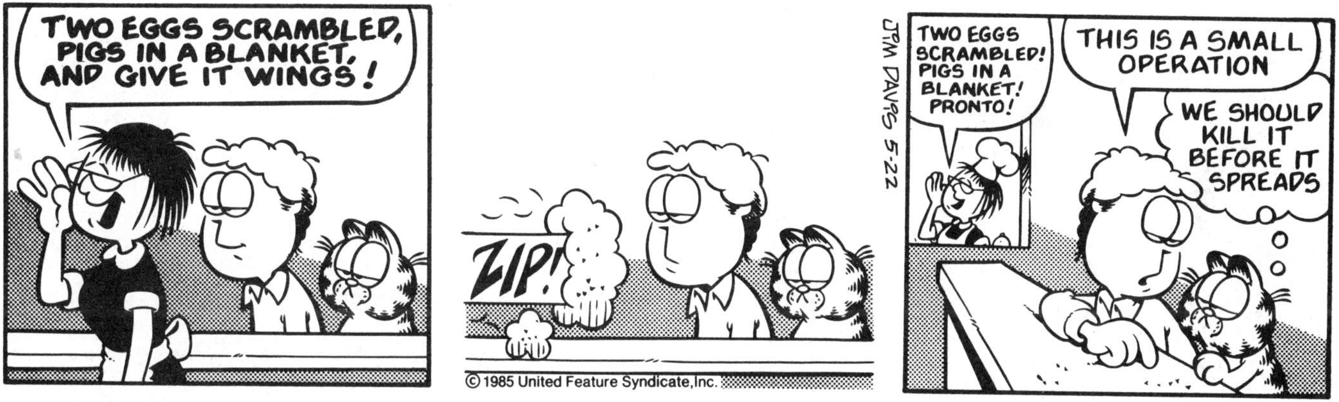
TWO EGGS SCRAMBLED, PIGS IN A BLANKET, AND GIVE IT WINGS!
ZIP!
© 1985 United Feature Syndicate, Inc.
JIM DAVIS 5-22
TWO EGGS SCRAMBLED! PIGS IN A BLANKET! PRONTO!
THIS IS A SMALL OPERATION
WE SHOULD KILL IT BEFORE IT SPREADS

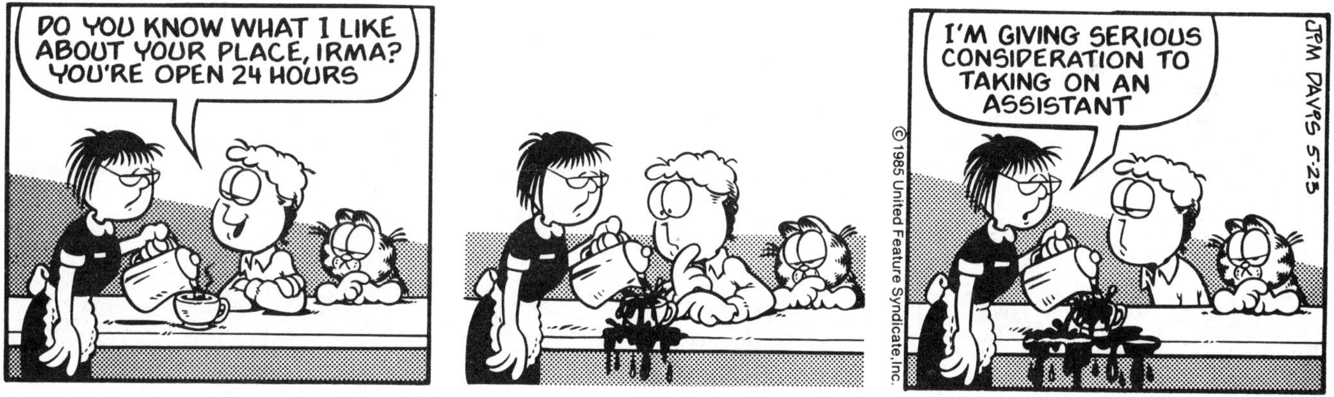
DO YOU KNOW WHAT I LIKE ABOUT YOUR PLACE, IRMA? YOU'RE OPEN 24 HOURS
© 1985 United Feature Syndicate, Inc.
JIM DAVIS 5-23
I'M GIVING SERIOUS CONSIDERATION TO TAKING ON AN ASSISTANT

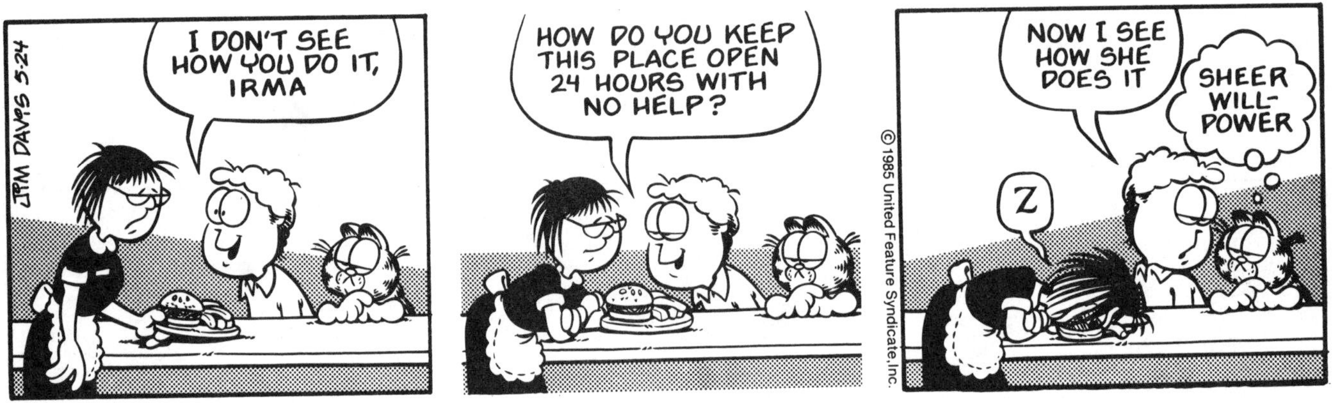
JIM DAVIS 5-24
I DON'T SEE HOW YOU DO IT, IRMA
HOW DO YOU KEEP THIS PLACE OPEN 24 HOURS WITH NO HELP?
© 1985 United Feature Syndicate, Inc.
NOW I SEE HOW SHE DOES IT
Z
SHEER WILL-POWER

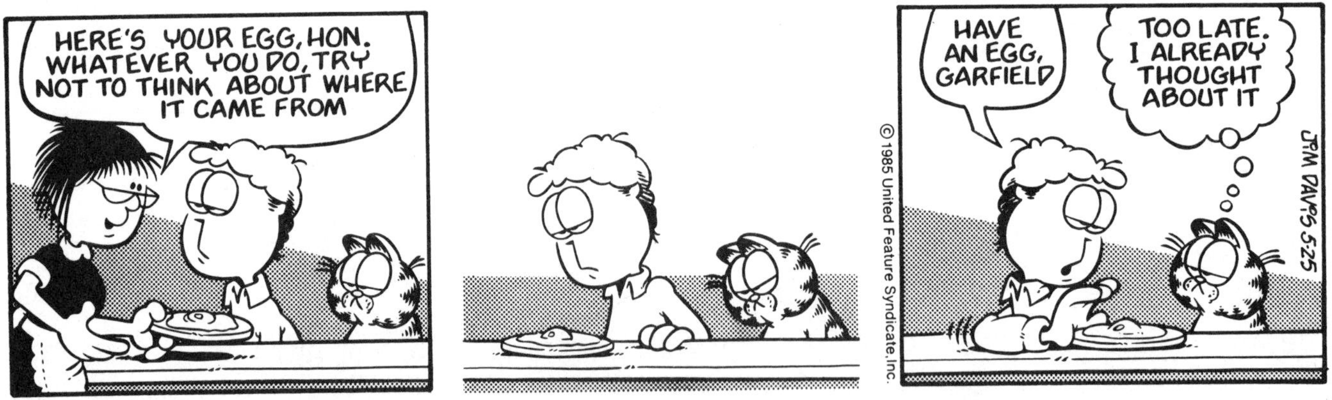
HERE'S YOUR EGG, HON. WHATEVER YOU DO, TRY NOT TO THINK ABOUT WHERE IT CAME FROM
© 1985 United Feature Syndicate, Inc.
HAVE AN EGG, GARFIELD
TOO LATE. I ALREADY THOUGHT ABOUT IT
JIM DAVIS 5-25

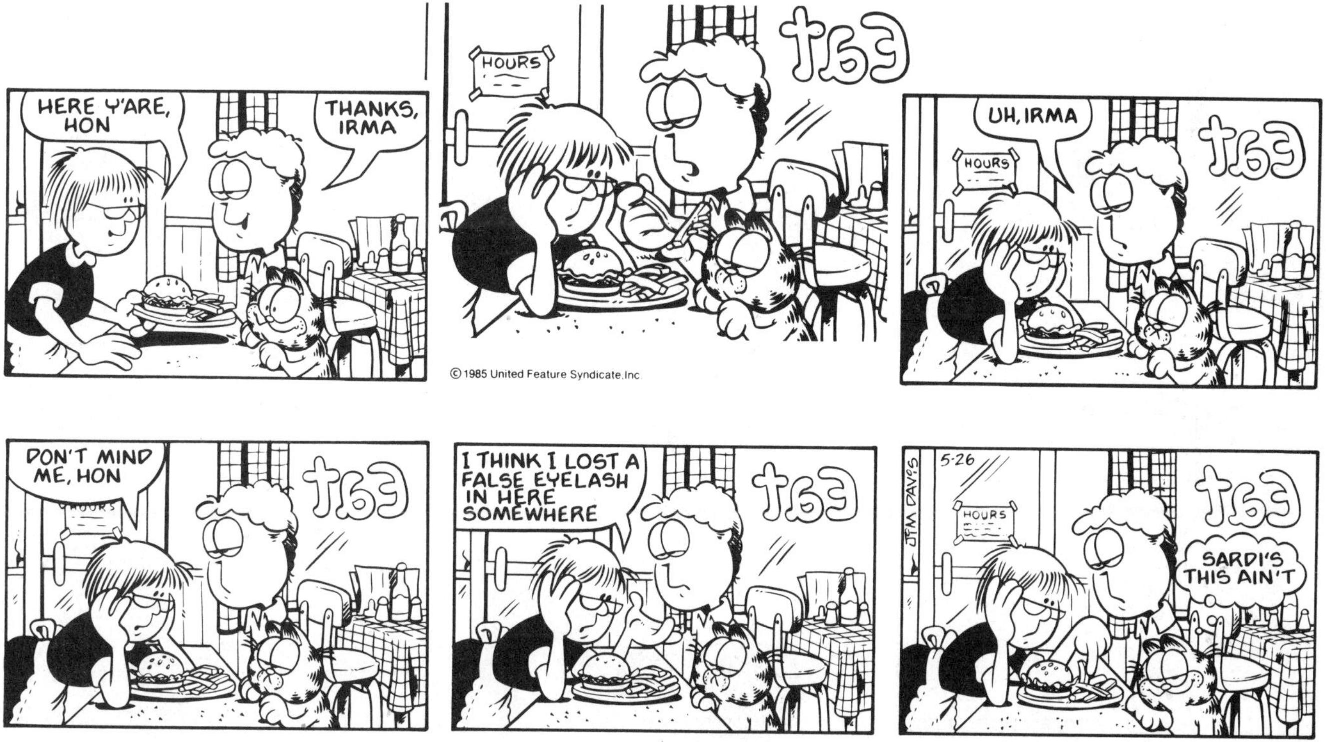
HERE Y'ARE, HON
THANKS, IRMA
HOURS
UH, IRMA
HOURS
DON'T MIND ME, HON
I THINK I LOST A FALSE EYELASH IN HERE SOMEWHERE
5-26
JIM DAVIS
HOURS
SARDI'S THIS AIN'T

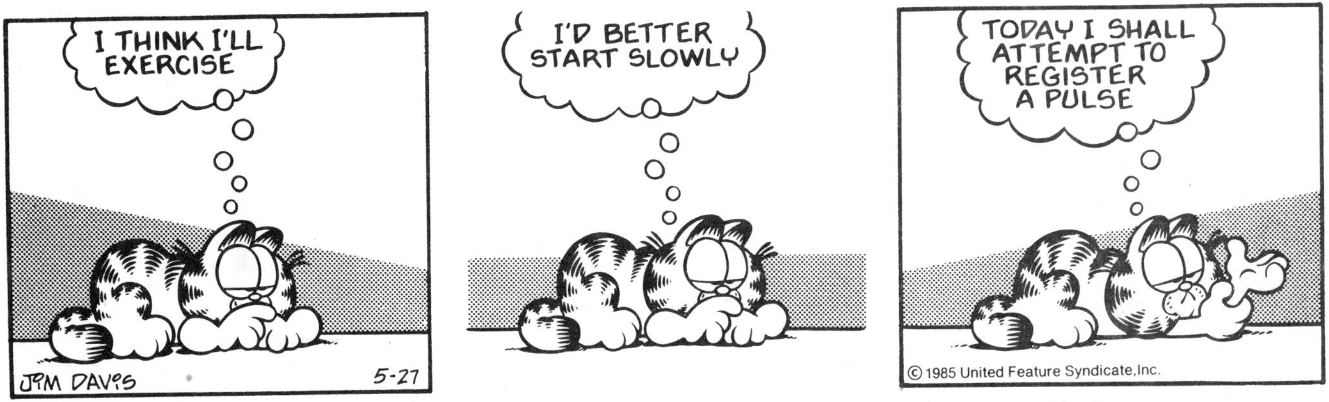
I THINK I'LL EXERCISE
JIM DAVIS
5-27
I'D BETTER START SLOWLY
TODAY I SHALL ATTEMPT TO REGISTER A PULSE
© 1985 United Feature Syndicate, Inc.

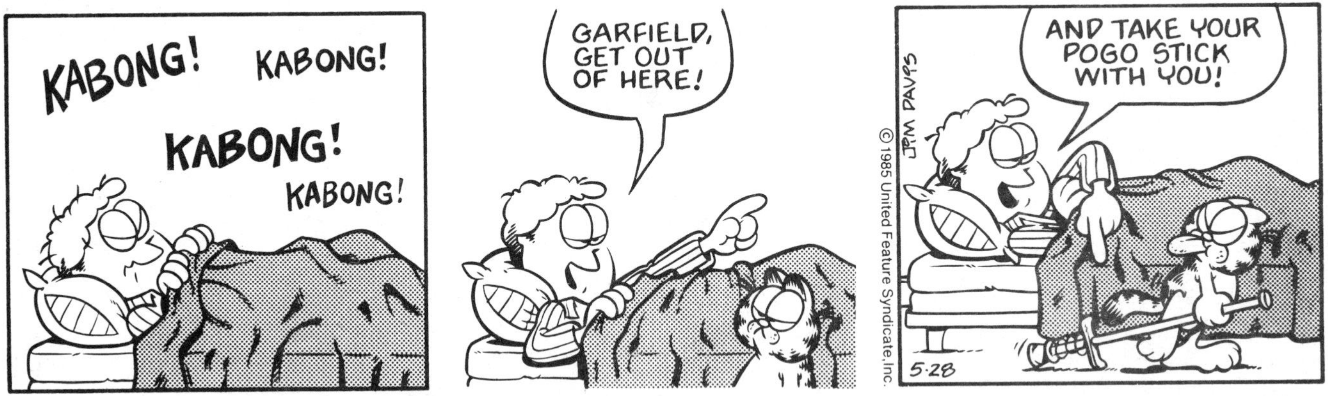
KABONG!
KABONG!
KABONG!
KABONG!
GARFIELD, GET OUT OF HERE!
© 1985 United Feature Syndicate, Inc.
JIM DAVIS
AND TAKE YOUR POGO STICK WITH YOU!
5-28

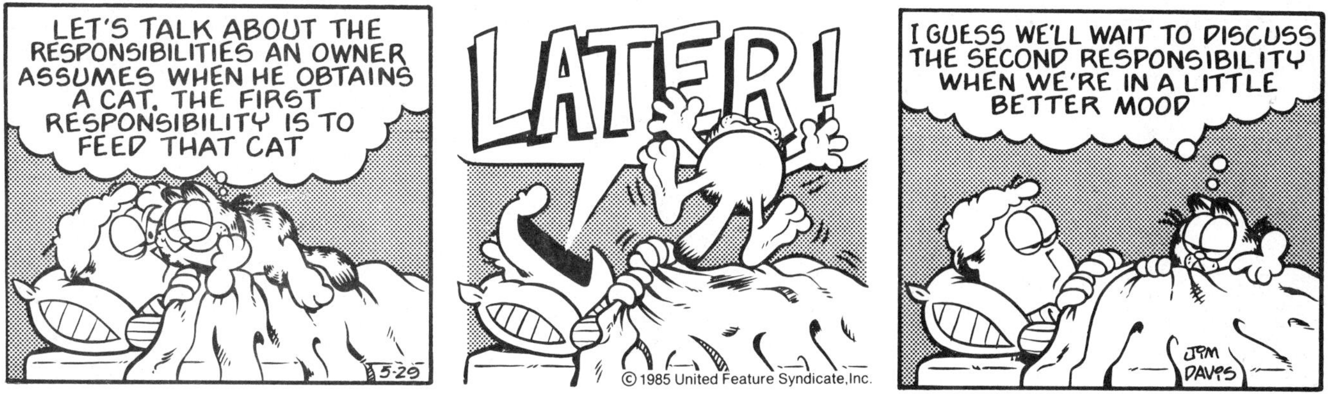
LET'S TALK ABOUT THE RESPONSIBILITIES AN OWNER ASSUMES WHEN HE OBTAINS A CAT. THE FIRST RESPONSIBILITY IS TO FEED THAT CAT
5-29
LATER!
I GUESS WE'LL WAIT TO DISCUSS THE SECOND RESPONSIBILITY WHEN WE'RE IN A LITTLE BETTER MOOD
JIM DAVIS

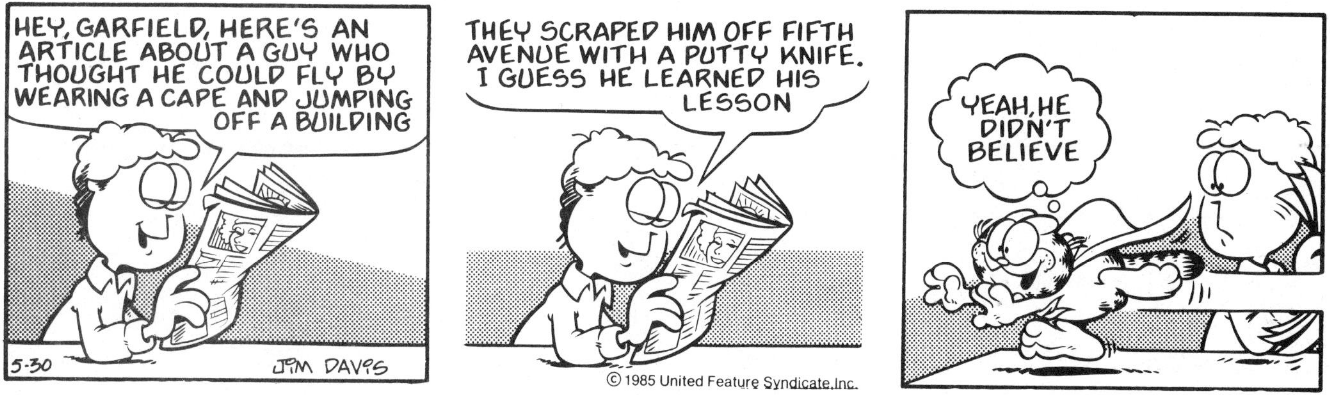
HEY, GARFIELD, HERE'S AN ARTICLE ABOUT A GUY WHO THOUGHT HE COULD FLY BY WEARING A CAPE AND JUMPING OFF A BUILDING
5-30
JIM DAVIS
THEY SCRAPED HIM OFF FIFTH AVENUE WITH A PUTTY KNIFE. I GUESS HE LEARNED HIS LESSON
YEAH, HE DIDN'T BELIEVE

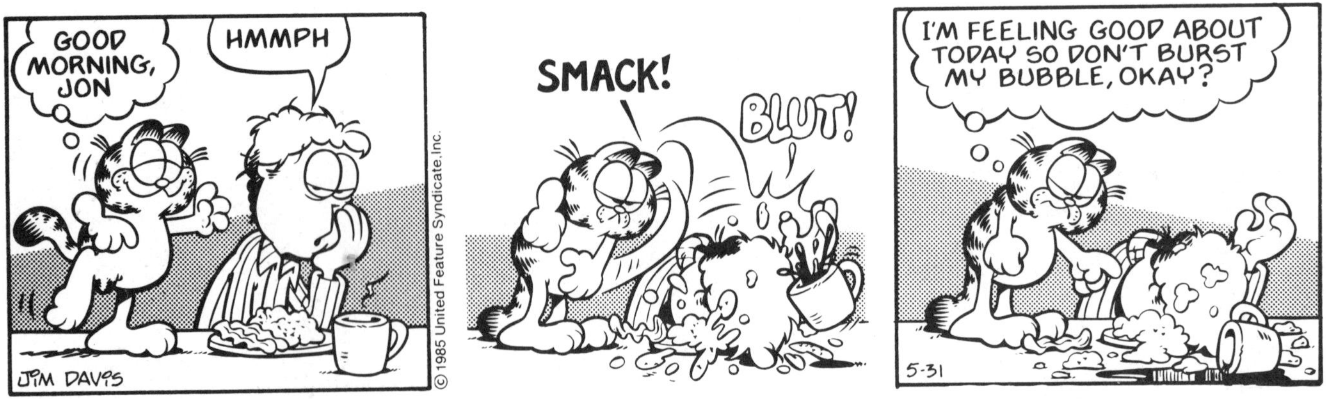
GOOD MORNING, JON
HMMPH
JIM DAVIS
© 1985 United Feature Syndicate, Inc.
SMACK!
BLUT!
I'M FEELING GOOD ABOUT TODAY SO DON'T BURST MY BUBBLE, OKAY?
5-31

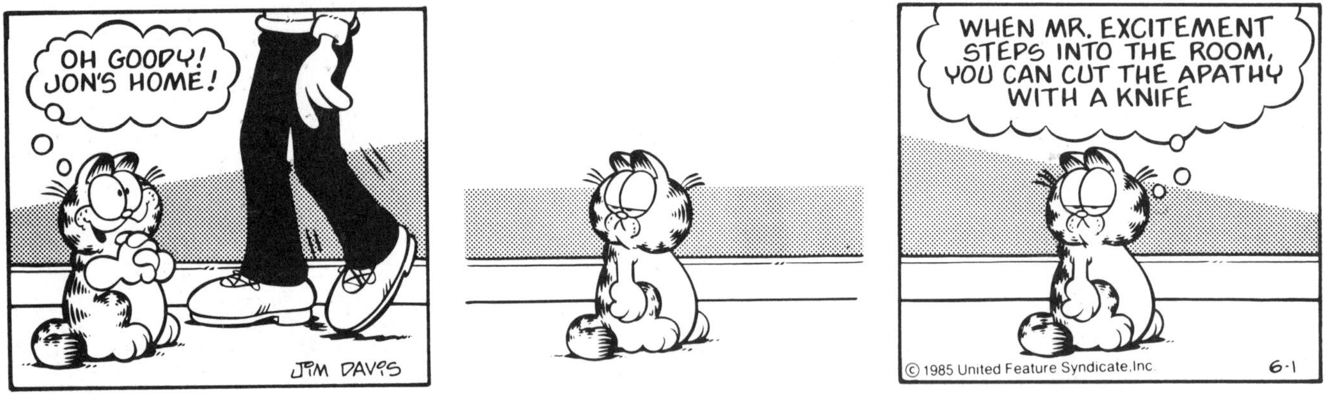
OH GOODY! JON'S HOME!
JIM DAVIS
WHEN MR. EXCITEMENT STEPS INTO THE ROOM, YOU CAN CUT THE APATHY WITH A KNIFE
© 1985 United Feature Syndicate, Inc.
6-1

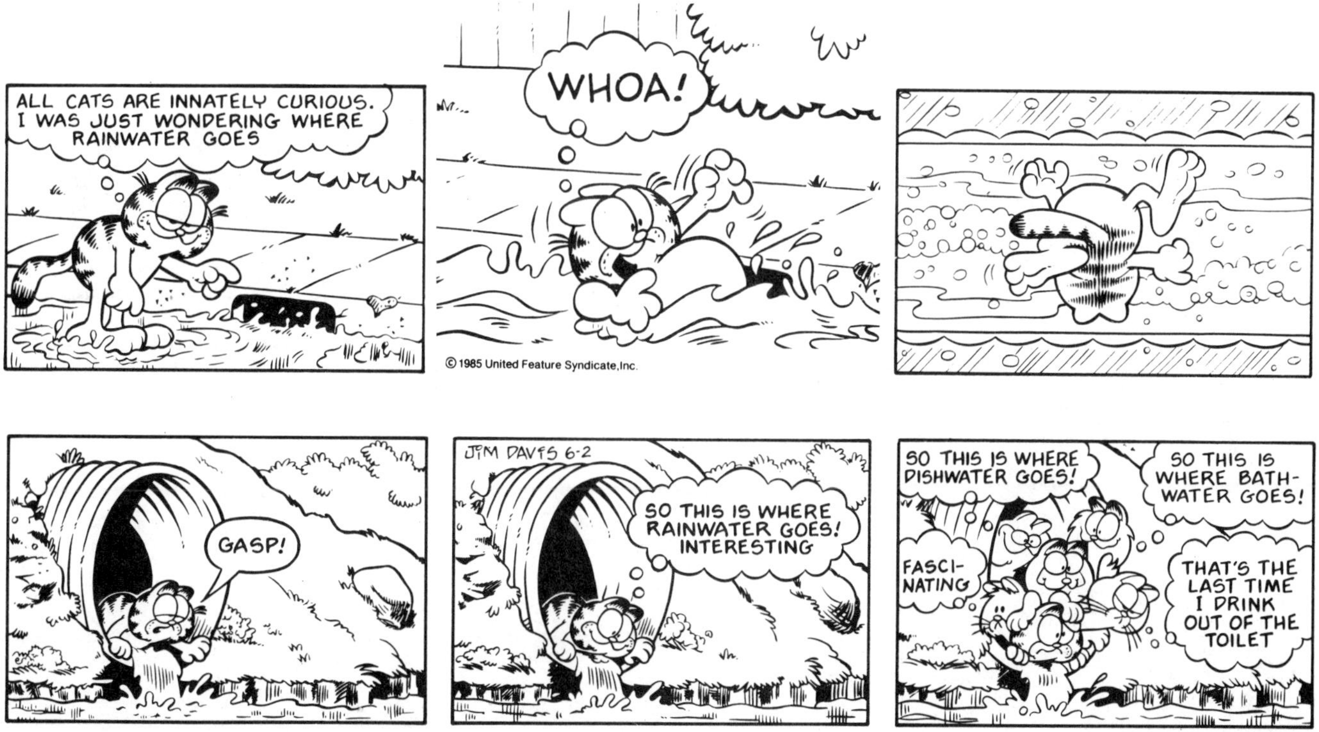
ALL CATS ARE INNATELY CURIOUS. I WAS JUST WONDERING WHERE RAINWATER GOES
WHOA!
© 1985 United Feature Syndicate, Inc.
GASP!
JIM DAVIS 6-2
SO THIS IS WHERE RAINWATER GOES! INTERESTING
SO THIS IS WHERE DISHWATER GOES!
SO THIS IS WHERE BATH-WATER GOES!
FASCI-NATING
THAT'S THE LAST TIME I DRINK OUT OF THE TOILET

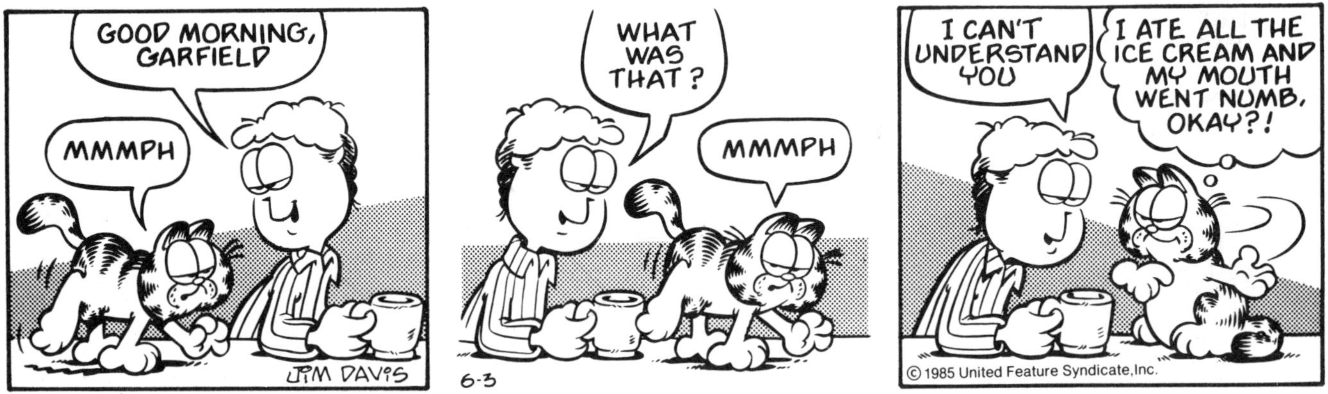
GOOD MORNING, GARFIELD
MMMPH
JIM DAVIS
WHAT WAS THAT?
MMMPH
6-3
I CAN'T UNDERSTAND YOU
I ATE ALL THE ICE CREAM AND MY MOUTH WENT NUMB, OKAY?!
© 1985 United Feature Syndicate, Inc.

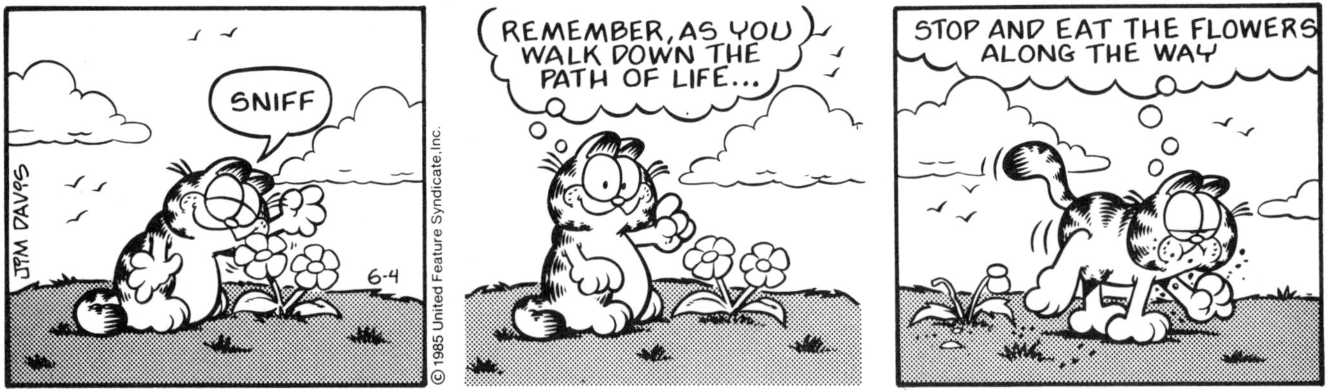
JIM DAVIS
SNIFF
6-4
© 1985 United Feature Syndicate, Inc.
REMEMBER, AS YOU WALK DOWN THE PATH OF LIFE...
STOP AND EAT THE FLOWERS ALONG THE WAY

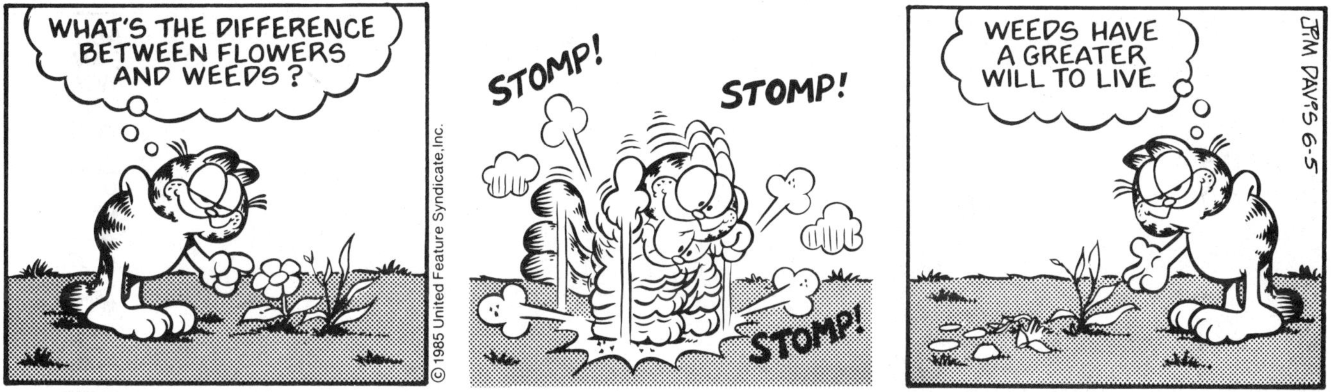
WHAT'S THE DIFFERENCE BETWEEN FLOWERS AND WEEDS?
© 1985 United Feature Syndicate, Inc.
STOMP!
STOMP!
STOMP!
WEEDS HAVE A GREATER WILL TO LIVE
JIM DAVIS 6-5

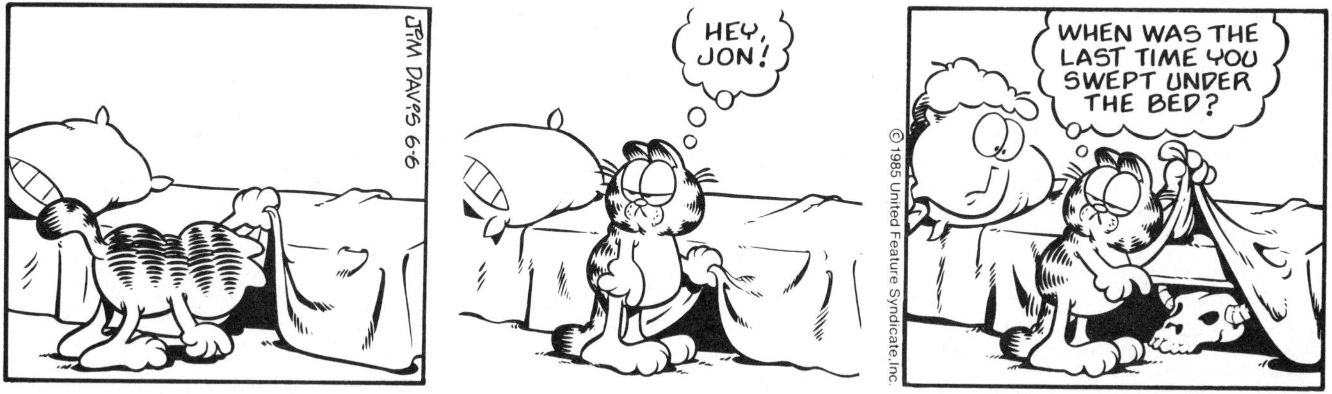
JIM DAVIS 6-6
HEY, JON!
© 1985 United Feature Syndicate, Inc.
WHEN WAS THE LAST TIME YOU SWEPT UNDER THE BED?

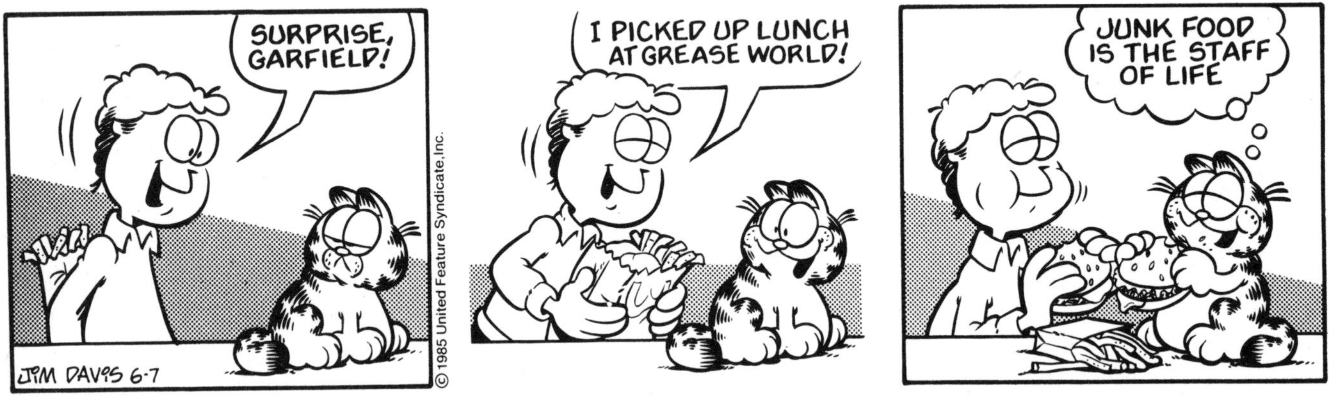
SURPRISE, GARFIELD!
JIM DAVIS 6-7
© 1985 United Feature Syndicate, Inc.
I PICKED UP LUNCH AT GREASE WORLD!
JUNK FOOD IS THE STAFF OF LIFE

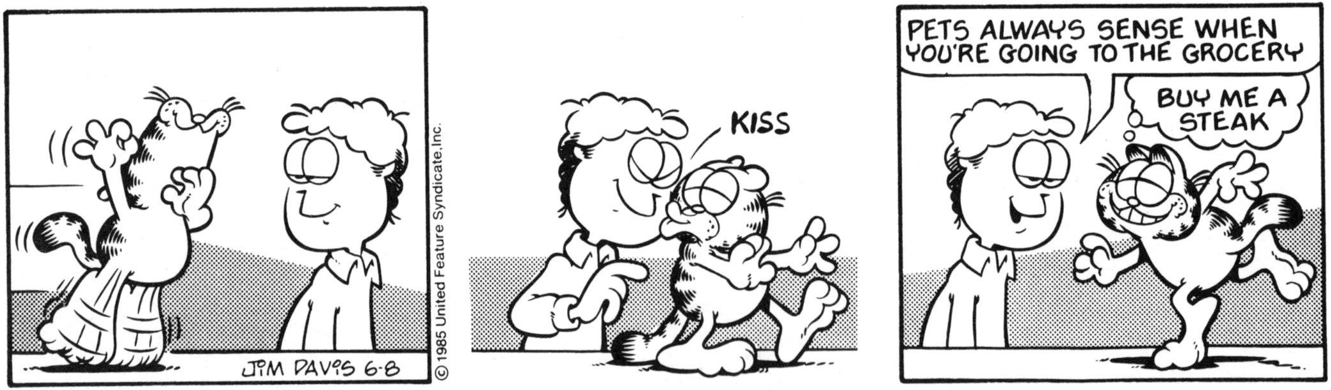
JIM DAVIS 6-8
© 1985 United Feature Syndicate, Inc.
KISS
PETS ALWAYS SENSE WHEN YOU'RE GOING TO THE GROCERY
BUY ME A STEAK

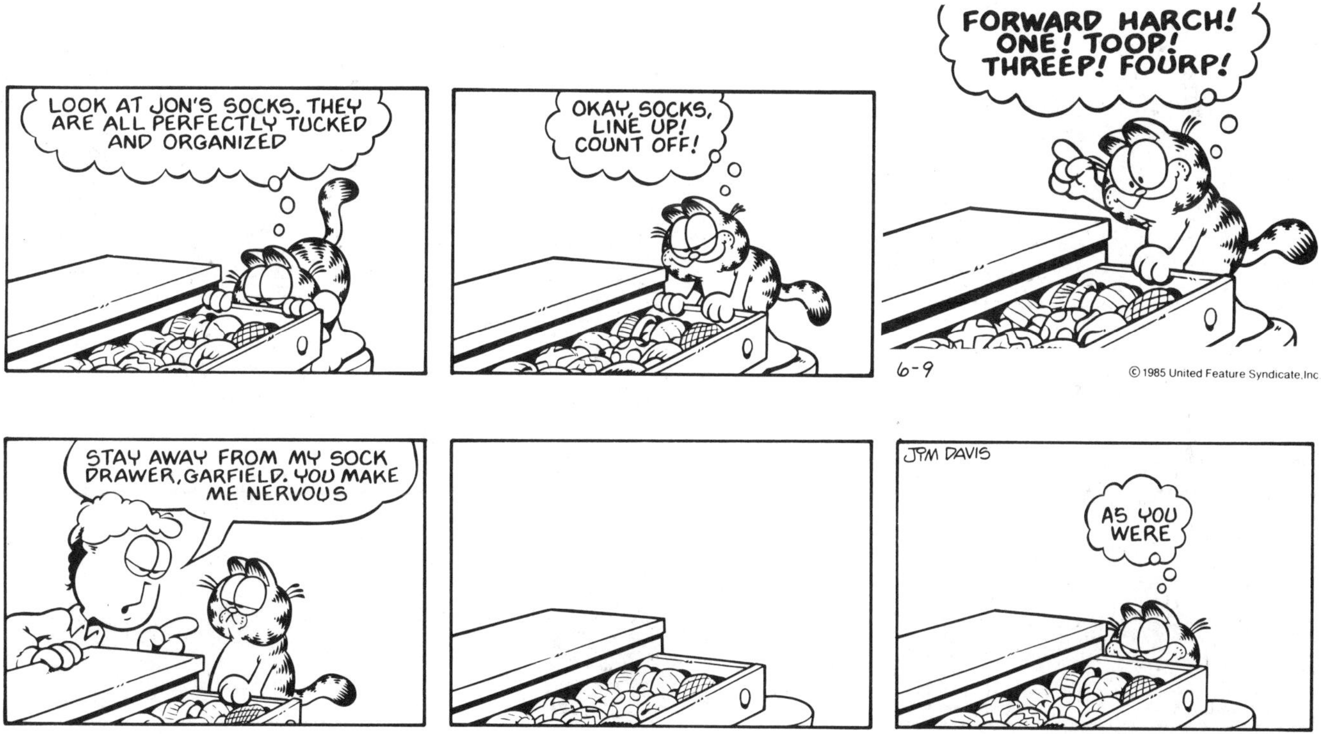

LOOK AT JON'S SOCKS. THEY ARE ALL PERFECTLY TUCKED AND ORGANIZED
OKAY, SOCKS, LINE UP! COUNT OFF!
FORWARD HARCH! ONE! TOOP! THREEP! FOURP!
6-9
© 1985 United Feature Syndicate, Inc
STAY AWAY FROM MY SOCK DRAWER, GARFIELD. YOU MAKE ME NERVOUS
JPM DAVIS
AS YOU WERE

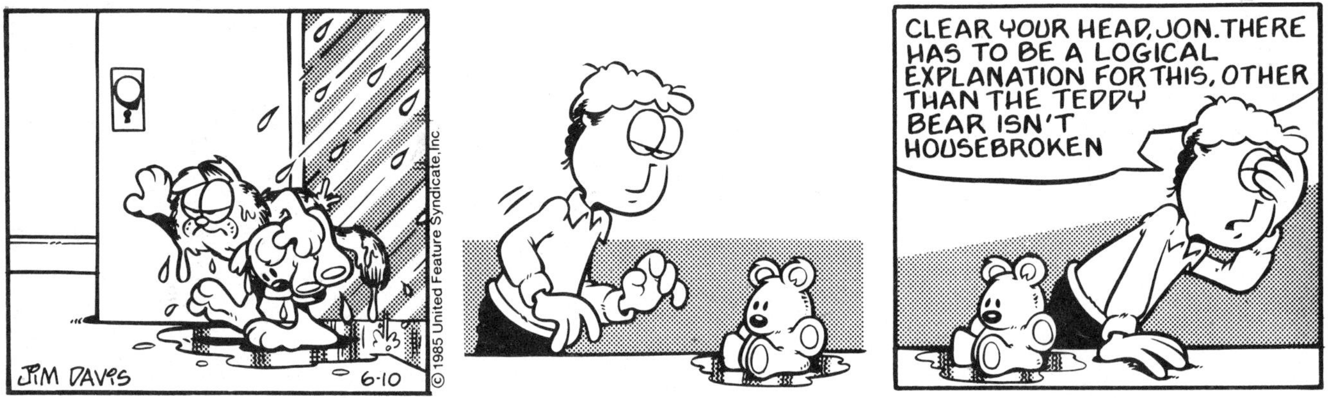

JIM DAVIS
6-10
© 1985 United Feature Syndicate, Inc.
CLEAR YOUR HEAD, JON. THERE HAS TO BE A LOGICAL EXPLANATION FOR THIS, OTHER THAN THE TEDDY BEAR ISN'T HOUSEBROKEN

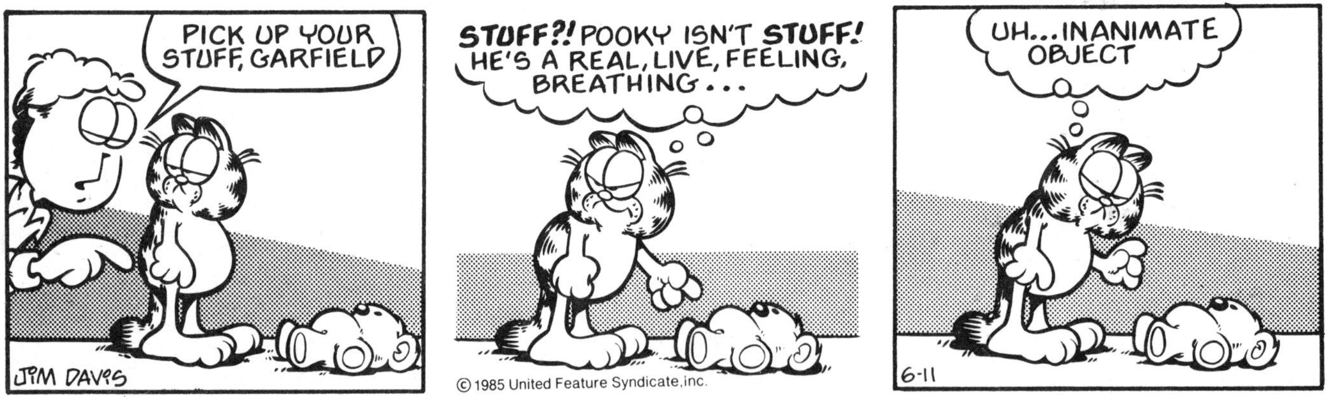

PICK UP YOUR STUFF, GARFIELD
JIM DAVIS
STUFF?! POOKY ISN'T **STUFF!** HE'S A REAL, LIVE, FEELING, BREATHING . . .
© 1985 United Feature Syndicate, inc.
UH...INANIMATE OBJECT
6-11

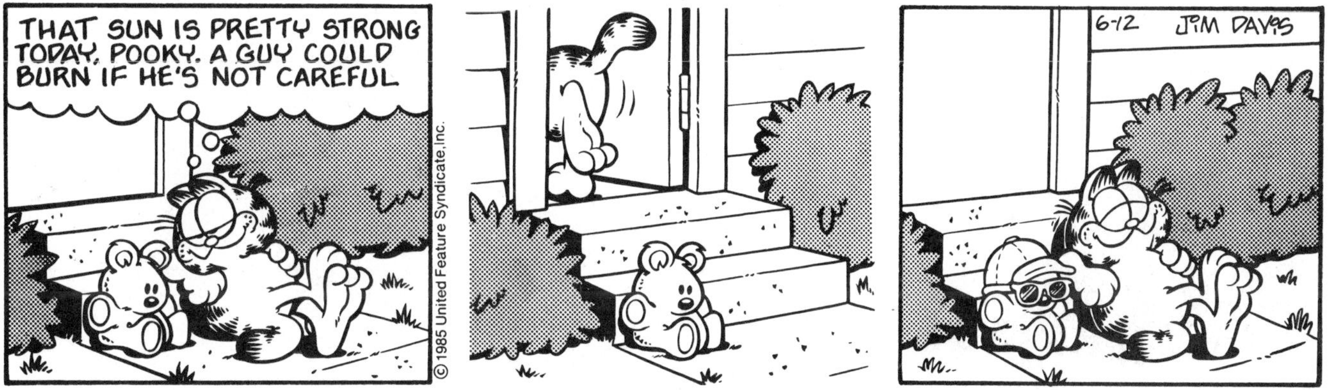
THAT SUN IS PRETTY STRONG TODAY, POOKY. A GUY COULD BURN IF HE'S NOT CAREFUL
© 1985 United Feature Syndicate, Inc.
6-12
JIM DAVIS

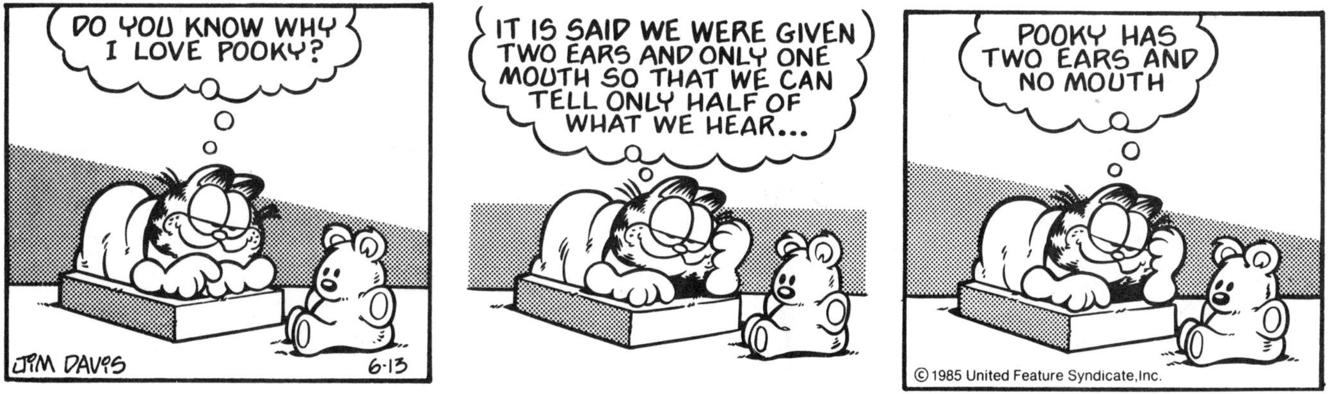
DO YOU KNOW WHY I LOVE POOKY?
JIM DAVIS
6-13
IT IS SAID WE WERE GIVEN TWO EARS AND ONLY ONE MOUTH SO THAT WE CAN TELL ONLY HALF OF WHAT WE HEAR...
POOKY HAS TWO EARS AND NO MOUTH
© 1985 United Feature Syndicate, Inc.

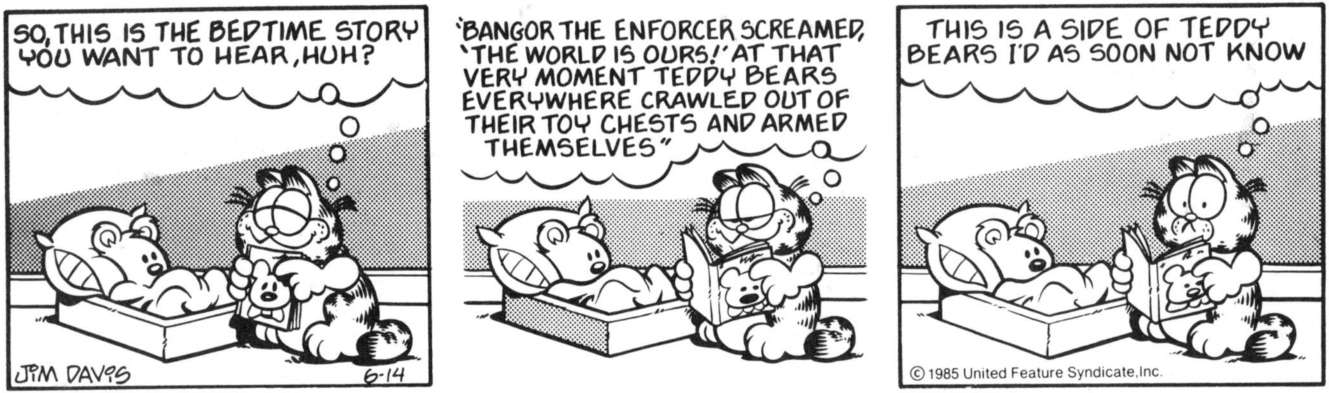
SO, THIS IS THE BEDTIME STORY YOU WANT TO HEAR, HUH?
JIM DAVIS
6-14
"BANGOR THE ENFORCER SCREAMED, 'THE WORLD IS OURS!' AT THAT VERY MOMENT TEDDY BEARS EVERYWHERE CRAWLED OUT OF THEIR TOY CHESTS AND ARMED THEMSELVES"
THIS IS A SIDE OF TEDDY BEARS I'D AS SOON NOT KNOW
© 1985 United Feature Syndicate, Inc.

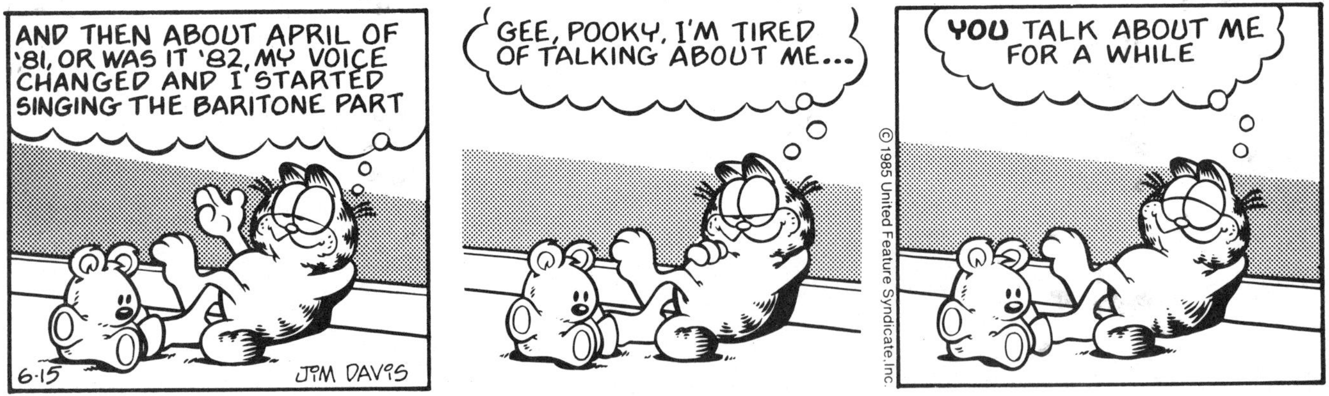
AND THEN ABOUT APRIL OF '81, OR WAS IT '82, MY VOICE CHANGED AND I STARTED SINGING THE BARITONE PART
6-15
JIM DAVIS
GEE, POOKY, I'M TIRED OF TALKING ABOUT ME...
© 1985 United Feature Syndicate, Inc.
YOU TALK ABOUT ME FOR A WHILE

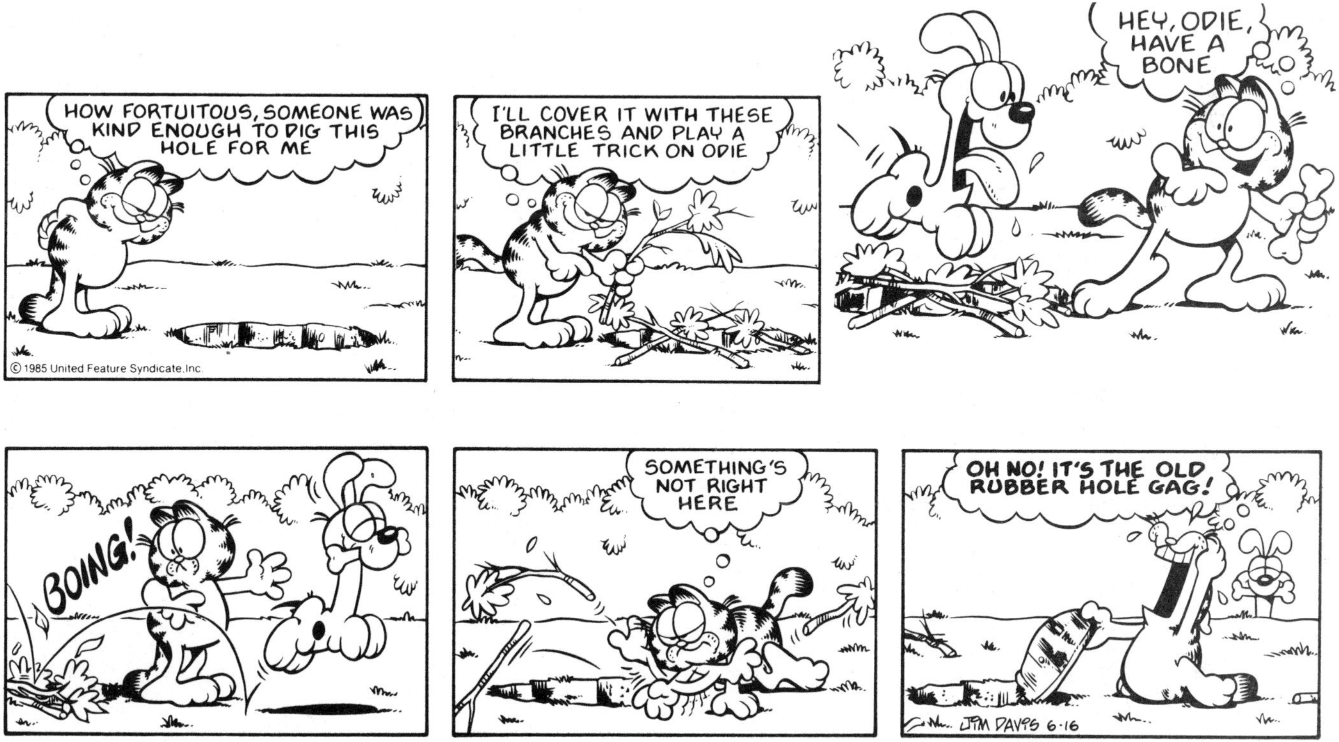

HOW FORTUITOUS, SOMEONE WAS KIND ENOUGH TO DIG THIS HOLE FOR ME
© 1985 United Feature Syndicate, Inc.
I'LL COVER IT WITH THESE BRANCHES AND PLAY A LITTLE TRICK ON ODIE
HEY, ODIE, HAVE A BONE
BOING!
SOMETHING'S NOT RIGHT HERE
OH NO! IT'S THE OLD RUBBER HOLE GAG!
JIM DAVIS 6-16

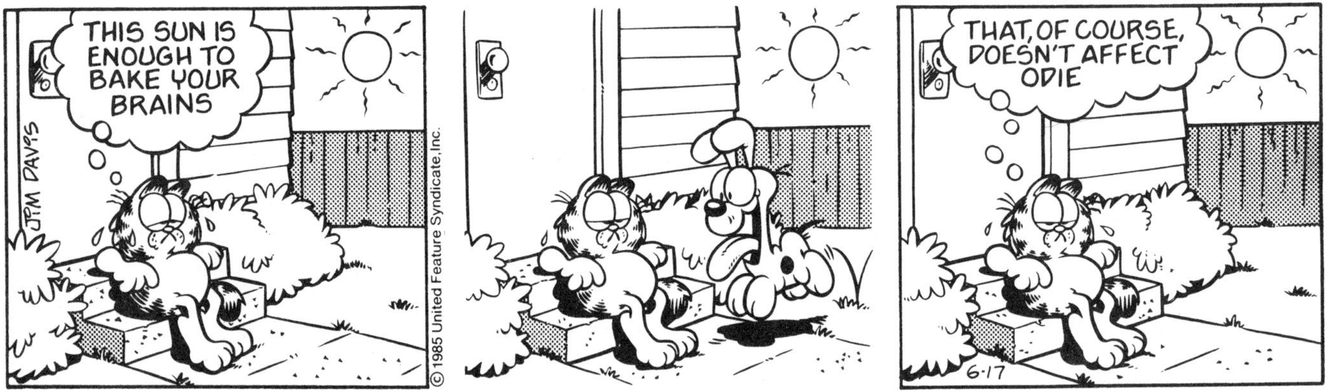
THIS SUN IS ENOUGH TO BAKE YOUR BRAINS
JIM DAVIS
© 1985 United Feature Syndicate, Inc.
THAT, OF COURSE, DOESN'T AFFECT ODIE
6-17

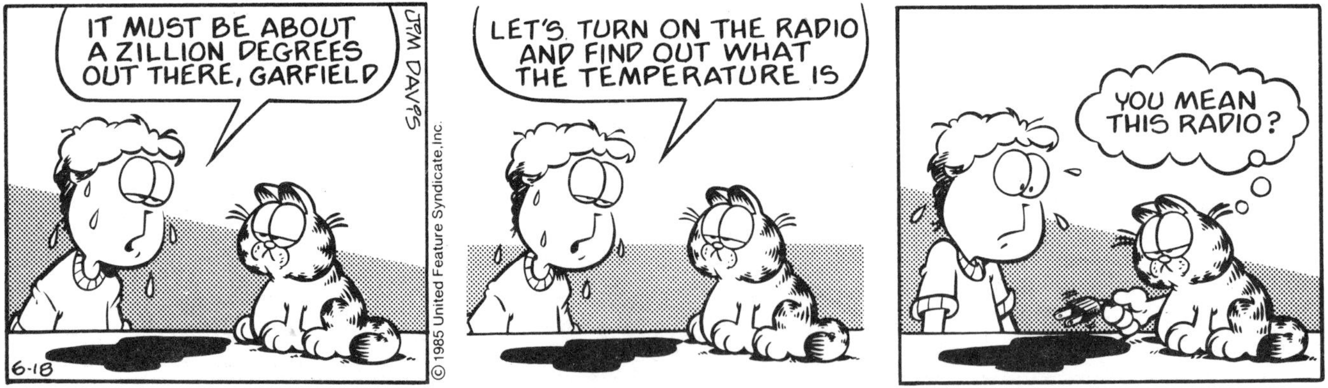
IT MUST BE ABOUT A ZILLION DEGREES OUT THERE, GARFIELD
JIM DAVIS
6-18
© 1985 United Feature Syndicate, Inc.
LET'S TURN ON THE RADIO AND FIND OUT WHAT THE TEMPERATURE IS
YOU MEAN THIS RADIO?

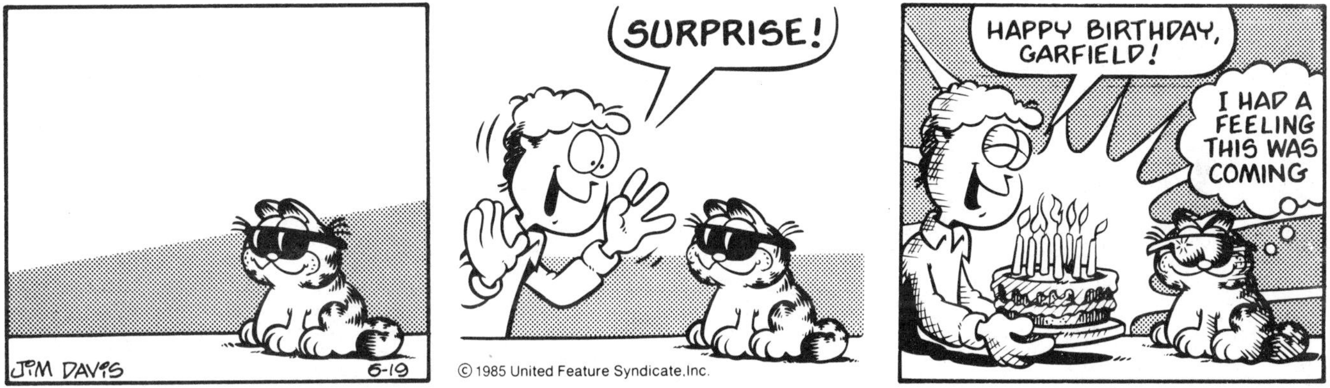
JIM DAVIS 6-19
SURPRISE!
HAPPY BIRTHDAY, GARFIELD!
I HAD A FEELING THIS WAS COMING

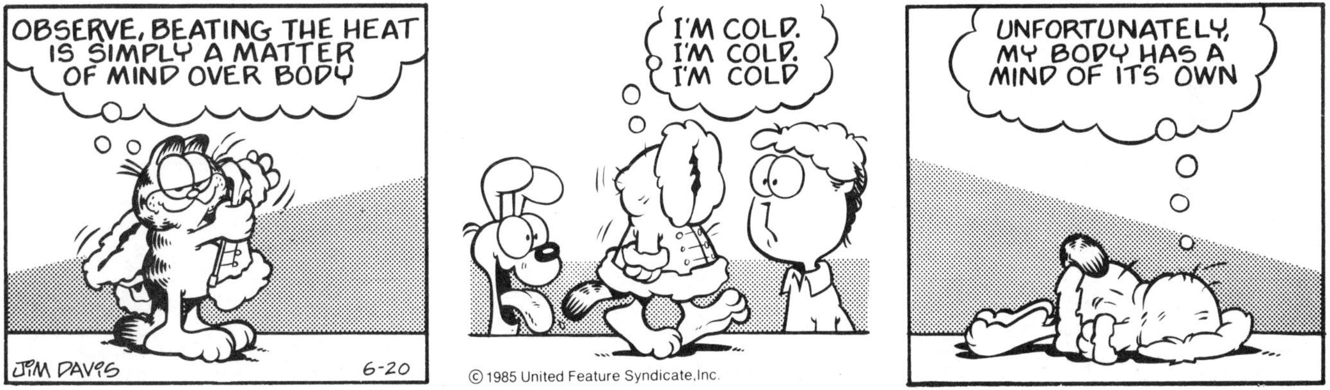
OBSERVE, BEATING THE HEAT IS SIMPLY A MATTER OF MIND OVER BODY
JIM DAVIS 6-20
I'M COLD. I'M COLD. I'M COLD
UNFORTUNATELY, MY BODY HAS A MIND OF ITS OWN

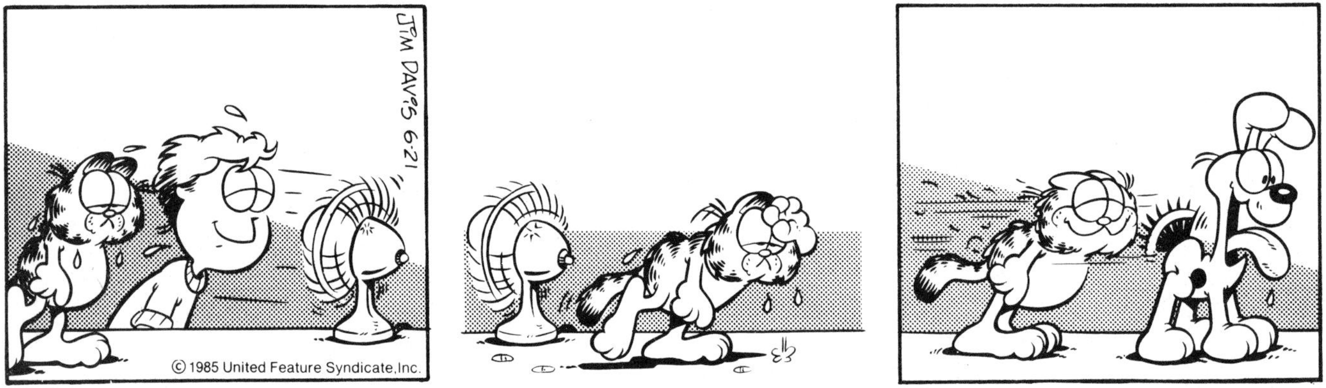
JIM DAVIS 6-21
© 1985 United Feature Syndicate, Inc.

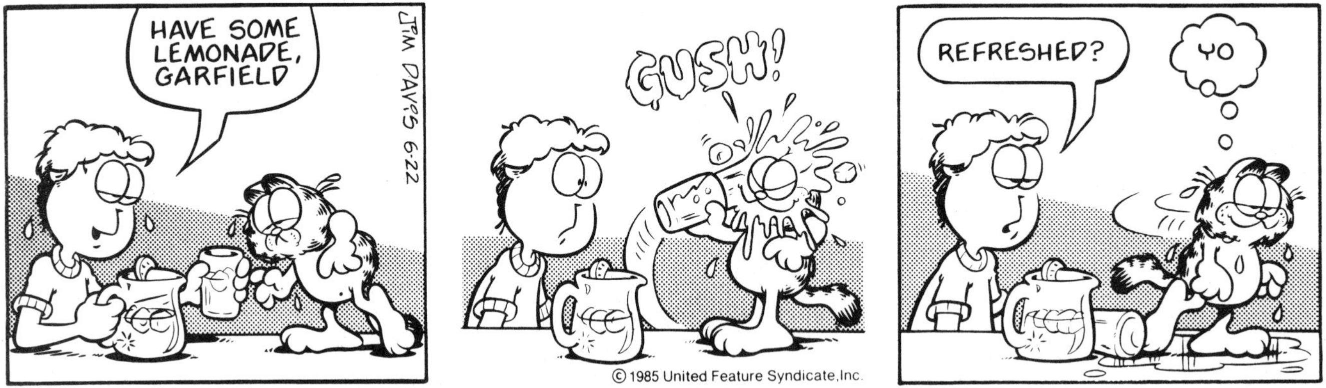
HAVE SOME LEMONADE, GARFIELD
JIM DAVIS 6-22
GUSH!
© 1985 United Feature Syndicate, Inc.
REFRESHED?
YO

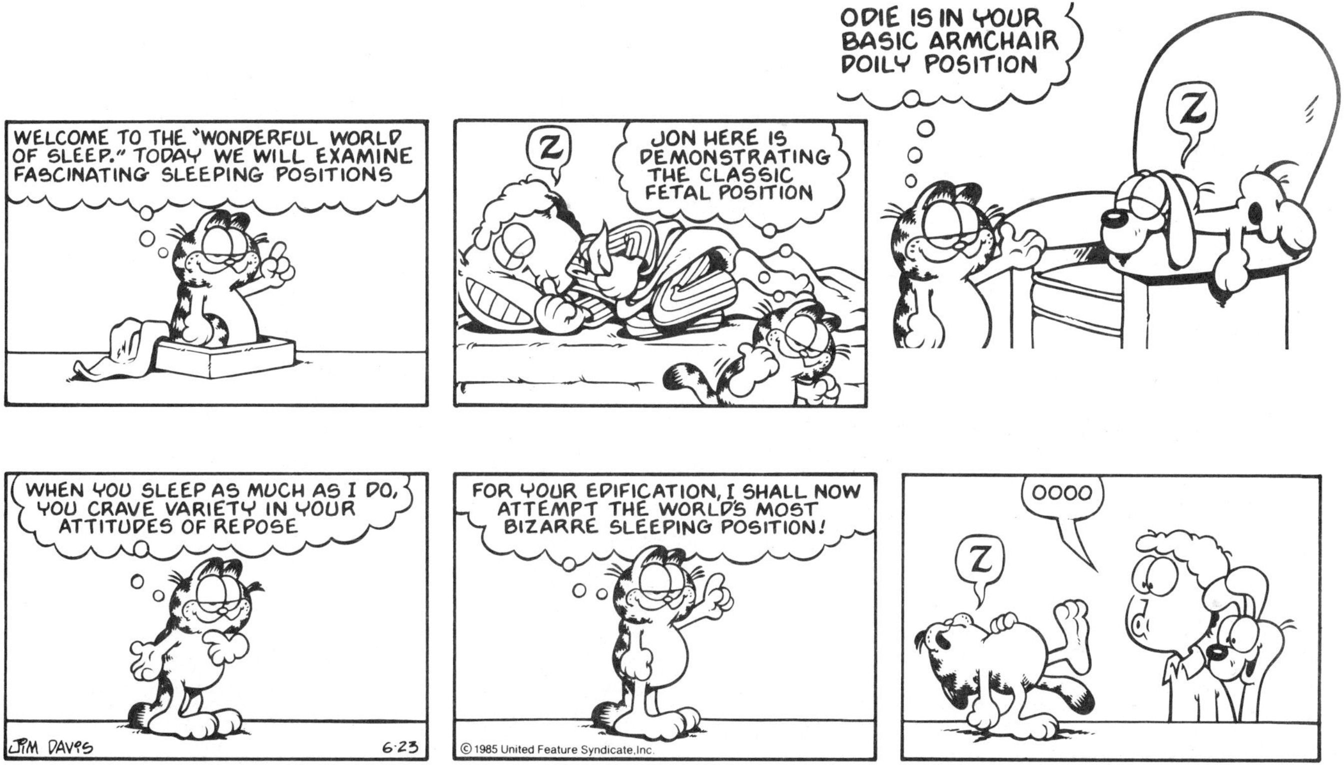
WELCOME TO THE "WONDERFUL WORLD OF SLEEP." TODAY WE WILL EXAMINE FASCINATING SLEEPING POSITIONS
Z
JON HERE IS DEMONSTRATING THE CLASSIC FETAL POSITION
ODIE IS IN YOUR BASIC ARMCHAIR DOILY POSITION
Z
WHEN YOU SLEEP AS MUCH AS I DO, YOU CRAVE VARIETY IN YOUR ATTITUDES OF REPOSE
JIM DAVIS
6-23
FOR YOUR EDIFICATION, I SHALL NOW ATTEMPT THE WORLD'S MOST BIZARRE SLEEPING POSITION!
© 1985 United Feature Syndicate, Inc.
Z
OOOO

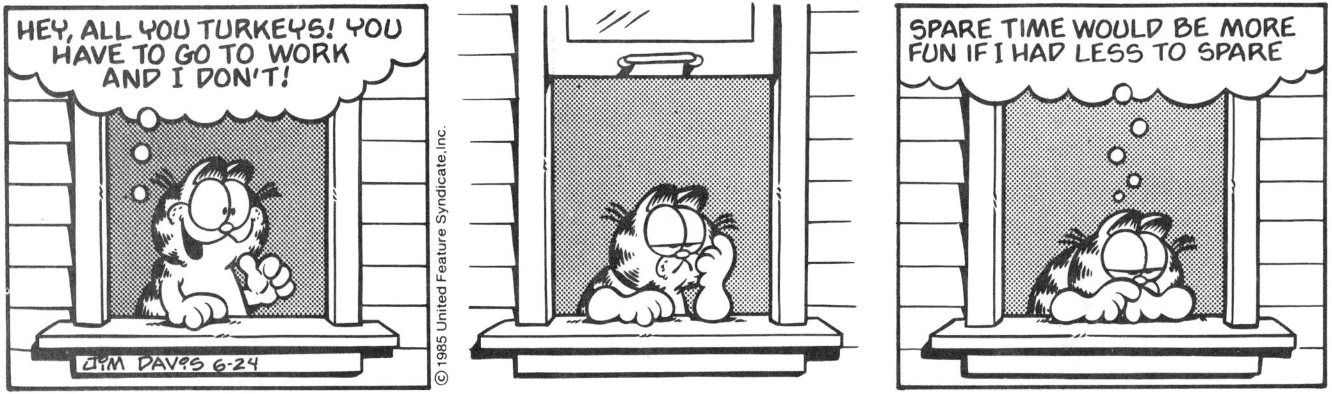
HEY, ALL YOU TURKEYS! YOU HAVE TO GO TO WORK AND I DON'T!
JIM DAVIS 6-24
© 1985 United Feature Syndicate, Inc.
SPARE TIME WOULD BE MORE FUN IF I HAD LESS TO SPARE

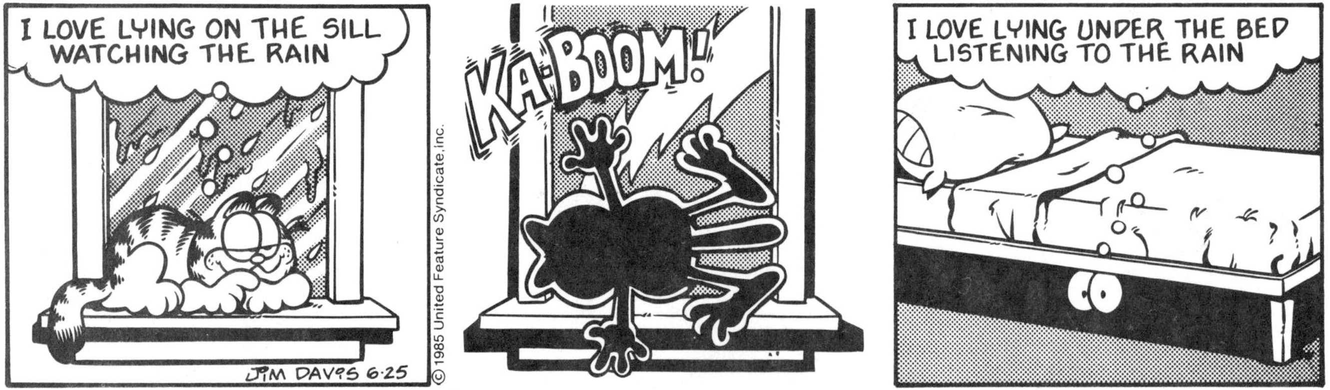
I LOVE LYING ON THE SILL WATCHING THE RAIN
JIM DAVIS 6-25
© 1985 United Feature Syndicate, Inc.
KA-BOOM!
I LOVE LYING UNDER THE BED LISTENING TO THE RAIN

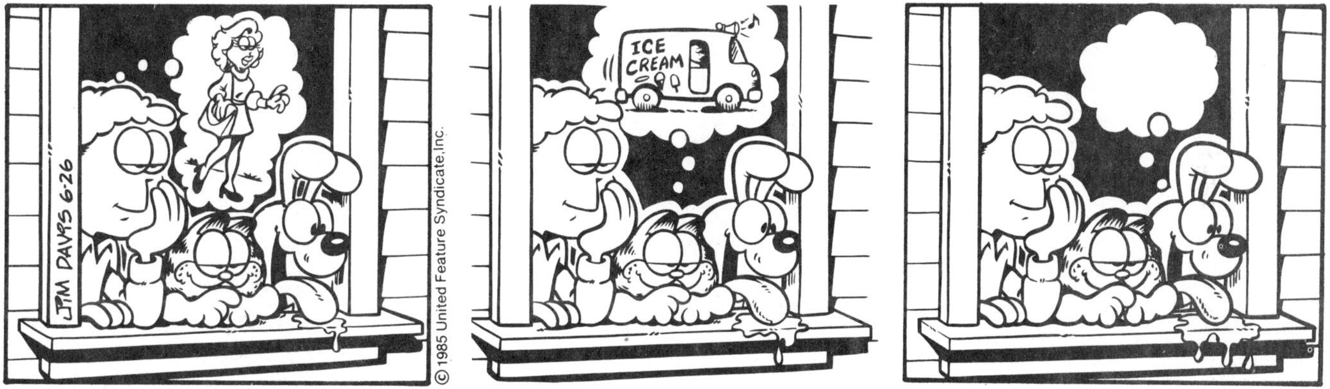
JIM DAVIS 6-26
© 1985 United Feature Syndicate, Inc.
ICE CREAM

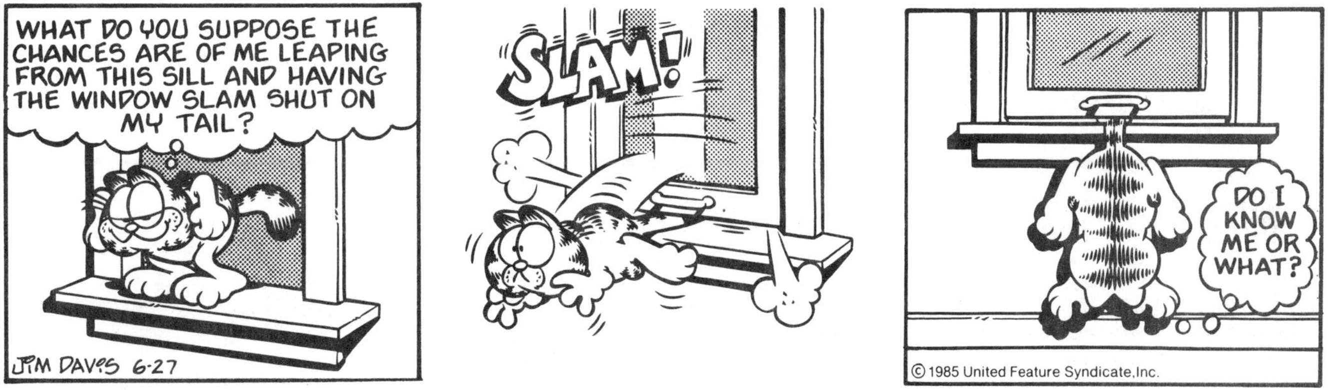
WHAT DO YOU SUPPOSE THE CHANCES ARE OF ME LEAPING FROM THIS SILL AND HAVING THE WINDOW SLAM SHUT ON MY TAIL?
JIM DAVIS 6-27
SLAM!
DO I KNOW ME OR WHAT?
© 1985 United Feature Syndicate, Inc.

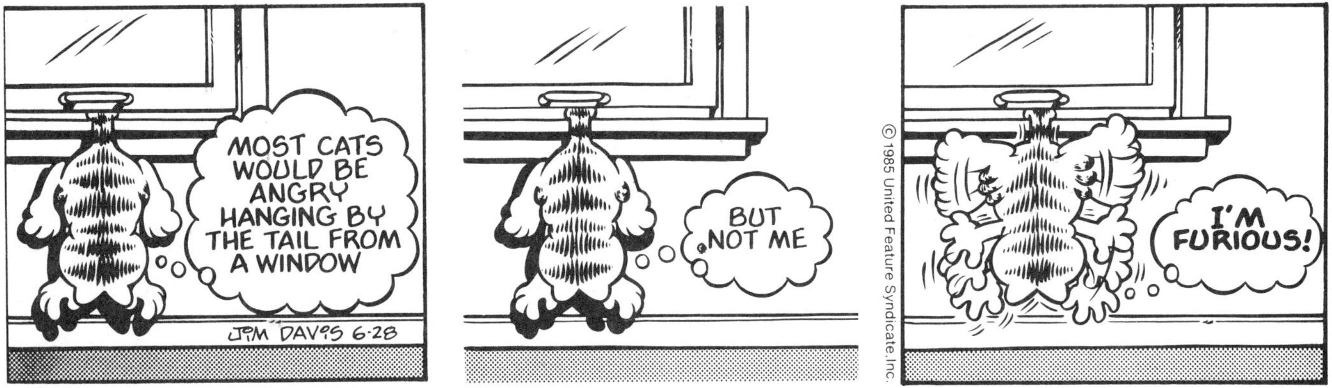
MOST CATS WOULD BE ANGRY HANGING BY THE TAIL FROM A WINDOW
JIM DAVIS 6-28
BUT NOT ME
I'M FURIOUS!

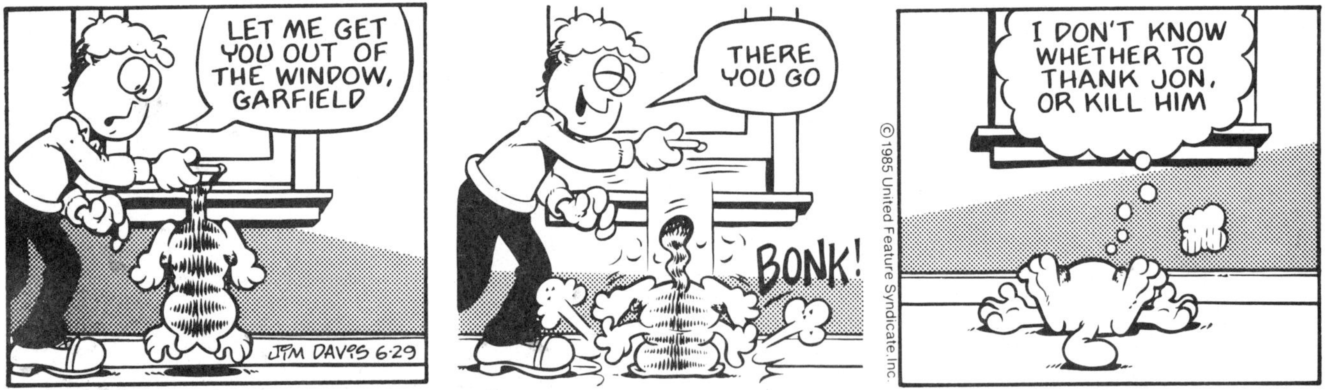
LET ME GET YOU OUT OF THE WINDOW, GARFIELD
JIM DAVIS 6-29
THERE YOU GO
BONK!
I DON'T KNOW WHETHER TO THANK JON, OR KILL HIM

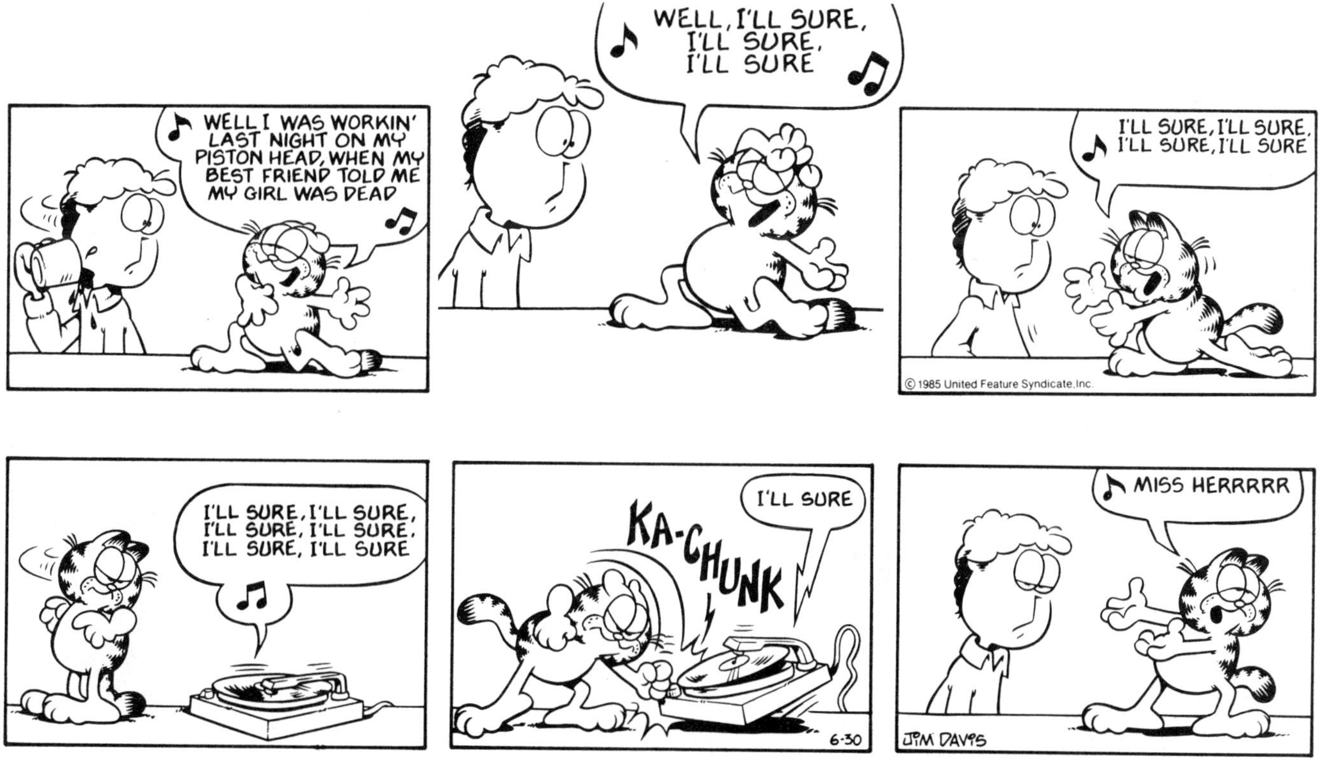
WELL I WAS WORKIN' LAST NIGHT ON MY PISTON HEAD, WHEN MY BEST FRIEND TOLD ME MY GIRL WAS DEAD
WELL, I'LL SURE, I'LL SURE, I'LL SURE
I'LL SURE, I'LL SURE, I'LL SURE, I'LL SURE
© 1985 United Feature Syndicate, Inc.
I'LL SURE, I'LL SURE, I'LL SURE, I'LL SURE, I'LL SURE, I'LL SURE
KA-CHUNK
I'LL SURE
6-30
MISS HERRRRR
JIM DAVIS

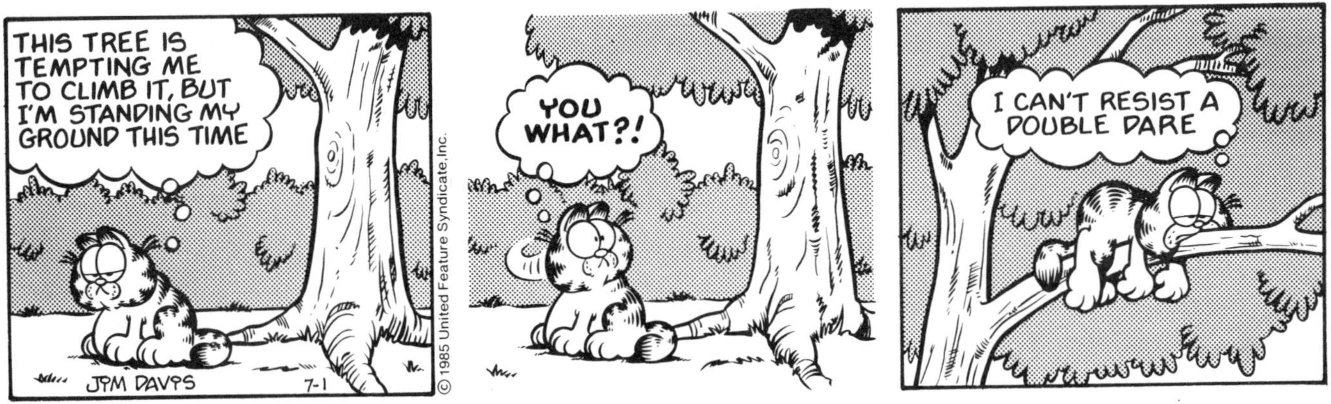
THIS TREE IS TEMPTING ME TO CLIMB IT, BUT I'M STANDING MY GROUND THIS TIME
JIM DAVIS
7-1
YOU WHAT?!
I CAN'T RESIST A DOUBLE DARE

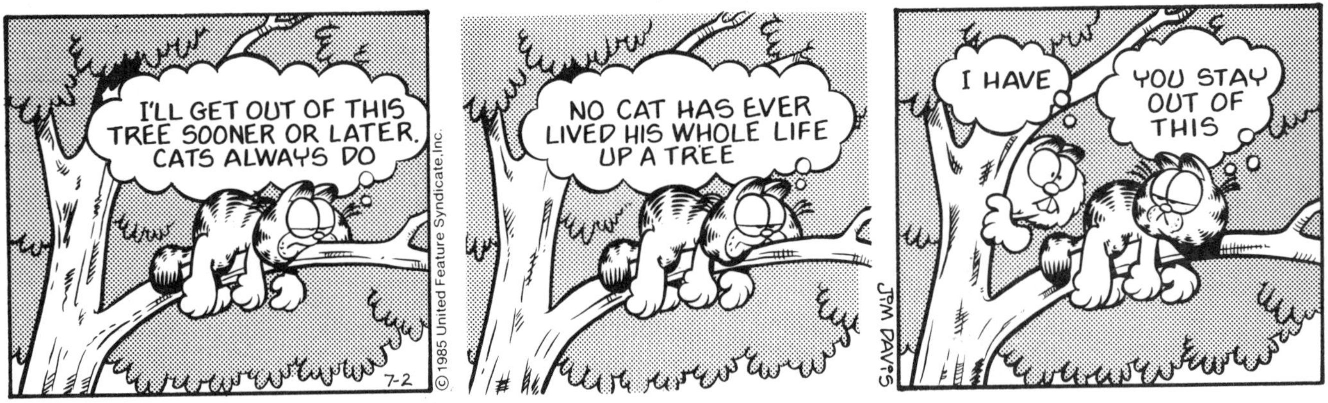
I'LL GET OUT OF THIS TREE SOONER OR LATER. CATS ALWAYS DO
7-2
NO CAT HAS EVER LIVED HIS WHOLE LIFE UP A TREE
JIM DAVIS
I HAVE
YOU STAY OUT OF THIS

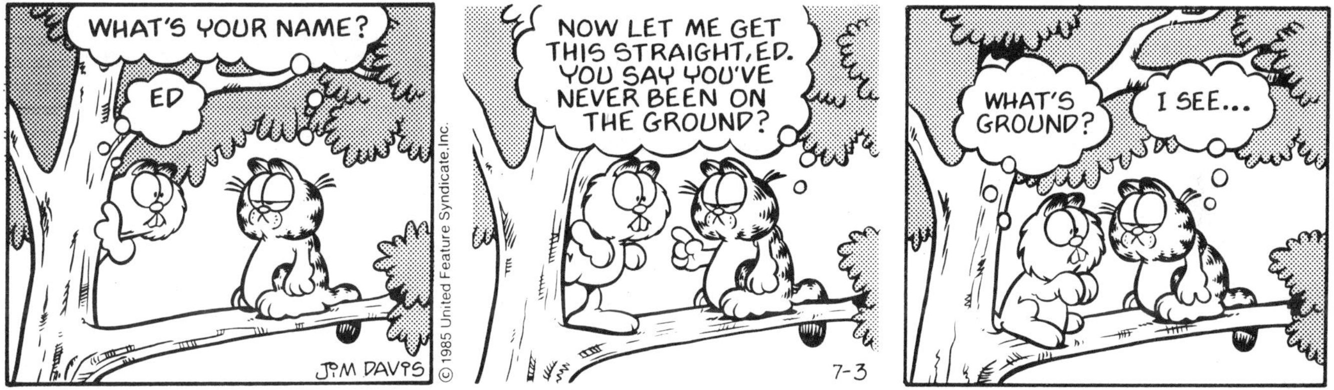
WHAT'S YOUR NAME?
ED
JIM DAVIS
© 1985 United Feature Syndicate, Inc.
NOW LET ME GET THIS STRAIGHT, ED. YOU SAY YOU'VE NEVER BEEN ON THE GROUND?
7-3
WHAT'S GROUND?
I SEE...

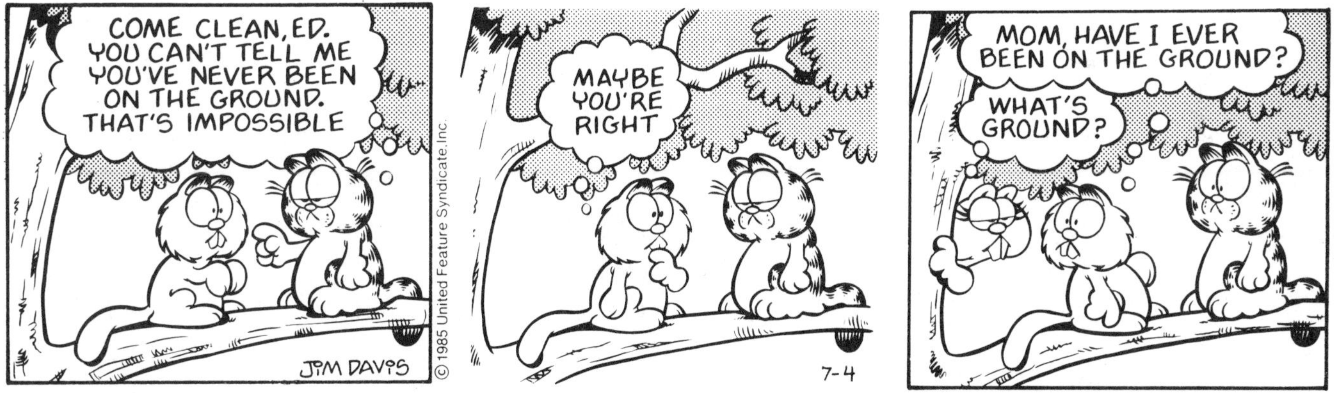
COME CLEAN, ED. YOU CAN'T TELL ME YOU'VE NEVER BEEN ON THE GROUND. THAT'S IMPOSSIBLE
JIM DAVIS
© 1985 United Feature Syndicate, Inc.
MAYBE YOU'RE RIGHT
7-4
MOM, HAVE I EVER BEEN ON THE GROUND?
WHAT'S GROUND?

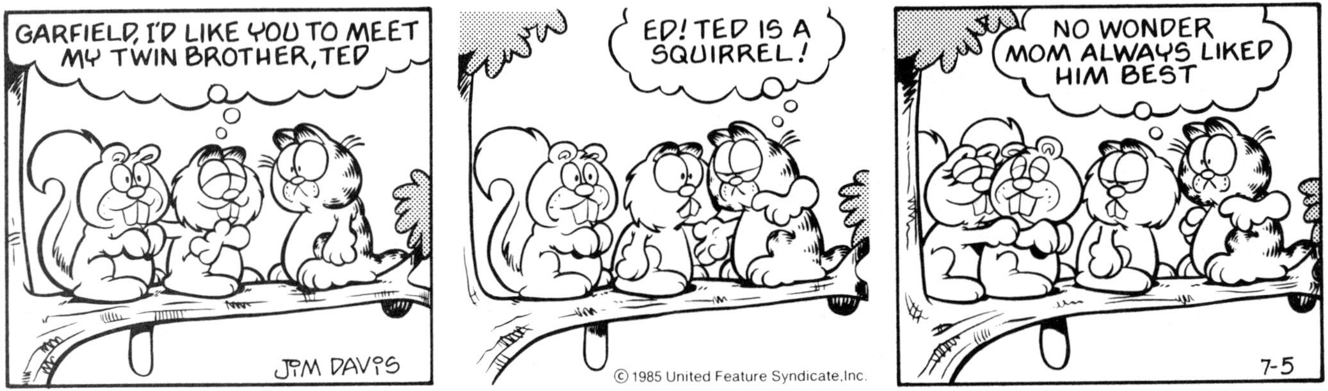
GARFIELD, I'D LIKE YOU TO MEET MY TWIN BROTHER, TED
JIM DAVIS
ED! TED IS A SQUIRREL!
© 1985 United Feature Syndicate, Inc.
NO WONDER MOM ALWAYS LIKED HIM BEST
7-5

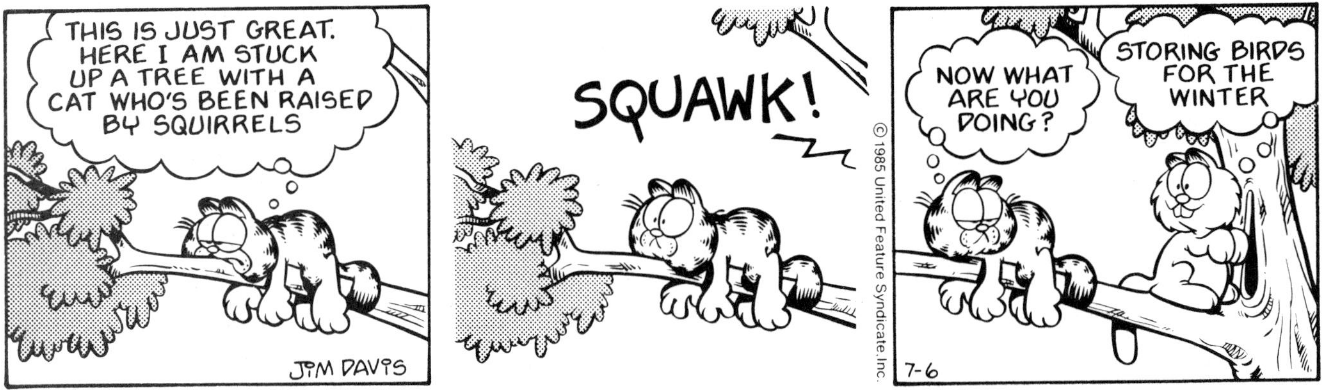
THIS IS JUST GREAT. HERE I AM STUCK UP A TREE WITH A CAT WHO'S BEEN RAISED BY SQUIRRELS
JIM DAVIS
SQUAWK!
© 1985 United Feature Syndicate, Inc.
NOW WHAT ARE YOU DOING?
STORING BIRDS FOR THE WINTER
7-6

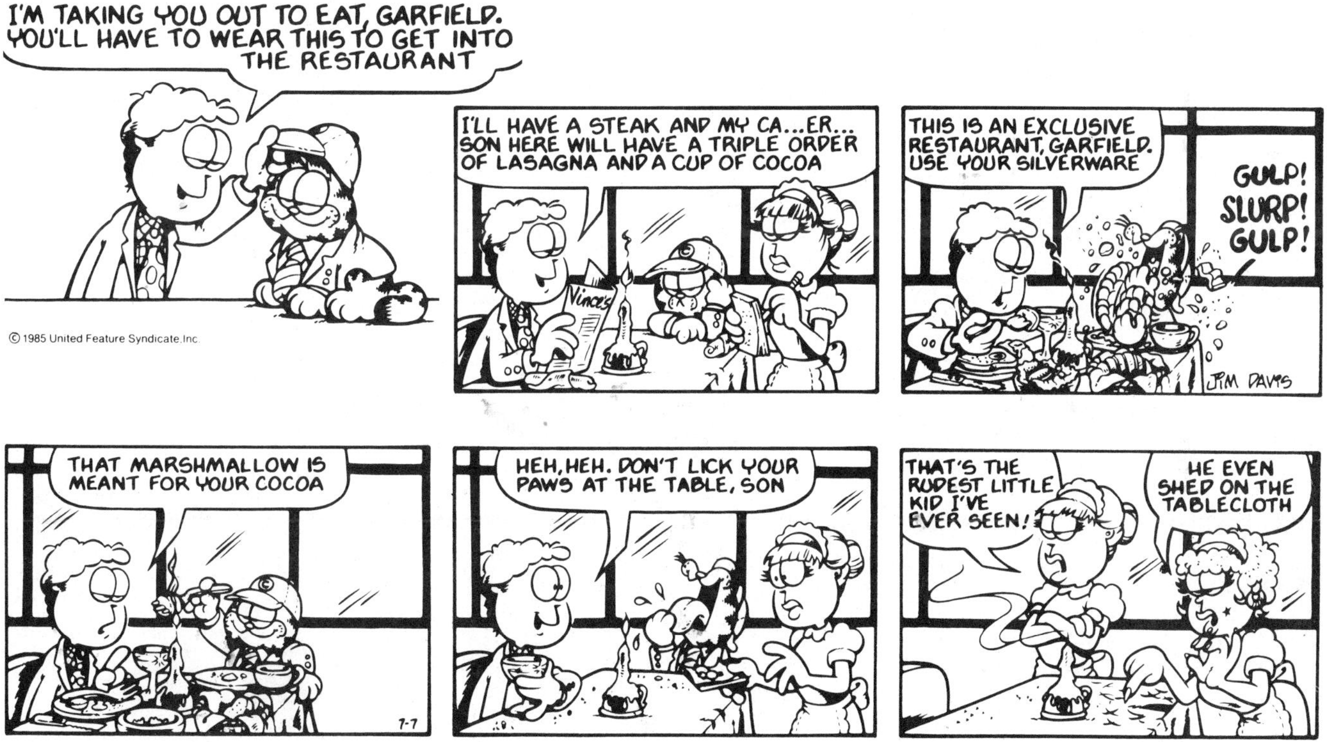
I'M TAKING YOU OUT TO EAT, GARFIELD. YOU'LL HAVE TO WEAR THIS TO GET INTO THE RESTAURANT
I'LL HAVE A STEAK AND MY CA...ER... SON HERE WILL HAVE A TRIPLE ORDER OF LASAGNA AND A CUP OF COCOA
Vince's
THIS IS AN EXCLUSIVE RESTAURANT, GARFIELD. USE YOUR SILVERWARE
GULP! SLURP! GULP!
JIM DAVIS
THAT MARSHMALLOW IS MEANT FOR YOUR COCOA
7-7
HEH, HEH. DON'T LICK YOUR PAWS AT THE TABLE, SON
THAT'S THE RUDEST LITTLE KID I'VE EVER SEEN!
HE EVEN SHED ON THE TABLECLOTH

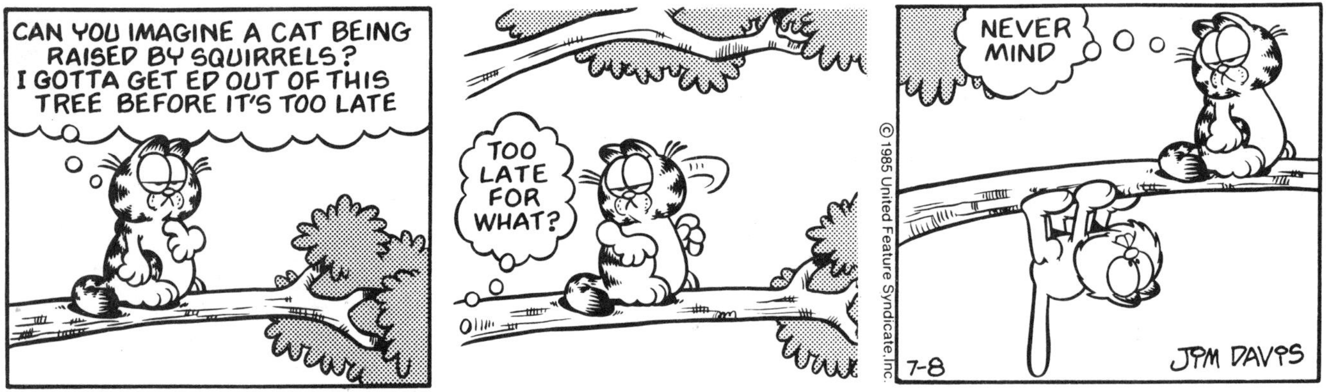
CAN YOU IMAGINE A CAT BEING RAISED BY SQUIRRELS? I GOTTA GET ED OUT OF THIS TREE BEFORE IT'S TOO LATE
TOO LATE FOR WHAT?
NEVER MIND
© 1985 United Feature Syndicate, Inc.
7-8
JIM DAVIS

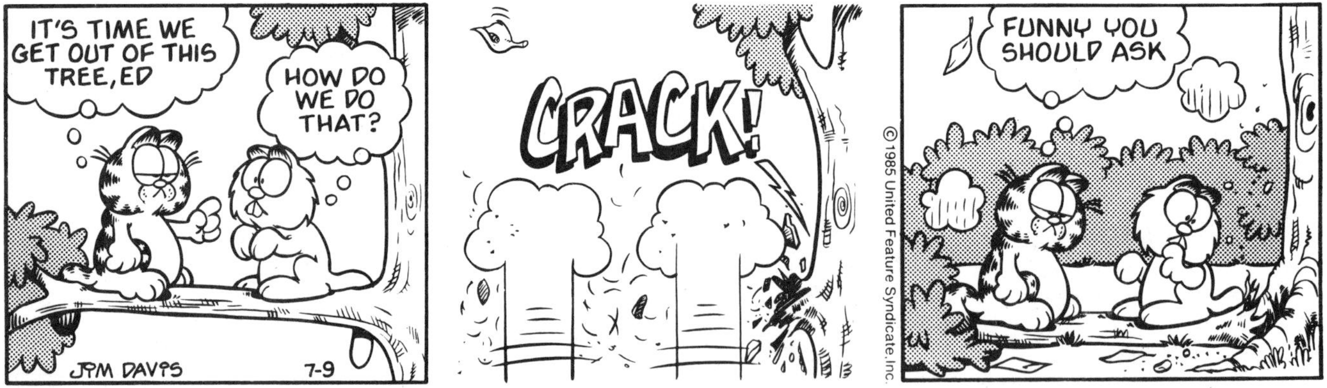
IT'S TIME WE GET OUT OF THIS TREE, ED
HOW DO WE DO THAT?
JIM DAVIS
7-9
CRACK!
FUNNY YOU SHOULD ASK
© 1985 United Feature Syndicate, Inc.

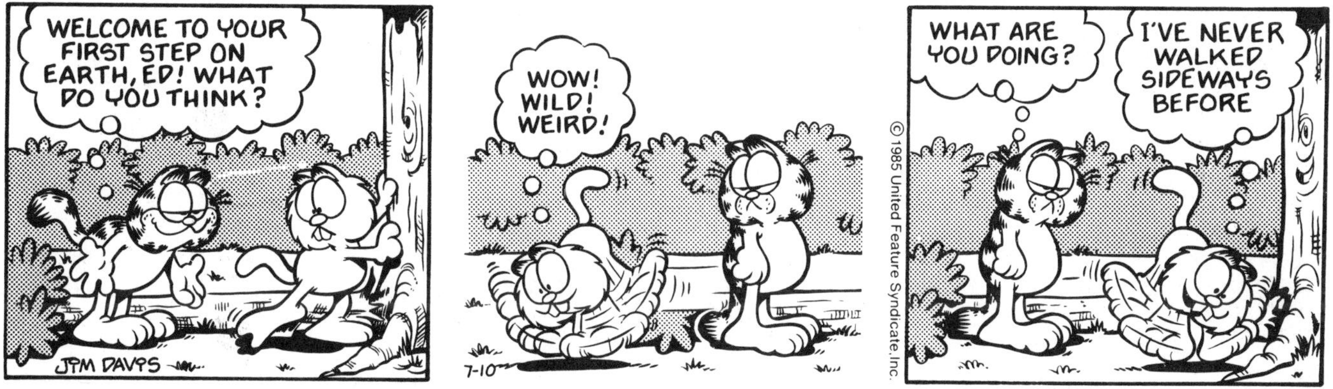
WELCOME TO YOUR FIRST STEP ON EARTH, ED! WHAT DO YOU THINK?
JIM DAVIS
WOW! WILD! WEIRD!
7-10
WHAT ARE YOU DOING?
I'VE NEVER WALKED SIDEWAYS BEFORE

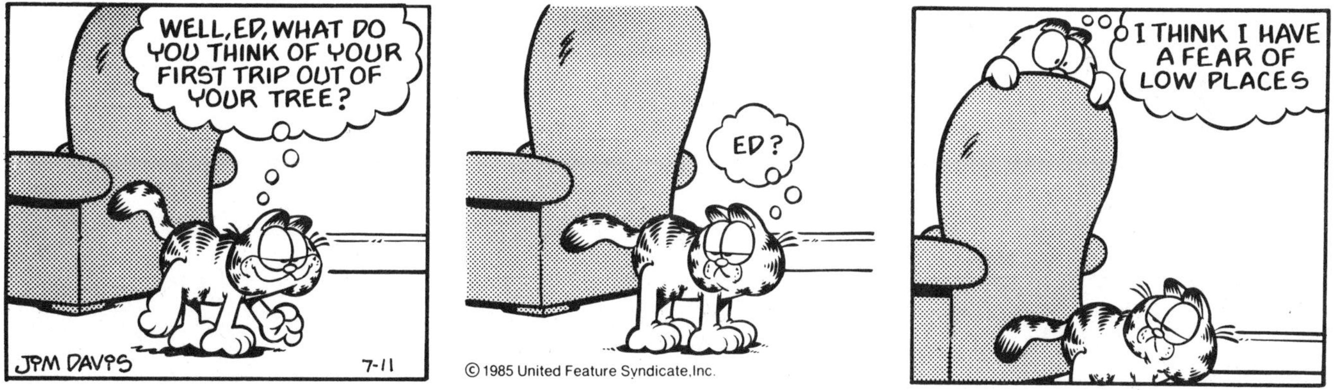
WELL, ED, WHAT DO YOU THINK OF YOUR FIRST TRIP OUT OF YOUR TREE?
JIM DAVIS
7-11
ED?
I THINK I HAVE A FEAR OF LOW PLACES

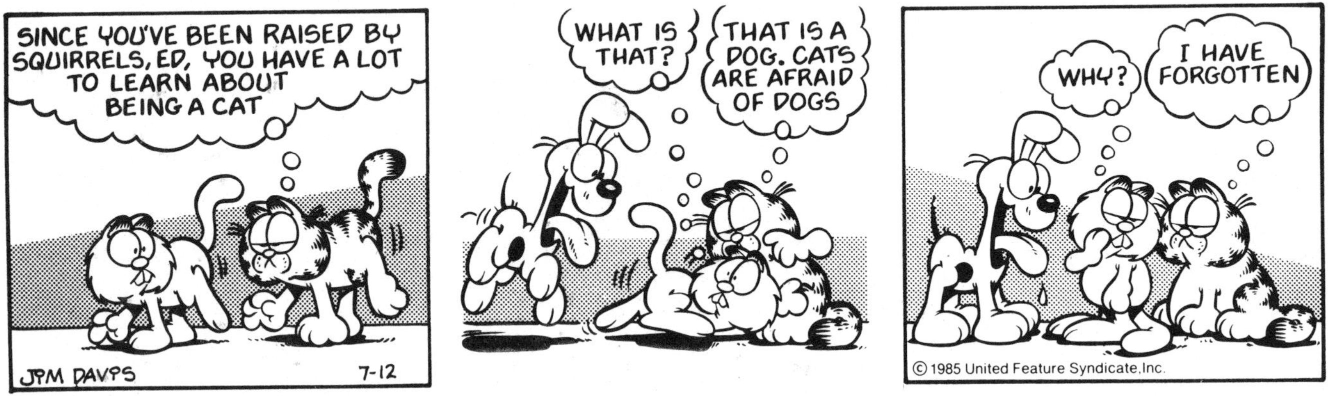
SINCE YOU'VE BEEN RAISED BY SQUIRRELS, ED, YOU HAVE A LOT TO LEARN ABOUT BEING A CAT
JIM DAVIS
7-12
WHAT IS THAT?
THAT IS A DOG. CATS ARE AFRAID OF DOGS
WHY?
I HAVE FORGOTTEN
© 1985 United Feature Syndicate, Inc.

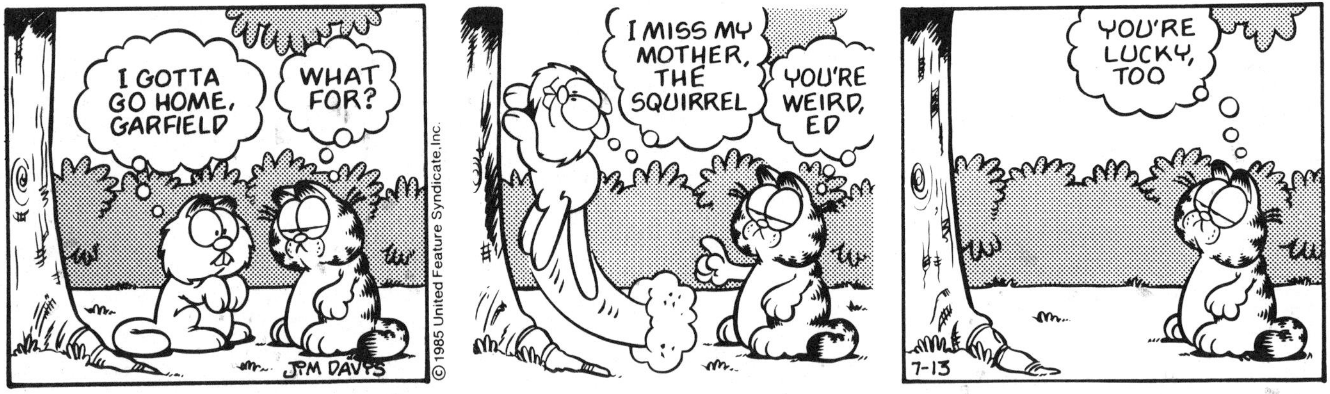
I GOTTA GO HOME, GARFIELD
WHAT FOR?
JIM DAVIS
© 1985 United Feature Syndicate, Inc.
I MISS MY MOTHER, THE SQUIRREL
YOU'RE WEIRD, ED
YOU'RE LUCKY, TOO
7-13

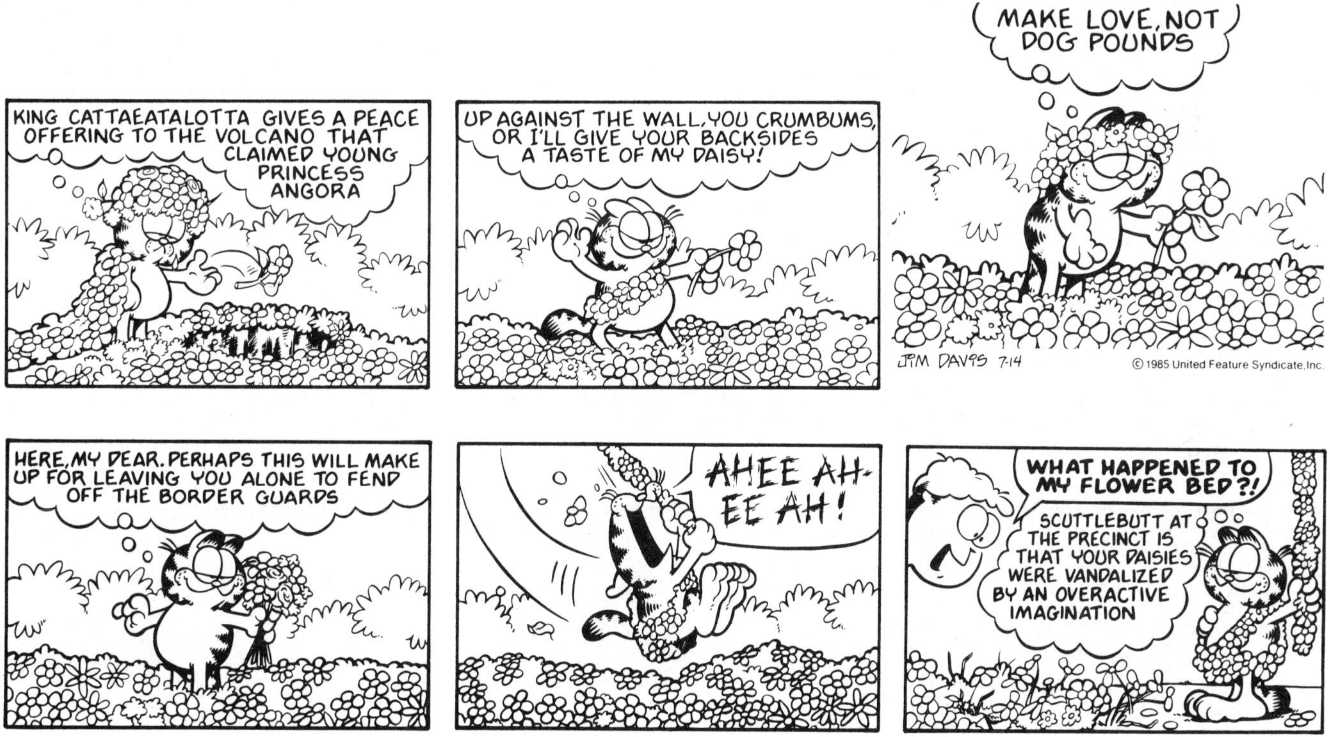
KING CATTAEATALOTTA GIVES A PEACE OFFERING TO THE VOLCANO THAT CLAIMED YOUNG PRINCESS ANGORA
UP AGAINST THE WALL, YOU CRUMBUMS, OR I'LL GIVE YOUR BACKSIDES A TASTE OF MY DAISY!
MAKE LOVE, NOT DOG POUNDS
JIM DAVIS 7-14
© 1985 United Feature Syndicate, Inc.
HERE, MY DEAR. PERHAPS THIS WILL MAKE UP FOR LEAVING YOU ALONE TO FEND OFF THE BORDER GUARDS
AHEE AH-EE AH!
WHAT HAPPENED TO MY FLOWER BED?!
SCUTTLEBUTT AT THE PRECINCT IS THAT YOUR DAISIES WERE VANDALIZED BY AN OVERACTIVE IMAGINATION

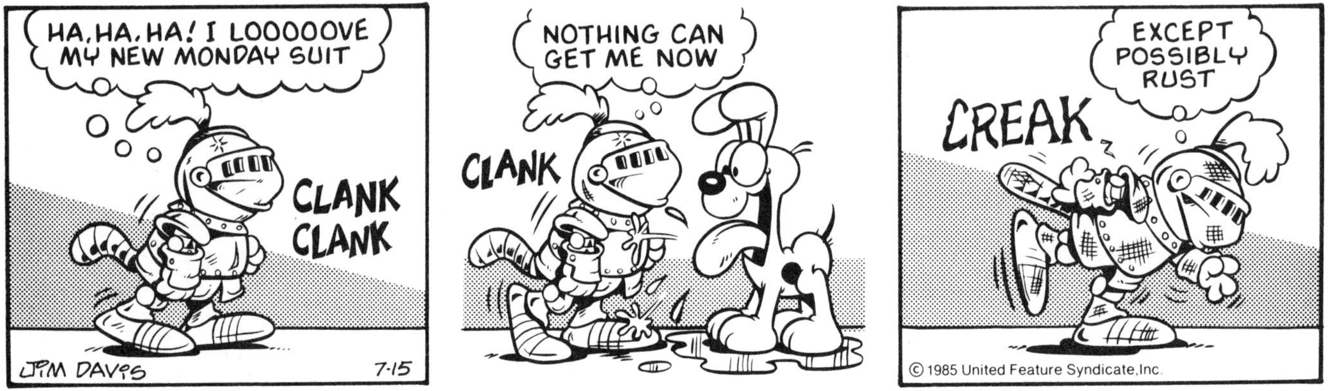
HA, HA, HA! I LOOOOOVE MY NEW MONDAY SUIT
CLANK CLANK
JIM DAVIS
7-15
CLANK
NOTHING CAN GET ME NOW
CREAK
EXCEPT POSSIBLY RUST

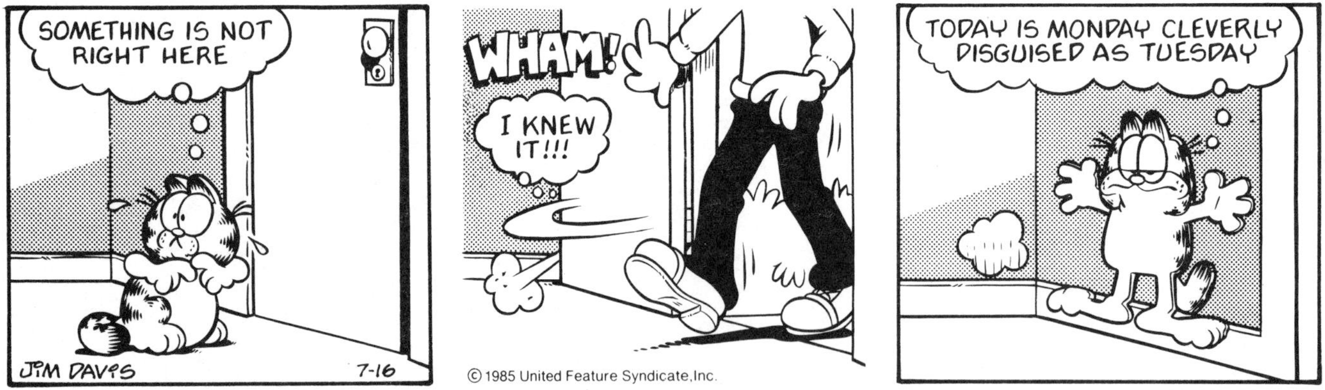
SOMETHING IS NOT RIGHT HERE
JIM DAVIS
7-16
WHAM!
I KNEW IT!!!
TODAY IS MONDAY CLEVERLY DISGUISED AS TUESDAY

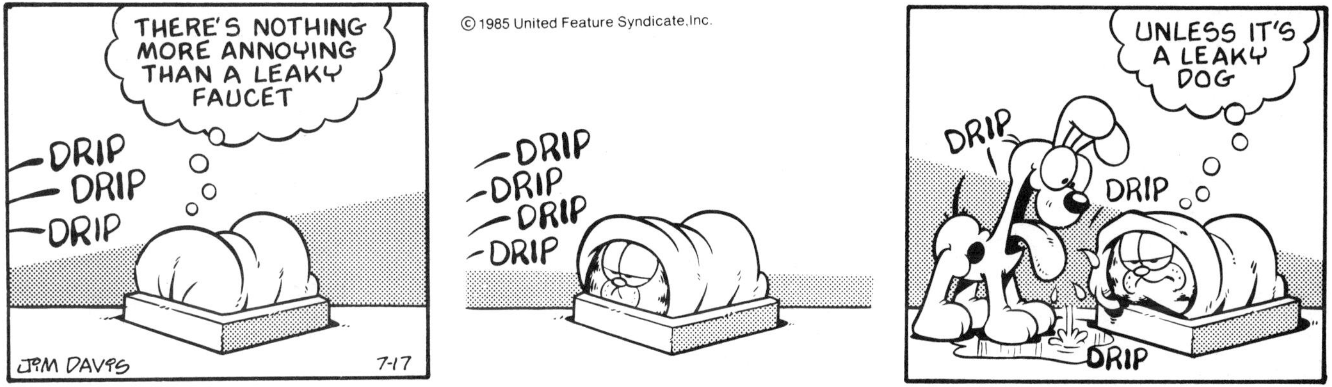
THERE'S NOTHING MORE ANNOYING THAN A LEAKY FAUCET
DRIP
DRIP
DRIP
JIM DAVIS
7-17
© 1985 United Feature Syndicate, Inc.
DRIP
DRIP
DRIP
DRIP
UNLESS IT'S A LEAKY DOG
DRIP
DRIP
DRIP

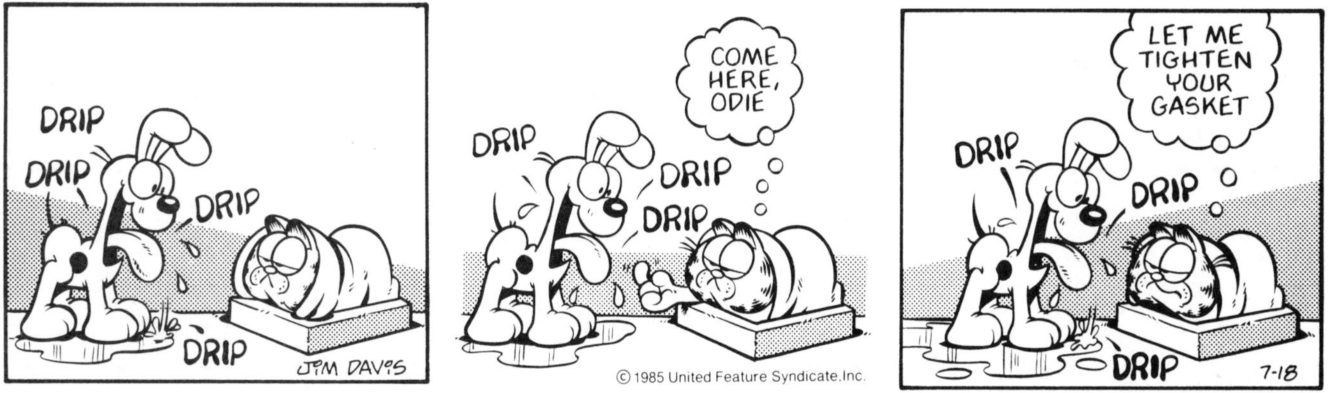
DRIP
DRIP
DRIP
DRIP
JIM DAVIS
COME HERE, ODIE
DRIP
DRIP
DRIP
© 1985 United Feature Syndicate, Inc.
LET ME TIGHTEN YOUR GASKET
DRIP
DRIP
DRIP
7-18

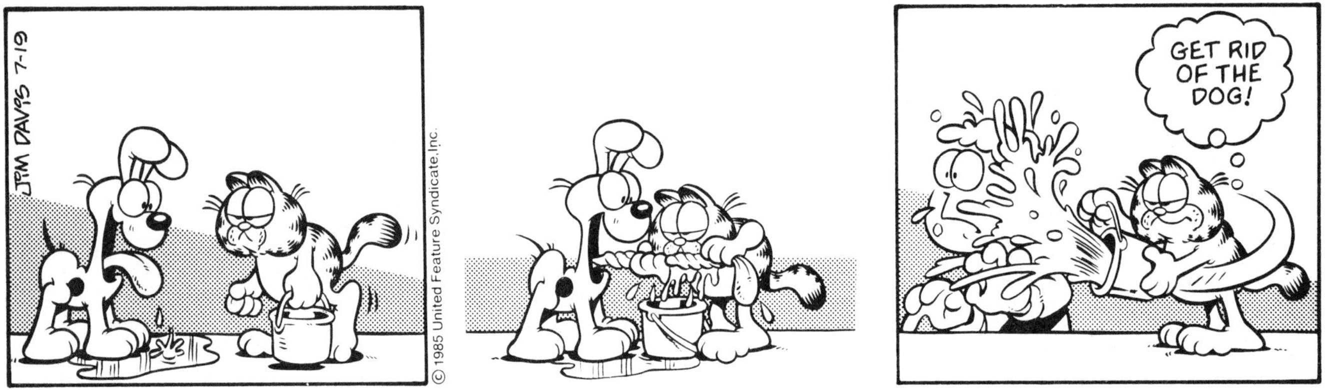
JIM DAVIS 7-19
© 1985 United Feature Syndicate, Inc.
GET RID OF THE DOG!

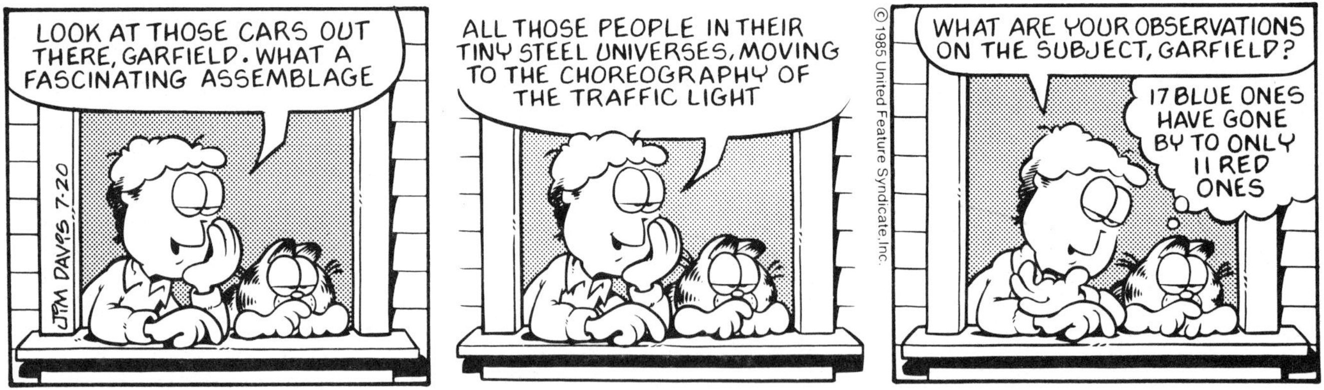
LOOK AT THOSE CARS OUT THERE, GARFIELD. WHAT A FASCINATING ASSEMBLAGE
JIM DAVIS 7-20
ALL THOSE PEOPLE IN THEIR TINY STEEL UNIVERSES, MOVING TO THE CHOREOGRAPHY OF THE TRAFFIC LIGHT
© 1985 United Feature Syndicate, Inc.
WHAT ARE YOUR OBSERVATIONS ON THE SUBJECT, GARFIELD?
17 BLUE ONES HAVE GONE BY TO ONLY 11 RED ONES

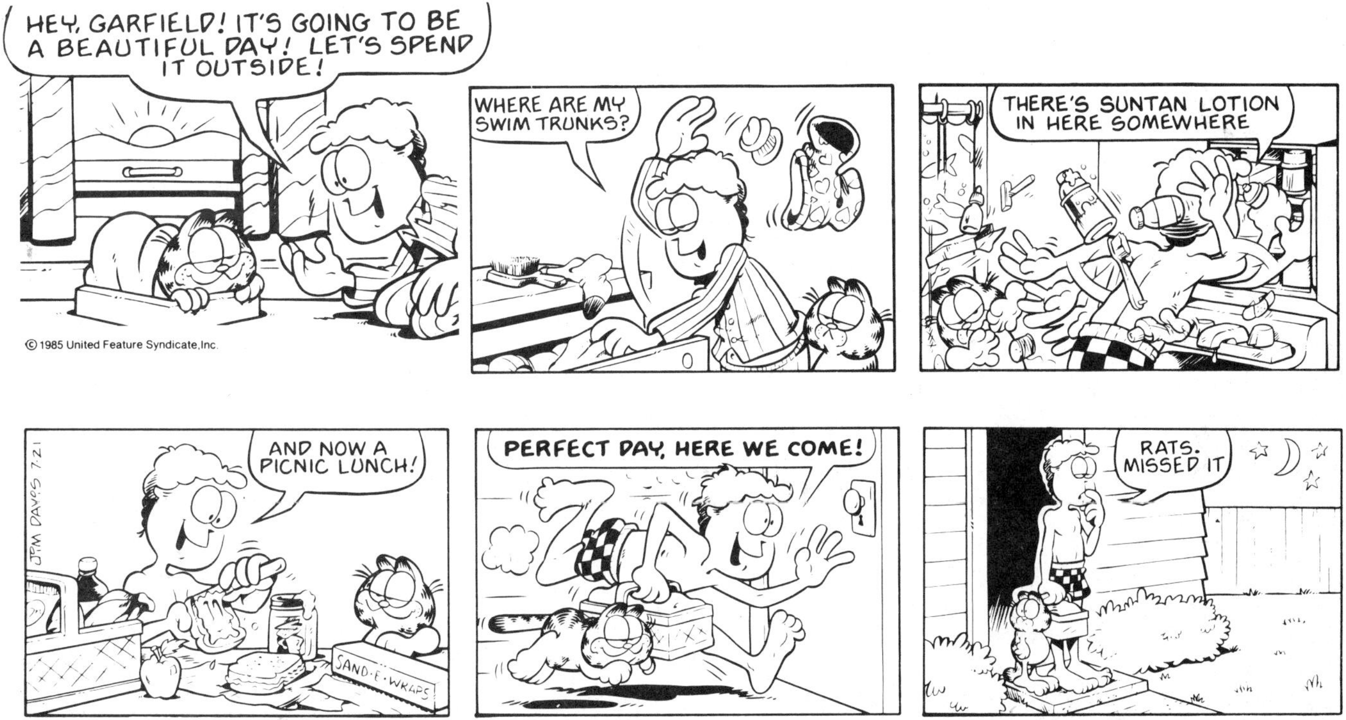

HEY, GARFIELD! IT'S GOING TO BE A BEAUTIFUL DAY! LET'S SPEND IT OUTSIDE!
© 1985 United Feature Syndicate, Inc.
WHERE ARE MY SWIM TRUNKS?
THERE'S SUNTAN LOTION IN HERE SOMEWHERE
JIM DAVIS 7·21
AND NOW A PICNIC LUNCH!
SAND·E·WRAPS
PERFECT DAY, HERE WE COME!
RATS. MISSED IT

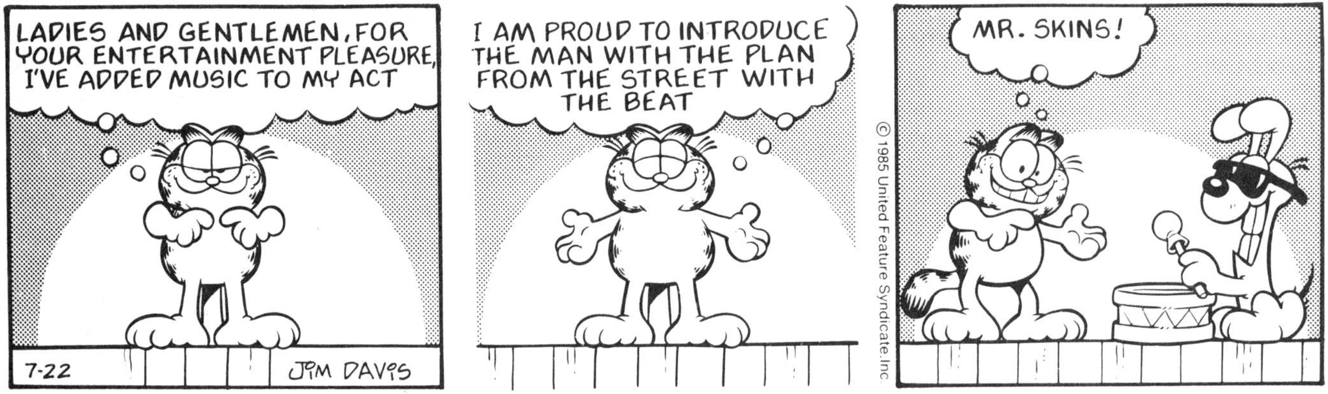
LADIES AND GENTLEMEN, FOR YOUR ENTERTAINMENT PLEASURE, I'VE ADDED MUSIC TO MY ACT
7-22
JIM DAVIS
I AM PROUD TO INTRODUCE THE MAN WITH THE PLAN FROM THE STREET WITH THE BEAT
© 1985 United Feature Syndicate, Inc.
MR. SKINS!

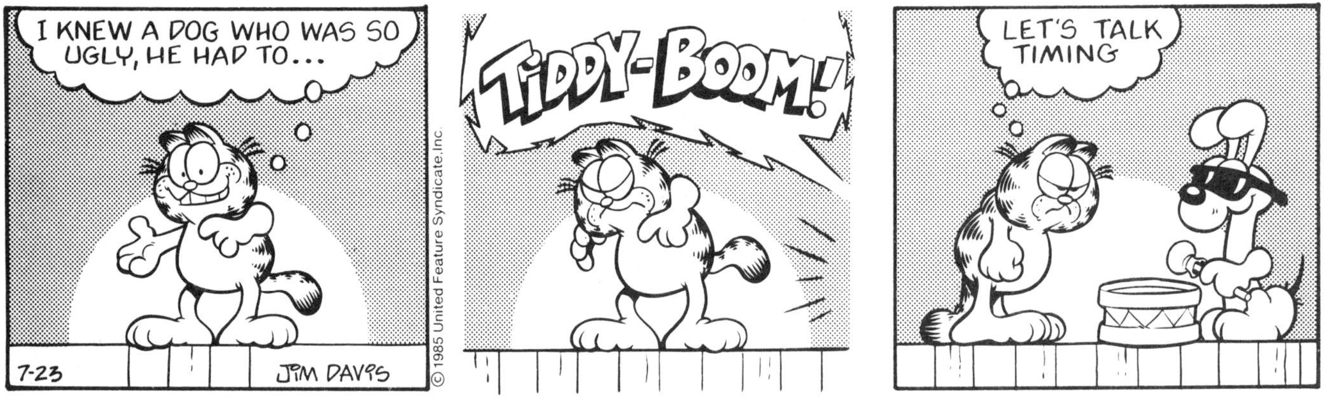
I KNEW A DOG WHO WAS SO UGLY, HE HAD TO...
7-23
JIM DAVIS
© 1985 United Feature Syndicate, Inc.
TIDDY-BOOM!
LET'S TALK TIMING

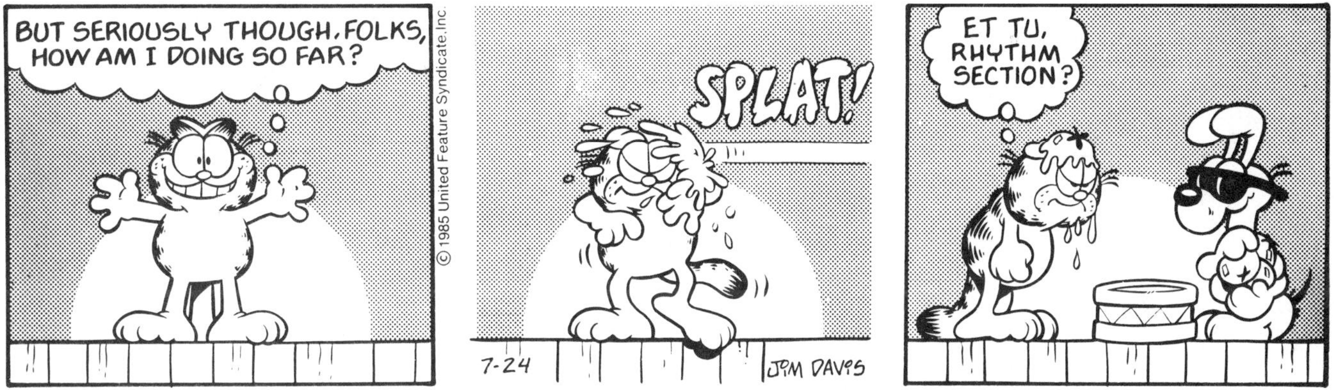
BUT SERIOUSLY THOUGH, FOLKS, HOW AM I DOING SO FAR?
© 1985 United Feature Syndicate, Inc.
SPLAT!
7-24
JIM DAVIS
ET TU, RHYTHM SECTION?

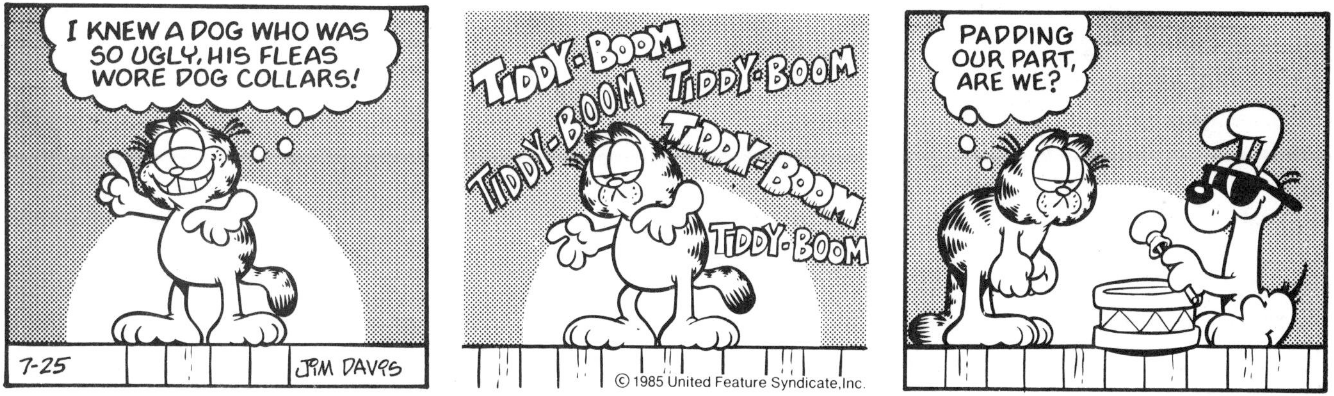
I KNEW A DOG WHO WAS SO UGLY, HIS FLEAS WORE DOG COLLARS!
7-25
JIM DAVIS
TIDDY-BOOM
TIDDY-BOOM
TIDDY-BOOM
TIDDY-BOOM
TIDDY-BOOM
© 1985 United Feature Syndicate, Inc.
PADDING OUR PART, ARE WE?

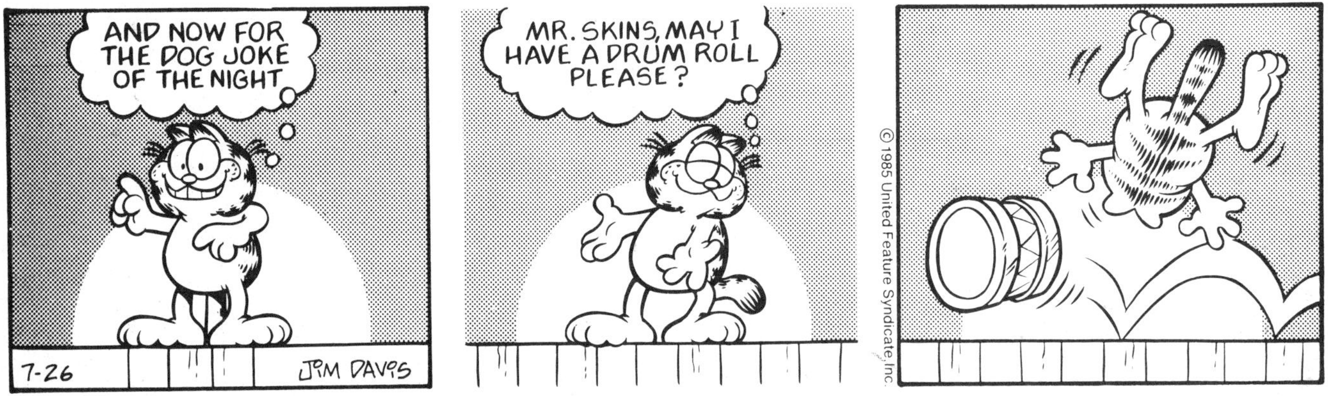
AND NOW FOR THE DOG JOKE OF THE NIGHT
7-26
JIM DAVIS
MR. SKINS, MAY I HAVE A DRUM ROLL PLEASE?
© 1985 United Feature Syndicate, Inc.

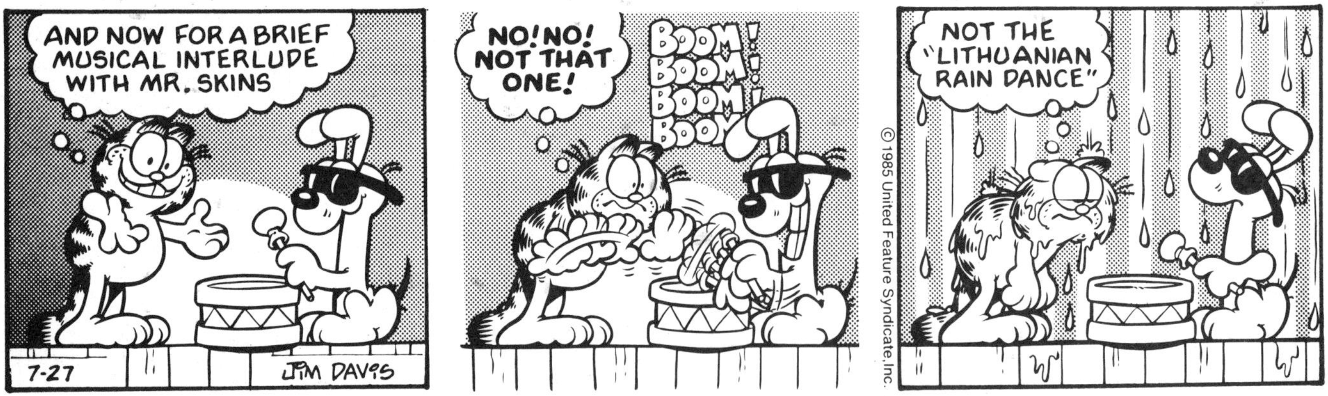
AND NOW FOR A BRIEF MUSICAL INTERLUDE WITH MR. SKINS
7-27
JIM DAVIS
NO! NO! NOT THAT ONE!
BOOM! BOOM! BOOM! BOOM
NOT THE "LITHUANIAN RAIN DANCE"
© 1985 United Feature Syndicate, Inc.

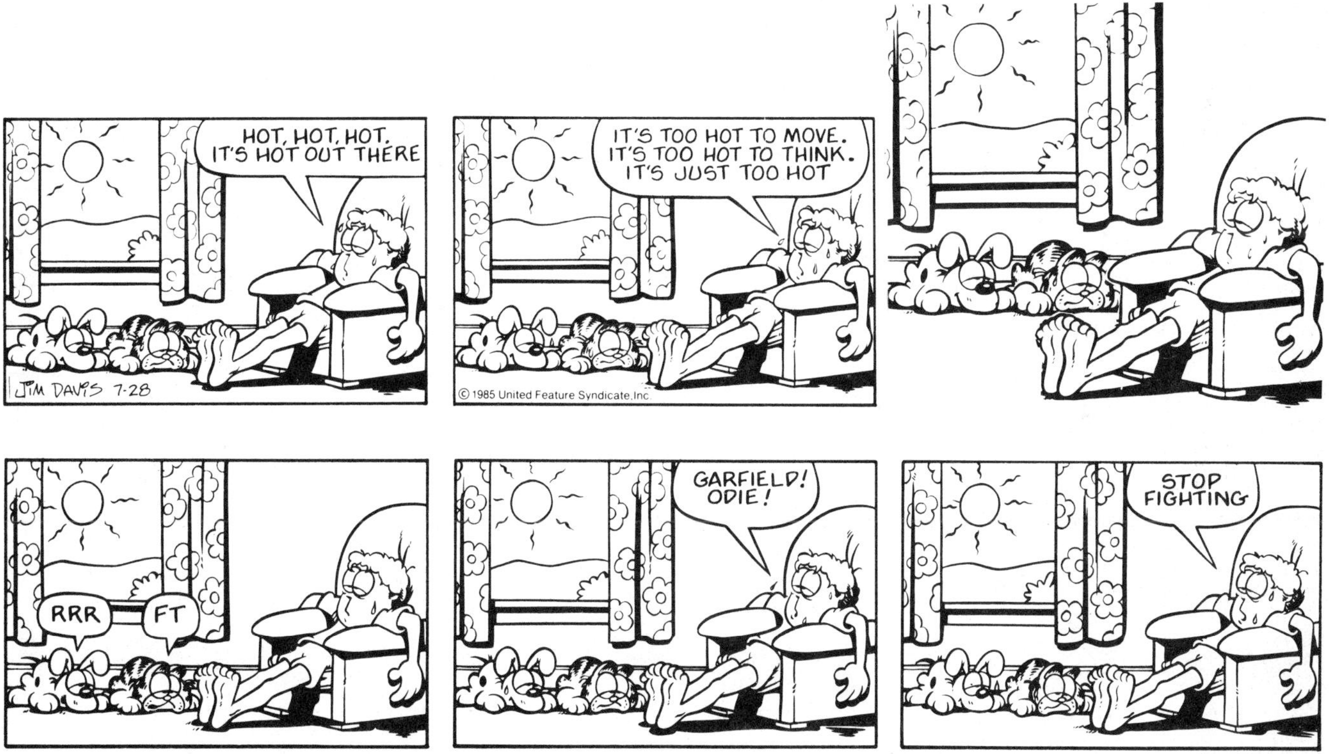

HOT, HOT, HOT. IT'S HOT OUT THERE
JIM DAVIS 7-28
IT'S TOO HOT TO MOVE. IT'S TOO HOT TO THINK. IT'S JUST TOO HOT
© 1985 United Feature Syndicate, Inc.
RRR
FT
GARFIELD! ODIE!
STOP FIGHTING

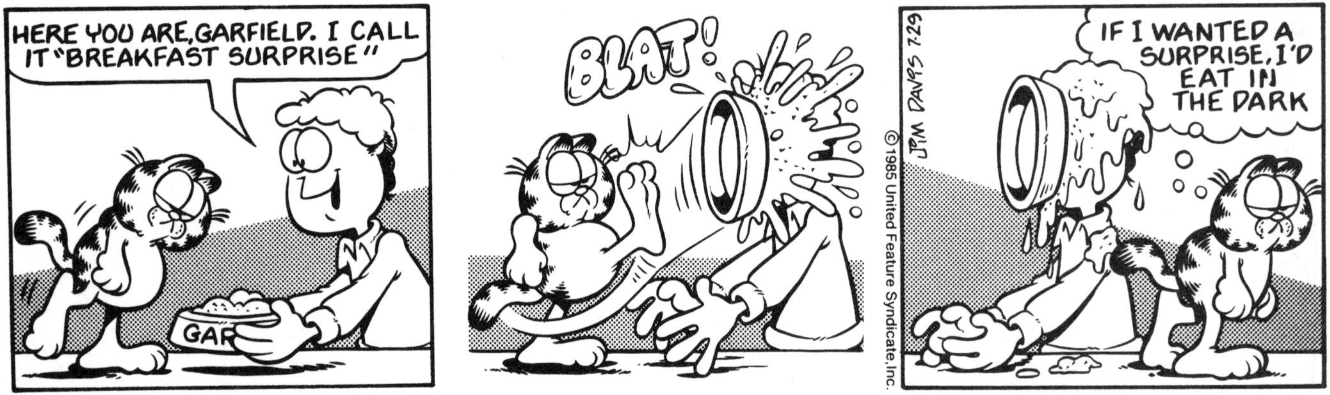
HERE YOU ARE, GARFIELD. I CALL IT "BREAKFAST SURPRISE"
GAR
BLAT!
JIM DAVIS 7-29
© 1985 United Feature Syndicate, Inc.
IF I WANTED A SURPRISE, I'D EAT IN THE DARK

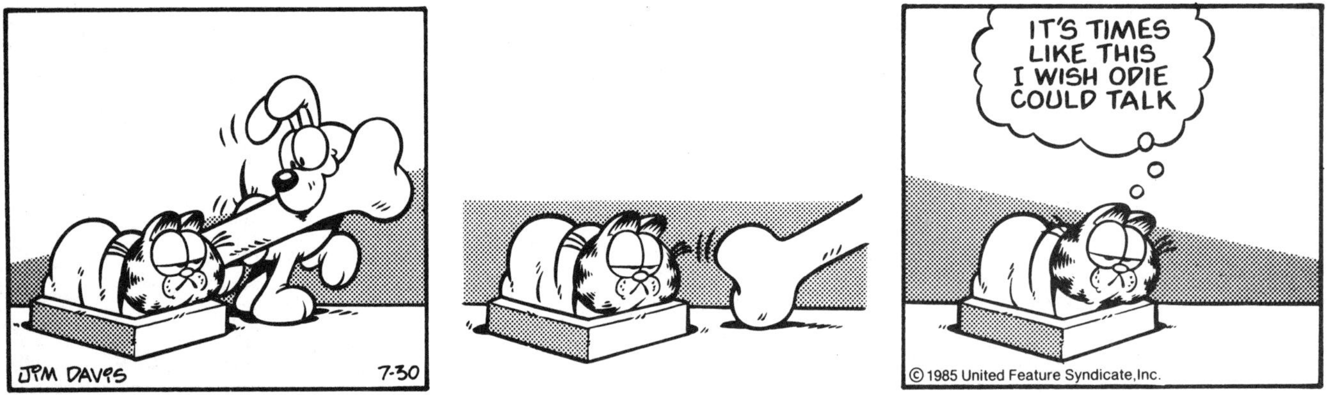
JIM DAVIS
7-30
IT'S TIMES LIKE THIS I WISH ODIE COULD TALK
© 1985 United Feature Syndicate, Inc.

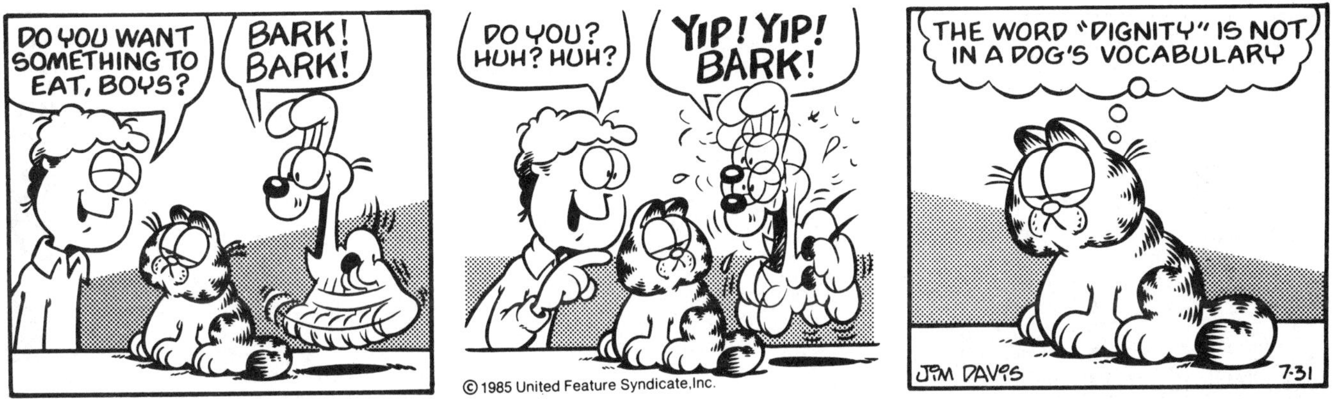
DO YOU WANT SOMETHING TO EAT, BOYS?
BARK! BARK!
DO YOU? HUH? HUH?
YIP! YIP! BARK!
THE WORD "DIGNITY" IS NOT IN A DOG'S VOCABULARY
JIM DAVIS
7-31

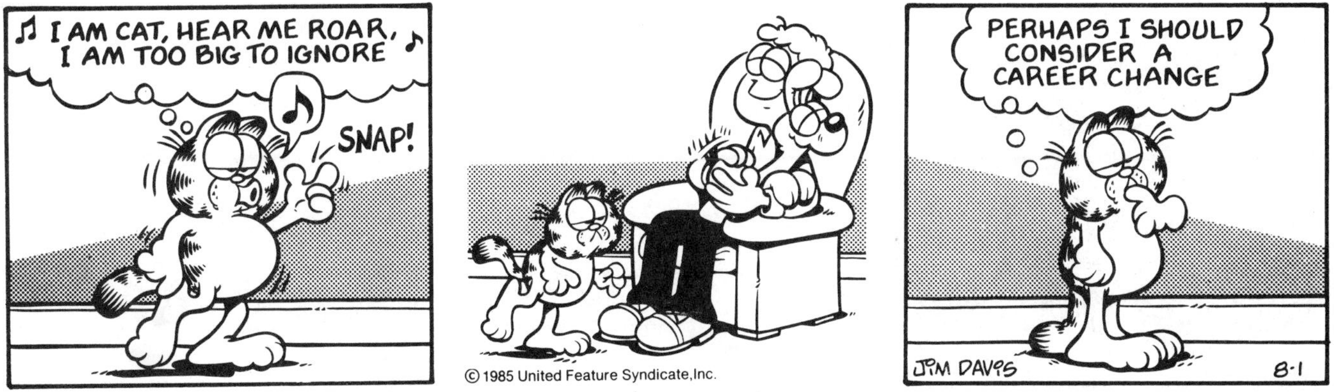
♫ I AM CAT, HEAR ME ROAR, I AM TOO BIG TO IGNORE ♪
SNAP!
PERHAPS I SHOULD CONSIDER A CAREER CHANGE
JIM DAVIS
8-1

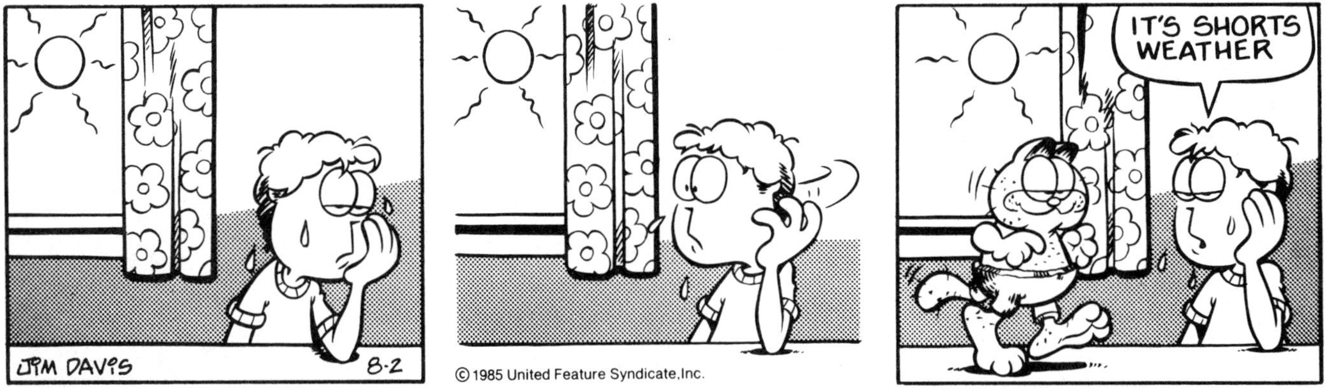
JIM DAVIS
8-2
IT'S SHORTS WEATHER

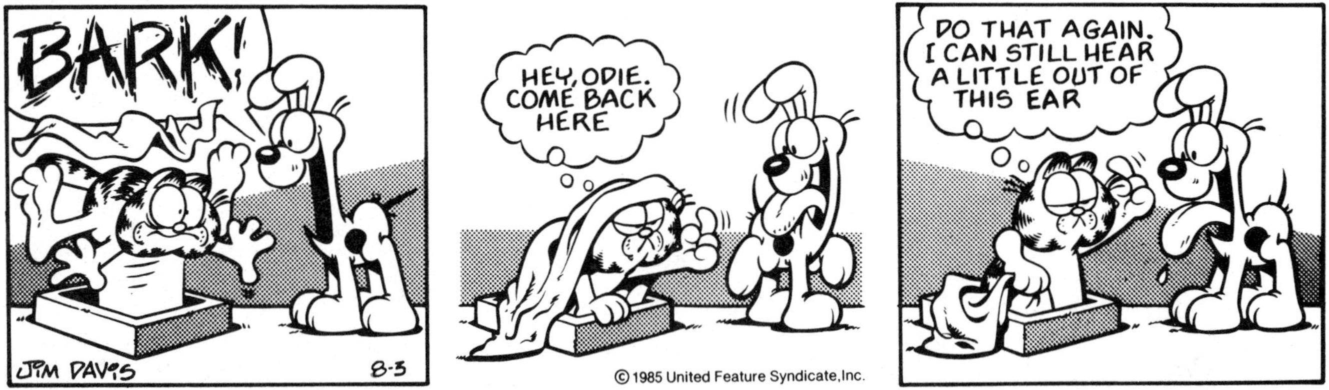
BARK!
JIM DAVIS
8-3
HEY, ODIE. COME BACK HERE
DO THAT AGAIN. I CAN STILL HEAR A LITTLE OUT OF THIS EAR

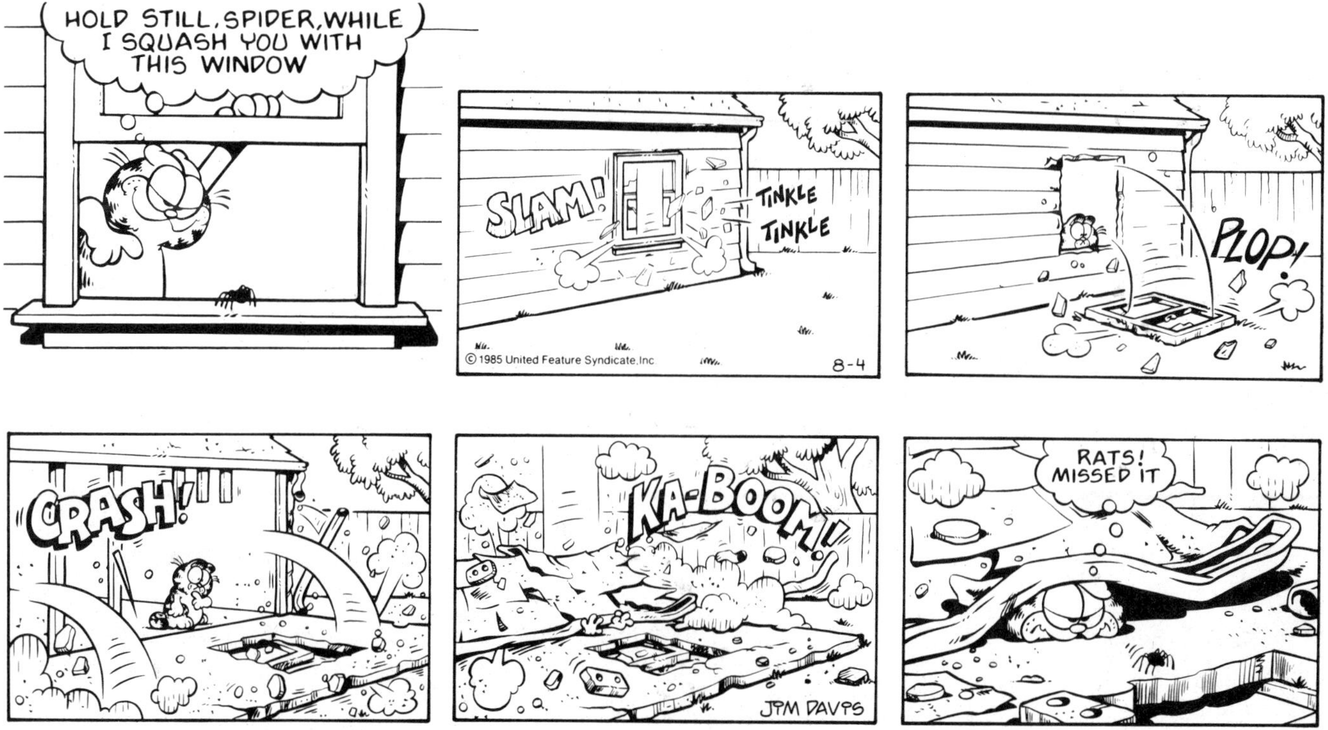
HOLD STILL, SPIDER, WHILE I SQUASH YOU WITH THIS WINDOW
SLAM!
TINKLE
TINKLE
© 1985 United Feature Syndicate, Inc.
8-4
PLOP!
CRASH!
KA-BOOM!
JIM DAVIS
RATS! MISSED IT

Garfield through the eyes of the little fans

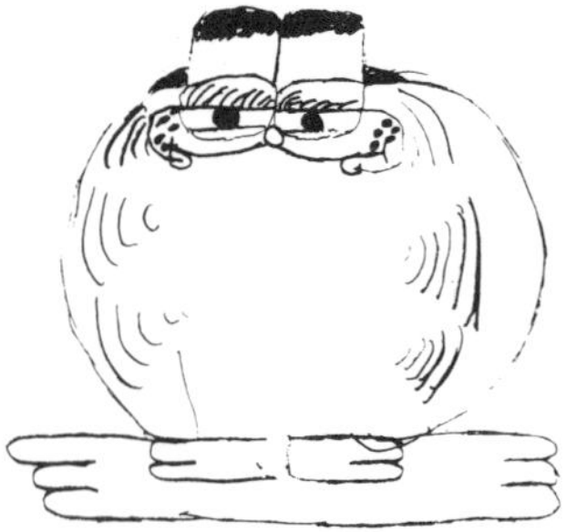

MICHAEL
ALPHA

Texas

KRISTEN
MUELLER

Pennsylvania

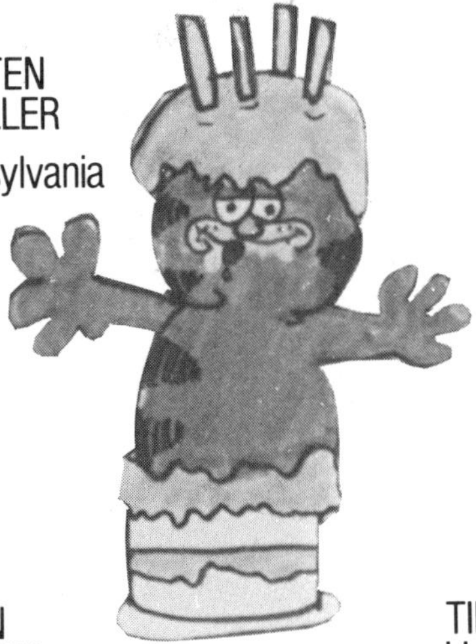

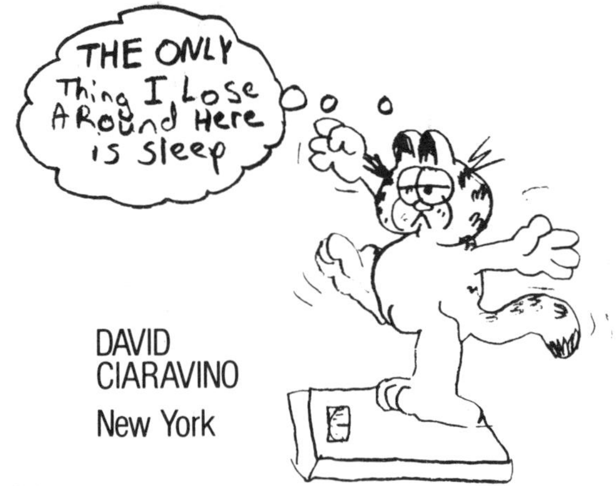
THE ONLY Thing I Lose ARound Here is Sleep

DAVID
CIARAVINO

New York

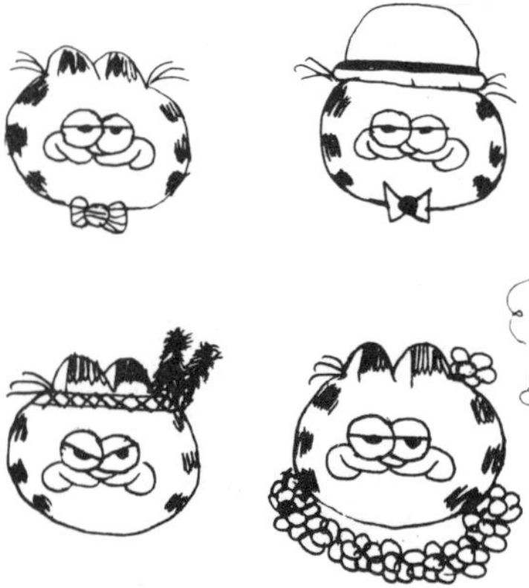
I ♡ HAWAII

CAROLYN
KLEEMANN

California

TIMMY
LUCIANI

Massachusetts

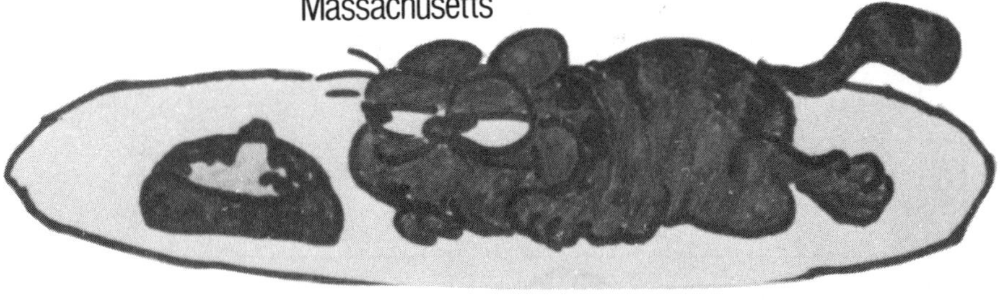

Third Edition

FRENCH VERB DRILLS

R. de Roussy de Sales

McGraw·Hill

New York   Chicago   San Francisco   Lisbon   London   Madrid   Mexico City
Milan   New Delhi   San Juan   Seoul   Singapore   Sydney   Toronto

2 3 4 5 6 7 8 9 10 11   QPD/QPD   3 2 1 0 9 8 7 6 5 4

ISBN 0-07-142087-8
Library of Congress control number 2004103588

Interior design by Rattray Design

McGraw-Hill books are available at special quantity discounts to use as premiums and sales promotions, or for use in corporate training programs. For more information, please write to the Director of Special Sales, Professional Publishing, McGraw-Hill, Two Penn Plaza, New York, NY 10121-2298. Or contact your local bookstore.

This book is printed on acid-free paper.

Contents

Part 2

Irregular Verbs 63

Introduction

Practice is an indispensable element of mastery in foreign language learning, as in other subject areas. *French Verb Drills* is an excellent supplement to basic classroom texts and is particularly valuable as a tool for individualized instruction and practice.

In a clear and concise way this book leads students to an understanding of how French verbs are formed and used. A variety of exercises reinforces the ability to manipulate the language in its written form, and many of the exercises can be easily converted to oral drills, thereby adding another dimension to practice. Students use the verbs in context, and the emphasis is on contemporary, colloquial use of the language.

There are several abbreviations that are used throughout the book. These are as follows:

f.	feminine
fam.	familiar
m.	masculine
pl.	plural
reg.	regular
s.	singular

French Verb Drills is divided into two parts. Part 1 offers concise explanations, charts, and focused examples of all French verb constructions, tenses, and moods, beginning with the present tense of regular and irregular verbs. Part 2 provides complete reference charts for common irregular verbs and verb groups. There are also an appendix offering students a final review of all the conjugations learned in the book, an answer key for self-correction, and a French–English/English–French index of verbs. This book should be an invaluable aid for students wishing to advance more quickly in their study of French, as well as for those who need additional understanding and practice for mastering classroom assignments.

Part 1

Regular Verbs

1 · Infinitive

All French verbs have infinitives ending in **-er, -ir,** or **-re.** Regular verbs are normally classified into three groups, according to their infinitive ending:

1. parl<u>er</u> (to speak)
2. fin<u>ir</u> (to finish)
3. vend<u>re</u> (to sell)

The stem of the verb is obtained by dropping the infinitive ending **-er, -ir,** or **-re** (i.e., leaving the stems **parl-, fin-,** and **vend-**).

2 · Present indicative of regular <u>-er</u> verbs

The present tense of regular -er verbs is formed by adding the endings **-e, -es, -e, -ons, -ez,** and **-ent** to the stem of the verb. The subject pronouns (**je, tu, il/elle/on, nous, vous, ils/elles**) are always used.

parler (to speak)

singular

je parl<u>e</u>	(I speak, I do speak, or I am speaking)
tu parl<u>es</u> (familiar singular)	(you speak, you do speak, or you are speaking)
or: vous parl<u>ez</u> (polite singular)	(you speak, you do speak, or you are speaking)
il parl<u>e</u>	(he speaks, he does speak, or he is speaking)
elle parl<u>e</u>	(she speaks, she does speak, or she is speaking)

on parle	(one speaks, we speak, or they speak; one does speak, we do speak, or they do speak; one is speaking, we are speaking, or they are speaking)

plural

nous parlons	(we speak, we do speak, or we are speaking)
vous parlez	(you speak, you do speak, or you are speaking)
ils parlent	(they [m.] speak, they do speak, or they are speaking)
elles parlent	(they [f.] speak, they do speak, or they are speaking)

In French, the second person singular (*you*) has two forms: the familiar form, using the pronoun **tu,** and the polite form, using the pronoun **vous.**

singular		*plural of both forms*
familiar form	tu parles (you speak)	vous parlez (you speak)
polite form	vous parlez	

The **-e** of **je** is dropped when the word that follows it begins with a vowel or a silent (mute) **h** (elision).

J'arrive.	(I'm coming.)
J'habite à Paris.	(I live in Paris.)

Use of tense

The present indicative is used in French as it is in English. However, with **depuis,** it is also used to express an action which took place in the past and is still going on at present.

Il pleut depuis deux jours.	(It has been raining for two days.)

The English progressive form (*-ing*) can be expressed in French with **être en train de** + the infinitive form of the verb.

Je suis en train de travailler.	(I am working.)

common regular -er verbs

admirer (to admire)	donner (to give)
aider (to help)	écouter (to listen to)
aimer (to love; to like)	entrer (to enter)
ajouter (to add)	étudier (to study)
apporter (to bring)	fermer (to close)
arriver (to arrive; to happen)	habiter (to live in)
brûler (to burn)	jouer (to play)
chanter (to sing)	monter (to climb, to go up)
compter (to count)	montrer (to show)
couper (to cut)	parler (to speak)
coûter (to cost)	penser (to think)
danser (to dance)	pleurer (to cry, weep)
déjeuner (to have lunch)	porter (to carry; to wear)
demander (to ask)	tomber (to fall)
demeurer (to remain, to stay)	travailler (to work)
dîner (to dine, to have dinner)	trouver (to find)

Exercise 1

Write the present tense of the following verbs.

1. demander je _____ tu _____ il/elle/on _____

                nous _____ vous _____ ils/elles _____

2. chanter je _____ tu _____ il/elle/on _____

                nous _____ vous _____ ils/elles _____

3. travailler je _____ tu _____ il/elle/on _____

                nous _____ vous _____ ils/elles _____

Exercise 2

Write the present tense of the following verbs.

1. étudier il/elle/on _____ vous _____

              j'_____ nous _____

2. donner tu _____ ils/elles _____

              vous _____ je _____

3. fermer   il/elle/on _____ nous _____

　　　　　　 tu _____ ils/elles _____

4. jouer   je _____ vous _____

　　　　　　 ils/elles _____ tu _____

5. dîner   nous _____ tu _____

　　　　　 je _____ vous _____

Exercise 3

Translate these phrases into French.

1. we speak _____

2. we are beginning _____

3. I do work _____

4. she helps _____

5. you love _____

6. he is listening _____

7. they (f.) count _____

8. I am falling _____

9. we find _____

10. we are arriving _____

11. he brings _____

12. we go up _____

13. she is wearing _____

14. we play _____

15. he does study _____

16. we admire _____

17. she finds _____

18. I am thinking _____

19. they (m.) ring _____

20. he cries _____

3 · Present indicative of regular -ir verbs and interrogative forms

-Ir verbs

The present tense of regular -ir verbs is formed by adding the endings -is, -is, -it, -issons, -issez, and -issent to the stem of the verb.

finir (to finish)

je finis   (I finish, I do finish, I am finishing)
tu finis
il/elle/on finit
nous finissons
vous finissez
ils/elles finissent

common regular -ir verbs
accomplir (to accomplish)
bâtir (to build)
choisir (to choose)
obéir (to obey)
punir (to punish)
remplir (to fill)
réussir (to succeed)

Note the group of irregular -ir verbs conjugated like **sortir** (*to go out*). They include **dormir** (*to sleep*), **mentir** (*to lie*), **partir** (*to leave*), **sentir** (*to feel*), and **servir** (*to serve*). See Part 2 of this handbook for conjugations and practice exercises for irregular verbs.

Exercise 4

Write the present tense of the following verbs.

1. obéir   j'_____ tu _____ il/elle/on _____

              nous _____ vous _____ ils/elles _____

2. réussir   je _____ tu _____ il/elle/on _____

              nous _____ vous _____ ils/elles _____

3. punir   je _____ tu _____ il/elle/on _____

   nous _____ vous _____ ils/elles _____

Exercise 5

Write the present tense of the following verbs.

1. bâtir   nous _____ il _____ je _____ tu _____

2. remplir   elle _____ vous _____ ils _____ nous _____

3. choisir   je _____ nous _____ tu _____ elle _____

4. accomplir il _____ vous _____ j'_____ ils _____

5. finir   vous _____ il _____ elles _____ tu _____

Interrogative forms

The French interrogative is formed:

> 1. with voice intonation (word order does not change)
>   <u>Vous</u> <u>aimez</u> <u>les</u> <u>chats</u>?   (Do you like cats?)

> 2. by placing **est-ce que** before the statement
>   <u>Est-ce que</u> vous aimez les chats?   (Do you like cats?)

> 3. by placing the pronoun *after* the verb and joining it with a hyphen (inversion)
>   <u>Aimez-vous</u> les chats?   (Do you like cats?)

In the inverted form, with the pronouns **il** and **elle**, a **t** is placed (and pronounced) between the verb and the pronoun, surrounded by closed-up hyphens in writing, unless the conjugated verb form already ends in **t**.

> <u>Aime-t-il</u> les chats?   (Does he like cats?)
> <u>Choisit-elle</u> un chat?   (Is she choosing a cat?)

Note that with the subject pronoun **je**, only the interrogative form with **est-ce que** is used, except, on occasion, with the verbs **être** (**suis-je?** *am I?*) and **avoir** (**ai-je?** *do I have?*), and a few others (**puis-je?** *may I?*).

Est-ce que j'obéis?			(Do I obey?)
Est-ce que tu obéis?	*or*	Obéis-tu?	(Do you obey?)
Est-ce qu'il obéit?	*or*	Obéit-il?	(Does he obey?)
Est-ce qu'elle obéit?	*or*	Obéit-elle?	(Does she obey?)
Est-ce que nous obéissons?	*or*	Obéissons-nous?	(Do we obey?)
Est-ce que vous obéissez?	*or*	Obéissez-vous?	(Do you obey?)
Est-ce qu'ils obéissent?	*or*	Obéissent-ils?	(Do they [m.] obey?)
Est-ce qu'elles obéissent?	*or*	Obéissent-elles?	(Do they [f.] obey?)

Exercise 6

Translate the following into French. (Use inversion except for questions whose subject is **je**).

1. Is he obeying? _____
2. Does she succeed? _____
3. Does he speak French? _____
4. Am I helping? _____
5. Do you dance? _____
6. Are you thinking? _____
7. Do I choose? _____
8. Are you listening? _____
9. Is he choosing a house? _____
10. Does she wear a hat? _____

4 • Present indicative of regular -re verbs and negative form

-Re forms

The present tense of **-re** verbs is formed by adding the endings **-s, -s, —, -ons, -ez,** and **-ent** to the stem of the verb.

vendre (to sell)

je vend<u>s</u>	(I sell, I do sell, I am selling)
tu vend<u>s</u>	
il/elle/on vend	
nous vend<u>ons</u>	
vous vend<u>ez</u>	
ils/elles vend<u>ent</u>	

common regular -re verbs

attendre (to wait)

défendre (to defend; to forbid)

descendre (to go down; to exit [a vehicle])

entendre (to hear)

perdre (to lose)

rendre (to give back)

répondre (to answer)

tendre (to stretch [out])

Exercise 7

Write the present tense form of the verb in the person indicated by the pronoun.

1. nous (répondre) _____

2. il (vendre) _____

3. elles (entendre) _____

4. je (défendre) _____

5. vous (perdre) _____

6. tu (rendre) _____

7. elle (tendre) _____

8. ils (descendre) _____

9. je (perdre) _____

10. tu (entendre) _____

Negative form

The negative is formed by placing **ne** before the verb and **pas** after it.

> *ne verb pas*
> Vous <u>ne</u> parlez <u>pas</u>.   (You do not speak; You are not speaking.)

The e of **ne** is dropped before a vowel or silent **h**.

> vous <u>n</u>'aimez pas   (you don't like)

In the negative interrogative form, the **ne** is placed before the verb and **pas** after the pronoun.

> *ne verb pronoun pas*
> <u>Ne</u> parlez-vous <u>pas</u>?   (Don't you speak? Aren't you speaking?)

This does not apply to the negative **est-ce que** form of questions. Word order does not change.

> <u>Est-ce que</u> vous <u>ne</u> parlez <u>pas</u>?   (Don't you speak? Aren't you speaking?)

Exercise 8

Translate the following into French.

1. they are losing _____
2. we don't hear _____
3. Don't you answer? _____
4. I don't forbid _____
5. Are they waiting? _____
6. Aren't they waiting? _____
7. I lose _____
8. she is giving back _____
9. they forbid _____
10. we aren't losing _____

5 · The imperative

To form the imperative, use the second person singular (**tu**) and first person plural (**nous**) forms of the present indicative, and the second person plural (**vous**) for both the polite form in the singular, and the familiar and polite plurals. The subject pronoun is not used in the imperative.

Both regular and irregular verbs follow this pattern. (See Part 2 of this handbook for conjugations of irregular verbs.)

familiar	*polite*	
tu	vous	nous
parle! (speak!)	parlez! (speak!)	parlons! (let's speak!)
finis! (finish!)	finissez! (finish!)	finissons! (let's finish!)
vends! (sell!)	vendez! (sell!)	vendons! (let's sell!)

Note that in the **tu** form of the imperative, for verbs ending in **-er**, an **s** is added when the verb is followed by the object pronouns **-y** or **-en**.

parler	Parles-en!	(Talk about it!)
aller	Vas-y!	(Go there! Go do it!)

Use of the imperative

The imperative is used, as in English, to express commands, orders, or suggestions.

Allons au cinéma ce soir.	(Let's go to the movies this evening.)
Lisez les fables de La Fontaine.	(Read the fables of La Fontaine.)
Mets ton imperméable!	(Put on your raincoat!)

Exercise 9

Translate the following commands into French.

1. Let's work! _____

2. Choose! (polite) _____

3. Obey! (fam. s.) _____

4. Listen! (polite) _____

5. Wait! (polite) _____

6. Let's think! _____

7. Let's study! _____

8. Come in! (polite) _____

9. Have dinner! (fam. s.) _____

10. Let's begin! _____

6 · The present participle

The present participle of all French verbs ends in **-ant.** To form the present participle of regular verbs, replace the **-ons** ending of the first person plural (**nous**) of the present indicative with **-ant.** Don't forget the **-iss-** between the stem and **-ant** in regular **-ir** verbs.

(nous) parl<u>ons</u>	→	parl<u>ant</u> (speaking)
(nous) finiss<u>ons</u>	→	finiss<u>ant</u> (finishing)
(nous) vend<u>ons</u>	→	vend<u>ant</u> (selling)

Sole exceptions: **être (étant),** *to be (being);* **avoir (ayant),** *to have (having);* and **savoir (sachant),** *to know (knowing).* (See Part 2 of this handbook for irregular verb forms.)

Usage

The present participle, or **-ant** form, of French verbs, is translated by the English *-ing* form.

The preposition **en** (*while, on, by, in, when*) governs the present participle form of French verbs. The present participle may, however, occur without **en.**

Il siffle <u>en travaillant.</u>	(He whistles while he works.)
<u>En voyant</u>...	(On/Upon seeing . . .)
<u>En entrant</u>...	(When/Upon entering . . .)
<u>Souffrant</u> atrocement, elle est allée chez le dentiste.	(Suffering terribly, she went to the dentist.)

Note that the present participle is invariable. However, it can be used as an adjective, where it agrees in gender and number with the noun.

<u>En les intéressant</u> à des choses intéressantes...	(By interesting them in interesting things . . .)

Exercise 10

Complete the following sentences by writing the verb in parentheses in the present participle.

1. En _____ (étudier) les verbes, on arrive à parler français correctement.

2. Il est entré en _____ (chanter) la Marseillaise.

3. En _____ (obéir), on apprend à commander.

4. C'est en _____ (écouter) le professeur que l'on apprend le français.

5. Finissons cet exercice en _____ (attendre) l'heure du dîner.

6. Il a fait une faute en _____ (compter) de un à dix.

7. C'est en _____ (descendre) l'escalier qu'il est tombé.

8. C'est en _____ (danser) qu'on devient bon danseur.

9. Les bons étudiants aident les autres en leur _____ (donner) des conseils en français.

10. Il s'est cassé une jambe en _____ (jouer) au football.

7 · The future

The future tense is formed by adding the endings **-ai, -as, -a, -ons, -ez,** and **-ont** to the infinitive. Drop the final **-e** before adding these endings to the infinitive of regular **-re** verbs.

parler	*finir*	*vendre*
je parlerai (I will speak)	je finirai	je vendrai
tu parleras	tu finiras	tu vendras
il/elle/on parlera	il/elle/on finira	il/elle/on vendra
nous parlerons	nous finirons	nous vendrons
vous parlerez	vous finirez	vous vendrez
ils/elles parleront	ils/elles finiront	ils/elles vendront

Certain irregular verbs (**aller, avoir, devoir, envoyer, être, faire, pleuvoir, pouvoir, recevoir, savoir, venir, voir,** and **vouloir**) have irregular stems in the future. They are listed with their conjugations in Section 10 and in Part 2 of this handbook.

Usage

The future tense in French expresses future time, as it does in English.

Je <u>parlerai</u> avec le prof plus tard.	(I'll speak with the teacher later.)
Est-ce que tu <u>attendras</u> Lucie?	(Will you wait for Lucie?)
Elles <u>choisiront</u> bientôt leurs cours.	(Soon, they'll choose their courses.)

As in English, future time is often expressed in French conversation and familiar writing by the present tense, or by the present tense of the verb **aller** (*to go*) preceding another verb in the infinitive.

Tu <u>déjeunes</u> au resto-U plus tard?	(You're having lunch later at the cafeteria?)
<u>Allez</u>-vous au cinéma ce soir?	(Are you going to the movies this evening?)
Je <u>vais</u> <u>voyager</u> en France cet été.	(I am going to travel in France this summer.)

Exercise 11

Write the future of the verb in the person indicated by the pronoun.

1. je (finir) _____
2. vous (chanter) _____
3. nous (choisir) _____
4. elle (attendre) _____
5. tu (perdre) _____
6. ils (écouter) _____
7. je (descendre) _____
8. on (répondre) _____
9. tu (réussir) _____
10. elles (guérir) _____

8 · The conditional

The present conditional is formed by adding the endings **-ais, -ais, -ait, -ions, -iez,** and **-aient** to the infinitive of the verb. Drop the final **-e** before adding these endings to the infinitive of regular verbs in **-re.**

parler	*finir*	*vendre*
je parlerais (I would speak)	je finirais	je vendrais
tu parlerais	tu finirais	tu vendrais
il/elle/on parlerait	il/elle/on finirait	il/elle/on vendrait
nous parlerions	nous finirions	nous vendrions
vous parleriez	vous finiriez	vous vendriez
ils/elles parleraient	ils/elles finiraient	ils/elles vendraient

The forms of verbs that have irregular stems in the present conditional (**aller, avoir, devoir, envoyer, être, faire, pleuvoir, pouvoir, recevoir, savoir, venir, voir,** and **vouloir**) are listed with their conjugations in Section 10 and in Part 2 of this handbook.

Usage

The conditional is used:

1. to express a hypothetical (contrary-to-fact) action (as in English), which might take place under certain conditions. Note that in a contrary-to-fact sentence, the verb following **si** is in the imperfect indicative (see Section 9).

   Si j'étais au Québec, je parlerais   (If I were in Quebec, I would speak French.)
   français.

2. to express a wish
   Je voudrais t'embrasser.   (I would like to kiss you.)

3. to make polite requests
   Pourriez-vous me prêter cinq euros?   (Could you lend me five euros?)

Exercise 12

Write the conditional form of the verb for the person indicated by the pronoun.

1. elles (répondre) _____

2. nous (finir) _____

3. on (choisir) _____

4. Pierre (arriver) _____

5. tu (penser) _____

6. vous (aimer) _____

7. je (perdre) _____

8. elles (attendre) _____

9. vous (choisir) _____

10. tu (réussir) _____

Exercise 13

Change the future to the conditional form, and translate into English.

1. nous obéirons _____

2. tu finiras _____

3. je commencerai _____

4. ils finiront _____

5. j'aimerai _____

6. vous déjeunerez _____

7. elle parlera _____

8. j'entendrai _____

9. elles travailleront _____

10. nous jouerons _____

Exercise 14

Translate the following phrases and sentences into French.

1. you will obey _____

2. I would think _____

3. we would listen _____

4. Would you wait? _____

5. I will sell _____

6. we would play _____

7. I shall answer. _____

8. they would admire _____

9. Will you come down? _____

10. They would not come down. _____

9 · The imperfect past

The imperfect past tense is formed by adding the endings **-ais, -ais, -ait, -ions, -iez,** and **-aient** to the stem of the verb in its first person plural (**nous**) form. For regular verbs in **-ir,** insert **-iss-** between the stem and the ending.

parler	*finir*	*vendre*
(nous parlons)	(nous finissons)	(nous vendons)
je parlais (I was speaking, used to speak)	je finissais	je vendais
tu parlais	tu finissais	tu vendais
il/elle/on parlait	il/elle/on finissait	il/elle/on vendait
nous parlions	nous finissions	nous vendions
vous parliez	vous finissiez	vous vendiez
ils/elles parlaient	ils/elles finissaient	ils/elles vendaient

Sole exception: The verb **être** has an irregular stem in the imperfect (**ét-**); the endings, however, are regular. (See Section 10 and Part 2 of this handbook for the stems of irregular verbs.)

Ils étaient à l'école secondaire   (Last year they were in high school.)
    l'année passée.

Usage

The imperfect expresses a continuous, ongoing, or repeated action that took place in the past, or a state, condition, or description in the past.

Il dormait quand je suis entré.   (He was sleeping when I came in.)
Autrefois, les hommes portaient   (In the past, men wore wigs.)
    des perruques.

Exercise 15

Write the imperfect (indicative) of the verb in the person indicated by the pronoun.

1. vous (choisir) _____
2. j' (entendre) _____
3. on (jouer) _____
4. je (travailler) _____
5. tu (demeurer) _____
6. nous (bâtir) _____
7. ils (accomplir) _____
8. je (remplir) _____
9. tu (perdre) _____
10. vous (descendre) _____
11. nous (vendre) _____
12. elle (dîner) _____
13. tu (écouter) _____
14. je (penser) _____
15. ils (porter) _____
16. il (demander) _____
17. nous (obćir) _____
18. elles (choisir) _____
19. nous (attendre) _____
20. je (descendre) _____

Review

Exercise 16

Translate the following phrases and sentences into English.

1. je finis _____
2. nous parlions _____

3. vous perdrez _____

4. je donnerais _____

5. ils dansaient _____

6. tu entreras _____

7. on vendait _____

8. vous habitiez _____

9. elles étudient _____

10. je bâtissais _____

11. Répondez à la question. _____

12. Aimez-vous Brahms? _____

13. Nous ne travaillons pas. _____

14. Est-ce que vous chantez? _____

15. Chantiez-vous? _____

16. Je suis en train de travailler. _____

17. Nous écoutions la radio. _____

18. Il joue du piano. _____

19. Écoutez-vous? _____

20. Ne réussiraient-elles pas? _____

Exercise 17

Write the following verbs in the tense or mood indicated in parentheses.

1. (present) descendre, je _____

2. (imperfect indicative) finir, nous _____

3. (future) attendre, j'_____

4. (conditional) chanter, je _____

5. (present) pleurer, elles _____

6. (imperfect indicative) réussir, vous _____

7. (imperative) parler (nous) _____

8. (imperative) écouter (vous) _____

9. (present) brûler, il _____

10. (imperfect indicative) trouver, vous _____

11. (future) compter, tu _____

12. (conditional) ajouter, nous _____

13. (future) apporter, ils _____

14. (present) aider, elle _____

15. (imperfect indicative) demander, vous _____

16. (present) obéir, ils _____

17. (present) répondre, nous _____

18. (future) perdre, je _____

19. (conditional) accomplir, on _____

20. (imperfect indicative) choisir, je _____

10 · <u>Être</u> and <u>avoir</u> (present, future, conditional, imperfect)

<u>être</u> (to be)

present	*future*	*conditional*	*imperfect*
(I am)	(I will be)	(I would be)	(I was, used to be)
je <u>suis</u>	je <u>serai</u>	je <u>serais</u>	j'<u>étais</u>
tu <u>es</u>	tu <u>seras</u>	tu <u>serais</u>	tu <u>étais</u>
il/elle/on <u>est</u>	il/elle/on <u>sera</u>	il/elle/on <u>serait</u>	il/elle/on <u>était</u>
nous <u>sommes</u>	nous <u>serons</u>	nous <u>serions</u>	nous <u>étions</u>
vous <u>êtes</u>	vous <u>serez</u>	vous <u>seriez</u>	vous <u>étiez</u>
ils/elles <u>sont</u>	ils/elles <u>seront</u>	ils/elles <u>seraient</u>	ils/elles <u>étaient</u>

imperative	*present participle*	*past participle*
sois! (be!)	<u>étant</u> (being)	<u>été</u> (been)
soyons! (let's be!)		
soyez! (be!)		

avoir (to have)

present (I have)	*future* (I shall have)	*conditional* (I would have)	*imperfect* (I was having, used to have)
j'ai	j'aurai	j'aurais	j'avais
tu as	tu auras	tu aurais	tu avais
il/elle/on a	il/elle/on aura	il/elle/on aurait	il/elle/on avait
nous avons	nous aurons	nous aurions	nous avions
vous avez	vous aurez	vous auriez	vous aviez
ils/elles ont	ils/elles auront	ils/elles auraient	ils/elles avaient

imperative	*present participle*	*past participle*
aie! (have!)	ayant (having)	eu (had)
ayons! (let's have!)		
ayez! (have!)		

idiomatic uses of avoir

avoir — ans (to be — years old)

avoir besoin de (to need)

avoir chaud (to be warm, hot)

avoir de la chance (to be lucky)

avoir envie de (to feel like)

avoir faim (to be hungry)

avoir froid (to be cold)

avoir honte (de) (to be ashamed [of])

avoir la parole (to have the floor [in a meeting])

avoir l'air de (to seem)

avoir l'habitude de (to be accustomed to)

avoir lieu (to take place)

avoir mal (à) (to have a pain, to have a[n] —ache)

avoir peur (de) (to be afraid [of])

avoir raison (to be right)

avoir soif (to be thirsty)

avoir sommeil (to be sleepy)

avoir tort (to be wrong)

il y a (there is, there are)

Exercise 18

Translate the following phrases and sentences into French.

1. I shall be _____

2. we are _____

3. you would be (fam. s.) _____

4. you would have (polite) _____

5. he used to be _____

6. let's be . . . ! _____

7. they (f.) are _____

8. I used to have _____

9. we have _____

10. we would have _____

11. one would be _____

12. you will be (polite) _____

13. he will have _____

14. we will be _____

15. she has _____

16. be . . . ! (fam. s.) _____

17. being _____

18. we were _____

19. having _____

20. you (fam. s.) are _____

21. let's have . . . ! _____

22. she used to be _____

23. I shall have _____

24. I would be _____

25. have . . . ! (fam. s.) _____

26. I am _____

27. he is _____

28. you (polite or pl.) used to live _____

29. he will work _____

30. she was speaking _____

31. they (m.) were _____

32. we are having _____

33. I used to be _____

34. I am warm. _____

35. He is hungry. _____

36. You are right. (polite) _____

37. I am wrong. _____

38. Are you sleeping? (polite) _____

39. She is eighteen years old. _____

40. there is _____

41. to seem _____

42. I am thirsty. _____

43. She is afraid. _____

44. there are _____

45. We're cold. _____

46. She is not ashamed. _____

47. We're not sleepy. _____

48. Am I wrong? _____

49. Are you right? (fam. s.) _____

50. Let's not be afraid. _____

11 · The past participle

The past participle of regular verbs is formed by adding -é for -er verbs, -i for -ir verbs, and -u for -re verbs to the stem of the verb.

parler
parlé (spoken)

finir
fini (finished)

vendre
vendu (sold)

Agreement of the past participle

With verbs that are conjugated in the **passé composé** with the auxiliary **être** (see Section 12), the past participle agrees in gender and number with the subject of the verb.

> <u>Nous</u> sommes arriv<u>és</u> à minuit.   (We arrived at midnight.)
> <u>Elle</u> est all<u>ée</u> voir sa famille.   (She went to see her family.)

With verbs that are conjugated in the **passé composé** with the auxiliary **avoir** (see Section 12), the past participle agrees with the direct object of the verb, but only when the direct object (noun or pronoun) is placed *before* the conjugated verb.

> J'ai fin<u>i</u> <u>la</u> <u>leçon</u>.   (I finished the lesson.)

In the above example, the past participle *does not agree* because the direct object follows the verb.

> <u>Quelle</u> <u>leçon</u> as-tu fin<u>ie</u>?   (Which lesson did you finish?)
> La leçon? Je ne <u>l'</u>ai pas trouv<u>ée</u>.   (The lesson? I didn't find it.)

In these examples, the past participle *does agree* with the direct object because the direct object, noun, or pronoun precedes the verb.

The past participle never shows agreement when the conjugated verb is preceded by the object pronoun **en:**

> Avez-vous des bananes?   (Do you have any bananas?)
> —Oui, j'<u>en</u> ai achet<u>é</u>.   (Yes, I bought some.)

12 · The <u>passé</u> composé

The **passé composé** is formed by combining the present tense of the verbs **avoir** or **être** as auxiliaries with the past participle of the verb being conjugated.

parler	*finir*	*vendre*
j'<u>ai</u> parl<u>é</u>	j'<u>ai</u> fin<u>i</u>	j'<u>ai</u> vend<u>u</u>
(I spoke; I have spoken; I did speak)	(I finished; I have finished I did finish)	(I sold; I have sold; I did sell)

tu as parlé	tu as fini	tu as vendu
il/elle/on a parlé	il/elle/on a fini	il/elle/on a vendu
nous avons parlé	nous avons fini	nous avons vendu
vous avez parlé	vous avez fini	vous avez vendu
ils/elles ont parlé	ils/elles ont fini	ils/elles ont vendu

arriver

je suis arrivé(e)
(I arrived; I have arrived; I did arrive)
tu es arrivé(e)
il/on est arrivé
elle est arrivée
nous sommes arrivé(e)s
vous êtes arrivé(e)(s)
ils sont arrivés
elles sont arrivées

descendre

je suis descendu(e)
(I went down; I have gone down; I did go down)
tu es descendu(e)
il/on est descendu
elle est descendue
nous sommes descendu(e)s
vous êtes descendu(e)(s)
ils sont descendus
elles sont descendues

Être or avoir?

Most French verbs are conjugated with the auxiliary **avoir.** However, the following verbs are conjugated with **être:**

aller
arriver
descendre
devenir
entrer
monter
mourir
naître
partir
retourner
revenir
sortir
tomber
venir

Several verbs conjugated with **être** have irregular past participles (**mourir, naître, venir).** See Part 2 of this handbook for past participles of these irregular verbs.

Usage

The **passé composé** commonly refers to past actions. It is the past tense most used in speaking and everyday language; it is often called the "conversational past."

The **passé composé** refers to a completed action or state, or a succession of past events. (It describes the same shade of past time or action, or succession of past events, which the **passé simple** depicts in literary or formal, written French.) It contrasts with the imperfect, which, you will recall, indicates ongoing, customary, repeated, or habitual action in the past.

Elle est partie à six heures.	(She left at six o'clock.)
Il les a vus. Puis, il a fermé la porte, et il est parti.	(He saw them. Then he shut the door and went away.)
Georges et Yvette m'ont dit bonjour.	(Georges and Yvette said hello to me.)

But the imperfect is used for past description or ongoing or habitual activities in the past:

Quand j'étais petite, nous allions au cinéma le vendredi soir.	(When I was little, we used to go to the movies on Friday nights.)
Il faisait beau quand elles sont sorties.	(It was nice out when they left.)

Exercise 19

Write the verb in the **passé composé** with the subject given.

1. (parler) elle _____

2. (monter) je (m.) _____

3. (finir) je _____

4. (chanter) je _____

5. (obéir) vous _____

6. (arriver) elles _____

7. (étudier) il _____

8. (tomber) elle _____

9. (trouver) je _____

10. (choisir) vous _____

11. (attendre) nous _____

12. (répondre) on _____

13. (entendre) tu _____

14. (descendre) nous (f.) _____

15. (aimer) elle _____

16. (perdre) tu _____

17. (bâtir) il _____

18. (punir) elle _____

19. (réussir) nous _____

20. (donner) on _____

13 · The passé simple

The **passé simple** is formed by adding the following endings to the stem of the verb: **-ai, -as, -a, âmes, -âtes,** and **-èrent** with **-er** verbs, and **-is, -is, -it, -îmes, -îtes,** and **-irent** with **-ir** and **-re** verbs.

parler	*finir*	*vendre*
je parlai (I spoke)	je finis (I finished)	je vendis (I sold)
tu parlas	tu finis	tu vendis
il/elle/on parla	il/elle/on finit	il/elle/on vendit
nous parlâmes	nous finîmes	nous vendîmes
vous parlâtes	vous finîtes	vous vendîtes
ils/elles parlèrent	ils/elles finirent	ils/elles vendirent

passé simple of avoir and être

avoir	*être*
j'eus (I had)	je fus (I was)
tu eus	tu fus
il/elle/on eut	il/elle/on fut
nous eûmes	nous fûmes
vous eûtes	vous fûtes
ils/elles eurent	ils/elles furent

Usage

The **passé simple** is used to depict a completed past action or state. Unlike the imperfect, it carries no idea of ongoing, customary, repeated, or habitual action. It is often called the literary or historical past and will be useful to you for reading purposes. It is not used in conversation or everyday writing.

Son grand-père <u>vendit</u> le terrain en 1930.　　　　(His grandfather sold the land in 1930.)

Note that in conversation or everyday writing, one would use the **passé composé** to express this thought.

Son grand-père <u>a</u> <u>vendu</u> le terrain en 1930.

Exercise 20

Write the verb in parentheses in the **passé simple,** using the subject given.

1. on (parler) _____
2. nous (perdre) _____
3. ils (bâtir) _____
4. elle (aimer) _____
5. vous (descendre) _____
6. ils (répondre) _____
7. nous (attendre) _____
8. vous (choisir) _____
9. j' (étudier) _____
10. elles (arriver) _____
11. vous (obéir) _____
12. je (chanter) _____
13. vous (finir) _____
14. je (réussir) _____
15. il (étudier) _____
16. nous (parler) _____
17. vous (attendre) _____

18. ils (remplir) _____

19. vous (accomplir) _____

20. ils (dîner) _____

Exercise 21

Rewrite the following sentences in the formal (literary) style, putting the underlined verbs in the **passé simple** instead of the **passé composé**. (This section gives the verb forms for the irregular verbs **avoir** and **être**; see Part 2 of this handbook for other irregular verb forms in the **passé simple**.)

1. La conquête romaine a enlevé _____ à la Gaule sa liberté politique.

2. Elle lui a donné _____ en échange la paix et la sécurité.

3. Jeanne d'Arc a sauvé _____ la France.

4. Richelieu a créé _____ l'Académie Française.

5. Louis XIV a écrit _____ son testament dans la tour du Temple, à Paris, le 25 décembre 1792.

6. Pendant la Deuxième Guerre mondiale, le gouvernement de Vichy a adopté _____ une politique de collaboration avec les Allemands.

7. Le 18 juin 1940, le général de Gaulle a invité _____ de Londres, les Français à la résistance.

8. Pascal a inventé _____ une machine à calculer.

9. Madame Curie a découvert _____ le radium.

10. Le skieur français a remporté _____ trois médailles d'or aux jeux Olympiques.

11. La France a perdu _____ ses colonies d'outre-mer dans les années 50 et 60.

12. François Mitterrand a été _____ le président de la France de 1981 à 1995.

14 · The present subjunctive

The present subjunctive is formed by adding **-e, -es, -e, -ions, -iez,** and **-ent** to the stem of the verb. For verbs in **-ir,** insert **-iss-** between the stem and the ending.

present subjunctive of regular verbs

parler	*finir*	*vendre*
que je parle	que je finisse	que je vende
(that I may speak)	(that I may finish)	(that I may sell)
que tu parles	que tu finisses	que tu vendes
qu'il/elle/on parle	qu'il/elle/on finisse	qu'il/elle/on vende
que nous parlions[1]	que nous finissions	que nous vendions
que vous parliez[1]	que vous finissiez	que vous vendiez
qu'ils/elles parlent	qu'ils/elles finissent	qu'ils/elles vendent

The subjunctive endings for all verbs are the same except for **être** and **avoir.**

present subjunctive of avoir and être

avoir	*être*
que j'aie	que je sois
(that I may have)	(that I may be)
que tu aies	que tu sois
qu'il/elle/on ait	qu'il/elle/on soit
que nous ayons	que nous soyons
que vous ayez	que vous soyez
qu'ils/elles aient	qu'ils/elles soient

See Part 2 of this handbook for the stems and present subjunctive forms of the other French verbs that are irregular in the subjunctive.

Use of the subjunctive mood

The indicative mood is so called because it indicates fact or certainty. The subjunctive mood is so called because it is usually found in a subjoined or subordinate clause. The subjunctive is most often used in subordinate clauses introduced by **que.**

1. It is used in the subordinate clause of sentences expressing emotion, such as joy, sorrow, or fear; wish or command; and uncertainty.

Je suis content que vous appreniez le subjonctif.   (I am glad that you are learning the subjunctive.)

Je regrette que vous le trouviez difficile.   (I'm sorry that you find it difficult.)

---

1. Note that the first and second person plural forms of the present subjunctive have the same spelling as those of the imperfect indicative. Context will help with meaning.

Le professeur veut que nous finissions cette leçon aujourd'hui.	(The instructor wants us to finish this lesson today.)
Je doute que vous la finissiez aujourd'hui.	(I doubt that you will finish it today.)

2. The subjunctive is used after impersonal expressions, except those that indicate a certainty or probability.

Il faut que je finisse cette leçon aujourd'hui.	(It is necessary that I finish this lesson today.)
Il est temps que nous partions.	(It is time that we leave.)
Il est nécessaire que vous étudiiez le subjonctif.	(It is necessary that you study the subjunctive.)

Note in the above example that there is a double -ii- in the **nous** and **vous** present subjunctive forms of **étudier** and other verbs whose stem ends in -i. (This spelling also occurs in the imperfect indicative.)

3. The subjunctive is also used in the clause following these conjunctions:
afin que (qu') (in order that)
bien que (qu') (although)
jusqu'à ce que (qu') (until)
malgré que (qu') (in spite of the fact that)
pour que (qu' (in order that)
pourvu que (qu') (provided that)
quoique (quoiqu') (although)
sans que (qu') (without)

Je vous l'explique pour que vous compreniez.	(I'm explaining it to you so that you'll understand.)
Il va attendre là-bas jusqu'à ce qu'elle finisse.	(He'll wait there until she's finished/she finishes.)

Use of the present subjunctive

The present subjunctive is used to show that the action of the verb in the subordinate clause goes on at the same time as, or later than, the action expressed by the verb in the governing (main) clause.

Furthermore, in most cases, the subject of the subordinate clause must differ from the subject of the governing clause.

Je veux qu'elle fasse cela demain.	(I want her to do that tomorrow.)
Nous doutons qu'il soit heureux à présent.	(We doubt that he is happy right now.)

Je ne crois pas qu'ils viennent à deux heures.	(I don't believe that they'll come at two o'clock.)
Il faut que Marie lui écrive une lettre tout de suite.	(It's necessary that Marie write him a letter immediately.)
Elle voudrait que je la voie demain.	(She would like me to see her tomorrow.)

Notice that the English equivalents are sometimes worded differently from the French. In English, the infinitive is often used when the subject of the subordinate clause differs from the subject of the governing verb. The word *that* (**que**), whose equivalent is required in French, is not always used in English.

Before starting Exercise 22, see Part 2 of this handbook for the conjugations in the present subjunctive of **écrire** (*to write*), **faire** (*to do, make*), **venir** (*to come*) (and its compounds), **pouvoir** (*to be able to*), **prendre** (*to take*) (and its compounds), **voir** (*to see*), etc.

Exercise 22

Write the verb in the present subjunctive using the subject pronoun given.

1. (attendre) Pourvu qu'elle _____
2. (monter) Il faut que nous _____
3. (aimer) Bien que vous _____
4. (dîner) Pourvu qu'ils _____
5. (chanter) Pour que tu _____
6. (vendre) Il est temps que vous _____
7. (être) Il est nécessaire qu'elles _____
8. (choisir) Afin qu'elles _____
9. (écouter) Il faut que j' _____
10. (perdre) Bien que tu _____
11. (avoir) Il est possible que nous _____
12. (finir) Il est temps que vous _____
13. (répondre) Il faut qu'on _____
14. (travailler) Quoique nous _____
15. (dîner) Pourvu que je _____
16. (avoir) Il est normal que tu _____
17. (écrire) Pour qu'ils _____
18. (être) Il n'est pas possible qu'elle _____

19. (finir) Afin que nous _____

20. (apprendre) Il faut que vous _____

21. (trouver) Pour qu'il _____

22. (bâtir) Il n'est pas nécessaire que je _____

23. (réussir) Pourvu que vous _____

24. (donner) Quoique je _____

25. (avoir) Malgré que nous _____

Exercise 23

Locate the subject of the verb, and write the verb in parentheses in the present subjunctive. Then try to get the gist of the entire quote.

1. <<Tout ce que je faisais d'inutile en ce lieu m'est alors remonté à la gorge et je n'ai eu qu'une hâte, c'est qu'on en (finir) _____ et que je retrouve ma cellule avec mon sommeil.>> —Albert Camus

2. <<Qu'Hélène nous (être) _____ rendue dans l'heure même. Ou c'est la guerre.>> —Jean Giraudoux

3. <<Vous m'apportez ce dossier pour que je le (contrôler) _____ .>> —Antoine de Saint-Exupéry

4. <<Pourvu que le cyanure ne/n' (être) _____ pas décomposé, malgré le papier d'argent!>> —André Malraux

5. <<Que ta vision (être) _____ à chaque instant nouvelle!>> —André Gide

6. <<—Vous ne voulez rien accepter des autres?
   —Si, puisque j'accepte bien que vous me (faire) _____ cadeau de votre temps.>> —Béatrix Beck

7. <<Ce qui me frappe, ce qui me désole, c'est qu'ils (être) _____ aussi apathiques sans être aveugles, ni inconscients. [...] (ils) ne se sentent responsables de rien, parce qu'ils ne croient pas pouvoir rien faire en ce monde.>> —Simone de Beauvoir

8. Sous le pont Mirabeau coule la Seine

   Et nos amours

   Faut-il qu'il m'en (souvenir) _____

   La joie venait toujours après la peine

   (Venir) _____ la nuit sonne l'heure

   Les jours s'en vont je demeure

          —Guillaume Apollinaire

9. <<Qu'est-ce que vous voulez alors que nous (faire) _____ de ces meubles,

   Philippe?>> —André Maurois

10. <<Mon armée? Ah, poltron! Ah, traître! pour leur mort

    Tu crois donc que ce bras ne (être) _____ pas assez fort.>> —Corneille

11. <<Il n'est, je le vois bien, si poltron sur la terre

    Qui ne (pouvoir) _____ trouver un plus poltron que soi.>> —La Fontaine

12. <<Mieux vaut qu'elle ne (être) _____ point là demain, quand on viendra

    lever le corps, dit-elle.>> —André Gide

15 • The past (or perfect) subjunctive and the pluperfect subjunctive

The past subjunctive

The past subjunctive (or perfect subjunctive), like the **passé composé**, is a compound tense formed with the present subjunctive of **avoir** or être + the past participle of the verb.

Jérémie est désolé que Jackie ne l'ait pas accompagné hier soir.	(Jérémie is sorry that Jackie didn't accompany him last night.)
Nous sommes contents que vous soyez arrivées à l'heure.	(We're happy you got here on time.)

parler	*finir*	*vendre*
que j'aie parlé	que j'aie fini	que j'aie vendu
(that I spoke)	(that I finished)	(that I sold)
que tu aies parlé	que tu aies fini	que tu aies vendu
qu'il/elle/on ait parlé	qu'il/elle/on ait fini	qu'il/elle/on ait vendu
que nous ayons parlé	que nous ayons fini	que nous ayons vendu
que vous ayez parlé	que vous ayez fini	que vous ayez vendu
qu'ils/elles aient parlé	qu'ils/elles aient fini	qu'ils/elles aient vendu

arriver

que je sois arrivé(e)   (that I arrived)

que tu sois arrivé(e)

qu'il/elle/on soit arrivé(e)

que nous soyons arrivé(e)s

que vous soyez arrivé(e)(s)

qu'ils/elles soient arrivé(e)s

The past subjunctive is used following the same expressions in the main clause as the present subjunctive. It indicates that the action or situation in the subordinate clause (after **que**) happened *before* the action or situation of the main (first or principal) clause.

Je suis heureuse que tu aies réussi à tes examens.	(I'm pleased [now] [that] you passed your exams [yesterday, last week, etc.]).
Vous ne croyiez pas que nous soyons partis?	(Didn't you believe that we had left [departed]?)

The pluperfect subjunctive

The pluperfect subjunctive is a compound verb form that shows past time with respect to the verb in the main clause. However, it is never used in conversation or everyday writing, and is seen only infrequently in twentieth and twenty-first century French literature.

For the conjugated forms of the pluperfect subjunctive with the auxiliaries **avoir** and **être,** see Sections 25 and 26 of this handbook.

Je ne croyais pas qu'ils fussent venus. (... qu'ils soient venus [modern form])	(I did not believe that they had come.)

Nous doutions qu'il eût jamais été heureux. (... qu'il ait... été... [modern form])

(We doubted that he had ever been happy.)

The seventeenth-century dramatist Corneille wrote:

Si Chimène se plaint qu'il a tué son père
(If Chimène laments that he killed her father . . .)
Il ne l'eût jamais fait si je l'eusse pu faire.

Note that modern French uses the conditional perfect and the pluperfect indicative:

Il ne l'aurait jamais fait si j'avais pu le faire.

(He would never have done it if I had been able to do it.)

For the conjugation of the pluperfect indicative (**j'avais pu**), expressing what one *had done* (the past of the past), and the conditional perfect (**il aurait fait**), expressing what one *would have done* (contrary-to-fact), see Sections 25 and 26 of this handbook.

Exercise 24

Write the past (perfect) subjunctive form of each verb, using the subject provided.

Nos amis sont contents...

1. que nous (f.) (venir) _____
2. que le professeur (être absent) _____
3. que mon amie (réussir) _____
4. que tu (attendre) _____
5. que la tempête (ne pas arriver) _____
6. que certains étudiants (donner la réponse) _____
7. que je/j' (voyager) _____
8. que l'enfant (m.) (ne pas tomber) _____
9. que ton oncle (téléphoner) _____
10. que nous (vendre la voiture) _____
11. que Marie-Laure (partir en vacances) _____
12. que leurs parents (acheter cette maison) _____

16 · The imperfect subjunctive

The imperfect subjunctive is formed by dropping the last letter of the first person singular of the **passé simple** (see Section 13) and adding the endings **-sse, -sses, -ât (-ît, -ût), -ssions, -ssiez, -ssent**.

Note the circumflex accent in the third person singular (**il/elle/on**) form. This conjugation pattern has no exceptions.

imperfect subjunctive

parler	*finir*	*vendre*
(passé simple: je parlai)	(passé simple: je finis)	(passé simple: je vendis)
que je parla<u>sse</u>	que je fini<u>sse</u>	que je vendi<u>sse</u>
(that I might speak)	(that I might finish)	(that I might sell)
que tu parla<u>sses</u>	que tu fini<u>sses</u>	que tu vendi<u>sses</u>
qu'il/elle/on parl<u>ât</u>	qu'il/elle/on fin<u>ît</u>	qu'il/elle/on vend<u>ît</u>
que nous parla<u>ssions</u>	que nous fini<u>ssions</u>	que nous vendi<u>ssions</u>
que vous parla<u>ssiez</u>	que vous fini<u>ssiez</u>	que vous vendi<u>ssiez</u>
qu'ils/elles parla<u>ssent</u>	qu'ils/elles fini<u>ssent</u>	qu'ils/elles vendi<u>ssent</u>

See Part 2 of this handbook for the irregular verb conjugations of the imperfect subjunctive.

Use of the imperfect subjunctive

This verb form is seen in very formal writing only. In French literary or historical writing, you may see the following:

Elle craignait qu'il ne <u>plût</u>.   (She was afraid that it might rain.)

French conversation and most present-day written texts use the present subjunctive in this case. Therefore, you would normally say:

Elle craignait qu'il ne <u>pleuve</u>.   (She was afraid that it might rain.)

Note in the above example the particle **ne** (without negative value), which is seen in subjunctive constructions after the verbal expressions **craindre (que)** (*to fear [that]*) and **avoir peur (que)** (*to fear [that]*) and the conjunctions **avant que** (*before*) and **à moins que** (*unless*).

Exercise 25

Write the present subjunctive form of the verbs given in the imperfect subjunctive below.

1. que je parlasse _____

2. que nous finissions _____

3. qu'il vendît _____

4. que nous tombassions _____

5. qu'on entendît _____

6. que tu perdisses _____

7. qu'ils chantassent _____

8. que vous punissiez _____

9. qu'elles dansassent _____

10. que j'ajoutasse _____

11. qu'ils choisissent _____

12. que je répondisse _____

17 · Reflexive verbs

In reflexive verbs (which also include reciprocal verbs in the plural, as well as idiomatic pronominal verbs), the action is considered to be performed by the subject on itself. Hence, the required use of object pronouns (reflexive pronouns) that reflect (i.e., are identical to) the subject of the verb.

<u>se</u> <u>laver</u> (to wash oneself)

present indicative

je <u>me</u> lave	(I wash [am washing] myself)
tu <u>te</u> laves	(you [fam.] wash yourself)
il/elle/on <u>se</u> lave	(he/she washes him/herself, we wash ourselves, people wash themselves, one washes oneself)
nous <u>nous</u> lavons	(we wash ourselves)
vous <u>vous</u> lavez	(you wash yourself/selves)
ils/elles <u>se</u> lavent	(they wash themselves)

imperative

Lave-<u>toi</u>!	(Wash yourself!)
Lavons-<u>nous</u>!	(Let's wash [ourselves]!)
Lavez-<u>vous</u>!	(Wash yourself/selves!)

Note the following:

1. The **e** of **me, te, se** is dropped when the word after it begins with a vowel or a silent (mute) **h** (elision).

Il <u>s'arrête</u> au feu rouge.	(He stops at the red light.)
Je <u>m'habille</u> tôt.	(I get dressed early.)

2. **Toi** is used instead of **te** in the imperative affirmative of the familiar form.

   Lave-<u>toi</u>! (Wash yourself!)   Dépêche-<u>toi</u>! (Hurry up!)

3. The verb **être** is used as the auxiliary with reflexive and all other pronominal verbs.

Je <u>me</u> <u>suis</u> <u>lavé</u>.	(I washed myself.)
Il <u>s'est</u> <u>marié</u>.	(He got married.)
Le prof <u>s'est</u> <u>rappelé</u> mon nom.	(The teacher remembered my name.)

Agreement of the past participle

With reflexive verbs in compound tenses, the past participle agrees in gender and in number with the preceding direct object (and therefore also with the subject of the verb).

<u>Je</u> <u>me</u> suis <u>lavé</u>.	(I washed myself = a man is writing this.)
<u>Je</u> <u>me</u> suis <u>lavée</u>.	(I washed myself = a woman is writing this.)
<u>Les</u> <u>enfants</u> <u>se</u> sont <u>lavés</u>.	(The children [mixed group] washed themselves.)

The reflexive pronoun is used as a direct object (preceding the verb), except in sentences where a following direct object comes to replace it:

Marianne <u>s'est</u> <u>lavé</u> <u>les</u> <u>cheveux</u>.	(Marianne washed her hair.)
Nous <u>nous</u> sommes <u>brossé</u> <u>les</u> <u>dents</u>.	(We brushed our teeth.)

In the two examples above, **les cheveux** and **les dents** (following the verbs) are the direct objects of the action; therefore, **se (s')** and **nous** become the indirect objects of the verb and there is no agreement of the past participle.

some common reflexive and pronominal verbs

s'amuser (to enjoy oneself)

s'appeler (to be named)

s'approcher (to approach)

s'arrêter (to stop)

s'asseoir[2] (to sit down)

se battre (to fight)

se coucher (to go to bed)

se dépêcher (to hurry)

s'en aller (to go away)

s'endormir (to go to sleep)

s'ennuyer (to get bored)

se fâcher (to get angry)

s'habiller (to get dressed)

se laver (to wash [oneself])

se lever (to get/stand up)

se marier (to get married)

se promener (to take a walk)

se rappeler (to recall/remember)

se reposer (to [take a] rest)

se réveiller (to wake up)

se souvenir de (to remember)

se taire (to be silent/quiet)

se tromper (to make a mistake/be wrong)

se trouver (to be [present]; to find oneself)

Exercise 26

Conjugate the verb **se coucher** in the present tense.

1. je _____

2. tu _____

3. il/elle/on _____

4. nous _____

5. vous _____

6. ils/elles _____

---

2. See Part 2 and the verb indexes at the back of the book for the conjugation of irregular verbs such as **s'asseoir, se battre, s'en aller, s'endormir, se souvenir de,** and **se taire** and for listings of other reflexive verbs.

Exercise 27

Conjugate the verb **s'habiller** in the future tense.

1. je _____
2. tu _____
3. il/elle/on _____
4. nous _____
5. vous _____
6. ils/elles _____

Exercise 28

Conjugate the verb **se promener** in the imperfect indicative tense.

1. je _____
2. tu _____
3. il/elle/on _____
4. nous _____
5. vous _____
6. ils/elles _____

Exercise 29

Conjugate the verb **s'amuser** in the **passé composé.** Give both the masculine and feminine forms.

1. je _____
2. je _____
3. tu _____
4. tu _____
5. il _____
6. elle _____
7. nous _____
8. nous _____
9. vous _____

10. vous _____

11. ils _____

12. elles _____

Exercise 30

Conjugate the verb **se lever** in the **passé simple**.

1. je _____

2. tu _____

3. il/elle/on _____

4. nous _____

5. vous _____

6. ils/elles _____

Exercise 31

Conjugate the verb **se tromper** in the present subjunctive.

1. que je _____

2. que tu _____

3. qu'il/qu'elle/qu'on _____

4. que nous _____

5. que vous _____

6. qu'ils/qu'elles _____

Review

Exercise 32

Translate the following phrases and sentences into English.

1. Je fus... _____

2. Nous parlions. _____

3. Il faut que... _____

4. Vous dîniez. _____

5. Ils ont invité... _____

6. Elles aimeraient... _____

7. Nous sommes entrés. _____

8. Pour que vous soyez... _____

9. Nous parlâmes. _____

10. Elles ont obéi. _____

11. Vous êtes descendus. _____

12. Ils répondirent. _____

13. Je remplissais... _____

14. Il pleuvait. _____

15. Elles arriveraient. _____

16. Nous avons faim. _____

17. Il est en train de dîner. _____

18. J'aurais honte. _____

19. Ils s'amusèrent. _____

20. Nous nous sommes dépêchés. _____

21. Aidez-moi! _____

22. Ils sont tombés. _____

23. Vous vous arrêterez. _____

24. Reposez-vous! _____

25. Afin que nous parlions... _____

26. Il eut... _____

27. Réveille-toi! _____

28. Nous partions. _____

29. On vend... _____

30. Nous n'attendrons pas. _____

31. Je choisis... _____

32. Il perdit. _____

33. Je vendis... _____

34. Ils auraient... _____

35. Nous donnons... _____

36. Il s'habillera. _____

37. Nous nous lavions. _____

38. Ils perdirent. _____

39. Il y avait... _____

40. Elles arrivent. _____

41. Elles ont aimé... _____

42. On vendra... _____

43. Nous nous promenions. _____

44. Ils se marieront. _____

45. Donnez-moi... ! _____

46. Partons! _____

47. En descendant... _____

48. Afin qu'il soit... _____

49. Vous restiez... _____

50. Ils ont fini. _____

Exercise 33

Translate the underlined words and phrases into English, and try to get the gist of the rest of the quotation.

1. <<Est-ce un si grand mal d'être entendu quand on parle, et de parler comme tout le monde?>> —La Bruyère

   _____

2. <<Comptons comme un pur néant tout ce qui finit.>> —Bossuet

   _____

3. <<Il ne faut pas vendre la peau de l'ours avant qu'on l'ait pris.>> —Proverbe

   _____

4. <<Aide-toi, et le ciel t'aidera.>> —Proverbe

   _____

5. <<La cigale <u>ayant</u> chanté tout l'été <u>se</u> <u>trouva</u> fort dépourvue quand la bise fut venue.>>
    —La Fontaine

    _____

6. <<<u>Il</u> <u>n'est</u> <u>pas</u> <u>donné</u> à l'homme de porter plus loin la vertu que Saint Louis.>> —Voltaire

    _____

7. <<Il <u>coûte</u> si peu aux grands à ne donner que des paroles.>> —La Bruyère

    _____

8. <<Combien tout ce que l'on dit est loin de <u>ce</u> <u>qu'on</u> <u>pense</u>.>> —Racine

    _____

9. <<Alexandre <u>pleura</u> de n'avoir point d'Homère.>> —Delille

    _____

10. <<<u>Sortant</u> d'un embarras <u>pour</u> <u>entrer</u> dans un autre.>> —Molière

    _____

11. <<Tout vous <u>a</u> <u>réussi</u>.>> —Racine

    _____

12. <<Un peuple libre <u>obéit</u>, mais il ne sert pas; il a des chefs et non des maîtres.>>
    —Jean-Jacques Rousseau

    _____

13. <<<u>Ne</u> <u>forçons</u> <u>point</u> notre talent.>> —La Fontaine

    _____

14. <<Et le cri de son peuple <u>est</u> <u>monté</u> jusqu'à lui.>> —Racine

    _____

15. <<<u>Levez-vous</u> vite orages désirés, qui devez emporter René dans les espaces enchantés.>>
    —Chateaubriand

    _____

16. <<J'ai <u>tendu</u> des cordes de clocher à clocher; des guirlandes de fenêtre à fenêtre; des chaînes
    d'or d'étoile à étoile, et je danse.>> —Rimbaud

    _____

    _____

17. <<On lui avait demandé s'il dansait bien, et il avait répondu avec confiance, qui donna envie de trouver qu'il dansait mal.>> —Saint-Simon

_____

_____

18. <<Il y a folie à tout âge.>> —Proverbe

_____

19. <<Mais il arriva que le petit prince, ayant longtemps marché à travers les sables, les rocs et les neiges, découvrit enfin une route. Et les routes vont toujours chez les hommes.>> —Antoine de Saint-Exupéry

_____

_____

20. <<Il se passa toute une année avant que je consentisse à revoir Gaston. [...] Puisque je ne voulais pas de lui, il fallait qu'il m'eût.>> —Elsa Triolet

_____

_____

18 • -Cer verbs that change -c- into -ç-

Verbs ending in **-cer** change **-c-** to **-ç-** before **-a-** or **-o-** in the ending to retain the soft **s** sound. Note that this change only occurs in tenses that have forms with **-a-** or **-o-** at the beginning of verb endings.

commencer (to begin)

present	*imperfect*	*passé simple*
je commence	je commençais	je commençai
tu commences	tu commençais	tu commenças
il/elle/on commence	il/elle/on commençait	il/elle/on commença
nous commençons	nous commencions	nous commençâmes
vous commencez	vous commenciez	vous commençâtes
ils/elles commencent	ils/elles commençaient	ils/elles commencèrent

other verbs like <u>commencer</u>

annoncer (to announce)

avancer (to advance)

forcer (to force)

lancer (to throw, to launch)

menacer (to threaten)

percer (to pierce)

placer (to place)

prononcer (to pronounce)

recommencer (to begin again)

remplacer (to replace)

renoncer (to renounce, give up)

19 • <u>-Ger</u> verbs that add a mute <u>-e-</u>

Verbs ending in **-ger** add a mute **-e-** before an **-a-** or an **-o-**, to retain the soft **g** sound. Note that this change only occurs in tenses that have forms with **-a-** or **-o-** at the beginning of verb endings.

<u>changer</u> (to change)

present	*imperfect*	*passé simple*
je change	je changeais	je changeai
tu changes	tu changeais	tu changeas
il/elle/on change	il/elle/on changeait	il/elle/on changea
nous changeons	nous changions	nous changeâmes
vous changez	vous changiez	vous changeâtes
ils/elles changent	ils/elles changeaient	ils/elles changèrent

other verbs like <u>changer</u>

arranger (to arrange)

bouger (to move)

corriger (to correct)

diriger (to direct)

échanger (to exchange)

forger (to forge)

interroger (to interrogate)

juger (to judge)

loger (to live [somewhere])
manger (to eat)
nager (to swim)
neiger (to snow)
partager (to share)
ranger (to put away)
songer (to dream, to think of)
voyager (to travel)

20 · Verbs with a mute -e- that changes into -è-

Verbs with a mute -e- in the syllable before the infinitive ending change the mute -e- to -è- in forms where the syllable following contains a mute -e-.

acheter (to buy)

present	*imperfect*	*future*
j'achète	j'achetais	j'achèterai
tu achètes	tu achetais	tu achèteras
il/elle/on achète	il/elle/on achetait	il/elle/on achètera
nous achetons	nous achetions	nous achèterons
vous achetez	vous achetiez	vous achèterez
ils/elles achètent	ils/elles achetaient	ils/elles achèteront

other verbs like acheter
achever (to finish)
amener (to bring)
élever (to erect; to raise)
emmener (to lead away)
enlever (to remove, to take off)
geler (to freeze)
lever (to raise, to lift)
mener (to lead)
peser (to weigh)
se promener (to take a walk)
se soulever (to raise [oneself] up)

21 · Verbs with an -é- that changes into -è-

Verbs with an -é- in the last syllable before the infinitive ending change the -é- to -è- when that syllable is stressed. Note that these verbs retain the -é- in the future and conditional.

espérer (to hope)

present	*imperfect*	*future*
j'espère	j'espérais	j'espérerai
tu espères	tu espérais	tu espéreras
il/elle/on espère	il/elle/on espérait	il/elle/on espérera
nous espérons	nous espérions	nous espérerons
vous espérez	vous espériez	vous espérerez
ils/elles espèrent	ils/elles espéraient	ils/elles espéreront

other verbs like espérer

céder (to yield, give in)
célébrer (to celebrate)
compléter (to complete)
considérer (to consider)
exagérer (to exaggerate)
inquiéter (to worry)
posséder (to possess)
préférer (to prefer)
répéter (to repeat)
sécher (to dry)
suggérer (to suggest)

22 · Verbs ending in -yer that change -y- into -i-

Verbs ending in -yer change -y- into -i- before -e.

envoyer (to send)	*ennuyer (to annoy, bore)*
present	
j'envoie	j'ennuie
tu envoies	tu ennuies

il/elle/on envoie
nous envoyons
vous envoyez
ils/elles envoient

il/elle/on ennuie
nous ennuyons
vous ennuyez
ils/elles ennuient

other verbs like envoyer and ennuyer
aboyer (to bark)
appuyer (to lean; to bear, support)
employer (to use)
essayer (to try)
essuyer (to wipe)
nettoyer (to clean)
payer (to pay)

23 • Verbs ending in -eler or -eter that double the consonant

Verbs ending in **-eler** or **-eter** double the consonant when the next syllable contains a mute **e.**

appeler (to call)

present indicative
j'appelle
tu appelles
il/elle/on appelle
nous appelons
vous appelez
ils/elles appellent

future
j'appellerai
tu appelleras
il/elle/on appellera
nous appellerons
vous appellerez
ils/elles appelleront

jeter (to throw [away])

present indicative
je jette
tu jettes
il/elle/on jette
nous jetons
vous jetez
ils/elles jettent

future
je jetterai
tu jetteras
il/elle/on jettera
nous jetterons
vous jetterez
ils/elles jetteront

other verbs like <u>appeler</u> and <u>jeter</u>

épeler (to spell)

projeter (to project; to plan)

rappeler (to recall, remember)

renouveler (to renew, renovate)

Exercise 34

Give the present indicative form of the verbs in parentheses, using the subject given.

1. nous (placer) _____

2. je (geler) _____

3. il (acheter) _____

4. vous (préférer) _____

5. tu (céder) _____

6. vous (envoyer) _____

7. il (aboyer) _____

8. elles (nettoyer) _____

9. nous (épeler) _____

10. elle (rappeler) _____

11. je (céder) _____

12. nous (célébrer) _____

13. ils (répéter) _____

14. vous (mener) _____

15. tu (achever) _____

16. nous (nager) _____

17. vous (voyager) _____

18. nous (échanger) _____

19. elle (suggérer) _____

20. je (bouger) _____

Exercise 35

Give the past imperfect (indicative) form of the verbs in parentheses, using the subjects given.

1. je (partager) _____
2. nous (voyager) _____
3. elles (prononcer) _____
4. tu (avancer) _____
5. on (appeler) _____
6. vous (commencer) _____
7. tu (annoncer) _____
8. vous (bouger) _____
9. ils (diriger) _____
10. il (élever) _____
11. elles (appeler) _____
12. vous (suggérer) _____
13. nous (amener) _____
14. vous (interroger) _____
15. ils (loger) _____
16. nous (songer) _____
17. tu (manger) _____
18. il (neiger) _____
19. je/j' (arranger) _____
20. elle (voyager) _____

Exercise 36

Write the following verbs in the tense or mood indicated in parentheses.

1. (present) commencer, je/j'_____
2. (future) acheter, on _____
3. (past imperfect [indicative]) corriger, elle _____
4. (passé simple) juger, je/j'_____
5. (future) menacer, il _____

6. (past imperfect [indicative]) interroger, vous _____

7. (passé simple) songer, nous _____

8. (present) posséder, on _____

9. (present) ennuyer, je/j' _____

10. (present) jeter, tu _____

11. (future) renouveler, nous _____

12. (past imperfect [indicative]) interroger, elles _____

13. (passé simple) voyager, nous _____

14. (future) céder, je/j' _____

15. (past imperfect [indicative]) projeter, nous _____

16. (present) envoyer, nous _____

17. (present) appuyer, il _____

18. (past imperfect [indicative]) appeler, elle _____

19. (passé simple) neiger, il _____

20. (past imperfect [indicative]) avancer, ils _____

24 • Être and avoir (all tenses)

infinitive	être (to be)	avoir (to have)
present participle	étant	ayant
past participle	été	eu
present indicative	je suis	j'ai
	tu es	tu as
	il/elle/on est	il/elle/on a
	nous sommes	nous avons
	vous êtes	vous avez
	ils/elles sont	ils/elles ont
future	je serai	j'aurai
	tu seras	tu auras
	il/elle/on sera	il/elle/on aura
	nous serons	nous aurons
	vous serez	vous aurez
	ils/elles seront	ils/elles auront

conditional	je serais	j'aurais
	tu serais	tu aurais
	il/elle/on serait	il/elle/on aurait
	nous serions	nous aurions
	vous seriez	vous auriez
	ils/elles seraient	ils/elles auraient
past imperfect (indicative)	j'étais	j'avais
	tu étais	tu avais
	il/elle/on était	il/elle/on avait
	nous étions	nous avions
	vous étiez	vous aviez
	ils/elles étaient	ils/elles avaient
passé composé	j'ai été	j'ai eu
	tu as été	tu as eu
	il/elle/on a été	il/elle/on a eu
	nous avons été	nous avons eu
	vous avez été	vous avez eu
	ils/elles ont été	ils/elles ont eu
passé simple	je fus	j'eus
	tu fus	tu eus
	il/elle/on fut	il/elle/on eut
	nous fûmes	nous eûmes
	vous fûtes	vous eûtes
	ils/elles furent	ils/elles eurent
present subjunctive	que je sois	que j'aie
	que tu sois	que tu aies
	qu'il/elle/on soit	qu'il/elle/on ait
	que nous soyons	que nous ayons
	que vous soyez	que vous ayez
	qu'ils/elles soient	qu'ils/elles aient
imperfect subjunctive	que je fusse	que j'eusse
	que tu fusses	que tu eusses
	qu'il/elle/on fût	qu'il/elle/on eût
	que nous fussions	que nous eussions
	que vous fussiez	que vous eussiez
	qu'ils/elles fussent	qu'ils/elles eussent
imperative	sois!	aie!
	soyons!	ayons!
	soyez!	ayez!

Exercise 37

Conjugate the verb **être** in the **passé simple**.

1. je/j'_____
2. tu _____
3. il/elle/on _____
4. nous _____
5. vous _____
6. ils/elles _____

Exercise 38

Conjugate the verb **avoir** in the **passé simple**.

1. je/j'_____
2. tu _____
3. il/elle/on _____
4. nous _____
5. vous _____
6. ils/elles _____

Exercise 39

Conjugate the verb **être** in the present subjunctive.

1. que je/j'_____
2. que tu _____
3. qu'il/elle/on _____
4. que nous _____
5. que vous _____
6. qu'ils/elles _____

Exercise 40

Conjugate the verb **avoir** in the present subjunctive.

1. que je/j' _____

2. que tu _____

3. qu'il/elle/on _____

4. que nous _____

5. que vous _____

6. qu'ils/elles _____

Exercise 41

Translate the following phrases into French.

1. I was _____

2. I had _____

3. you have been _____

4. he has had _____

5. we have been _____

6. she used to have _____

7. I shall be _____

8. you will have _____

9. I would have _____

10. let us be _____

11. they were having _____

12. being _____

13. that I may be _____

14. that you may have _____

15. that you might be _____

16. they will be _____

17. that we might have _____

18. she used to be _____

19. he had _____

20. we have had _____

25 • Compound tenses with <u>avoir</u>

Compound tenses are formed, as in English, by combining various tenses of the auxiliary verbs **avoir** and **être** with the past participle; the **passé composé** (see Section 12) is one such compound tense, formed with the present tense of the auxiliary verbs.

past infinitive	avoir parlé	(to have spoken)
participle <u>passé</u> <u>composé</u>	ayant parlé	(having spoken)
<u>passé</u> <u>composé</u>	j'ai parlé	(I have spoken, I spoke)
	tu as parlé	
	il/elle/on a parlé	
	nous avons parlé	
	vous avez parlé	
	ils/elles ont parlé	
pluperfect indicative	j'avais parlé	(I had spoken)
	tu avais parlé	
	il/elle/on avait parlé	
	nous avions parlé	
	vous aviez parlé	
	ils/elles avaient parlé	
past perfect indicative (literary)	j'eus parlé	(I had spoken)
	tu eus parlé	
	il/elle/on eut parlé	
	nous eûmes parlé	
	vous eûtes parlé	
	ils/elles eurent parlé	
future perfect	j'aurai parlé	(I will have spoken)
	tu auras parlé	
	il/elle/on aura parlé	
	nous aurons parlé	
	vous aurez parlé	
	ils/elles auront parlé	
conditional perfect	j'aurais parlé	(I would have spoken)
	tu aurais parlé	
	il/elle/on aurait parlé	
	nous aurions parlé	
	vous auriez parlé	
	ils/elles auraient parlé	

past (perfect) subjunctive	que j'aie parlé	(that I [may] have spoken, that I spoke)
	que tu aies parlé	
	qu'il/elle/on ait parlé	
	que nous ayons parlé	
	que vous ayez parlé	
	qu'ils/elles aient parlé	
pluperfect subjunctive (literary)	que j'eusse parlé	(that I [might] have spoken)
	que tu eusses parlé	
	qu'il/elle/on eût parlé	
	que nous eussions parlé	
	que vous eussiez parlé	
	qu'ils/elles eussent parlé	

26 · Compound tenses with ĕtre

Remember that the past participle usually agrees in gender and number with the subject of verbs conjugated with **être**.

past infinitive	être arrivé(e)(s)	(to have arrived)
participle passé composé	étant arrivé(e)(s)	(having arrived)
passé composé	je suis arrivé(e)	(I have arrived, I arrived)
	tu es arrivé(e)	
	il est arrivé	
	elle est arrivée	
	on est arrivé	
	nous sommes arrivé(e)s	
	vous êtes arrivé(e)(s)	
	ils sont arrivés	
	elles sont arrivées	
pluperfect indicative	j'étais arrivé(e)	(I had arrived)
	tu étais arrivé(e)	
	il était arrivé	
	elle était arrivée	
	on était arrivé	
	nous étions arrivé(e)s	
	vous étiez arrivé(e)(s)	

	ils étaient arrivés	
	elles étaient arrivées	
past perfect indicative *(literary)*	je fus arrivé(e)	(I had arrived)
	tu fus arrivé(e)	
	il fut arrivé	
	elle fut arrivée	
	on fut arrivé	
	nous fûmes arrivé(e)s	
	vous fûtes arrivé(e)(s)	
	ils furent arrivés	
	elles furent arrivées	
future perfect	je serai arrivé(e)	(I will have arrived)
	tu seras arrivé(e)	
	il sera arrivé	
	elle sera arrivée	
	on sera arrivé	
	nous serons arrivé(e)s	
	vous serez arrivé(e)(s)	
	ils seront arrivés	
	elles seront arrivées	
conditional perfect	je serais arrivé(e)	(I would have arrived)
	tu serais arrivé(e)	
	il serait arrivé	
	elle serait arrivée	
	on serait arrivé	
	nous serions arrivé(e)s	
	vous seriez arrivé(e)(s)	
	ils seraient arrivés	
	elles seraient arrivées	
perfect subjunctive	que je sois arrivé(e)	(that I [may] have arrived)
	que tu sois arrivé(e)	
	qu'il soit arrivé	
	qu'elle soit arrivée	
	qu'on soit arrivé	
	que nous soyons arrivé(e)s	
	que vous soyez arrivé(e)(s)	
	qu'ils soient arrivés	
	qu'elles soient arrivées	

pluperfect subjunctive *(literary)*	que je fusse arrivé(e)	(that I [might] have arrived)
	que tu fusses arrivé(e)	
	qu'il fût arrivé	
	qu'elle fût arrivée	
	qu'on fût arrivé	
	que nous fussions arrivé(e)s	
	que vous fussiez arrivé(e)(s)	
	qu'ils fussent arrivés	
	qu'elles fussent arrivées	

Exercise 42

Translate the following phrases and sentences into English.

1. j'avais admiré _____

2. il aurait aimé _____

3. elle a étudié _____

4. j'aurais fini _____

5. nous avons joué _____

6. nous avons perdu _____

7. tu auras trouvé _____

8. on eut donné _____

9. elle eût donné _____

10. nous eussions espéré _____

11. vous seriez arrivé _____

12. je suis allée _____

13. j'étais arrivé _____

14. j'ai été _____

15. tu avais attendu _____

16. Elles s'étaient trompées. _____

17. ils auraient déclaré _____

18. Ils s'étaient arrêtés. _____

19. Il faut que vous étudiiez. _____

20. Nous nous sommes dépêchés. _____

Exercise 43

Translate the following phrases and sentences into French.

1. You would have gone down. _____

2. He will sell. _____

3. we might have bought _____

4. We had slept. _____

5. One would have heard. _____

6. you had hoped _____

7. She had arrived. _____

8. I was coming down. _____

9. he had said _____

10. We would have studied. _____

11. I have had _____

12. we have been _____

13. You will have finished. _____

14. They (f.) would have gotten up. _____

15. I will have waited _____

16. he would have arrived _____

17. I (m.) had arrived. _____

18. You (fam.) had waited. _____

19. You (polite) would have waited. _____

20. She said that he might have spoken. _____

27 • Passive voice

In the active voice, the subject of the verb performs the action, while in the passive voice, it receives the action.

> *active voice*
>
> <u>Le prof</u> <u>enseigne</u> ce cours.   (The instructor teaches this course.)

passive voice

Ce cours <u>est</u> <u>enseigné</u> (par le professeur).

(This course is taught [by the instructor]).

The passive voice is formed by combining the past participle of a verb with a conjugated form of the verb **être.** It is used in all the verb tenses. Note that in the passive voice the past participle behaves like an adjective, that is, it agrees in gender and number with the subject of **être.**

Ce prof <u>est</u> <u>aimé</u> de tous ses étudiants.	(This professor is liked by all his students.)
Ces cafés <u>étaient</u> beaucoup <u>fréquentés</u> du temps des existentialistes.	(These cafés were very popular [frequented] in the time of the existentialists.)
Cette pièce de théâtre <u>a</u> <u>été</u> <u>écrite</u> en japonais.	(That play was written in Japanese.)
Ces dames <u>avaient</u> <u>été</u> <u>embauchées</u> avant le début de l'année.	(Those women had been hired before the beginning of the year.)

French has several equivalents of the passive voice that do not involve **être** + past participle. They include active verb forms with the subject **on** (*people, we, they, one*), third person verb forms with the reflexive pronoun **se,** and other active voice constructions.

<u>On</u> <u>a</u> <u>volé</u> mon auto.	(My car was stolen.)
<u>On</u> <u>a</u> <u>signé</u> le traité de paix.	(The peace treaty was signed.)
<u>On</u> <u>vend</u> des livres dans les librairies. (Les livres <u>se</u> <u>vendent</u> dans les librairies.)	(Books are sold in bookstores.)
Ici, <u>on</u> <u>parle</u> français. (Le français <u>se</u> <u>parle</u> ici.)	(French is spoken here.)
Ce journal <u>se</u> <u>lit</u> beaucoup.	(This newspaper is read a lot.)
<u>Cela</u> <u>m'a</u> <u>fait</u> <u>plaisir.</u>	(I was pleased.)

Exercise 44

Translate the following sentences into English.

1. On a corrigé les erreurs.

   _____

2. La fenêtre est ouverte.

   _____

3. Il a été dit beaucoup de choses.

   _____

4. Ce livre se vend dans toutes les librairies.

   _____

5. En France, on va au bureau de poste pour payer ses factures.

   _____

6. Le sénateur est accompagné de sa femme.

   _____

7. La maison sera construite cette année.

   _____

8. On a signé un armistice.

   _____

9. On a terminé la guerre.

   _____

10. Cela a été décidé hier.

   _____

Part 2

Irregular Verbs

28 · Vouloir, pouvoir, savoir

infinitive	vouloir	pouvoir	savoir
	(to wish, want)	(to be able, can)	(to know)
present participle	voulant	pouvant	sachant
past participle	voulu	pu	su
present indicative	je veux	je peux	je sais
	tu veux	tu peux	tu sais
	il/elle/on veut	il/elle/on peut	il/elle/on sait
	nous voulons	nous pouvons	nous savons
	vous voulez	vous pouvez	vous savez
	ils/elles veulent	ils/elles peuvent	ils/elles savent
imperfect indicative	je voulais	je pouvais	je savais
	tu voulais	tu pouvais	tu savais
	il/elle/on voulait	il/elle/on pouvait	il/elle/on savait
	nous voulions	nous pouvions	nous savions
	vous vouliez	vous pouviez	vous saviez
	ils/elles voulaient	ils/elles pouvaient	ils/elles savaient
future	je voudrai	je pourrai	je saurai
	tu voudras	tu pourras	tu sauras
	il/elle/on voudra	il/elle/on pourra	il/elle/on saura
	nous voudrons	nous pourrons	nous saurons
	vous voudrez	vous pourrez	vous saurez
	ils/elles voudront	ils/elles pourront	ils/elles sauront
conditional	je voudrais	je pourrais	je saurais
	tu voudrais	tu pourrais	tu saurais
	il/elle/on voudrait	il/elle/on pourrait	il/elle/on saurait
	nous voudrions	nous pourrions	nous saurions
	vous voudriez	vous pourriez	vous sauriez
	ils/elles voudraient	ils/elles pourraient	ils/elles sauraient

passé simple (literary)	je voulus	je pus	je sus
	tu voulus	tu pus	tu sus
	il/elle/on voulut	il/elle/on put	il/elle/on sut
	nous voulûmes	nous pûmes	nous sûmes
	vous voulûtes	vous pûtes	vous sûtes
	ils/elles voulurent	ils/elles purent	ils/elles surent
passé composé	j'ai voulu	j'ai pu	j'ai su
	tu as voulu	tu as pu	tu as su
	il/elle/on a voulu	il/elle/on a pu	il/elle/on a su
	nous avons voulu	nous avons pu	nous avons su
	vous avez voulu	vous avez pu	vous avez su
	ils/elles ont voulu	ils/elles ont pu	ils/elles ont su
present subjunctive	que je veuille	que je puisse	que je sache
	que tu veuilles	que tu puisses	que tu saches
	qu'il/elle/on veuille	qu'il/elle/on puisse	qu'il/elle/on sache
	que nous voulions	que nous puissions	que nous sachions
	que vous vouliez	que vous puissiez	que vous sachiez
	qu'ils/elles veuillent	qu'ils/elles puissent	qu'ils/elles sachent
imperfect subjunctive (literary)	que je voulusse	que je pusse	que je susse
	que tu voulusses	que tu pusses	que tu susses
	qu'il/elle/on voulût	qu'il/elle/on pût	qu'il/elle/on sût
	que nous voulussions	que nous pussions	que nous sussions
	que vous voulussiez	que vous pussiez	que vous sussiez
	qu'ils/elles voulussent	qu'ils/elles pussent	qu'ils/elles sussent
imperative	veuille!¹	(imperative of pouvoir not used)	sache!
	veuillons!		sachons!
	veuillez!		sachez!

There are two forms of the first person singular of **pouvoir: je peux** and **je puis.**

Puis-je entrer?   (May I come in?)
Est-ce que je peux entrer?   (May I come in?)

_____

1. Note that the imperative forms of **vouloir** are used only in very formal situations.

The present tense of **pouvoir** is often translated as *I can.*

<u>Pouvez-vous</u> (<u>Pourriez-vous</u>) me   (Can you [Could you] lend me a euro?)
    prêter un euro?

Exercise 45

Complete each sentence with the present tense of the verb in parentheses.

1. (pouvoir) Vous _____ entrer.

2. (vouloir) _____ -vous du sucre?

3. (pouvoir) _____ -je entrer?

4. (savoir) Je/J' _____ ma leçon.

5. (savoir) Ils ne _____ pas danser.

6. (vouloir) Je/J' _____ de l'eau.

7. (pouvoir) Il _____ écrire au président.

8. (savoir) Elle le _____ .

9. (pouvoir) Nous _____ nous reposer demain.

10. (savoir) Tu _____ jouer au tennis.

11. (vouloir) Elles _____ aller au cinéma.

Exercise 46

Translate the following phrases into French.

1. I want _____

2. I can _____

3. he knew _____

4. we used to know _____

5. I have been able _____

6. we could _____

7. she would like to _____

8. I shall know _____

9. we have known _____

10. he was able _____

Exercise 47

Translate the following phrases into English.

1. je veux _____
2. elle pouvait _____
3. nous saurons _____
4. il put _____
5. qu'elle sût _____
6. nous voulions _____
7. on saurait _____
8. nous sûmes _____
9. elles ont pu _____
10. vous voulûtes _____
11. puis-je? _____
12. je sais _____
13. sache! _____
14. ils peuvent _____
15. nous voudrions _____
16. qu'elle veuille _____
17. que nous puissions _____
18. que vous sussiez _____
19. tu as su _____
20. pouvant _____

29 • Dormir, prendre, ouvrir

infinitive	dormir	prendre	ouvrir
	(to sleep)	(to take)	(to open)
present participle	dormant	prenant	ouvrant
past participle	dormi	pris	ouvert

present indicative	je dors	je prends	j'ouvre
	tu dors	tu prends	tu ouvres
	il/elle/on dort	il/elle/on prend	il/elle/on ouvre
	nous dormons	nous prenons	nous ouvrons
	vous dormez	vous prenez	vous ouvrez
	ils/elles dorment	ils/elles prennent	ils/elles ouvrent
imperfect indicative	je dormais	je prenais	j'ouvrais
	tu dormais	tu prenais	tu ouvrais
	il/elle/on dormait	il/elle/on prenait	il/elle/on ouvrait
	nous dormions	nous prenions	nous ouvrions
	vous dormiez	vous preniez	vous ouvriez
	ils/elles dormaient	ils/elles prenaient	ils/elles ouvraient
future	je dormirai	je prendrai	j'ouvrirai
	tu dormiras	tu prendras	tu ouvriras
	il/elle/on dormira	il/elle/on prendra	il/elle/on ouvrira
	nous dormirons	nous prendrons	nous ouvrirons
	vous dormirez	vous prendrez	vous ouvrirez
	ils/elles dormiront	ils/elles prendront	ils/elles ouvriront
conditional	je dormirais	je prendrais	j'ouvrirais
	tu dormirais	tu prendrais	tu ouvrirais
	il/elle/on dormirait	il/elle/on prendrait	il/elle/on ouvrirait
	nous dormirions	nous prendrions	nous ouvririons
	vous dormiriez	vous prendriez	vous ouvririez
	ils/elles dormiraient	ils/elles prendraient	ils/elles ouvriraient
passé simple (literary)	je dormis	je pris	j'ouvris
	tu dormis	tu pris	tu ouvris
	il/elle/on dormit	il/elle/on prit	il/elle/on ouvrit
	nous dormîmes	nous prîmes	nous ouvrîmes
	vous dormîtes	vous prîtes	vous ouvrîtes
	ils/elles dormirent	ils/elles prirent	ils/elles ouvrirent
passé composé	j'ai dormi	j'ai pris	j'ai ouvert
	tu as dormi	tu as pris	tu as ouvert
	il/elle/on a dormi	il/elle/on a pris	il/elle/on a ouvert
	nous avons dormi	nous avons pris	nous avons ouvert
	vous avez dormi	vous avez pris	vous avez ouvert
	ils/elles ont dormi	ils/elles ont pris	ils/elles ont ouvert
present subjunctive	que je dorme	que je prenne	que j'ouvre
	que tu dormes	que tu prennes	que tu ouvres
	qu'il/elle/on dorme	qu'il/elle/on prenne	qu'il/elle/on ouvre

	que nous dormions	que nous prenions	que nous ouvrions
	que vous dormiez	que vous preniez	que vous ouvriez
	qu'ils/elles dorment	qu'ils/elles prennent	qu'ils/elles ouvrent
imperfect subjunctive *(literary)*	que je dormisse	que je prisse	que j'ouvrisse
	que tu dormisses	que tu prisses	que tu ouvrisses
	qu'il/elle/on dormît	qu'il/elle/on prît	qu'il/elle/on ouvrît
	que nous dormissions	que nous prissions	que nous ouvrissions
	que vous dormissiez	que vous prissiez	que vous ouvrissiez
	qu'ils/elles dormissent	qu'ils/elles prissent	qu'ils/elles ouvrissent
imperative	dors!	prends!	ouvre!
	dormons!	prenons!	ouvrons!
	dormez!	prenez!	ouvrez!

verbs conjugated like <u>dormir</u>

s'endormir (to fall asleep)

mentir (to lie)

partir (to go away)

sentir (to feel; to smell)

servir (to serve)

sortir (to go out [conjugated with **être**])

verbs conjugated like <u>prendre</u>

apprendre (to learn)

comprendre (to understand)

reprendre (to take back; to continue)

surprendre (to surprise)

verbs conjugated like <u>ouvrir</u>

couvrir (to cover)

découvrir (to discover)

offrir (to offer)

recouvrir (to cover [again])

souffrir (to suffer)

Exercise 48

Write the following verbs in the tense and person indicated.

1. present indicative

    (dormir)   je/j'_____

    (prendre)   nous _____

    (ouvrir)   elles _____

2. imperfect indicative

    (sortir)   je/j'_____

    (offrir)   il _____

    (prendre)   nous _____

    (comprendre)   vous _____

3. future

    (ouvrir)   elle _____

    (prendre)   je/j'_____

    (servir)   vous _____

    (découvrir)   ils _____

4. passé simple

    (dormir)   on _____

    (comprendre)   je/j'_____

    (offrir)   vous _____

    (recouvrir)   elles _____

5. present subjunctive

    (ouvrir)   qu'elle _____

    (prendre)   que nous _____

    (sortir)   qu'ils _____

    (apprendre)   que tu _____

6. past participle

    (sortir) _____

    (apprendre) _____

    (dormir) _____

7. imperfect subjunctive

   (apprendre)   que je/j' _____

   (dormir)   que nous _____

   (ouvrir)   qu'ils _____

Exercise 49

Translate the following phrases into English.

1. je partis _____

2. nous comprenions _____

3. vous sentirez _____

4. elle a pris _____

5. il ouvrira _____

6. j'ai découvert _____

7. elle offrirait _____

8. que nous nous comprenions _____

9. que vous dormiez _____

10. tu reprends _____

11. je dors _____

12. qu'il dormît _____

13. ouvrez! _____

14. elle surprenait _____

15. je surpris _____

16. il a compris _____

17. nous sommes sortis _____

18. elle est partie _____

19. on partit _____

20. nous offririons _____

Exercise 50

Translate the following phrases and sentences into French.

1. I am leaving. _____
2. He is sleeping. _____
3. we took _____
4. she has taken _____
5. They will understand. _____
6. They do understand. _____
7. he was serving _____
8. that one may feel _____
9. that we might go out _____
10. I shall offer _____
11. I do offer _____
12. I am taking _____
13. she took _____
14. We left. _____
15. You have gone out. _____
16. She has slept. _____
17. we feel _____
18. Go out! _____
19. Let's leave! _____
20. he opened _____

30 • Aller*², venir*, voir

infinitive	*aller*	*venir*	*voir*
	(to go)	(to come)	(to see)
present participle	allant	venant	voyant
past participle	allé	venu	vu

---

2. The asterisk (*) indicates that the verb is conjugated in compound tenses with the auxiliary verb **être.**

present indicative	je vais	je viens	je vois
	tu vas	tu viens	tu vois
	il/elle/on va	il/elle/on vient	il/elle/on voit
	nous allons	nous venons	nous voyons
	vous allez	vous venez	vous voyez
	ils/elles vont	ils/elles viennent	ils/elles voient
imperfect indicative	j'allais	je venais	je voyais
	tu allais	tu venais	tu voyais
	il/elle/on allait	il/elle/on venait	il/elle/on voyait
	nous allions	nous venions	nous voyions
	vous alliez	vous veniez	vous voyiez
	ils/elles allaient	ils/elles venaient	ils/elles voyaient
future	j'irai	je viendrai	je verrai
	tu iras	tu viendras	tu verras
	il/elle/on ira	il/elle/on viendra	il/elle/on verra
	nous irons	nous viendrons	nous verrons
	vous irez	vous viendrez	vous verrez
	ils/elles iront	ils/elles viendront	ils/elles verront
conditional	j'irais	je viendrais	je verrais
	tu irais	tu viendrais	tu verrais
	il/elle/on irait	il/elle/on viendrait	il/elle/on verrait
	nous irions	nous viendrions	nous verrions
	vous iriez	vous viendriez	vous verriez
	ils/elles iraient	ils/elles viendraient	ils/elles verraient
passé simple (literary)	j'allai	je vins	je vis
	tu allas	tu vins	tu vis
	il/elle/on alla	il/elle/on vint	il/elle/on vit
	nous allâmes	nous vînmes	nous vîmes
	vous allâtes	vous vîntes	vous vîtes
	ils/elles allèrent	ils/elles vinrent	ils/elles virent
passé composé	je suis allé(e)	je suis venu(e)	j'ai vu
	tu es allé(e)	tu es venu(e)	tu as vu
	il/elle/on est allé(e)	il/elle/on est venu(e)	il/elle/on a vu
	nous sommes allé(e)s	nous sommes venu(e)s	nous avons vu
	vous êtes allé(e)(s)	vous êtes venu(e)(s)	vous avez vu
	ils/elles sont allé(e)s	ils/elles sont venu(e)s	ils/elles ont vu

present subjunctive	que j'aille	que je vienne	que je voie
	que tu ailles	que tu viennes	que tu voies
	qu'il/elle/on aille	qu'il/elle/on vienne	qu'il/elle/on voie
	que nous allions	que nous venions	que nous voyions
	que vous alliez	que vous veniez	que vous voyiez
	qu'ils/elles aillent	qu'ils/elles viennent	qu'ils/elles voient
imperfect subjunctive (literary)	que j'allasse	que je vinsse	que je visse
	que tu allasses	que tu vinsses	que tu visses
	qu'il/elle/on allât	qu'il/elle/on vînt	qu'il/elle/on vît
	que nous allassions	que nous vinssions	que nous vissions
	que vous allassiez	que vous vinssiez	que vous vissiez
	qu'ils/elles allassent	qu'ils/elles vinssent	qu'ils/elles vissent
imperative	va!	viens!	vois!
	allons!	venons!	voyons!
	allez!	venez!	voyez!

idiomatic expressions with the verb aller

Comment allez-vous? (How are you?)

Je vais bien. (I am fine.)

Il va travailler. (He is going to work.)

Cette robe lui va bien. (This dress suits her well [fits her].)

Tu t'en vas déjà? (s'en aller) (You're leaving already?)

verbs conjugated like venir

appartenir (to belong)

convenir (to suit)

devenir* (to become)

provenir* de (to result from)

revenir* (to come back)

se souvenir* de (to remember)

verbs conjugated like voir

apercevoir (to catch sight of, notice)

prévoir (to predict)

revoir (to see [again])

Exercise 51

Write the following verbs in the tense and person indicated.

1. present indicative

   (aller) je/j' _____

   (venir) il _____

   (voir) nous _____

   (aller) vous _____

   (revenir) je/j' _____

2. past imperfect (indicative)

   (venir) je/j' _____

   (aller) tu _____

   (voir) nous _____

   (apercevoir) je/j' _____

   (devenir) vous _____

3. future

   (revoir) tu _____

   (venir) elle _____

   (aller) je/j' _____

   (voir) nous _____

   (revenir) ils _____

4. passé composé

   (voir) je/j' _____

   (aller) nous _____

   (venir) elles _____

   (revoir) nous _____

   (aller) tu _____

5. passé simple

   (aller) il _____

   (voir) je/j' _____

   (revoir) nous _____

(venir) je/j' _____

(devenir) elles _____

6. present subjunctive

(voir) que je/j' _____

(aller) qu'il _____

(venir) que nous _____

(devenir) qu'elles _____

(revoir) que vous _____

Exercise 52

Translate the following phrases and sentences into English.

1. il vit _____

2. je vois _____

3. elle allait _____

4. nous venons _____

5. je verrai _____

6. on alla _____

7. nous avons vu _____

8. nous sommes venus _____

9. je suis devenue _____

10. Allons enfants de la patrie! _____

11. Elle vient d'entrer. _____

12. Il va venir. _____

13. Venez voir. _____

14. Nous allons bien. _____

15. Ce chapeau vous va bien. _____

16. Revenez nous voir. _____

17. Voyons! _____

18. Nous irons au bois. _____

19. Il veut s'en aller à midi. _____

20. Elle reviendra à Pâques. _____

Exercise 53

Translate the following phrases and sentences into French.

1. I saw _____

2. He went to school. _____

3. We're going to learn French. _____

4. How is she? _____

5. Go see her! _____

6. we have seen _____

7. I shall return. _____

8. We used to go to France. _____

9. He will come back soon. _____

10. What has become of her? _____

11. Everything's going well. _____

12. we were seeing _____

13. she has seen _____

14. Come here! _____

15. I'm coming. _____

16. He came to class. _____

17. You (fam.) will come back. _____

18. I see. _____

19. The red coat suits her well. _____

20. It goes well with her hat. _____

Exercise 54

Give the English equivalent of the underlined French words. Then, try to get the gist of the entire quote.

1. <<Je suis venu, calme orphelin,

   Riche de mes seuls yeux tranquilles,

   Vers les hommes des grandes villes;

   Ils ne m'ont pas trouvé malin.>> —Verlaine

   _____

   _____

2. <<Vous verrez dans une seule vie toutes les extrémités des choses humaines.>> —Bossuet

    _____

3. <<Mais mon regard, peu à peu, devenait savant et apprenait à distinguer les moindres clartés. Et bientôt, très loin derrière les transparences, je vis le feu lui-même. Et je ne vis plus que le feu.>> —Nora Mitrani

    _____

    _____

4. <<Tout le monde ne sait pas voir.>> —Fontenelle

    _____

5. <<La plus grande ville que le soleil eût jamais vue.>> —Bossuet

    _____

6. <<Les grandes pensées viennent du cœur.>> —Vauvenargues

    _____

7. <<Il te vient un vrai coup sur la tête lorsque tu t'aperçois que tout cela, finalement, était une entreprise de pouvoir.>> —Dominique Desanti

    _____

8. <<Je crains que ce groupe ne vienne pas assez sur le devant.>> —Didier

    _____

9. <<Du haut de ce balcon votre malheureux frère vint tomber tout sanglant.>> —Delille

    _____

10. <<Va, je ne te hais pas.>> —Corneille

    _____

11. <<Tout ce que je fais me vient naturellement, c'est sans étude.>> —Molière

    _____

12. <<Quiconque a beaucoup vu
    Peut avoir beaucoup retenu.>> —La Fontaine

    _____

13. <<Voir au milieu de la nuit, dans le plus beau lieu du monde, une personne qu'il adorait, la voir sans qu'elle sût qu'il la voyait, et la voir tout occupée de choses qui avaient du rapport à lui... >> —Mme de La Fayette

    _____

    _____

31 • Faire, mettre, connaître

infinitive	faire	mettre	connaître
	(to do, make)	(to put)	(to know, be acquainted with)
present participle	faisant	mettant	connaissant
past participle	fait	mis	connu
present indicative	je fais	je mets	je connais
	tu fais	tu mets	tu connais
	il/elle/on fait	il/elle/on met	il/elle/on connaît
	nous faisons	nous mettons	nous connaissons
	vous faites	vous mettez	vous connaissez
	ils/elles font	ils/elles mettent	ils/elles connaissent
imperfect indicative	je faisais	je mettais	je connaissais
	tu faisais	tu mettais	tu connaissais
	il/elle/on faisait	il/elle/on mettait	il/elle/on connaissait
	nous faisions	nous mettions	nous connaissions
	vous faisiez	vous mettiez	vous connaissiez
	ils/elles faisaient	ils/elles mettaient	ils/elles connaissaient
future	je ferai	je mettrai	je connaîtrai
	tu feras	tu mettras	tu connaîtras
	il/elle/on fera	il/elle/on mettra	il/elle/on connaîtra
	nous ferons	nous mettrons	nous connaîtrons
	vous ferez	vous mettrez	vous connaîtrez
	ils/elles feront	ils/elles mettront	ils/elles connaîtront
conditional	je ferais	je mettrais	je connaîtrais
	tu ferais	tu mettrais	tu connaîtrais
	il/elle/on ferait	il/elle/on mettrait	il/elle/on connaîtrait
	nous ferions	nous mettrions	nous connaîtrions
	vous feriez	vous mettriez	vous connaîtriez
	ils/elles feraient	ils/elles mettraient	ils/elles connaîtraient
passé simple (literary)	je fis	je mis	je connus
	tu fis	tu mis	tu connus
	il/elle/on fit	il/elle/on mit	il/elle/on connut
	nous fîmes	nous mîmes	nous connûmes
	vous fîtes	vous mîtes	vous connûtes
	ils/elles firent	ils/elles mirent	ils/elles connurent

passé composé	j'ai fait	j'ai mis	j'ai connu
	tu as fait	tu as mis	tu as connu
	il/elle/on a fait	il/elle/on a mis	il/elle/on a connu
	nous avons fait	nous avons mis	nous avons connu
	vous avez fait	vous avez mis	vous avez connu
	ils/elles ont fait	ils/elles ont mis	ils/elles ont connu
present subjunctive	que je fasse	que je mette	que je connaisse
	que tu fasses	que tu mettes	que tu connaisses
	qu'il/elle/on fasse	qu'il/elle/on mette	qu'il/elle/on connaisse
	que nous fassions	que nous mettions	que nous connaissions
	que vous fassiez	que vous mettiez	que vous connaissiez
	qu'ils/elles fassent	qu'ils/elles mettent	qu'ils/elles connaissent
imperfect subjunctive (literary)	que je fisse	que je misse	que je connusse
	que tu fisses	que tu misses	que tu connusses
	qu'il/elle/on fît	qu'il/elle/on mît	qu'il/elle/on connût
	que nous fissions	que nous missions	que nous connussions
	que vous fissiez	que vous missiez	que vous connussiez
	qu'ils/elles fissent	qu'ils/elles missent	qu'ils/elles connussent
imperative	fais!	mets!	connais!
	faisons!	mettons!	connaissons!
	faites!	mettez!	connaissez!

verb conjugated like <u>faire</u>
satisfaire (to satisfy)

verbs conjugated like <u>mettre</u>
commettre (to commit)
se mettre à (to begin, start)
permettre (to allow)
promettre (to promise)
remettre (to put back; to postpone)

verbs conjugated like <u>connaître</u>
apparaître (to appear)
disparaître (to disappear)
paraître (to seem)
reconnaître (to recognize)

Idiomatic uses of <u>faire</u>

The verb **faire** is used very frequently in French. It expresses many types of actions, including the pursuit of academic disciplines, sports, arts and hobbies, housekeeping activities, transference of emotions, and descriptions of the weather. The following list of idioms with **faire** is in alphabetical order according to the identifying word:

faire attention (à) (to pay attention [to], to mind)

il fait beau (it's good weather [out])

se faire beau (belle) (to dress up, get dressed up)

faire de la bicyclette (du cyclisme) (to go bike riding)

faire du bien (à) (to do [some] good [for])

faire les cartes (to read the [fortune-telling] cards)

faire du cent à l'heure (to go a hundred kilometers an hour)

faire la chambre (to clean/make up the room)

il fait chaud (it's hot [out])

faire ses chaussures (to polish one's shoes)

chemin faisant (on the road, on the way)

faire la cour (à) (to court)

faire une course (des courses) (to do an errand [errands])

faire de la couture (to sew)

faire la cuisine (to cook)

faire son droit (to study law)

faire de l'exercice (to exercise)

Vous êtes fait(e)! (You've had it!)

il fait frais (it's cool [out])

il fait froid (it's cold [out])

il fait jour (it's daylight)

faire la lessive (to do the laundry)

faire le lit (to make the bed)

faire mal (à) (to hurt [someone])

faire du mal (à) (to harm)

faire une malle (les valises) (to pack a trunk [one's bags])

faire le marché (to do the shopping)

il fait mauvais (it's bad weather [out])

faire le ménage (to clean house)

faire le mort (to play dead)

faire de la musique (to do, make music)

il fait noir (it's dark, nighttime)

faire partie de (to belong to)

faire une partie de tennis (to play a game of tennis)

faire de la peine (à) (to hurt [someone's] feelings)

faire de la peinture (to paint [fine art])

faire peur (à) (to frighten [someone])

faire de la photographie (to do photography)

faire des pieds et des mains (to move heaven and earth)

faire plaisir (à) (to please [someone])

faire la pluie et le beau temps (to get one's way)

faire de la poésie (to do, write poetry)

faire une promenade (to take a walk, go on an outing)

ne pas s'en faire (not to worry)

faire du ski (to ski, go skiing)

il se fait tard (it's getting late)

faire la vaisselle (to do the dishes)

faire de la vitesse (to speed [while driving])

Exercise 55

Write the verb in parentheses in the tense and person indicated.

1. present indicative

   (faire) je/j'_____

   (faire) elles _____

   (mettre) je/j'_____

   (permettre) nous _____

   (connaître) tu _____

2. future

   (paraître) il _____

   (promettre) je/j'_____

   (faire) nous _____

   (remettre) tu _____

   (paraître) elles _____

3. past participle

   (faire) _____

   (connaître) _____

(mettre) _____

4. present participle

(faire) _____

(connaître) _____

5. <u>passé</u> <u>simple</u>

(mettre) elle _____

(permettre) nous _____

(faire) vous _____

(paraître) ils _____

(reconnaître) je/j' _____

6. present subjunctive

(faire) que je _____

(mettre) que nous _____

(paraître) qu'ils _____

(apparaître) que vous _____

(disparaître) que je/j' _____

Exercise 56

Translate the following phrases and sentences into English.

1. nous faisions _____

2. tu fis _____

3. qu'il fasse _____

4. nous mettons _____

5. on a mis _____

6. vous commettiez _____

7. nous promettons _____

8. que vous disparaissiez _____

9. je connus _____

10. elle connut _____

11. Faites le marché! _____

12. Il fera beau demain. _____

13. Ils ont fait une partie de tennis. _____

14. Savez-vous faire la cuisine? _____

15. Elles font du basket-ball. _____

16. Nous allons faire une promenade. _____

17. Cela vous fait plaisir. _____

18. Il se faisait tard. _____

19. Ne vous en faites pas. _____

20. Que ferez-vous demain? _____

Exercise 57

Translate the following phrases and sentences into French.

1. I knew _____

2. they promised _____

3. we are appearing _____

4. he has allowed _____

5. I will not allow _____

6. we are committing _____

7. she is promising _____

8. I shall recognize _____

9. let us allow! _____

10. He'll do the cooking. _____

11. She used to be in photography. _____

12. You were speeding. _____

13. She scares me. _____

14. We studied law. _____

15. They took a walk. _____

16. We packed our trunks. _____

17. He dressed up for the occasion. _____

18. You've had it! _____

19. Do you want to study music? _____

20. Tomorrow, the weather will be bad. _____

32 • Impersonal verbs (falloir, pleuvoir, neiger)

Some verbs are used only in the third person masculine singular (**il**). These are called impersonal verbs.

infinitive	falloir	pleuvoir	neiger
	(to be necessary, must)	(to rain)	(to snow)
present participle	(present participle of falloir not used)	pleuvant	neigeant
past participle	fallu	plu	neigé
present indicative	il faut	il pleut	il neige
imperfect indicative	il fallait	il pleuvait	il neigeait
future	il faudra	il pleuvra	il neigera
conditional	il faudrait	il pleuvrait	il neigerait
passé simple (literary)	il fallut	il plut	il neigea
passé composé	il a fallu	il a plu	il a neigé
present subjunctive	qu'il faille	qu'il pleuve	qu'il neige
imperfect subjunctive (literary)	qu'il fallût	qu'il plût	qu'il neigeât

some common uses of impersonal expressions

il y a (there is, there are)

il y avait une fois (once upon a time)

Il fait beau. (The weather is fine [It's a beautiful day].)

Il fait froid. (It's cold [out].)

il convient de dire... (it is fitting to say . . .)

Il est une heure. (It's one o'clock.)

Il faut que je m'en aille.[3] (I must [it is necessary that I] leave.)

Il paraît qu'elle parle français. (It seems that she speaks French.)

Il reste du champagne. (There is some champagne left.)

Exercise 58

Write the verb **falloir** in the forms indicated.

1. (present indicative) il _____

2. (passé simple) il _____

---

3. See Part 1 (Section 14) for use of the subjunctive after impersonals.

3. (present subjunctive) qu'il _____

4. (future) il _____

5. (past participle) _____

Exercise 59

Write the verb **pleuvoir** in the forms indicated.

1. (passé simple) il _____

2. (passé composé) il _____

3. (future) il _____

4. (imperfect subjunctive) qu'il _____

5. (conditional) il _____

Exercise 60

Translate the underlined words into English.

1. <<Il pleure dans mon cœur _____

2. Comme il pleut sur la ville. _____

   Quelle est cette langueur

   Qui pénètre mon cœur?>> —Verlaine

33 • Battre, boire, conduire

infinitive	battre	boire	conduire
	(to beat)	(to drink)	(to drive)
present participle	battant	buvant	conduisant
past participle	battu	bu	conduit
present indicative	je bats	je bois	je conduis
	tu bats	tu bois	tu conduis
	il/elle/on bat	il/elle/on boit	il/elle/on conduit
	nous battons	nous buvons	nous conduisons
	vous battez	vous buvez	vous conduisez
	ils/elles battent	ils/elles boivent	ils/elles conduisent

imperfect indicative	je battais	je buvais	je conduisais
	tu battais	tu buvais	tu conduisais
	il/elle/on battait	il/elle/on buvait	il/elle/on conduisait
	nous battions	nous buvions	nous conduisions
	vous battiez	vous buviez	vous conduisiez
	ils/elles battaient	ils/elles buvaient	ils/elles conduisaient
future	je battrai	je boirai	je conduirai
	tu battras	tu boiras	tu conduiras
	il/elle/on battra	il/elle/on boira	il/elle/on conduira
	nous battrons	nous boirons	nous conduirons
	vous battrez	vous boirez	vous conduirez
	ils/elles battront	ils/elles boiront	ils/elles conduiront
conditional	je battrais	je boirais	je conduirais
	tu battrais	tu boirais	tu conduirais
	il/elle/on battrait	il/elle/on boirait	il/elle/on conduirait
	nous battrions	nous boirions	nous conduirions
	vous battriez	vous boiriez	vous conduirions
	ils/elles battraient	ils/elles boiraient	ils/elles conduiraient
<u>passé</u> <u>simple</u> *(literary)*	je battis	je bus	je conduisis
	tu battis	tu bus	tu conduisis
	il/elle/on battit	il/elle/on but	il/elle/on conduisit
	nous battîmes	nous bûmes	nous conduisîmes
	vous battîtes	vous bûtes	vous conduisîtes
	ils/elles battirent	ils/elles burent	ils/elles conduisirent
<u>passé</u> <u>composé</u>	j'ai battu	j'ai bu	j'ai conduit
	tu as battu	tu as bu	tu as conduit
	il/elle/on a battu	il/elle/on a bu	il/elle/on a conduit
	nous avons battu	nous avons bu	nous avons conduit
	vous avez battu	vous avez bu	vous avez conduit
	ils/elles ont battu	ils/elles ont bu	ils/elles ont conduit
present subjunctive	que je batte	que je boive	que je conduise
	que tu battes	que tu boives	que tu conduises
	qu'il/elle/on batte	qu'il/elle/on boive	qu'il/elle/on conduise
	que nous battions	que nous buvions	que nous conduisions
	que vous battiez	que vous buviez	que vous conduisiez
	qu'ils/elles battent	qu'ils/elles boivent	qu'ils/elles conduisent
imperfect subjunctive (literary)	que je battisse	que je busse	que je conduisisse

	que tu battisses	que tu busses	que tu conduisisses
	qu'il/elle/on battît	qu'il/elle/on bût	qu'il/elle/on conduisît
	que nous battissions	que nous bussions	que nous conduisissions
	que vous battissiez	que vous bussiez	que vous conduisissiez
	qu'ils/elles battissent	qu'ils/elles bussent	qu'ils/elles conduisissent
imperative	bats!	bois!	conduis!
	battons!	buvons!	conduisons!
	battez!	buvez!	conduisez!

verb conjugated like battre
combattre (to combat, fight)

verbs conjugated like conduire
construire (to build, construct)
produire (to produce)
réduire (to reduce)
reproduire (to reproduce)
traduire (to translate)

Exercise 61

Write the verb **battre** in the forms indicated.

1. (present indicative) je/j'_____

2. (past participle) _____

3. (future) il _____

4. (present subjunctive) que nous _____

5. (passé composé) vous _____

Exercise 62

Write the verb **boire** in the forms indicated.

1. (passé simple) je/j'_____

2. (passé composé) je/j'_____

3. (conditional) vous _____

4. (imperative [tu]) _____

5. (imperative [nous]) _____

Exercise 63

Write the verb **conduire** in the forms indicated.

1. (imperfect indicative) nous _____

2. (present subjunctive) que vous _____

3. (present participle) _____

4. (imperfect subjunctive) qu'on _____

34 • Courir, craindre, croire

infinitive	courir	craindre	croire
	(to run)	(to fear)	(to believe)
present participle	courant	craignant	croyant
past participle	couru	craint	cru
present indicative	je cours	je crains	je crois
	tu cours	tu crains	tu crois
	il/elle/on court	il/elle/on craint	il/elle/on croit
	nous courons	nous craignons	nous croyons
	vous courez	vous craignez	vous croyez
	ils/elles courent	ils/elles craignent	ils/elles croient
imperfect indicative	je courais	je craignais	je croyais
	tu courais	tu craignais	tu croyais
	il/elle/on courait	il/elle/on craignait	il/elle/on croyait
	nous courions	nous craignions	nous croyions
	vous couriez	vous craigniez	vous croyiez
	ils/elles couraient	ils/elles craignaient	ils/elles croyaient
future	je courrai	je craindrai	je croirai
	tu courras	tu craindras	tu croiras
	il/elle/on courra	il/elle/on craindra	il/elle/on croira
	nous courrons	nous craindrons	nous croirons
	vous courrez	vous craindrez	vous croirez
	ils/elles courront	ils/elles craindront	ils/elles croiront

conditional	je courrais	je craindrais	je croirais
	tu courrais	tu craindrais	tu croirais
	il/elle/on courrait	il/elle/on craindrait	il/elle/on croirait
	nous courrions	nous craindrions	nous croirions
	vous courriez	vous craindriez	vous croiriez
	ils/elles courraient	ils/elles craindraient	ils/elles croiraient
passé simple (literary)	je courus	je craignis	je crus
	tu courus	tu craignis	tu crus
	il/elle/on courut	il/elle/on craignit	il/elle/on crut
	nous courûmes	nous craignîmes	nous crûmes
	vous courûtes	vous craignîtes	vous crûtes
	ils/elles coururent	ils/elles craignirent	ils/elles crurent
passé composé	j'ai couru	j'ai craint	j'ai cru
	tu as couru	tu as craint	tu as cru
	il/elle/on a couru	il/elle/on a craint	il/elle/on a cru
	nous avons couru	nous avons craint	nous avons cru
	vous avez couru	vous avez craint	vous avez cru .
	ils/elles ont couru	ils/elles ont craint	ils/elles ont cru
present subjunctive	que je coure	que je craigne	que je croie
	que tu coures	que tu craignes	que tu croies
	qu'il/elle/on coure	qu'il/elle/on craigne	qu'il/elle/on croie
	que nous courions	que nous craignions	que nous croyions
	que vous couriez	que vous craigniez	que vous croyiez
	qu'ils/elles courent	qu'ils/elles craignent	qu'ils/elles croient
imperfect subjunctive (literary)	que je courusse	que je craignisse	que je crusse
	que tu courusses	que tu craignisses	que tu crusses
	qu'il/elle/on courût	qu'il/elle/on craignît	qu'il/elle/on crût
	que nous courussions	que nous craignissions	que nous crussions
	que vous courussiez	que vous craignissiez	que vous crussiez
	qu'ils/elles courussent	qu'ils/elles craignissent	qu'ils/elles crussent

imperative	cours!	crains!	crois!
	courons!	craignons!	croyons!
	courez!	craignez!	croyez!

verbs conjugated like <u>craindre</u>
éteindre (to extinguish; to turn out [lights, etc.])
peindre (to paint)
plaindre (to pity)
se plaindre (to complain)

Exercise 64

Translate the following phrases and sentences into French.

1. I ran. _____

2. we feared _____

3. I believed _____

4. I used to believe _____

5. Is she running? _____

6. they would believe _____

7. I will fear _____

8. they did fear _____

9. you believe _____

10. Let's run! _____

Exercise 65

Translate the following phrases and sentences into English.

1. Il courut. _____

2. qu'elle craigne _____

3. nous croyions _____

4. elle crut _____

5. Il courra. _____

6. Elles coururent. _____

7. Courez! _____

8. tu croiras _____

9. Que craignez-vous? _____

10. Je crains que vous couriez trop. _____

35 • Devoir, dire, écrire

infinitive	devoir	dire	écrire
	(to owe, ought, must, to be obliged, to have to)	(to say)	(to write)
present participle	devant	disant	écrivant
past participle	dû	dit	écrit
present indicative	je dois	je dis	j'écris
	tu dois	tu dis	tu écris
	il/elle/on doit	il/elle/on dit	il/elle/on écrit
	nous devons	nous disons	nous écrivons
	vous devez	vous dites	vous écrivez
	ils/elles doivent	ils/elles disent	ils/elles écrivent
imperfect indicative	je devais	je disais	j'écrivais
	tu devais	tu disais	tu écrivais
	il/elle/on devait	il/elle/on disait	il/elle/on écrivait
	nous devions	nous disions	nous écrivions
	vous deviez	vous disiez	vous écriviez
	ils/elles devaient	ils/elles disaient	ils/elles écrivaient
future	je devrai	je dirai	j'écrirai
	tu devras	tu diras	tu écriras
	il/elle/on devra	il/elle/on dira	il/elle/on écrira
	nous devrons	nous dirons	nous écrirons
	vous devrez	vous direz	vous écrirez
	ils/elles devront	ils/elles diront	ils/elles écriront
conditional	je devrais	je dirais	j'écrirais
	tu devrais	tu dirais	tu écrirais
	il/elle/on devrait	il/elle/on dirait	il/elle/on écrirait
	nous devrions	nous dirions	nous écririons
	vous devriez	vous diriez	vous écririez
	ils/elles devraient	ils/elles diraient	ils/elles écriraient

passé simple (literary)	je dus	je dis	j'écrivis
	tu dus	tu dis	tu écrivis
	il/elle/on dut	il/elle/on dit	il/elle/on écrivit
	nous dûmes	nous dîmes	nous écrivîmes
	vous dûtes	vous dîtes	vous écrivîtes
	ils/elles durent	ils/elles dirent	ils/elles écrivirent
passé composé	j'ai dû	j'ai dit	j'ai écrit
	tu as dû	tu as dit	tu as écrit
	il/elle/on a dû	il/elle/on a dit	il/elle/on a écrit
	nous avons dû	nous avons dit	nous avons écrit
	vous avez dû	vous avez dit	vous avez écrit
	ils/elles ont dû	ils/elles ont dit	ils/elles ont écrit
present subjunctive	que je doive	que je dise	que j'écrive
	que tu doives	que tu dises	que tu écrives
	qu'il/elle/on doive	qu'il/elle/on dise	qu'il/elle/on écrive
	que nous devions	que nous disions	que nous écrivions
	que vous deviez	que vous disiez	que vous écriviez
	qu'ils/elles doivent	qu'ils/elles disent	qu'ils/elles écrivent
imperfect subjunctive (literary)	que je dusse	que je disse	que j'écrivisse
	que tu dusses	que tu disses	que tu écrivisses
	qu'il/elle/on dût	qu'il/elle/on dît	qu'il/elle/on écrivît
	que nous dussions	que nous dissions	que nous écrivissions
	que vous dussiez	que vous dissiez	que vous écrivissiez
	qu'ils/elles dussent	qu'ils/elles dissent	qu'ils/elles écrivissent
imperative	(imperative of devoir not used)	dis!	écris!
		disons!	écrivons!
		dites!	écrivez!

Exercise 66

Translate the following sentences into English.

1. J'écrirai au président (à la présidente).

_____

2. Il faut que je lui écrive.

_____

3. Oui, vous devriez lui écrire.

_____

4. On dit que vous devez trente-cinq euros au coiffeur.

_____

5. Oui, je lui dois trente-cinq euros.

_____

6. Je disais que j'allais écrire à mon sénateur.

_____

7. Vous devez avoir quelque chose d'important à lui dire.

_____

8. Écrivez-vous beaucoup?

_____

9. Non, mais j'écrivais beaucoup autrefois.

_____

10. Elle dit qu'elle a écrit une lettre à son sénateur.

_____

Exercise 67

Translate the following sentences into French.

1. I wrote the book.

_____

2. We are writing a book.

_____

3. You must be Michelle's husband.

_____

4. We have to work.

_____

5. She should write a book.

_____

6. He has written a book.

_____

7. He did not write that book.

   _____

8. I owe (à) my friend ten euros.

   _____

9. Let's write to our senator!

   _____

10. I was saying that she has to write a book.

   _____

36 • Lire, mourir*⁴, naître*

infinitive	*lire*	*mourir*	*naître*
	(to read)	(to die)	(to be born)
present participle	lisant	mourant	naissant
past participle	lu	mort	né
present indicative	je lis	je meurs	je nais
	tu lis	tu meurs	tu nais
	il/elle/on lit	il/elle/on meurt	il/elle/on naît
	nous lisons	nous mourons	nous naissons
	vous lisez	vous mourez	vous naissez
	ils/elles lisent	ils/elles meurent	ils/elles naissent
imperfect indicative	je lisais	je mourais	je naissais
	tu lisais	tu mourais	tu naissais
	il/elle/on lisait	il/elle/on mourait	il/elle/on naissait
	nous lisions	nous mourions	nous naissions
	vous lisiez	vous mouriez	vous naissiez
	ils/elles lisaient	ils/elles mouraient	ils/elles naissaient
future	je lirai	je mourrai	je naîtrai
	tu liras	tu mourras	tu naîtras
	il/elle/on lira	il/elle/on mourra	il/elle/on naîtra
	nous lirons	nous mourrons	nous naîtrons
	vous lirez	vous mourrez	vous naîtrez
	ils/elles liront	ils/elles mourront	ils/elles naîtront

---

4. The asterisk (*) indicates that the verb is conjugated in compound tenses with the auxiliary verb **être**.

conditional	je lirais	je mourrais	je naîtrais
	tu lirais	tu mourrais	tu naîtrais
	il/elle/on lirait	il/elle/on mourrait	il/elle/on naîtrait
	nous lirions	nous mourrions	nous naîtrions
	vous liriez	vous mourriez	vous naîtrions
	ils/elles liraient	ils/elles mourraient	ils/elles naîtraient
passé simple (literary)	je lus	je mourus	je naquis
	tu lus	tu mourus	tu naquis
	il/elle/on lut	il/elle/on mourut	il/elle/on naquit
	nous lûmes	nous mourûmes	nous naquîmes
	vous lûtes	vous mourûtes	vous naquîtes
	ils/elles lurent	ils/elles moururent	ils/elles naquirent
passé composé	j'ai lu	je suis mort(e)	je suis né(e)
	tu as lu	tu es mort(e)	tu es né(e)
	il/elle/on a lu	il/elle/on est mort(e)	il/elle/on est né(e)
	nous avons lu	nous sommes mort(e)s	nous sommes né(e)s
	vous avez lu	vous êtes mort(e)(s)	vous êtes né(e)(s)
	ils/elles ont lu	ils/elles sont mort(e)s	ils/elles sont né(e)s
present subjunctive	que je lise	que je meures	que je naisse
	que tu lises	que tu meures	que tu naisses
	qu'il/elle/on lise	qu'il/elle/on meure	qu'il/elle/on naisse
	que nous lisions	que nous mourions	que nous naissions
	que vous lisiez	que vous mouriez	que vous naissiez
	qu'ils/elles lisent	qu'ils/elles meurent	qu'ils/elles naissent
imperfect subjunctive (literary)	que je lusse	que je mourusse	que je naquisse
	que tu lusses	que tu mourusses	que tu naquisses
	qu'il/elle/on lût	qu'il/elle/on mourût	qu'il/elle/on naquît
	que nous lussions	que nous mourussions	que nous naquissions
	que vous lussiez	que vous mourussiez	que vous naquissiez
	qu'ils/elles lussent	qu'ils/elles mourussent	qu'ils/elles naquissent
imperative	lis!	meurs!	nais!
	lisons!	mourons!	naissons!
	lisez!	mourez!	naissez!

Exercise 68

Translate the following phrases and sentences into English.

1. Elle est morte. _____

2. Nous mourons de faim. _____

3. Il meurt. _____

4. Nous lisions. _____

5. on lut _____

6. Vous lisiez. _____

7. il naquit (il est né) _____

8. elle naquit (elle est née) _____

9. nous naquîmes (nous sommes nés) _____

10. qu'il meure! _____

Exercise 69

Translate the following phrases and sentences into French.

1. He will die one day. _____

2. She was born in Paris. _____

3. We read the newspapers. _____

4. She is reading a book. _____

5. Many have died. _____

6. I am dying. _____

7. He is dead. _____

8. I will read this article. _____

9. We have read the book. _____

10. Before dying . . . _____

37 · Plaire, recevoir, rire

infinitive	*plaire*	*recevoir*	*rire*
	(to please)	(to receive)	(to laugh)
present participle	plaisant	recevant	riant
past participle	plu	reçu	ri
present indicative	je plais	je reçois	je ris
	tu plais	tu reçois	tu ris
	il/elle/on plaît	il/elle/on reçoit	il/elle/on rit
	nous plaisons	nous recevons	nous rions
	vous plaisez	vous recevez	vous riez
	ils/elles plaisent	ils/elles reçoivent	ils/elles rient
imperfect indicative	je plaisais	je recevais	je riais
	tu plaisais	tu recevais	tu riais
	il/elle/on plaisait	il/elle/on recevait	il/elle/on riait
	nous plaisions	nous recevions	nous riions
	vous plaisiez	vous receviez	vous riiez
	ils/elles plaisaient	ils/elles recevaient	ils/elles riaient
future	je plairai	je recevrai	je rirai
	tu plairas	tu recevras	tu riras
	il/elle/on plaira	il/elle/on recevra	il/elle/on rira
	nous plairons	nous recevrons	nous rirons
	vous plairez	vous recevrez	vous rirez
	ils/elles plairont	ils/elles recevront	ils/elles riront
conditional	je plairais	je recevrais	je rirais
	tu plairais	tu recevrais	tu rirais
	il/elle/on plairait	il/elle/on recevrait	il/elle/on rirait
	nous plairions	nous recevrions	nous ririons
	vous plairiez	vous recevriez	vous ririez
	ils/elles plairaient	ils/elles recevraient	ils/elles riraient
passé simple (literary)	je plus	je reçus	je ris
	tu plus	tu reçus	tu ris
	il/elle/on plut	il/elle/on reçut	il/elle/on rit
	nous plûmes	nous reçûmes	nous rîmes
	vous plûtes	vous reçûtes	vous rîtes
	ils/elles plurent	ils/elles reçurent	ils/elles rirent

passé composé	j'ai plu	j'ai reçu	j'ai ri
	tu as plu	tu as reçu	tu as ri
	il/elle/on a plu	il/elle/on a reçu	il/elle/on a ri
	nous avons plu	nous avons reçu	nous avons ri
	vous avez plu	vous avez reçu	vous avez ri
	ils/elles ont plu	ils/elles ont reçu	ils/elles ont ri
present subjunctive	que je plaise	que je reçoive	que je rie
	que tu plaises	que tu reçoives	que tu ries
	qu'il/elle/on plaise	qu'il/elle/on reçoive	qu'il/elle/on rie
	que nous plaisions	que nous recevions	que nous riions
	que vous plaisiez	que vous receviez	que vous riiez
	qu'ils/elles plaisent	qu'ils/elles reçoivent	qu'ils/elles rient
imperfect subjunctive (literary)	que je plusse	que je reçusse	que je risse
	que tu plusses	que tu reçusses	que tu risses
	qu'il/elle/on plût	qu'il/elle/on reçût	qu'il/elle/on rît
	que nous plussions	que nous reçussions	que nous rissions
	que vous plussiez	que vous reçussiez	que vous rissiez
	qu'ils/elles plussent	qu'ils/elles reçussent	qu'ils/elles rissent
imperative	plais!	reçois!	ris!
	plaisons!	recevons!	rions!
	plaisez!	recevez!	riez!

verbs conjugated like plaire
déplaire (to displease)
se taire* (to quiet down, be silent)

verb conjugated like rire
sourire (to smile)

Exercise 70

Translate the following phrases and sentences into French.

1. I am laughing. _____

2. he will receive _____

3. we were pleasing _____

4. I have pleased _____

5. she does receive _____

6. you have received _____

7. Laugh! _____

8. one would receive _____

9. that he may receive _____

10. pleasing _____

11. I will please _____

12. we would receive _____

13. You will laugh. _____

14. She is laughing. _____

15. that I may please _____

16. they do receive _____

17. you received _____

18. He laughed. _____

19. Let's laugh! _____

20. Don't laugh! _____

Exercise 71

Translate the underlined words into English, and try to get the gist of the entire quote.

1. <<Riez de ma faiblesse.>> —Corneille

   _____

2. <<Rira bien qui rira le dernier.>> —Proverbe

   _____

3. <<Plus on est de fous, plus on rit.>> —Proverbe

_____

4. <<Votre fille me plut, je prétendis lui plaire.

   Elle est de mes serments seule dépositaire.>> —Racine

_____

_____

5. <<La fortune se plaît à faire de ces coups.>> —La Fontaine

_____

6. <<Plût à Dieu vous savoir en chemin présentement!>> —Mme de Sévigné

_____

7. <<Vous plaît-il, don Juan, nous éclaircir ces beaux mystères?>> —Molière

_____

8. Elle a été reçue à l'Académie française.

_____

9. <<Recevez par cette lettre un pouvoir absolu sur tout le palais.>> —Montesquieu

_____

10. <<La terre ne rit plus à l'homme comme auparavant.>> —Bossuet

38 • Suivre, tenir, vaincre

infinitive	suivre	tenir	vaincre
	(to follow)	(to hold)	(to conquer)
present participle	suivant	tenant	vainquant
past participle	suivi	tenu	vaincu
present indicative	je suis	je tiens	je vaincs
	tu suis	tu tiens	tu vaincs
	il/elle/on suit	il/elle/on tient	il/elle/on vainc
	nous suivons	nous tenons	nous vainquons
	vous suivez	vous tenez	vous vainquez
	ils/elles suivent	ils/elles tiennent	ils/elles vainquent

imperfect indicative	je suivais	je tenais	je vainquais
	tu suivais	tu tenais	tu vainquais
	il/elle/on suivait	il/elle/on tenait	il/elle/on vainquait
	nous suivions	nous tenions	nous vainquions
	vous suiviez	vous teniez	vous vainquiez
	ils/elles suivaient	ils/elles tenaient	ils/elles vainquaient
future	je suivrai	je tiendrai	je vaincrai
	tu suivras	tu tiendras	tu vaincras
	il/elle/on suivra	il/elle/on tiendra	il/elle/on vaincra
	nous suivrons	nous tiendrons	nous vaincrons
	vous suivrez	vous tiendrez	vous vaincrez
	ils/elles suivront	ils/elles tiendront	ils/elles vaincront
conditional	je suivrais	je tiendrais	je vaincrais
	tu suivrais	tu tiendrais	tu vaincrais
	il/elle/on suivrait	il/elle/on tiendrait	il/elle/on vaincrait
	nous suivrions	nous tiendrions	nous vaincrions
	vous suivriez	vous tiendriez	vous vaincriez
	ils/elles suivraient	ils/elles tiendraient	ils/elles vaincraient
passé simple (literary)	je suivis	je tins	je vainquis
	tu suivis	tu tins	tu vainquis
	il/elle/on suivit	il/elle/on tint	il/elle/on vainquit
	nous suivîmes	nous tînmes	nous vainquîmes
	vous suivîtes	vous tîntes	vous vainquîtes
	ils/elles suivirent	ils/elles tinrent	ils/elles vainquirent
passé composé	j'ai suivi	j'ai tenu	j'ai vaincu
	tu as suivi	tu as tenu	tu as vaincu
	il/elle/on a suivi	il/elle/on a tenu	il/elle/on a vaincu
	nous avons suivi	nous avons tenu	nous avons vaincu
	vous avez suivi	vous avez tenu	vous avez vaincu
	ils/elles ont suivi	ils/elles ont tenu	ils/elles ont vaincu
present subjunctive	que je suive	que je tienne	que je vainque
	que tu suives	que tu tiennes	que tu vainques
	qu'il/elle/on suive	qu'il/elle/on tienne	qu'il/elle/on vainque
	que nous suivions	que nous tenions	que nous vainquions
	que vous suiviez	que vous teniez	que vous vainquiez
	qu'ils/elles suivent	qu'ils/elles tiennent	qu'ils/elles vainquent

imperfect subjunctive (*literary*)	que je suivisse	que je tinsse	que je vainquisse
	que tu suivisses	que tu tinsses	que tu vainquisses
	qu'il/elle/on suivît	qu'il/elle/on tînt	qu'il/elle/on vainquît
	que nous suivissions	que nous tinssions	que nous vainquissions
	que vous suivissiez	que vous tinssiez	que vous vainquissiez
	qu'ils/elles suivissent	qu'ils/elles tinssent	qu'ils/elles vainquissent
imperative	suis!	tiens!	vaincs!
	suivons!	tenons!	vainquons!
	suivez!	tenez!	vainquez!

verb conjugated like <u>suivre</u>
poursuivre (to pursue; to follow through)

verbs conjugated like <u>tenir</u>
appartenir à (to belong to)
contenir (to contain)
obtenir (to obtain, get)
retenir (to retain)

verb conjugated like <u>vaincre</u>
convaincre (to convince)

Exercise 72

Translate the following phrases and sentences into French.

1. I hold _____

2. he was following _____

3. we will conquer _____

4. you followed _____

5. I follow _____

6. you will hold _____

7. you do follow _____

8. Follow me! _____

9. I would follow _____

10. they conquered _____

11. conquering _____

12. I will conquer _____

13. we have conquered _____

14. they are conquered _____

15. I'll follow. _____

16. you are followed _____

17. You will be followed. _____

18. You have been followed. _____

19. the following example _____

20. She was holding the cat. _____

39 · <u>Vivre</u>, <u>valoir</u>

infinitive	*vivre*	*valoir*
	(to live)	(to be worth)
present participle	vivant	valant
past participle	vécu	valu
present indicative	je vis	je vaux
	tu vis	tu vaux
	il/elle/on vit	il/elle/on vaut
	nous vivons	nous valons
	vous vivez	vous valez
	ils/elles vivent	ils/elles valent
imperfect indicative	je vivais	je valais
	tu vivais	tu valais
	il/elle/on vivait	il/elle/on valait
	nous vivions	nous valions
	vous viviez	vous valiez
	ils/elles vivaient	ils/elles valaient
future	je vivrai	je vaudrai
	tu vivras	tu vaudras
	il/elle/on vivra	il/elle/on vaudra

	nous vivrons	nous vaudrons
	vous vivrez	vous vaudrez
	ils/elles vivront	ils/elles vaudront
conditional	je vivrais	je vaudrais
	tu vivrais	tu vaudrais
	il/elle/on vivrait	il/elle/on vaudrait
	nous vivrions	nous vaudrions
	vous vivriez	vous vaudriez
	ils/elles vivraient	ils/elles vaudraient
passé simple (literary)	je vécus	je valus
	tu vécus	tu valus
	il/elle/on vécut	il/elle/on valut
	nous vécûmes	nous valûmes
	vous vécûtes	vous valûtes
	ils/elles vécurent	ils/elles valurent
passé composé	j'ai vécu	j'ai valu
	tu as vécu	tu as valu
	il/elle/on a vécu	il/elle/on a valu
	nous avons vécu	nous avons valu
	vous avez vécu	vous avez valu
	ils/elles ont vécu	ils/elles ont valu
present subjunctive	que je vive	que je vaille
	que tu vives	que tu vailles
	qu'il/elle/on vive	qu'il/elle/on vaille
	que nous vivions	que nous valions
	que vous viviez	que vous valiez
	qu'ils/elles vivent	qu'ils/elles vaillent
imperfect subjunctive (literary)	que je vécusse	que je valusse
	que tu vécusses	que tu valusses
	qu'il/elle/on vécût	qu'il/elle/on valût
	que nous vécussions	que nous valussions
	que vous vécussiez	que vous valussiez
	qu'ils/elles vécussent	que ils/elles valussent
imperative	vis!	vaux![5]
	vivons!	valons!
	vivez!	valez!

---

5. The imperative of **valoir** is hardly ever used.

The verb **valoir** is most often used in the impersonal form (**il vaut mieux** + infinitive/**que** + subjunctive, *it would be better/best if/that*). It also means *to be worth/to cost.*

Il <u>vaut</u> <u>mieux</u> <u>que</u> tu laisses tomber
   ce cours.

(It's best if you drop that course.)

Combien <u>vaut</u> cette voiture?

(How much does that car cost?)

Exercise 73

Translate into English.

1. Depuis quand est-ce que vous vivez à Montréal?

2. J'ai essayé de vendre mes livres, mais ils ne valaient pas beaucoup.

3. Il vaut mieux que nous commencions tout de suite.

4. Mozart ne vécut que 33 ans.

5. Vive le Roi!

Exercise 74

Translate into French.

1. How much is a diploma worth?

2. She lived in Lyon for three years.

3. Long live the president!

4. It would be better to leave before noon.

5. When I was a child we lived near a lake.

_____

6. How much does that motorcycle cost? (use **valoir**)

_____

40 · S'asseoir*⁶

infinitive	s'asseoir (to sit down, take a seat)		
present participle	s'asseyant	*or*⁷	s'assoyant
past participle	assis		
present indicative	je m'assieds	*or*	je m'assois
	tu t'assieds		tu t'assois
	il/elle/on s'assied		il/elle/on s'assoit
	nous nous asseyons		nous nous assoyons
	vous vous asseyez		vous vous assoyez
	ils/elles s'asseyent		ils/elles s'assoient
imperfect indicative	je m'asseyais	*or*	je m'assoyais
	tu t'asseyais		tu s'assoyais
	il/elle/on s'asseyait		il/elle/on s'assoyait
	nous nous asseyions		nous nous assoyions
	vous vous asseyiez		vous vous assoyiez
	ils/elles s'asseyaient		ils/elles s'assoyaient
future	je m'assiérai	*or*	je m'assoirai
	tu t'assiéras		tu t'assoiras
	il/elle/on s'assiéra		il/elle/on s'assoira
	nous nous assiérons		nous nous assoirons
	vous vous assiérez		vous vous assoirez
	ils/elles s'assiéront		ils/elles s'assoiront

_____

6. The asterisk (*) indicates that the verb is conjugated in compound tenses with the auxiliary verb **être**.

7. The forms of **s'asseoir** with -ie- or -ey- (**Je m'assieds, Asseyez-vous!**) are used more commonly than those with -oi-
and -oy-.

conditional	je m'assiérais	*or*	je m'assoirais
	tu t'assiérais		tu t'assoirais
	il/elle/on s'assiérait		il/elle/on s'assoirait
	nous nous assiérions		nous nous assoirions
	vous vous assiériez		vous vous assoiriez
	ils/elles s'assiéraient		ils/elles s'assoiraient
passé simple (literary)	je m'assis		
	tu t'assis		
	il/elle/on s'assit		
	nous nous assîmes		
	vous vous assîtes		
	ils/elles s'assirent		
passé composé	je me suis assis(e)		
	tu t'es assis(e)		
	il/elle/on s'est assis(e)		
	nous nous sommes assis(es)		
	vous vous êtes assis(e)(s)		
	ils/elles se sont assis(es)		
present subjunctive	que je m'asseye	*or*	que je m'assoie
	que tu t'asseyes		que tu t'assoies
	qu'il/elle/on s'asseye		qu'il/elle/on s'assoie
	que nous nous asseyions		que nous nous assoyions
	que vous vous asseyiez		que vous vous assoyiez
	qu'ils/elles s'asseyent		qu'ils/elles s'assoient
imperfect subjunctive (literary)	que je m'assisse		
	que tu t'assisses		
	qu'il/elle/on s'assît		
	que nous nous assissions		
	que vous vous assissiez		
	qu'ils/elles s'assissent		
imperative	assieds-toi!	*or*	assois-toi!
	asseyons-nous!		assoyons-nous!
	asseyez-vous!		assoyez-vous!

Exercise 75

Translate into English.

1. Asseyez-vous!

_____

2. Je me suis assis devant la porte.

_____

3. Il faut que tu t'asseyes.

_____

4. Asseyons-nous maintenant.

_____

5. Nous nous sommes assises dans le train.

_____

Exercise 76

Translate into French.

1. Sit down here. (fam.)

_____

2. Let's sit down.

_____

3. O.K., I'll sit down (*present tense*), if you wish.

_____

4. They (f.) sat down while waiting.

_____

5. She asked me to sit down.

_____

Review

Exercise 77

Translate the underlined words into English, and try to get the gist of the entire quote.

1. <<Seigneur, je sais que je ne sais qu'une chose; c'est qu'il est bon de vous suivre.>> —Pascal

   _____

2. <<Qui m'aime me suive.>> —Proverbe

   _____

3. <<D'où tenez-vous ce pouvoir de traverser la vie en la perturbant avec arrogance... ?>> —Tahar Ben Jelloun

   _____

4. <<Une goutte d'eau tient quelque chose du vaste océan.>> —Voltaire

   _____

5. <<Un tiens vaut mieux que deux tu auras.>> —Proverbe

   _____

6. <<Alexis et Henriette la suivirent, dociles. Elle marchait devant, menant sa bicyclette: "On va se mettre là, si vous avez un moment", dit-elle en s'asseyant sur le petit mur de pierre... >> —Elsa Triolet

   _____

   _____

   _____

7. <<Elle ne me voyait pas. Elle était absorbée par ses prières. Je m'assis à côté d'elle... Elle ressemblait étrangement à l'Assise. Moins corpulente, elle avait cependant les mêmes gestes, la même façon de s'asseoir. J'arrêtai de prier et me mis à la regarder avec inquiétude.>> —Tahar Ben Jelloun

   _____

   _____

   _____

   _____

8. <<À vaincre sans péril on triomphe sans gloire.>> —Corneille

_____

9. <<On ne vainc qu'en combattant.>> —Rotrou

_____

10. <<Je suis vaincu du temps, je cède à ses outrages.>> —Malherbe

_____

Appendix: Final Review

This extra opportunity for review will reinforce your command of the conjugations you have learned throughout the book.

Present tense

Exercise 78

Express the following in English.

1. elle vend _____

2. je réussis _____

3. elles ne comprennent pas _____

4. Vous levez-vous bientôt? _____

5. ils répondent _____

6. Ils s'aiment depuis cinq ans. _____

7. nous choisissons _____

8. Je reçois ton paquet. _____

9. Vous dites toujours la vérité. _____

10. Tu te dépêches. _____

Exercise 79

Give French equivalents of the following sentences.

1. Where do they sell maps? _____

2. When do we go out? _____

3. I'm going to phone Chantal. _____

4. We're correcting the essays. _____

5. He doesn't believe you. _____

6. They're opening the store. _____

7. I hope to see Rachelle. _____

8. Are you sleeping? _____

9. We remember our school. _____

10. It's starting to snow. _____

Imperative

Exercise 80

Read the following situations in English, and react with an appropriate imperative form in French.

1. Your roommate is sleeping way too late this morning.

   _____

2. A person leaving the subway car in front of you is about to miss a step.

   _____

3. You suggest to your friends that the three of you go shopping together.

   _____

4. You think your parents should take the train (instead of driving).

   _____

5. You indicate to your friend that this is your subway stop; the two of you need to get off.

   _____

6. You tell your students to pronounce these words.

   _____

7. Tell your children not to get married too young.

   _____

8. You want to take a walk with a group of co-workers.

   _____

9. You tell your friend not to forget his backpack.

   _____

10. You invite your professor to sit down.

   _____

11. You ask your boyfriend/girlfriend to promise you something.

   _____

12. You want to play tennis with your next-door neighbor.

   _____

13. You tell your mother not to get angry.

   _____

14. You tell your little nephew to sleep well.

   _____

15. You tell a good friend not to worry.

   _____

16. You inadvertently interrupt someone (you don't know).

   _____

17. Tell a group of young campers to make their beds.

   _____

18. Tell your friend to stop smoking.

   _____

19. Tell the kids not to cry.

   _____

20. Tell them it's time to tidy up the room.

   _____

Present participle

Exercise 81

Complete each sentence with the appropriate present participle. Choose from among the suggested verbs in each group.

1. **écouter, forger, lire**

   En _____ on devient forgeron.

   J'apprends en _____ beaucoup.

   Il fait le ménage en _____ la radio.

2. **aller, se baigner, promener**

En _____ à la banque, j'ai perdu mon portefeuille.

Elle court en _____ le chien.

Nous chantons en _____

3. **conduire, faire, réfléchir**

Tu t'es amusée en _____ de la peinture.

Il ne faut pas parler au téléphone en _____.

Je quitte la maison en _____ déjà à mon travail.

4. **interroger, jouer, s'occuper**

En _____ au volley-ball, elle oublie ses soucis.

Il peut travailler un peu en _____ de ses enfants.

L'agent de police a beaucoup appris en _____ le suspect.

5. **lancer, nager, ouvrir**

En _____ ce nouveau produit, elles ont dû travailler très dur.

Je me suis détendue en _____.

Il a souri en _____ cette lettre.

Future and conditional

Exercise 82

Change the following verb forms from the future to the conditional, or from the conditional to the future, retaining the same subject pronoun.

1. tu répondras _____
2. j'irai _____
3. nous aurions _____
4. elles parleraient _____
5. il vaudra mieux _____
6. tu vivras _____
7. elles riront _____
8. je plairai _____
9. nous viendrions _____
10. on suivra _____

Exercise 83

Give French equivalents for the following phrases and sentences.

1. Will she run with us? _____

2. Would he tell the truth? _____

3. You (fam.) should write to your mother. _____

4. O.K., I'll write her tomorrow. _____

5. My nephew will be born in a few days. _____

6. I would drink some wine if I weren't working. _____

    _____

7. Will you (polite) do the dishes? _____

8. How long will they live in Italy? _____

9. They would be able to stay longer if their visas were valid. _____

    _____

10. I'd like to stay for three months. _____

Imperfect indicative

Exercise 84

Express the following in French.

1. I was thinking _____

2. she used to travel _____

3. your (fam.) name was . . . _____

4. They always got up at seven. _____

5. He always said that he was happy. _____

6. It was beautiful (out). _____

7. We knew each other very well. _____

8. She was starving (dying of hunger). _____

9. You (polite) were in the midst of finishing your work. _____

    _____

10. It rained every day. _____

11. We had to leave early. _____

12. They could call each other often. _____

Exercise 85

Read the following extracts from a short story, <<La vie privée ou Alexis Slavsky>> (1945), by Elsa Triolet, and write the infinitives shown in the imperfect tense. An artist, Alexis, and his companion Henriette are living in Lyon during the German occupation of France.

<<Quel répit après les mois d'hôtel [...] Alexis ne (sortir) (1) _____ presque pas. Henriette (aller) (2) _____ et (venir) (3) _____, (faire) (4) _____ la cuisine, (laver) (5) _____ la vaisselle, (éplucher) (6) _____ les légumes, (raccommoder) (7) _____ les chaussettes [...] (arranger) (8) _____ une robe, (se laver) (9) _____ dans la cuisine, (lire) (10) _____ des romans policiers ou autres, (jouer) (11) _____ avec le petit chat tigré qu'elle avait ramassé dans la rue (Henriette [avoir] [12] _____ une passion pour les chats de gouttière), (sortir) (13) _____, (revenir) (14) _____ chargée de paquets [...] Il (commencer) (15) _____ à faire froid, il (pleuvoir) (16) _____, il (faire) (17) _____ ignoble [...] Alexis (craindre) (18) _____ le froid plus que tout au monde. Parfois, ils (sortir) (19) _____ ensemble [...] (ils) (s'en aller) (20) _____ entre ces maisons, souvent silencieux [...] L'effroyable nudité de Lyon leur (convenir) (21) _____ [...] Les couleurs à l'huile, la toile [...] (se faire) (22) _____ rares, et puisque c'était ainsi, Alexis (prendre) (23) _____ plaisir à faire des petites gouaches sur n'importe quel petit bout de papier [...] Cette peinture (satisfaire) (24) _____ sa misère intérieure [...] Il (faire) (25) _____ plusieurs gouaches par jour, les jetant par terre autour de lui, les regardant pendant qu'il (se promener) (26) _____ à travers la pièce... >>

Passé composé and passé simple

Exercise 86

Rewrite the following **passé simple** forms in the **passé composé**.

1. ils suivirent _____

2. vous crûtes _____

3. je naquis _____

4. nous reçûmes _____

5. tu craignis _____

6. elle vécut _____

7. vous lûtes _____

8. j'allai _____

9. elles se souvinrent _____

10. tu t'assis _____

Exercise 87

Translate the following into French. Use the **passé composé.**

1. Where did you put the menu? _____

2. They traveled to Senegal in May. _____

3. He and I met for the first time last week. _____

_____

4. This is the suitcase she left in front of my door. _____

_____

5. I bought three books that I gave to the children. _____

_____

6. Which lessons did he study? _____

7. Your sisters? I saw them at the market. _____

8. We woke up too late to go. _____

9. How many times did you try to call? _____

10. Who arrived after me? _____

Present subjunctive

Exercise 88

Translate the English sentences into French. Choose from among the following expressions for the main clause of each sentence and use the present subjunctive in the subordinate clause: **craindre que, douter que, être désolé(e) que, il est important que, il est indispensable que, il est nécessaire que, il est normal que, il est possible que, il est temps que, il faut que, ne pas croire (penser) que, regretter que, vouloir que**

1. I want you to repeat that. _____

2. It's necessary that they choose. _____

3. It's time for us to leave. _____

4. He doubts that we're finishing. _____

5. She regrets that there's an exam today. _____

6. It's possible that he's right. _____

7. I'm afraid that you're wrong. _____

8. It's normal that it's (it be) cold in January. _____

9. He's sorry that I'm selling the house. _____

10. It's important for you to know Paris. _____

11. We have to pack the bags. _____

12. It's possible that she's coming. _____

13. I don't think that he'll change. _____

14. It's indispensable that you go to sleep early. _____

_____

Exercise 89

Use the following conjunctions to translate the English sentences into French: **afin que, bien que, jusqu'à ce que, pour que, pourvu que, quoique, sans que**

1. I'll wait until you come. _____

2. He left without her knowing (it). _____

3. She's explaining it so that we'll understand. _____

4. We're leaving even though it's raining. _____

5. I'll go provided that you come too. _____

6. They work so that their family can be more comfortable. _____

_____

7. You left school even though you were successful (were succeeding)? _____

_____

Past perfect subjunctive

Exercise 90

Give your opinion about some events that happened yesterday by completing the following sentence with the correct verb form.

Je suis surpris(e) que/qu'...

1. mon ami (réussir) _____ à son examen.

2. tu (oublier) _____ de venir en cours.

3. le professeur (se souvenir) _____ de moi.

4. vous (venir) _____ en retard.

5. il (voir) _____ trois films comiques.

6. tu (craindre) _____ mon chien.

7. vous (ne pas se raser) _____.

8. nos amis (se réveiller) _____ à six heures.

9. elle (manger) _____ de la viande.

10. ils (rire) _____ du président.

11. tu (pouvoir) _____ venir.

12. nous (aller) _____ à la plage.

13. vous (se reposer) _____ l'après-midi.

14. tu (reconnaître) _____ mon frère.

15. elle (prendre) _____ le train.

16. vous (se retrouver) _____ au café.

17. Pierre (mettre) _____ les valises dans la voiture.

18. nous (préférer) _____ le restaurant vietnamien.

19. ils (apprendre) _____ la leçon si vite.

20. elles (conduire) _____ cet autobus.

Reflexive verbs

Exercise 91

Translate the italicized words into French. In choosing tense and mood, play close attention to the English equivalents.

1. *I wash myself* tous les matins. _____
2. *They met each other* à midi. _____
3. *We hurried* d'arriver à l'heure. _____
4. *Wake up!* _____
5. *She gets angry* facilement. _____
6. *You looked at each other* curieusement. _____
7. Quand *will we get dressed?* _____
8. *I remember* de vous. _____
9. *They would love to take a walk.* _____
10. *He got bored* en cours. _____
11. *They'll marry* au mois de juin. _____
12. *You brush your teeth* après les repas. _____
13. *We used to phone each other* le soir. _____
14. *Marcel fell asleep* tout de suite. _____
15. *Go to bed* tôt ce soir! _____
16. *Her name is* Amélie. _____
17. *They had fun* dans le parc. _____
18. Il faut que *I go away.* _____
19. *We stopped* au feu rouge. _____
20. Excusez-moi. *I made a mistake* de numéro. _____

Verbs with spelling changes

Exercise 92

Change the following forms from singular to plural, or from plural to singular.

1. je paie _____
2. je voyage _____
3. tu commences _____
4. nous achetons _____
5. nous nous ennuyons _____
6. ils jettent _____
7. vous vous appelez _____
8. vous espérez _____
9. je prononce _____
10. nous nous levons _____

Exercise 93

Translate the following from English to French.

1. They hope to leave. _____
2. You used to begin at eight. _____
3. We're changing clothes. _____
4. It was snowing this morning. _____
5. They call every day. _____
6. I was traveling every summer. _____
7. You (fam.) try to speak. _____
8. She throws out the old newspapers. _____
9. I get bored easily. _____
10. We'll celebrate tomorrow. _____

Compound tenses with <u>avoir</u> and <u>être</u>

Exercise 94

Change the following from the **passé composé** to the pluperfect (**plus-que-parfait**).

1. je suis arrivée _____
2. il a mangé _____
3. nous avons pris _____
4. le prof est venu _____
5. vous avez couru _____
6. elles ont dîné _____

Exercise 95

Change the following from the future perfect to the conditional perfect.

1. nous serons descendus _____
2. elle aura commencé _____
3. nos amis auront fini _____
4. elle sera devenue _____
5. vous aurez mangé _____
6. Tu auras eu ton diplôme. _____

Exercise 96

Translate the following into English.

1. il sera arrivé _____
2. nous avons compris _____
3. elles auraient lu _____
4. Tu étais partie très tôt. _____
5. Mes étudiants avaient terminé avant-hier. _____
6. Si nous étions venus, nous aurions vu ce film. _____

Exercise 97

Translate the following into French. Use compound tenses with the auxiliary verbs **avoir** or **être**.

1. he had known _____

2. we will have arrived _____

3. Napoleéon died in 1821. _____

4. He had lived on that street. _____

5. When did you fall? _____

6. Did you understand that essay? _____

The passive voice

Exercise 98

Translate the following into English.

1. Nous avons été appelés à une heure. _____

2. Le français se parle ici. _____

3. On vend des vêtements chauds en automne. _____

   _____

4. Le président est toujours accompagné de ses gardes du corps. _____

   _____

5. Les essais historiques seront écrits par les membres de cette classe. _____

   _____

6. S'il faisait soleil, est-ce que les tomates seraient cultivées ici? _____

   _____

7. Les images furent reproduites dans tous les journaux. _____

   _____

8. Les bandes dessinées se lisent beaucoup chez nous. _____

   _____

9. Ces candidats ont été refusés par les électeurs. _____

   _____

10. La porte était fermée tous les jours à sept heures. _____

    _____

Exercise 99

Translate the following into French.

1. This book is very often read. _____

2. She will be chosen. _____

3. We have been followed. _____

4. The teacher was called at three o'clock. _____

   _____

5. This class would be taught by an assistant. _____

   _____

6. Peace was declared in 1918. _____

7. These flowers are studied by biologists. _____

   _____

8. That house used to be surrounded by trees. _____

   _____

9. These magazines will be published tomorrow. _____

   _____

10. My clothes were made in France. _____

Overall review

Exercise 100

Complete the following interview with the requested verb forms. Note the subject, the infinitive, and the verb tense.

Amélie Nothomb est une romancière belge, encore jeune, qui a passé son enfance et sa première jeunesse au Japon avant de rentrer en Belgique.

1. —Comment (**passer,** present) _____-vous votre temps libre?

2. Je/J' (**lire,** present) _____ beaucoup, presque autant que je/j'
   (**écrire,** present) _____.

3. A côté de cela, je/j' (**aller,** present) _____ beaucoup au cinéma.

4. Lorsque je/j' (**étudier,** imperfect) _____ à l'Université, je/j' (**aller,** imperfect)
   _____ voir un film par jour.

5. C'est pour vous dire que je/j' (**aller**, imperfect) _____ tout voir—même les commerciaux—, de Bergman aux films américains.

6. Et je/j' (**garder**, <u>passé composé</u>) _____ ce côté omnivore en matière de cinéma.

7. Je/J' (**supposer**, present) _____ que cela (**provenir**, present) _____ du fait que lorsque je/j' (**arriver**, <u>passé composé</u>) _____ en Europe à 17 ans, je/j' (**être**, imperfect) _____ seule.

8. Je/J' (**ne pas avoir**, imperfect) _____ d'amis.

9. Pendant longtemps, pour m'occuper, je/j' (**aller**, imperfect) _____ au cinéma.

10. Et j'en (**devenir**, <u>passé composé</u>) _____ rapidement une fan.

11. D'autant plus que ce/c' (**être**, imperfect) _____ la seule culture européenne abordable pour moi.

12. Avant, je ne/n' (**connaître**, imperfect) _____ l'Europe qu'à travers la littérature classique.

13. Alors, je/j' (**essayer**, imperfect) _____ de découvrir l'Europe plus actuelle à travers le cinéma.

14. En général, je/j' (**aller**, present) _____ aux cinémas UGC.

15. Le Kinépolis (**être**, present) _____ bien trop loin et comme je/j' (**ne pas conduire**, present) _____....

16. Par contre, il (**exister**, present) _____ encore un bon vieux cinéma à Bruxelles, le Movy, non loin de la gare du Midi.

17. Ce/C' (**être**, present) _____ probablement un des derniers cinémas au monde (**fonctionner**, present participle) _____ encore au charbon de bois et cela (**donner**, present) _____ une image d'une qualité très particulière.

Exercise 101

Read the following extracts from *La Peste* (1947), by Albert Camus, and translate the underlined French words and phrases into English. Write your answers in the spaces provided.

<u>Ils</u> <u>suivirent</u>[1] un petit couloir dont les murs <u>étaient</u> <u>peints</u>[2] en vert clair et où <u>flottait</u>[3] une lumière d'aquarium. Juste <u>avant d'arriver</u>[4] à une double porte vitrée, derrière laquelle <u>on</u> <u>voyait</u>[5] un curieux mouvement d'ombres, Tarrou <u>fit entrer</u>[6] Rambert dans une très petite salle, entièrement tapissée de placards. <u>Il</u> <u>ouvrit</u>[7] l'un d'eux, <u>tira</u>[8] d'un stérilisateur deux masques de gaze hydrophile,

en tendit[9] un à Rambert et l'invita à s'en couvrir[10]. Le journaliste demanda si cela servait à quelque chose[11] et Tarrou répondit[12] que non, mais que cela donnait confiance aux autres[13].

<<Ce n'est pas cela[14], dit Rambert. J'ai toujours pensé que j'étais[15] étranger à cette ville et que je n'avais rien à faire avec vous[16]. Mais maintenant que j'ai vu ce que j'ai vu, je sais que je suis d'ici, que je le veuille ou non[17]. Cette histoire nous concerne tous[18].>>

Personne ne répondit[19] et Rambert parut s'impatienter[20].

<<Vous le savez bien[21] d'ailleurs! Ou sinon que feriez-vous[22] dans cet hôpital? Avez-vous donc choisi, vous, et renoncé[23] au bonheur?>>

Ni Tarrou ni Rieux ne répondirent encore[24]. Le silence dura longtemps[25], jusqu'à ce qu'on approchât[26] de la maison du docteur. Et Rambert, de nouveau, posa sa dernière question[27], avec plus de force encore. Et seul Rieux se tourna vers lui[28]. Il se souleva[29] avec effort:

<<Pardonnez-moi[30], Rambert, dit-il[31], mais je ne le sais pas[32]. Restez avec nous puisque vous le désirez[33].>>

1. _____
2. _____
3. _____
4. _____
5. _____
6. _____
7. _____
8. _____
9. _____
10. _____
11. _____
12. _____
13. _____
14. _____
15. _____
16. _____
17. _____

18. _____
19. _____
20. _____
21. _____
22. _____
23. _____
24. _____
25. _____
26. _____
27. _____
28. _____
29. _____
30. _____
31. _____
32. _____
33. _____

Answer Key

When there is more than one possible answer, alternate answers are given in parentheses and, when needed, separated by slashes.

Exercise 1

1. je demande, tu demandes, il/elle/on demande, nous demandons, vous demandez, ils/elles demandent 2. je chante, tu chantes, il/elle/on chante, nous chantons, vous chantez, ils/elles chantent 3. je travaille, tu travailles, il/elle/on travaille, nous travaillons, vous travaillez, ils/elles travaillent

Exercise 2

1. il/elle/on étudie, vous étudiez, j'étudie, nous étudions 2. tu donnes, ils/elles donnent, vous donnez, je donne 3. il/elle/on ferme, nous fermons, tu fermes, ils/elles ferment 4. je joue, vous jouez, ils/elles jouent, tu joues 5. nous dînons, tu dînes, je dîne, vous dînez

Exercise 3

1. nous parlons 2. nous commençons 3. je travaille 4. elle aide 5. vous aimez (tu aimes) 6. il écoute 7. elles comptent 8. je tombe 9. nous trouvons 10. nous arrivons 11. il apporte 12. nous montons 13. elle porte 14. nous jouons 15. il étudie 16. nous admirons 17. elle trouve 18. je pense 19. ils sonnent 20. il pleure (il crie)

Exercise 4

1. j'obéis, tu obéis, il/elle/on obéit, nous obéissons, vous obéissez, ils/elles obéissent 2. je réussis, tu réussis, il/elle/on réussit, nous réussissons, vous réussissez, ils/elles réussissent 3. je punis, tu punis, il/elle/on punit, nous punissons, vous punissez, ils/elles punissent

Exercise 5

1. nous bâtissons, il bâtit, je bâtis, tu bâtis 2. elle remplit, vous remplissez, ils remplissent, nous remplissons 3. je choisis, nous choisissons, tu choisis, elle choisit 4. il accomplit, vous accomplissez, j'accomplis, ils accomplissent 5. vous finissez, il finit, elles finissent, tu finis

Exercise 6

1. Obéit-il? 2. Réussit-elle? 3. Parle-t-il français? 4. Est-ce que j'aide? 5. Dansez-vous? (Danses-tu?) 6. Pensez-vous? (Penses-tu?) 7. Est-ce que je choisis? 8. Écoutez-vous? (Écoutes-tu?) 9. Choisit-il une maison? 10. Porte-t-elle un chapeau?

Exercise 7

1. nous répondons 2. il vend 3. elles entendent 4. je défends 5. vous perdez 6. tu rends 7. elle tend 8. ils descendent 9. je perds 10. tu entends

Exercise 8

1. ils/elles perdent 2. nous n'entendons pas 3. Ne répondez-vous pas? (Ne réponds-tu pas?) 4. je ne défends pas 5. Attendent-ils/elles? 6. N'attendent-ils/elles pas? 7. je perds 8. elle rend 9. ils/elles défendent 10. nous ne perdons pas

Exercise 9

1. Travaillons! 2. Choisissez! 3. Obéis! 4. Écoutez! 5. Attendez! 6. Pensons! 7. Étudions! 8. Entrez! 9. Dîne!
10. Commençons!

Exercise 10

1. étudiant 2. chantant 3. obéissant 4. écoutant 5. attendant 6. comptant 7. descendant 8. dansant 9. donnant
10. jouant

Exercise 11

1. je finirai 2. vous chanterez 3. nous choisirons 4. elle attendra 5. tu perdras 6. ils écouteront 7. je descendrai
8. on répondra 9. tu réussiras 10. elles guériront

Exercise 12

1. elles répondraient 2. nous finirions 3. on choisirait 4. Pierre arriverait 5. tu penserais 6. vous aimeriez 7. je
perdrais 8. elles attendraient 9. vous choisiriez 10. tu réussirais

Exercise 13

1. nous obéirions (we would obey) 2. tu finirais (you [fam.] would finish) 3. je commencerais (I would begin)
4. ils finiraient (they would finish) 5. j'aimerais (I would like, love) 6. vous déjeuneriez (you [polite or pl.] would
have lunch) 7. elle parlerait (she would speak) 8. j'entendrais (I would hear) 9. elles travailleraient (they [f.] would
work) 10. nous jouerions (we would play)

Exercise 14

1. vous obéirez (tu obéiras) 2. je penserais 3. nous écouterions 4. Attendriez-vous? (Attendrais-tu?) 5. je vendrai
6. nous jouerions 7. Je répondrai. 8. ils/elles admireraient 9. Descendrez-vous? (Descendras-tu?) 10. Ils/Elles ne
descendraient pas.

Exercise 15

1. vous choisissiez 2. j'entendais 3. on jouait 4. je travaillais 5. tu demeurais 6. nous bâtissions 7. ils accomplis-
saient 8. je remplissais 9. tu perdais 10. vous descendiez 11. nous vendions 12. elle dînait 13. tu écoutais 14. je
pensais 15. ils portaient 16. il demandait 17. nous obéissions 18. elles choisissaient 19. nous attendions 20. je
descendais

Exercise 16

1. I finish (am finishing) 2. we were speaking (used to speak) 3. you (polite or pl.) will lose 4. I would give
5. they (m.) used to dance (were dancing) 6. you (fam.) will enter 7. one (people/they) were selling (used to sell)
8. you (polite or pl.) lived (were living/used to live) 9. they (f.) study (are studying) 10. I was building (used to
build) 11. Answer (polite or pl.) the question. 12. Do you (polite or pl.) like Brahms? 13. We aren't working (don't
work). 14. Do you (polite or pl.) sing? 15. Were you (polite or pl.) singing (did you used to sing)? 16. I am (in
the midst of) working. 17. We were listening (used to listen) to the radio. 18. He plays (is playing) the piano.
19. Are you (polite or pl.) listening? 20. Wouldn't they (f.) succeed?

Exercise 17

1. je descends 2. nous finissions 3. j'attendrai 4. je chanterais 5. elles pleurent 6. vous réussissiez 7. Parlons!
8. Écoutez! 9. il brûle 10. vous trouviez 11. tu compteras 12. nous ajouterions 13. ils apporteront 14. elle aide
15. vous demandiez 16. ils obéissent 17. nous répondons 18. je perdrai 19. on accomplirait 20. je choisissais

Exercise 18

1. je serai 2. nous sommes 3. tu serais 4. vous auriez 5. il était 6. soyons... ! 7. elles sont 8. j'avais 9. nous avons
10. nous aurions 11. on serait 12. vous serez 13. il aura 14. nous serons 15. elle a 16. sois... ! 17. étant 18. nous
étions 19. ayant 20. tu es 21. ayons... ! 22. elle était 23. j'aurai 24. je serais 25. aie... ! 26. je suis 27. il est

28. vous viviez 29. il travaillera 30. elle parlait 31. ils étaient 32. nous avons 33. j'étais 34. J'ai chaud. 35. Il a faim. 36. Vous avez raison. 37. J'ai tort. 38. Dormez-vous? 39. Elle a dix-huit ans. 40. il y a 41. avoir l'air 42. J'ai soif. 43. Elle a peur. 44. il y a 45. Nous avons froid. 46. Elle n'a pas honte. 47. Nous n'avons pas sommeil. 48. Est-ce que j'ai tort? (Ai-je tort?) 49. As-tu raison? 50. N'ayons pas peur.

Exercise 19

1. elle a parlé 2. je suis monté 3. j'ai fini 4. j'ai chanté 5. vous avez obéi 6. elles sont arrivées 7. il a étudié 8. elle est tombée 9. j'ai trouvé 10. vous avez choisi 11. nous avons attendu 12. on a répondu 13. tu as entendu 14. nous sommes descendues 15. elle a aimé 16. tu as perdu 17. il a bâti 18. elle a puni 19. nous avons réussi 20. on a donné

Exercise 20

1. on parla 2. nous perdîmes 3. ils bâtirent 4. elle aima 5. vous descendîtes 6. ils répondirent 7. nous attendîmes 8. vous choisîtes 9. j'étudiai 10. elles arrivèrent 11. vous obéîtes 12. je chantai 13. vous finîtes 14. je réussis 15. il étudia 16. nous parlâmes 17. vous attendîtes 18. ils remplirent 19. vous accomplîtes 20. ils dînèrent

Exercise 21

1. enleva 2. donna 3. sauva 4. créa 5. écrivit 6. adopta 7. invita 8. inventa 9. découvrit 10. remporta 11. perdit 12. fut

Exercise 22

1. attende 2. montions 3. aimiez 4. dînent 5. chantes 6. vendiez 7. soient 8. choisissent 9. [j']écoute 10. perdes 11. ayons 12. finissiez 13. réponde 14. travaillions 15. dîne 16. aies 17. écrivent 18. soit 19. finissions 20. appreniez 21. trouve 22. bâtisse 23. réussissiez 24. donne 25. ayons

Exercise 23

1. finisse (All the useless activity I was doing in that place then rose up to gag me, and I got impatient for one thing only, that they finish with it so I could get back to my cell, and my sleep.) 2. soit (Let Helen be rendered up to us within the hour. Or it's war.) 3. contrôle (Bring me that file so I can check it.) 4. soit (Provided that [Let's hope that] the cyanide hasn't decomposed in spite of the tin foil wrapping!) 5. soit (May your vision be at each moment renewed!) 6. fassiez (You don't want to accept anything from others? Of course I do, since I'm accepting the gift of your time.) 7. soient (What strikes me and saddens me is that they are so apathetic without being blind or unconscious. . . . They don't feel responsible for anything, because they don't think they can do anything in this world.) 8. souvienne, Vienne (The Seine flows under the Mirabeau bridge / And our love / Must I remember it? / Joy always came after the pain / May night come may the hour ring / The days pass I remain) 9. fassions (And so what do you want us to do with this furniture, Philippe?) 10. soit (My army? Oh, you scoundrel! Ah, you traitor! For their death / Do you think this arm would not be strong enough?) 11. puisse (I see that there's no scoundrel on earth / Who could not find one more base than himself.) 12. soit (It would be better if she were not here tomorrow, when they come to remove the body, she said.)

Exercise 24

1. soyons venues 2. ait été absent 3. ait réussi 4. aies attendu 5. ne soit pas arrivée 6. aient donné la réponse 7. j'aie voyagé 8. ne soit pas tombé 9. ait téléphoné 10. ayons vendu la voiture 11. soit partie en vacances 12. aient acheté cette maison

Exercise 25

1. que je parle 2. que nous finissions 3. qu'il vende 4. que nous tombions 5. qu'on entende 6. que tu perdes 7. qu'ils chantent 8. que vous punissiez 9. qu'elles dansent 10. que j'ajoute 11. qu'ils choisissent 12. que je réponde

Exercise 26

1. je me couche 2. tu te couches 3. il/elle/on se couche 4. nous nous couchons 5. vous vous couchez 6. ils/elles se couchent

Exercise 27

1. je m'habillerai 2. tu t'habilleras 3. il/elle/on s'habillera 4. nous nous habillerons 5. vous vous habillerez 6. ils/elles s'habilleront

Exercise 28

1. je me promenais 2. tu te promenais 3. il/elle/on se promenait 4. nous nous promenions 5. vous vous promeniez 6. ils/elles se promenaient

Exercise 29

1. je me suis amusé 2. je me suis amusée 3. tu t'es amusé 4. tu t'es amusée 5. il s'est amusé 6. elle s'est amusée 7. nous nous sommes amusés 8. nous nous sommes amusées 9. vous vous êtes amusé(s) 10. vous vous êtes amusée(s) 11. ils se sont amusés 12. elles se sont amusées

Exercise 30

1. je me levai 2. tu te levas 3. il/elle/on se leva 4. nous nous levâmes 5. vous vous levâtes 6. ils/elles se levèrent

Exercise 31

1. que je me trompe 2. que tu te trompes 3. qu'il/qu'elle/qu'on se trompe 4. que nous nous trompions 5. que vous vous trompiez 6. qu'ils/qu'elles se trompent

Exercise 32

1. I was . . . 2. We were speaking (used to speak). 3. It is necessary that (One must) . . . 4. You (polite or pl.) were having dinner (used to have dinner . . .). 5. They (m.) invited . . . 6. They (f.) would like (would love) . . . 7. We (m. or mixed) went in (entered). 8. So that you'll be (polite or pl.) . . . 9. We spoke. 10. They (f.) obeyed. 11. You (pl., m. or mixed) came down. 12. They (m.) answered. 13. I was filling (used to fill) . . . 14. It was raining (used to rain). 15. They (f.) would arrive. 16. We're hungry. 17. He's (in the midst of) eating (having dinner). 18. I'd be ashamed. 19. They (m. or mixed) had a good time (had fun). 20. We (m. or mixed) hurried. 21. Help me! (polite or pl.) 22. They (m. or mixed) fell. 23. You (polite or pl.) will stop. 24. Rest! (Take a rest!) (polite or pl.) 25. So that we may (can) speak . . . 26. He had . . . 27. Wake up! (fams. s.) 28. We were leaving (used to leave). 29. They (People) sell . . . (One sells . . .) 30. We will not wait. 31. I am choosing . . . 32. He lost. 33. I sold . . . 34. They (m. or mixed) would have . . . 35. We give (are giving) . . . 36. He will get dressed. 37. We were washing (used to wash) ourselves. 38. They (m. or mixed) lost. 39. There was (were) . . . 40. They (f.) arrive (are arriving). 41. They (f.) liked (loved) . . . 42. They (People) will sell . . . (One will sell . . .) 43. We were taking (used to take) a walk. 44. They (m. or mixed) will get married. 45. Give me . . . ! (polite or pl.) 46. Let's leave! 47. Going down . . . (While descending . . .) 48. So that (In order that) he may (he'll) be . . . 49. You (polite or pl.) remained (stayed/were staying) . . . 50. They (m. or mixed) finished.

Exercise 33

1. to be heard when one speaks / to speak (Is it such a bad thing to be heard when one speaks, and to speak as all the others do?) 2. Let's count / finishes (ends) (Let us consider all that is finished [left behind] as total nothingness.) 3. One must not sell / before it's been taken (killed) (You may not sell the bearskin before the bear is taken.) 4. Help yourself / Heaven will help you (Help yourself and Heaven will help you.) 5. having sung / found herself (itself) (The grasshopper, having sung all summer, found herself in dire need at the coming of the winter wind.) 6. It isn't given (It's not given) (Man has not been granted the privilege of bearing virtue any farther than Saint Louis [Louis IX] [did].) 7. It costs (It costs the mighty so little simply to pass along their words.) 8. what one thinks (believes) (What we say is very far from what we think.) 9. cried (wept) (Alexander wept for not having a Homer.) 10. Coming out / in order to enter (Getting out of one dilemma just to enter another. [Out of the frying pan into the fire.]) 11. was a success (for you) (For you, everything was a success.) 12. obeys (A free people obeys, but is not servile; it has leaders, not masters.) 13. Let's not force (Let us not force our talent.) 14. rose up (came up) (And the cry of his people rose up to him.) 15. Rise up (Rise up quickly, o welcome storms, to sweep René up to the enchanted places.) 16. I stretched (I have stretched) (I flung [I have flung]) ropes from bell-

tower to belltower, garlands from window to window, golden chains from star to star, and I dance.) 17. They had asked him / he had answered / made them want to find (discover) that he danced badly. (They had asked him if he danced well, and he had answered with confidence, giving them the desire to discover that he danced badly.) 18. There is (Every age has its madness. [There is madness at every age.]) 19. it happened / having walked for a long time / discovered (found) (But it happened that the little prince, having walked long across the sands, the rocks and the snows, finally came upon a road. And roads always lead to the houses of men.) 20. A whole year went by before I agreed / . . . I wanted nothing to do with him, it was necessary that he have me (he had to have me) (An entire year passed before I agreed to see Gaston again. . . . since I wanted nothing to do with him, he had to have me [it was imperative that he have me.])

Exercise 34

1. nous plaçons 2. je gèle 3. il achète 4. vous préférez 5. tu cèdes 6. vous envoyez 7. il aboie 8. elles nettoient 9. nous épelons 10. elle rappelle 11. je cède 12. nous célébrons 13. ils répètent 14. vous menez 15. tu achèves 16. nous nageons 17. vous voyagez 18. nous échangeons 19. elle suggère 20. je bouge

Exercise 35

1. je partageais 2. nous voyagions 3. elles prononçaient 4. tu avançais 5. on appelait 6. vous commenciez 7. tu annonçais 8. vous bougiez 9. ils dirigeaient 10. il élevait 11. elles appelaient 12. vous suggériez 13. nous amenions 14. vous interrogiez 15. ils logeaient 16. nous songions 17. tu mangeais 18. il neigeait 19. j'arrangeais 20. elle voyageait

Exercise 36

1. je commence 2. on achètera 3. elle corrigeait 4. je jugeai 5. il menacera 6. vous interrogiez 7. nous songeâmes 8. on possède 9. j'ennuie 10. tu jettes 11. nous renouvellerons 12. elles interrogeaient 13. nous voyageâmes 14. je céderai 15. nous projetions 16. nous envoyons 17. il appuie 18. elle appelait 19. il neigea 20. ils avançaient

Exercise 37

1. je fus 2. tu fus 3. il/elle/on fut 4. nous fûmes 5. vous fûtes 6. ils/elles furent

Exercise 38

1. j'eus 2. tu eus 3. il/elle/on eut 4. nous eûmes 5. vous eûtes 6. ils/elles eurent

Exercise 39

1. que je sois 2. que tu sois 3. qu'il/elle/on soit 4. que nous soyons 5. que vous soyez 6. qu'ils/elles soient

Exercise 40

1. que j'aie 2. que tu aies 3. qu'il/elle/on ait 4. que nous ayons 5. que vous ayez 6. qu'ils/elles aient

Exercise 41

1. j'étais 2. j'avais (j'ai eu/j'eus) 3. vous avez été (tu as été) 4. il a eu 5. nous avons été 6. elle avait 7. je serai 8. vous aurez (tu auras) 9. j'aurais 10. soyons 11. ils (elles) avaient 12. étant 13. que je sois 14. que vous ayez (que tu aies) 15. que vous soyez (que tu sois) 16. ils (elles) seront 17. que nous ayons 18. elle était 19. il avait (il a eu/il eut) 20. nous avons eu

Exercise 42

1. I had admired 2. he would have liked (loved) 3. she studied (has studied) 4. I would have finished 5. we played (have played) 6. we lost (have lost) 7. you (fam.) will have found 8. one had given 9. she might have given 10. we might have hoped 11. you (polite, m.s.) would have arrived 12. I (f.) went 13. I (m.s.) had arrived 14. I have been 15. you (fam.) had waited 16. They (f.) had been mistaken (made a mistake). 17. they (m. or mixed) would have declared (stated) 18. They (m. or mixed) had stopped. 19. You (polite or pl.) must study. (It's necessary that you study.) 20. We (m. or mixed) hurried.

Exercise 43

1. Vous seriez descendu(e)(s). (Tu serais descendu[e].) 2. Il vendra. 3. que nous ayons (eussions) acheté 4. Nous avions dormi. 5. On aurait entendu. 6. vous aviez espéré (tu avais espéré) 7. Elle était arrivée. 8. Je descendais. 9. il avait dit 10. Nous aurions étudié. 11. j'ai eu 12. nous avons été 13. vous aurez fini (terminé) (tu aurais fini) 14. Elles se seraient levées. 15. j'aurai attendu 16. il serait arrivé 17. j'étais arrivé 18. Vous aviez attendu. (Tu avais attendu.) 19. Tu aurais attendu. 20. Elle dit (passé simple) qu'il eût parlé. (Elle a dit qu'il aurait parlé.)

Exercise 44

1. The errors were corrected. (We [They] corrected the errors.) 2. The window is open. 3. Many things were said. 4. This book is sold in all bookstores. 5. In France, one goes (we/they go) to the post office to pay one's (our/their) bills. 6. The senator is accompanied by his wife. 7. The house will be built this year. 8. An armistice was signed. (They signed an armistice.) 9. The war was finished (ended). (They finished/ended the war.) 10. That was decided yesterday.

Exercise 45

1. pouvez 2. Voulez 3. Puis 4. [Je] sais 5. savent 6. [Je] veux 7. peut 8. sait 9. pouvons 10. sais 11. veulent

Exercise 46

1. je veux 2. je peux 3. il savait 4. nous savions 5. j'ai pu 6. nous pouvions (nous avons pu) 7. elle voudrait 8. je saurai 9. nous avons su 10. il pouvait

Exercise 47

1. I want 2. she could (was able to) 3. we will (shall) know 4. he could (was able) 5. that she might know 6. we wanted 7. one (we/they) would know 8. we knew (found out) 9. they (f.) could (have been able) 10. you (polite or pl.) wanted (tried) 11. may I? 12. I know 13. know! (fam.) 14. they can (are able) 15. we would want 16. that she may want 17. that we may be able 18. that you (polite or pl.) might know 19. you (fam.) have known (found out) 20. being able

Exercise 48

1. je dors, nous prenons, elles ouvrent 2. je sortais, il offrait, nous prenions, vous compreniez 3. elle ouvrira, je prendrai, vous servirez, ils découvriront 4. on dormit, je compris, vous offrîtes, elles recouvrirent 5. qu'elle ouvre, que nous prenions, qu'ils sortent, que tu apprennes 6. sorti, appris, dormi 7. que j'apprisse, que nous ouvrissions, qu'ils ouvrissent

Exercise 49

1. I left 2. we understood (used to understand) 3. you (polite or pl.) will feel 4. she took (has taken) 5. he will (shall) open 6. I discovered (found out) 7. she would offer 8. that we may understand each other 9. that you (polite or pl.) may sleep 10. you (fam.) continue (pick up again) 11. I sleep (am sleeping) 12. that he might sleep 13. open (polite or pl.) (up)! 14. she used to surprise 15. I surprised 16. he understood 17. we (m. or mixed) went out 18. she left (has left) 19. one (we/they) left 20. we would offer

Exercise 50

1. je pars (je m'en vais) 2. Il dort. 3. nous avons pris (nous prîmes) 4. elle a pris 5. Ils/Elles comprendront. 6. Ils/Elles comprennent. 7. il servait 8. qu'on sente 9. que nous sortions (que nous sortissions) 10. j'offrirai 11. j'offre 12. je prends 13. elle a pris (elle prit) 14. nous sommes parti(e)s (nous partîmes); nous nous en sommes allé[e]s (nous nous en allâmes) 15. Vous êtes sorti(e)(s). (Vous sortîtes.) (Tu es sorti[e].) (Tu sortis.) 16. Elle a dormi. 17. nous sentons 18. Sortez! (Sors!) 19. Partons! (Allons-nous-en!) 20. il a ouvert (il ouvrit)

Exercise 51

1. je vais, il vient, nous voyons, vous allez, je reviens 2. je venais, tu allais, nous voyions, j'apercevais, vous deveniez 3. tu reverras, elle viendra, j'irai, nous verrons, ils reviendront 4. j'ai vu, nous sommes allé(e)s, elles sont venues,

nous avons revu, tu es allé(e) 5. il alla, je vis, nous revîmes, je vins, elles devinrent 6. que je voie, qu'il aille, que nous venions, qu'elles deviennent, que vous revoyiez

Exercise 52

1. he saw (he lived) (he lives) 2. I see 3. she used to go (was going) 4. we come (are coming) 5. I will (shall) see 6. one (we/they) went 7. we have seen (we saw) 8. we (m. or mixed) came (we have come) 9. I (f.) became (I have become) 10. Come (Let's go) children of the homeland! 11. She just came in (entered). 12. He's going to come. 13. Come (polite or pl.) see. 14. We're doing well. (We're fine.) 15. This hat suits you well (looks good on you) (polite or pl.). 16. Come back (polite or pl.) to see us. 17. Let's see! (Come now!) 18. We'll go to the woods. 19. He wants to leave (to take off) at noon. 20. She'll come back (return) at Easter.

Exercise 53

1. j'ai vu (je vis) 2. Il est allé (Il alla) à l'école. 3. Nous apprendrons (Nous allons apprendre) le français. 4. Comment va-t-elle? 5. Va (Allez) la voir! 6. nous avons vu 7. Je reviendrai. 8. Nous allions en France. 9. Il reviendra bientôt. 10. Qu'est-ce qu'elle est devenue? 11. Tout va bien. 12. nous voyions 13. elle a vu 14. Viens (Venez) ici! 15. Je viens. (J'arrive.) 16. Il est venu (Il vint) en cours. 17. Tu reviendras. 18. Je vois. 19. Le manteau rouge lui va bien. 20. Il va bien avec son chapeau.

Exercise 54

1. I came / They didn't find me (I came, a calm orphan, Rich only by virtue of my tranquil eyes, To men in the great cities; They didn't find me clever.) 2. You will see (In a single life you will see all the extremes of human things.) 3. my look (my perception) was gradually becoming skilled and was learning to distinguish / I saw (the) fire (But my perception was gradually becoming wise and learning to distinguish the tiniest luminescences. And soon, very far behind the transparency, I saw fire itself. And then I saw nothing (I no longer saw anything) but fire.) 4. Everyone doesn't know (Not everyone knows) how to see. (Everyone doesn't know [Not everyone knows] how to see.) 5. the sun had ever seen (The biggest [greatest] city the sun had ever seen.) 6. Great thoughts come from the heart. 7. You suffer (There comes to you) a real blow to the head when you realize (You suffer [There comes to you] a real blow to the head when you realize that all of it, finally, was founded on [an enterprise of] power.) 8. I fear that this group doesn't come (I fear that this group doesn't come far enough forward [to the front.]) 9. your unfortunate brother fell (suddenly) (Your unfortunate brother fell suddenly, bloodied, from the top of this balcony.) 10. Go (away) (Go [away], I do not hate you.) 11. All that I do comes to me (All that I do comes to me naturally, without study.) 12. has seen a great deal (a lot) (Whoever [He who] has seen a lot, may have retained a great deal.) 13. To see in the middle of the night / to see her without her knowing that he was seeing (was looking at) her, and to see her completely occupied with things (In the most beautiful place on earth, in the middle of the night, to see the person he worshiped, to see her without her knowing that he was seeing [was looking at] her, and to see her completely occupied with things that concerned him.)

Exercise 55

1. je fais, elles font, je mets, nous permettons, tu connais 2. il paraîtra, je promettrai, nous ferons, tu remettras, elles paraîtront 3. fait, connu, mis 4. faisant, connaissant 5. elle mit, nous permîmes, vous fîtes, ils parurent, je reconnus 6. que je fasse, que nous mettions, qu'ils paraissent, que vous apparaissiez, que je disparaisse

Exercise 56

1. we were doing (making) (we used to do, make) 2. you (fam.) made (did) 3. that he may do (make) 4. we put 5. one (we/they) put (has put) 6. you (polite or pl.) were committing (used to commit) 7. we promise 8. that you (polite or pl.) may disappear 9. I knew (I met) 10. she knew (she met) 11. Go (polite or pl.) do the shopping! 12. Tomorrow will be beautiful (weather). 13. They (m. or mixed) played a game of tennis. 14. Do you (polite or pl.) know how to cook? 15. They (f.) play basketball. 16. We're going to take a walk. 17. That pleases you (polite or pl.). 18. It was getting late (in the day). 19. Don't worry (polite or pl.) 20. What will you do (polite or pl.) tomorrow?

Exercise 57

1. je connaissais (je savais) 2. ils/elles ont promis (ils/elles promirent) 3. nous apparaissons 4. il a permis 5. je ne permettrai pas 6. nous commettons 7. elle promet 8. je reconnaîtrai 9. permettons! 10. Il fera la cuisine. 11. Elle faisait de la photographie. 12. Vous faisiez (Tu faisais) de la vitesse. 13. Elle me fait peur. 14. Nous avons fait (Nous fîmes) notre droit. 15. Ils/Elles ont fit (Ils/Elles firent) une promenade. 16. Nous avons fait (Nous fîmes) les (nos) malles. 17. Il s'est fait (Il se fit) beau à cette occasion. 18. Tu es fait(e)! (Vous êtes fait[e][s]!) 19. Veux-tu (Voudrais-tu/Voulez-vous/Voudriez-vous) faire de la musique (faire des études de musique)? 20. Il fera mauvais demain.

Exercise 58

1. il faut 2. il fallut 3. qu'il faille 4. il faudra 5. fallu

Exercise 59

1. il plut 2. il a plu 3. il pleuvra 4. qu'il pleuve 5. il pleuvrait

Exercise 60

1. It cries (weeps) / 2. it rains (It weeps in my heart / As it rains on the town / What is this languor that pierces my heart?)

Exercise 61

1. je bats 2. battu 3. il battra 4. que nous battions 5. vous avez battu

Exercise 62

1. je bus 2. j'ai bu 3. vous boiriez 4. bois! 5. buvons!

Exercise 63

1. nous conduisions 2. que vous conduisiez 3. conduisant 4. qu'on conduisît

Exercise 64

1. Je courus. (J'ai couru/Je courais.) 2. nous craignions (nous avons craint/nous craignîmes) 3. j'ai cru (je crus/je croyais) 4. je croyais 5. Court-elle? 6. ils/elles croiraient 7. je craindrai 8. ils/elles ont craint 9. vous croyez (tu crois) 10. Courons!

Exercise 65

1. He ran. 2. that she may fear 3. we used to believe (were believing/believed) 4. she believed 5. He will run. 6. They (f.) ran. 7. Run! (polite or pl.) 8. you (fam.) will believe 9. What do you fear (are you afraid of)? (polite or pl.) 10. I fear (I'm afraid) that you're running too much.

Exercise 66

1. I will write to the president. 2. I must (It is necessary that I) write to him (her). 3. Yes, you (polite or pl.) should write to him (her). 4. They say that you (polite or pl.) owe the hairdresser (barber) thirty-five euros. 5. Yes, I owe him thirty-five euros. 6. I was saying that I was going to write to my senator. 7. You (polite or pl.) must have something important to tell him (her). 8. Do you (polite or pl.) write a lot? 9. No, but in the past I used to write a lot. 10. She says that she wrote a letter to her senator.

Exercise 67

1. J'ai écrit (J'écrivis) le livre. 2. Nous écrivons un livre. 3. Vous devez (Tu dois) être le mari de Michelle. 4. Nous devons travailler. 5. Elle devrait écrire un livre. 6. Il a écrit un livre. 7. Il n'a pas écrit ce livre-là. 8. Je dois dix euros à mon ami(e). 9. Écrivons à notre sénateur! 10. Je disais qu'elle doit (devrait) écrire un livre.

Exercise 68

1. She died. (She is dead.) 2. We're dying of hunger. (We're starving.) 3. He's dying. 4. We were reading (used to read). 5. one read 6. You (polite or pl.) were reading (used to read). 7. he was born 8. she was born 9. we were born 10. may he (let him) die!

Exercise 69

1. Il mourra un jour. 2. Elle est née (naquit) à Paris. 3. Nous lisons (avons lu, lûmes) les journaux. 4. Elle lit un livre. 5. Beaucoup (de gens, de personnes) sont mort(e)s. 6. Je meurs. 7. Il est mort. 8. Je lirai cet article. 9. Nous avons lu le livre. 10. Avant de mourir...

Exercise 70

1. Je ris. 2. il recevra 3. nous plaisions 4. j'ai plu 5. elle reçoit 6. vous avez (tu as) reçu 7. Riez! (Ris!) 8. on recevrait 9. qu'il reçoive 10. plaisant 11. je plairai 12. nous recevrions 13. Vous rirez. (Tu riras.) 14. Elle rit. 15. que je plaise 16. ils/elles reçoivent 17. vous reçûtes (tu reçus) (vous avez reçu [tu as reçu]) 18. Il rit. (Il a ri.) 19. Rions! 20. Ne riez pas! (Ne ris pas!)

Exercise 71

1. Laugh (Laugh at my weakness.) 2. He laughs best who laughs last. 3. the more you (they) laugh (The more crazies [madmen] [there are] the more you [they] laugh.) 4. pleased me (I liked) (Your daughter pleased me, I aspired to pleased her. She is the sole depository [recipient] of my vows.) 5. Fortune enjoys (is happy) (Fortune enjoys creating such blows.) 6. Please God . . . (Please God to know you'll soon be en route [on the way here]). 7. Does it please you (Would you be kind enough) (Don Juan, would it please you to shed light upon these beautiful mysteries [secrets]?) 8. She was accepted (She was accepted [received] by the French Academy.) 9. Receive (Accept) (Receive [Accept] by this letter absolute power over the entire palace.) 10. no longer laughs (The earth no longer laughs at man as it once did.)

Exercise 72

1. je tiens 2. il suivait 3. nous vaincrons 4. vous suivîtes (tu suivis) (vous avez suivi [tu as suivi]) 5. je suis 6. vous tiendrez (tu tiendras) 7. vous suivez (tu suis) 8. Suivez-moi! (Suis-moi!) 9. je suivrais 10. ils/elles vainquirent (ils/elles ont vaincu) 11. vainquant 12. je vaincrai 13. nous avons vaincu 14. ils/elles ont été vaincu(e)s 15. je suivrai 16. vous êtes suivi(e)(s) (tu es suivi[e]) 17. Vous allez être suivi(e)(s). (Tu vas être suivi[e].) 18. Vous avez été suivi(e)(s). (Tu as été suivi[e].) 19. l'exemple suivant 20. Elle tenait le chat.

Exercise 73

1. How long have you (polite or pl.) been living in Montreal? 2. I tried to sell my books, but they weren't worth much. 3. It's better if (that) we start right away. 4. Mozart only lived 33 years. 5. Long live the King!

Exercise 74

1. Combien vaut un diplôme? (Combien un diplôme vaut-il?) 2. Elle a vécu (vécut) à Lyon pendant trois ans. 3. Vive le président (la présidente)! 4. Il vaudrait mieux partir avant midi. 5. Quand j'étais enfant nous habitions près d'un lac. 6. Combien vaut cette moto?

Exercise 75

1. Sit down! (polite or pl.) 2. I (m.s.) sat down in front of the door. 3. You (fam.) must sit down. (It's necessary that you sit down.) 4. Let's sit down now. 5. We (f.) sat down (took our seats) in the train.

Exercise 76

1. Assieds-toi ici. 2. Asseyons-nous. 3. D'accord, je m'assieds, si vous voulez (si tu veux). 4. Elles s'assirent (se sont assises) en attendant. 5. Elle m'a prié de m'asseoir.

Exercise 77

1. I know that I know only / to follow you (Lord, I know that I know only one thing; that is it is good to follow you.) 2. He who loves me follows me. 3. do you have (get) (Where do you get the power to pass through life arrogantly disturbing it?) 4. holds (retains) (A single drop of water retains something of the vast ocean.) 5. a "here you are" ("take it") (A "here you are" is worth more than two "you'll have." [A bird in the hand is worth two in the bush.]) 6. followed her / She was walking / guiding / We'll sit there, if you have a moment / she said, sitting down (Alexis and Henriette followed her, docilely. She walked before them, guiding her bicycle. "We'll sit there, if you have a moment," she said, sitting down on the low stone wall . . .) 7. She didn't see me. She was absorbed / I sat down next to her. . . . She resembled / she had / the same way of sitting. I stopped praying and began to look at her (She didn't see me. She was absorbed in her prayers. I sat down next to her . . . She strangely resembled the "Seated One." Less heavy, still she had the same gestures, the same way of sitting. I stopped praying and began to look at her anxiously.) 8. to triumph (win) (He who wins without danger triumphs without glory.) 9. You win only by fighting (if you fight). 10. I am bested by time, I yield to its outrages.

Exercise 78

1. she sells 2. I succeed (I succeeded) 3. they (f.) don't understand 4. Are you (polite or pl.) getting up soon? 5. they (m. or mixed) answer 6. They've loved each other for five years. 7. we choose 8. I receive your (fam.) package. 9. You (polite or pl.) always tell the truth. 10. You're (fam.) hurrying (rushing).

Exercise 79

1. Où vend-on (vendent-ils) des cartes? (Où est-ce que les cartes se vendent?) 2. Quand sortons-nous? 3. Je vais téléphoner à Chantal. 4. Nous corrigeons les essais. 5. Il ne vous (te) croit pas. 6. Ils/Elles ouvrent le magasin. 7. J'espère voir Rachelle. 8. Dormez-vous? (Dors-tu?) 9. Nous nous souvenons de notre école. 10. Il commence à neiger.

Exercise 80 (suggested answers)

1. Réveille-toi! 2. Faites attention! 3. Faisons le marché! (Allons au magasin!) 4. Prenez le train! (Ne conduisez pas!) 5. Descendons ici! 6. Prononcez ces mots! 7. Ne vous mariez pas trop jeunes. 8. Promenons-nous! (Allons nous promener!/Allons faire une promenade!/Faisons une promenade!) 9. N'oublie pas ton sac à dos! 10. Asseyez-vous. 11. Promets-moi quelque chose. 12. Jouons au tennis. (Faisons une partie de tennis.) 13. Ne te fâche pas. 14. Dors bien. 15. Ne t'inquiète pas. (Ne t'en fais pas.) 16. Pardonne-moi. (Excuse-moi.) 17. Faites vos lits! 18. Arrête de fumer! (Ne fume plus!) 19. Ne pleurez pas. 20. Rangeons la chambre. (Rangez la chambre.)

Exercise 81

1. forgeant, lisant, écoutant 2. allant, promenant, nous baignant 3. faisant, conduisant, réfléchissant 4. jouant, s'occupant, interrogeant 5. lançant, nageant, ouvrant

Exercise 82

1. tu répondrais 2. j'irais 3. nous aurons 4. elles parleront 5. il vaudrait mieux 6. tu vivrais 7. elles riraient 8. je plairais 9. nous viendrons 10. on suivrait

Exercise 83

1. Courra-t-elle avec nous? 2. Dirait-il la vérité? 3. Tu devrais écrire à ta mère. 4. D'accord, je lui écrirai (écris) demain. 5. Mon neveu naîtra dans quelques jours. 6. Je boirais du vin, si je ne travaillais pas. 7. Ferez-vous la vaisselle? (Laverez-vous la vaisselle?) 8. Combien de temps vivront-ils en Italie? 9. Ils/Elles pourraient rester plus longtemps, si leur visa était valable. 10. J'aimerais (Je voudrais) rester trois mois.

Exercise 84

1. je pensais (je réfléchissais) 2. elle voyageait 3. tu t'appelais... 4. Ils/Elles se levaient toujours à sept heures. 5. Il disait toujours qu'il était heureux (content). 6. Il faisait beau. 7. Nous nous connaissions très bien. 8. Elle

mourait de faim. 9. Vous étiez en train de finir (terminer) votre travail. 10. Il pleuvait tous les jours. 11. Nous devions (avons dû) partir tôt. 12. Ils/Elles pouvaient se téléphoner (s'appeler) souvent.

Exercise 85

1. sortait 2. allait 3. venait 4. faisait 5. lavait 6. épluchait 7. raccommodait 8. arrangeait 9. se lavait 10. lisait 11. jouait 12. avait 13. sortait 14. revenait 15. commençait 16. pleuvait 17. faisait 18. craignait 19. sortaient 20. s'en allaient 21. convenait 22. se faisaient 23. prenait 24. satisfaisait 25. faisait 26. se promenait

Exercise 86

1. ils ont suivi 2. vous avez cru 3. je suis né(e) 4. nous avons reçu 5. tu as craint 6. elle a vécu 7. vous avez lu 8. je suis allé(e) 9. elles se sont souvenues 10. tu t'es assis(e)

Exercise 87

1. Où as-tu (avez-vous) mis le menu? 2. Ils ont voyagé au Sénégal en mai. 3. Lui et moi, nous nous sommes rencontrés pour la première fois la semaine dernière. 4. Voici la valise qu'elle a laissée devant ma porte. 5. J'ai acheté trois livres que j'ai donnés aux enfants. 6. Quelles leçons a-t-il étudiées? 7. Tes (Vos) sœurs? Je les ai vues au marché. 8. Nous nous sommes réveillé(e)s trop tard pour (y) aller. 9. Combien de fois as-tu (avez-vous) essayé d'appeler (de téléphoner)? 10. Qui est arrivé après moi?

Exercise 88

1. Je veux que tu répètes (que vous répétiez) cela. 2. Il faut qu'ils/elles choisissent. (Il est nécessaire qu'ils/elles choisissent.) 3. Il est temps que nous partions. 4. Il doute que nous finissions (terminions). 5. Elle regrette (Elle est désolée) qu'il y ait un examen aujourd'hui. 6. Il est possible qu'il ait raison. 7. Je crains (J'ai peur) que tu aies (que vous ayez) tort. 8. Il est normal qu'il fasse froid en janvier. 9. Il regrette (Il est désolé) que je vende la maison. 10. Il est important que tu connaisses (que vous connaissiez) Paris. 11. Il faut (Il est nécessaire) que nous fassions les valises. 12. Il est possible qu'elle vienne. 13. Je ne pense pas qu'il change. (Je doute qu'il change.) 14. Il est indispensable que tu t'endormes (vous vous endormiez) tôt.

Exercise 89

1. J'attendrai jusqu'à ce que tu viennes (vous veniez). 2. Il est parti sans qu'elle le sache. 3. Elle l'explique pour que (afin que) nous comprenions. 4. Nous partons bien qu'il (quoiqu'il) pleuve. 5. J'irai pourvu que tu viennes (vous veniez) aussi. 6. Ils travaillent pour que (afin que) leur famille puisse être plus confortable. 7. Tu as (vous avez) quitté l'école quoi que (bien que) tu réussisses (vous réussissiez)?

Exercise 90

1. ait réussi 2. aies oublié 3. se soit souvenu 4. soyez venu(e)(s) 5. ait vu 6. aies craint 7. ne vous soyez pas rasé(s) 8. se soient réveillés 9. ait mangé 10. aient ri 11. aies pu 12. soyons allé(e)s 13. vous soyez reposé(e)(s) 14. aies reconnu 15. ait pris 16. vous soyez retrouvé(e)s 17. ait mis 18. ayons préféré 19. aient appris 20. aient conduit

Exercise 91

1. Je me lave 2. Ils/Elles se sont retrouvé(e)s (se retrouvèrent) 3. Nous nous sommes dépêché(e)s (nous nous dépêchâmes) 4. Réveille-toi! (Réveillez-vous!) 5. Elle se fâche 6. Vous vous êtes regardé(e)s (vous vous regardâtes) 7. nous habillerons-nous 8. Je me souviens 9. Ils/Elles aimeraient se promener (faire une promenade). 10. Il s'est ennuyé (Il s'ennuyait/Il s'ennuya) 11. Ils se marieront 12. Tu te brosses (Vous vous brossez) les dents 13. Nous nous téléphonions (Nous nous appelions) 14. Marcel s'est endormi (s'endormit) 15. Couche-toi (Couchez-vous) 16. Elle s'appelle 17. Ils/Elles se sont amusé(e)s (s'amusèrent) 18. je m'en aille (je parte) 19. Nous nous sommes arrêté(e)s (nous nous arrêtâmes) 20. Je me suis trompé(e)

Exercise 92

1. nous payons 2. nous voyageons 3. vous commencez 4. j'achète 5. je m'ennuie 6. il jette 7. tu t'appelles 8. tu espères 9. nous prononçons 10. je me lève

Exercise 93

1. Ils/Elles espèrent partir (s'en aller). 2. Tu commençais (Vous commenciez) à huit heures. 3. Nous changeons de vêtements. 4. Il neigeait ce matin. 5. Ils/Elles appellent (téléphonent) tous les jours. 6. Je voyageais chaque été. 7. Tu essaies de parler. 8. Elle jette les vieux journaux. 9. Je m'ennuie facilement. 10. Nous célébrerons (allons célébrer) demain.

Exercise 94

1. j'étais arrivée 2. il avait mangé 3. nous avions pris 4. le prof était venu 5. vous aviez couru 6. elles avaient dîné

Exercise 95

1. nous serions descendus 2. elle aurait commencé 3. nous amis auraient fini 4. elle serait devenue 5. vous auriez mangé 6. Tu aurais eu ton diplôme.

Exercise 96

1. he will have arrived 2. we understood (did understand) 3. they (f.) would have read 4. You (f. s.)had left very early. 5. My students had finished the day before yesterday. 6. If we had come, we would have seen that film.

Exercise 97

1. il avait su (avait connu) 2. nous serons arrivé(e)s 3. Napoléon est mort en 1821. 4. Il avait vécu dans cette rue. 5. Quand es-tu tombé(e)? (Quand êtes-vous tombé(e)(s)?) 6. As-tu (Avez-vous) compris cet essai?

Exercise 98

1. We (m. or mixed) were called at one o'clock. 2. French is spoken here. 3. Warm clothing is sold in the fall. (They sell warm clothing in the fall.) 4. The president is always accompanied by his bodyguards. 5. The historical essays will be written by the members of this class. 6. If it were sunny, would tomatoes be grown here? 7. The images (pictures) were reproduced in all the newspapers. 8. Comics are read a lot at our house (in our country). 9. Those candidates were refused (turned down) by the voters. 10. The door was closed (shut) every day at seven o'clock.

Exercise 99

1. Ce livre est lu très souvent. 2. Elle sera choisie (élue). 3. Nous avons été suivi(e)s. (Nous fûmes suivi[e]s.) 4. Le professeur a été appelé à trois heures. (Le professeur fut appelé à trois heures.) 5. Cette classe (Ce cours) serait enseigné(e) par un assistant. 6. La paix a été déclarée en 1918. (La paix fut déclarée en 1918.) 7. Ces fleurs sont étudiées par les biologistes. 8. Cette maison était entourée d'arbres. 9. Ces revues seront publiées (vont être publiées) demain. 10. Mes vêtements ont été faits en France. (Mes vêtements furent faits en France.)

Exercise 100

1. passez-vous 2. Je lis; j'écris 3. je vais 4. j'étudiais; j'allais 5. j'allais 6. j'ai gardé 7. Je suppose; cela provient; je suis arrivée; j'étais 8. Je n'avais pas 9. j'allais 10. j'en suis devenue 11. c'était 12. je ne connaissais 13. j'essayais 14. je vais 15. Le Kinépolis est; je ne conduis pas 16. il existe 17. C'est; fonctionnant; cela donne

Exercise 101

1. They followed 2. were painted 3. floated 4. before arriving 5. one saw 6. ushered (made enter) 7. He opened 8. pulled (out) 9. handed (offered) 10. invited him to cover himself (his face) with it 11. asked if that was good for anything 12. answered 13. gave the others confidence (made the others more confident) 14. It's not that 15. I always thought I was 16. I had nothing to do with you 17. I have seen what I have seen. I know that I am from here, whether I want to be or not 18. concerns us all (we are all involved) 19. No one answered 20. seemed to get impatient 21. You know it (all too) well 22. what would you be doing 23. So, have you chosen and given up 24. still did not answer 25. lasted a long time 26. until they were getting near (approaching) 27. asked his final question 28. turned toward him 29. He raised himself 30. Pardon me 31. he said 32. I don't know it 33. Stay with us since that's what you want (you want it)

Index of Verbs

The number after each verb indicates the section in which that verb, or a similarly conjugated verb, will be found.

The abbreviation *reg.* indicates that the verb is regular. Regular -er, -ir, and -re verbs are presented in Part 1, Sections 1–17.

An asterisk (*) indicates that the verb is conjugated with être.

French–English

A

aboyer (to bark), 22

accepter (to accept), reg.

accompagner (to accompany), reg.

accomplir (to accomplish), reg.

acheter (to buy), 20

achever (to finish, complete), 20

admirer (to admire), reg.

adorer (to adore, worship), reg.

adopter (to adopt), reg.

aider (to help, aid), reg.

aimer (to love; to like), reg.

ajouter (to add), reg.

*aller (to go), 30

*s'en aller (to leave, go away), 17, 30

amener (to bring [a person]), 20

*s'amuser (to enjoy oneself), reg., 17

annoncer (to announce), 18

apercevoir (to notice, catch sight of), 30

*s'apercevoir (to realize), 17, 30

apparaître (to appear), 31

appartenir (to belong), 30, 38

appeler (to call), 23

*s'appeler (to be named, called), 17, 23

apporter (to bring), reg.

apprendre (to learn), 29

*s'approcher (to approach, come closer), reg., 17

appuyer (to lean; to bear, support), 22

arranger (to arrange), 19

*s'arrêter (to stop), reg., 17

*arriver (to arrive), reg.

*s'asseoir (to sit [down]), 17, 40

attendre (to wait), reg.

avancer (to advance), 18

avoir (to have), 10, 24

B

*se baigner (to take a bath; to go swimming), reg., 17

baisser (to lower), reg.

*se baisser (to bend down), reg., 17

bâtir (to build), reg.

battre (to beat), 33

*se battre (to fight), 17, 33

blesser (to wound, injure), reg.

C

D

dire (to say), 35

diriger (to direct), 19

disparaître (to disappear), 31

donner (to give), reg.

dormir (to sleep), 29

douter (to doubt), reg.

durer (to last), reg.

E

échanger (to exchange), 19

éclaircir (to illuminate, enlighten), reg.

écouter (to listen to), reg.

écrire (to write), 35

élever (to erect; to raise [a child]), 20

embaucher (to hire), reg.

emmener (to lead away), 20

empêcher (to prevent), reg.

employer (to employ, use), 22

emporter (to take away, carry off), reg.

*s'endormir (to go to sleep, fall asleep), 17, 29

enlever (to remove, take off), 20

ennuyer (to annoy; to bore), 22

*s'ennuyer (to get bored), 17, 22

enseigner (to teach), reg.

entendre (to hear), reg.

enterrer (to bury), reg.

entourer (to surround), reg.

*entrer (to enter), reg.

envelopper (to wrap up), reg.

envoyer (to send), 22

épeler (to spell), 23

éplucher (to peel [vegetables]), reg.

espérer (to hope), 21

essayer (to try), 22

essuyer (to wipe), 22

éteindre (to extinguish [fire]; to turn out [lights, etc.]), 34

être (to be), 10, 24

étudier (to study), reg.

exagérer (to exaggerate), 21

excuser (to excuse), reg.

exister (to exist), reg.

expliquer (to explain), reg.

F

*se fâcher (to get angry), reg., 17

faire (to do, make), 31

falloir (il faut) (to have to, be necessary), 32

fermer (to close), reg.

finir (to finish), reg.

flotter (to float), reg.

fonctionner (to function; to work [machine]), reg.

forcer (to force), 18

forger (to forge), 19

frapper (to strike, hit), reg.

fréquenter (to frequent, go to), reg.

fumer (to smoke), reg.

G

gagner (to earn, win), reg.

garder (to keep), reg.

geler (to freeze), 20

guérir (to cure; to get well), reg.

H

*s'habiller (to get dressed), reg., 17

habiter (to live, dwell), reg.

I

*s'impatienter (to get impatient), reg., 17

inquiéter (to worry [someone]), 21

*s'inquiéter (to get worried, worry), 17, 21

intéresser (to interest), reg.

interroger (to interrogate, question), 19

inventer (to invent), reg.

inviter (to invite), reg.

English–French

be (present) (*se trouver, reg., 17)

be able (pouvoir, 28)

be acquainted with (connaître, 31)

be afraid of (craindre, 34)

be better (valoir [il vaut mieux], 39)

be born (*naître, 36)

be called (*s'appeler, 17, 23)

be fitting (convenir, 30, 38)

be lacking (manquer, reg.)

be named (*s'appeler, 17, 23)

be necessary (falloir [il faut], 32)

be obliged to (devoir, 35)

be quiet, silent (*se taire, 17, 37)

be suitable (convenir, 30, 38)

be worth (valoir, 39)

be wrong (*se tromper, reg., 17)

bear (down) (appuyer, 22)

beat (battre, 33)

become (*devenir, 30, 38)

beg (prier, reg.)

begin (commencer, 18)

begin (*se mettre à, 17, 31)

begin again (recommencer, 18)

believe (croire, 34)

belong (appartenir, 30, 38)

bend down (*se baisser, reg., 17)

bore (ennuyer, 22)

break (casser, reg.)

break (a limb) (*se casser, reg., 17)

breathe (respirer, reg.)

bring (a person) (amener, 20)

bring (an object) (apporter, reg.)

brush (brosser, reg.)

brush (one's hair) (*se brosser [les cheveux], reg., 17)

build (bâtir, reg.)

build (construire, 33)

burn (brûler, reg.)

bury (enterrer, reg.)

buy (acheter, 20)

C

call (appeler, 23)

call (téléphoner, reg.)

can (pouvoir, 28)

care for (soigner, reg.)

carry (porter, reg.)

carry off (emporter, reg.)

carry off (remporter, reg.)

catch sight of (apercevoir, 30)

celebrate (célébrer, 21)

change (changer, 19)

chase away (chasser, reg.)

check (out) (contrôler, reg.)

choose (choisir, reg.)

claim (prétendre, reg.)

clean (nettoyer, 22)

climb (up, in) (*monter, reg.)

close (fermer, reg.)

combat (combattre, 33)

come (*venir, 30, 38)

come back home (*revenir, 30, 38)

come back up (*remonter, reg.)

come closer (*s'approcher, reg., 17)

come from (*provenir de, 30, 38)

command (commander, reg.)

commit (commettre, 31)

complain (*se plaindre, 17, 34)

complete (achever, 20)

complete (compléter, 21)

concern (concerner, reg.)

conquer (vaincre, 38)

consent (consentir, reg.)

consider (considérer, 21)

construct (construire, 33)

contain (contenir, 30, 38)

continue (continuer, reg.)

continue (reprendre, 29)

control (contrôler, reg.)

convince (convaincre, 38)

correct (corriger, 19)

cost (coûter, reg.)

cough (tousser, reg.)

count (compter, reg.)

cover (couvrir, 29)

cover (again) (recouvrir, 29)

create (créer, reg.)

cross (traverser, reg.)

cry (pleurer, reg.)

cry out (crier, reg.)

cultivate (cultiver, reg.)

cure (guérir, reg.)

cut (couper, reg.)

D

dance (danser, reg.)

decide (décider, reg.)

declare (déclarer, reg.)

defend (défendre, reg.)

depart (*partir, 29)

depress (désoler, reg.)

derive (*provenir [de], 30, 38)

desire (désirer, reg.)

die (*mourir, 36)

dine (dîner, reg.)

direct (diriger, 19)

disappear (disparaître, 31)

discover (découvrir, 29)

displease (déplaire, 37)

disturb (perturber, reg.)

do (faire, 31)

doubt (douter, reg.)

draw (dessiner, reg.)

dream (rêver, reg.)

dream (songer, 19)

drink (boire, 33)

drive (conduire, 33)

drive (rouler, reg.)

dry (sécher, 21)

dwell (habiter, reg.)

E

earn (gagner, reg.)

eat (manger, 19)

employ (employer, 22)

enjoy oneself (*s'amuser, reg., 17)

enlighten (éclaircir, reg.)

enter (*entrer, reg.)

erect (élever, 20)

exaggerate (exagérer, 21)

exchange (échanger, 19)

excuse (excuser, reg.)

exist (exister, reg.)

exit (a vehicle) (*descendre, reg.)

explain (expliquer, reg.)

extinguish (light, fire) (éteindre, 34)

F

fail (manquer, reg.)

fall (down) (*tomber, reg.)

fall asleep (*s'endormir, 17, 29)

fear (craindre, 34)

feel (sentir, 29)

fight (*se battre, 17, 33)

fight (combattre, 33)

fill (remplir, reg.)

find (trouver, reg.)

find (oneself) (*se trouver, reg., 17)

find again (retrouver, reg.)

finish (achever, 20)

finish (finir, reg.)

finish (terminer, reg.)

fish (pêcher, reg.)

float (flotter, reg.)

flow (couler, reg.)

fly (voler, reg.)

fold (plier, reg.)

follow (suivre, 38)

forbid (défendre, reg.)

force (forcer, 18)

foresee (prévoir, 30)

forge (forger, 19)

forget (oublier, reg.)

freeze (geler, 20)

frequent (fréquenter, reg.)

fulfill (remplir, reg.)

function (fonctionner, reg.)

G

get (obtenir, 30, 38)

get angry (*se fâcher, reg., 17)

get bored (*s'ennuyer, 17, 22)

get dressed (*s'habiller, reg., 17)

get impatient (*s'impatienter, reg., 17)

get married (*se marier, reg., 17)

get up (*se lever, 17, 20)

get well (guérir, reg.)

get worried (*s'inquiéter, 17, 21)

give (donner, reg.)

give back (rendre, reg.)

give up (renoncer, 18)

go (*aller, 30)

go away (*s'en aller, 17, 30)

go (back) home (*rentrer, reg.)

go by (time) (*se passer, reg., 17)

go down (*descendre, reg.)

go out (*sortir, 29)

go swimming (*se baigner, reg., 17)

go to (fréquenter, reg.)

go to bed (*se coucher, reg., 17)

go to sleep (*s'endormir, 17, 29)

go up (*monter, reg.)

grow (cultiver, reg.)

guide (mener, 20)

H

have (avoir, 10, 24)

have dinner (dîner, reg.)

have lunch (déjeuner, reg.)

have to (devoir, 35)

have to (falloir [il faut], 32)

hear (entendre, reg.)

heat (up) (chauffer, reg.)

help (aider, reg.)

hide (cacher, reg.)

hire (embaucher, reg.)

hit (frapper, reg.)

hold (tenir, 30, 38)

hope (espérer, 21)

house (loger, 19)

hunt (chasser, reg.)

hurry (*se dépêcher, reg., 17)

hurry (*se presser, reg., 17)

I

illuminate (éclaircir, reg.)

injure (blesser, reg.)

injure oneself (*se blesser, reg., 17)

interest (intéresser, reg.)

interrogate (interroger, 19)

invent (inventer, reg.)

invite (inviter, reg.)

involve (concerner, reg.)

J

judge (juger, 19)

jump (sauter, reg.)

K

keep (garder, reg.)

kill (tuer, reg.)

know (connaître, 31)

know (a fact) (savoir, 28)

sit (down) (*s'asseoir, 17, 40)

sleep (dormir, 29)

smile (sourire, 37)

smoke (fumer, reg.)

snow (neiger [il neige], 19, 32)

sound (sonner, reg.)

speak (parler, reg.)

spell (épeler, 23)

spend (dépenser, reg.)

start (commencer, 18)

start (*se mettre à, 17, 31)

state (déclarer, reg.)

stay (demeurer, reg.)

stay (*rester, reg.)

steal (voler, reg.)

stick (coller, reg.)

stop (*s'arrêter, reg., 17)

stretch (out) (tendre, reg.)

strike (frapper, reg.)

study (étudier, reg.)

stir (remuer, reg.)

succeed (réussir, reg.)

suffer (souffrir, 29)

suggest (suggérer, 21)

support (appuyer, 22)

suppose (supposer, reg.)

surprise (surprendre, 29)

surround (entourer, reg.)

swim (nager, 19)

T

take (prendre, 29)

take a bath (*se baigner, reg., 17)

take a walk (*se promener, 17, 20)

take away (emporter, reg.)

take back (reprendre, 29)

take care of (soigner, reg.)

take off (enlever, 20)

talk (parler, reg.)

teach (enseigner, reg.)

tear (déchirer, reg.)

telephone (téléphoner, reg.)

tell (dire, 35)

tell (raconter, reg.)

tell a falsehood (mentir, 29)

terminate (terminer, reg.)

think (penser, reg.)

think (réfléchir, reg.)

think of (songer, 19)

threaten (menacer, 18)

throw (lancer, 18)

throw (away) (jeter, 23)

tighten (serrer, reg.)

touch (toucher, reg.)

translate (traduire, 33)

travel (voyager, 19)

traverse (traverser, reg.)

triumph (triompher, reg.)

try (essayer, 22)

turn (oneself) around (*se tourner, reg., 17)

U

uncover (découvrir, 29)

understand (comprendre, 29)

undress (oneself) (*se déshabiller, reg., 17)

upholster (tapisser, reg.)

use (employer, 22)

W

wait (attendre, reg.)

wake up (*se réveiller, reg., 17)

walk (a dog) (promener, 20)

walk, take a (*se promener, 17, 20)

want (désirer, reg.)

want to (vouloir, 28)

wash (laver, reg.)

wash oneself (*se laver, reg., 17)

wear (porter, reg.)

weep (pleurer, reg.)

weigh (peser, 20)

win (gagner, reg.)

win (remporter, reg.)

win (triompher, reg.)

wipe (essuyer, 22)

work (travailler, reg.)

work (machine) (fonctionner, reg.)

worry (*s'inquiéter, 17, 21)

worry (someone) (inquiéter, 21)

worship (adorer, reg.)

wound (blesser, reg.)

wrap up (envelopper, reg.)

write (écrire, 35)

Y

yield (céder, 21)